William Henry Odenheimer, Frederic M Bird

Songs of the Spirit

Hymns of praise and prayer to God the Holy Ghost

William Henry Odenheimer, Frederic M Bird

Songs of the Spirit
Hymns of praise and prayer to God the Holy Ghost

ISBN/EAN: 9783742821652

Manufactured in Europe, USA, Canada, Australia, Japa

Cover: Foto ©Angelika Wolter / pixelio.de

Manufactured and distributed by brebook publishing software (www.brebook.com)

William Henry Odenheimer, Frederic M Bird

Songs of the Spirit

Songs of the Spirit.

Hymns of Praise and Prayer

TO

GOD THE HOLY GHOST.

EDITED BY

The Right Rev. WILLIAM HENRY ODENHEIMER, D.D.,

AND

FREDERIC M. BIRD.

"I believe in the Holy Ghost, the Lord and Giver of Life."

NEW YORK:
ANSON D. F. RANDOLPH & COMPANY,
770 Broadway.

Entered according to Act of Congress, in the year 1871, by
ANSON D. F. RANDOLPH AND COMPANY,
In the Office of the Librarian of Congress at Washington.

Press of
JOHN WILSON AND SON,
Cambridge.

ROBERT RUTTER,
Binder,
84 Beekman Street, N.Y.

TO

ALL WHO BELIEVE THAT

𝕲𝖔𝖉 𝖙𝖍𝖊 𝕳𝖔𝖑𝖞 𝕲𝖍𝖔𝖘𝖙 𝖎𝖘 𝖙𝖍𝖊 𝕷𝖔𝖗𝖉 𝖆𝖓𝖉 𝕷𝖎𝖋𝖊 𝕲𝖎𝖛𝖊𝖗,

AND WHO INVOKE, IN PRAYER AND PRAISE,

HIS GRACIOUS POWER

TO PREPARE THE CHURCH AND THE DISCIPLE'S HEART FOR THE

SECOND COMING OF

OUR LORD AND SAVIOUR JESUS CHRIST.

PREFATORY NOTE.

IN the Second Charge of the Bishop of New Jersey (A.D. 1865), entitled "The Church's Power in her Controversy with Antichrist," whilst earnestly advocating the duty and privilege of direct addresses to GOD the HOLY GHOST, as the divine Administrator for CHRIST of this Dispensation, the following language was employed:—

"*We must pray to the Holy Ghost*, as to the Father and to the Son, or we do not pray in the fulness of the Evangelical development of the duty. To pray is to address our petition to God; but the God Whom we Christians worship is Father, Son, and Holy Ghost. Every petition to God simply, in our Liturgy, is a prayer to the Three Persons of the one Divine Nature; but this is not always distinctly before our minds, and I desire to bring it out with emphasis.

"The devotional treasures of the whole Church, and of all holy men who have composed petitions to the Third Person of the adorable Trinity, in *Hymns* as well as in Prayers, are spread out before us, and we can use them, at our will, in our private, family, and social devotions."

In the above quotation may be found the origin and design of this Collection of Hymns to the HOLY GHOST.

PREFATORY NOTE.

We have fallen on evil times. We want power, spiritual power, for the increase of purity, unity, charity. Now "GOD spake once, and twice have I also heard the same, that *power belongeth unto* GOD."

W. H. O.

BURLINGTON, N.J., A.D. 1871.

INTRODUCTION.

THIS volume is meant to be in some sort a contribution to the history of doctrine; containing what Christian men in many lands and ages have held and sung as to their Enlightener and Sanctifier. It was at first intended to restrict our selections to direct addresses to the HOLY GHOST; but much matter of interest being found, which, though not bearing this form, dealt altogether with our subject, the plan was enlarged, and the three Introductory Parts or Chapters added. Less emphasis every way, however, is laid on these than on the body of the book; they are a porch of the Temple, not the Temple itself.

The scope of the work, and we hope its spirit, are thoroughly Catholic. All religious bodies and all schools of thought which recognize the Deity of the HOLY GHOST are allowed to have their say in these pages: if some are represented more fully than others, it is because they had more to say or said it better. The amount of material may surprise our readers, considering how little on this subject is found in ordinary Hymnals and Collections of sacred verse. Little indeed has been written

here, compared with the enormous mass of lyrics which celebrate the SON of GOD; but the whole domain of Hymnody has been pretty thoroughly ransacked, and its treasures drawn upon with no sparing hand. As a rule, whatever seemed noticeable, whether from intrinsic or extrinsic reasons, has been admitted; many pieces which cannot claim much poetic merit may be found interesting historically, either from the value that has been put upon them by Christian congregations, or as illustrating the thought and feeling of the age or school in which they were produced.

It was not deemed wise or practicable to attempt any division of the subject as such. The ordinary operations of the SPIRIT are everywhere celebrated through the following pages in a way which defies classification; and His special relations to the Bible, to Creation, to the natural light of Reason and Conscience, etc., are mentioned here and there, for the most part incidentally, in connection with these. A lingual and chronological arrangement fitted the purpose of the book, and was indeed the only one which could be intelligently followed.

Few of the hymns have been taken at second hand; and the text may be relied on as *unaltered and unabridged* in nearly or quite every case except where the contrary is stated.

The idea of this work originated with Bishop Odenheimer, as intimated in his Prefatory Note; and he gathered a good deal of material toward its execution.

INTRODUCTION.

Afterwards transferring his MSS. to me, the plan and scope of it have been enlarged; and for the details of selection, arrangement, and annotation, I am responsible.

I am indebted to Dr. E. A. Washburn, the Rev. S. W. Duffield, and the Hon. E. C. Benedict, for translations from the Latin, kindly made for this work; to Thomas H. Gill, Esq., for an original hymn; to the Rev. B. M. Schmucker, D.D., of Reading, Pa., for some of the notes on the German and Latin hymns; to David Creamer, Esq., of Baltimore, and others, for the loan of a few important books not in my own library. Mr. Daniel Sedgwick of 93 Sun Street, Bishopsgate, London, has supplied some points of information elsewhere inaccessible: indeed no Collection can be thoroughly made without help from the immense information and long experience of this veteran hymnologist.

F. M. B.

SPOTSWOOD, N.J., September, 1871.

TABLE OF CONTENTS.

INTRODUCTORY.

Part I.

PRAYERS FOR THE HOLY GHOST.

	Author.	Date.	Page.
O Lord, Thy wing outspread	WILLIAM JOHN BLEW.	1851	5
O Thou that hearest prayer	JOHN BURTON.	1824	6
O God of Love and Power	JOHN MASON NEALE.	1844	8
Ere the world, with light invested	W. H. BATHURST.	1831	9
O for that flame of living fire	,,	,,	10
Lord, show Thy glory as of old	,,	,,	11
Full of weakness and of sin	,,	,,	12
For another Pentecost	BENJAMIN GOUGH.	1865	13
Come from the four winds	,,	,,	14
Come, ye who desire	,,	,,	16
Saviour, I Thy word believe	A. M. TOPLADY.	1759	17
Jesus is gone up on high	THOMAS KELLY.	1806	19
Enthroned on high, Almighty Lord	THOMAS HAWEIS.	1792	20
Father, if justly still we claim	JOHN WESLEY.	1739	21
Leave us not comfortless	JOSIAH CONDER.	1836	23
Father, if Thou my Father art	CHARLES WESLEY.	1740	23
Father of our dying Lord	,,	1742	25
Father, glorify Thy Son	,,	1746	26
Jesus, we hang upon the word	,,	,,	27
Saviour and Prince of Peace	,,	,,	28
Jesus, our exalted Head	,,	,,	29
Jesus, we on the word depend	,,	,,	31
Saviour, Lord, Who at Thy Death	,,	,,	32
Father, admit our lawful claim	,,	,,	33

TABLE OF CONTENTS

	Author.	Date.	Page.
Hear all the Saviour's cry	CHARLES WESLEY.	1746	34
Jesus, Lord, in pity hear us	,,	,,	36
O Thou Who by Thy Blood	,,	,,	37
Son of God, for Thee we languish	,,	,,	38

Part II.

THE STORY OF PENTECOST.

Above the starry spheres	AMBROSE?	d. 397	45
Christ had regained the sky	,,	,,	47
Now our prayers are heard	From the Latin.		49
Round roll the weeks	HILARY?	d. 368	50
Gladsome feast!	,,	,,	52
Now prompt, O Muse	From the Latin.		53
The illustrious day	ADAM ST. VICTOR.	ab. 1170	54
A year's swift months	From the Latin.		57
All laud and worship	NOTKER?	912	58
We keep the Feast of Pentecost	From the Greek.		59
The tuneful sound of music	JOHN OF DAMASCUS.	ab. 780	60
He Who with His mighty hand	COSMAS.	ab. 760	61
Holy Gift, surpassing	JOSEPH OF THE STUDIUM.	ab. 830	62
I will not leave you comfortless	GEORGE V. COX.	1845	63
Hail the joyful day's return	ROBERT CAMPBELL.	1850	65
Midnight clouds are rolled away	CHARLES L. FORD.	1858	66
Exceeding faithful in Thy word	GEORGE WITHER.	1623	67
Nay, startle not	CHRISTOPHER HARVIE.	1640	69
Thy heavenly kingdom here below	JOSEPH BEAUMONT.	1652	71
Tongues of fire from Heaven	JEREMY TAYLOR.	1655	72
When Christ His body	HENRY MORE.	1668	73
Welcome, white day!	HENRY VAUGHAN.	1654	75
At Pentecost, illustrious day	SIMON BROWNE.	1720	78
Now Christ ascends above	WILLIAM HAMMOND.	1745	80
When the blest day of Pentecost	JOSEPH HART.	1759	82
Granted is the Saviour's prayer	CHARLES WESLEY.	1739	83
Father of everlasting grace	,,	1746	85
Rejoice, rejoice, ye fallen race	,,	1742	87
Sinners, your hearts lift up	,,	,,	89

TABLE OF CONTENTS.

	Author.	Date.	Page.
Let songs of praises fill the sky	Thomas Cotterill.	1819	90
There was a lowly upper room	C. F. Alexander.	1840	91
The Day of Pentecost	Archer T. Gurney.	1862	93
Once the soft dews of night	Eliza Humphreys.	1856	94
Christ our Sun on us arose	R. F. Littledale.	1867	95
One the descending Flame	John Keble.	1846	96
When God of old came down	,,	1827	98
Day divine, when sudden	Thomas H. Gill.	1850	100
Would the Spirit more completely	,,	,,	101

Part III.

THE FRUITS OF THE SPIRIT.

But who shall comfort	Charlotte M. Noel.	1862	107
Jehovah, let me now adore Thee	B. Crasselius.	1697	109
His Holy Spirit dwelleth	Paul Gerhardt.	1656	111
Awake, Thou Spirit, Who of old	C. H. Bogatzky.	1749	112
Dear Dove, Thy prisoner may I be	Faithful Teate.	1669	114
My soul doth magnify the Lord	John Mason.	1683	116
The Love of the Spirit I sing	John Ryland.	1796	118
Dear Lord, and shall Thy Spirit rest	Anne Steele.	1760	119
The God of grace will never leave	John Fawcett.	1782	121
That we might walk with God	Benjamin Beddome.	d. 1795	122
Away with our fears	Charles Wesley.	1746	123
Sinners, lift up your hearts	,,	,,	124
Whither shall a creature run	,,	1767	126
Drink deep of the Spirit	John Barclay.	1776	127
O love ye the Spirit indwelling	,,	,,	129
The Spirit in the Word	Thomas Gibbons.	1769	130
The Spirit in our hearts	H. U. Onderdonk.	1826	131
Blest be the God Who men inspired	S. B. Haslam.	1824	132
I would not grieve my dearest Lord	,,	1833	133
Lord, 'twas a time of wondrous Love		1800	134
As blows the wind			135
Not bound by chains	Ingram Cobbin.		
	C. Wordsworth.	1862	136
Thou Who framedst this goodly	J. H. Alexander.	1844	138
O God, when wilt Thou come	,,	,,	139

xiv TABLE OF CONTENTS.

	Author.	Date.	Page.
Be joyful in the Lord, ye lands!	J. H. ALEXANDER.	1844	140
Our blest Redeemer	HARRIET AUBER.	1829	141
We cannot see the wondrous Hand	JANE CREWDSON.	1864	142
Brethren, let us join to raise		1832	143
May Thy Spirit, bright and holy	ADA CAMBRIDGE.	1866	144
Bright Presence! may my soul	THOMAS H. GILL.	1849	147
Why hasteth on this pilgrim throng	,,	1850	150
Alas these pilgrims faint and worn	,,	1854	151
O smitten soul	,,	1855	153
Do we only give Thee heed	,,	1849	155
Thy happy ones a strain begin	,,	1846	156
Lord, am I precious in Thy sight	,,	1849	157
Our God, our God! Thou shinest	,,	1846	158
O Son of God, Who wentest up	ARTHUR M. MORGAN.	1856	160

HYMNS TO THE HOLY GHOST.

LATIN HYMNS.

	Author.	Date.	Page.
VENI CREATOR SPIRITUS	Uncertain.		167
First Version	GEORGE WITHER.	1623	168
Second Version	WILLIAM DRUMMOND.	1623	169
Third ,,	JOHN COSIN.	1627	171
Fourth ,,	Old Version Psalms.		172
Fifth ,,	NAHUM TATE.	1703	174
Sixth ,,	JOHN DRYDEN.	d. 1700	175
Seventh ,,	ISAAC WILLIAMS.	1839	177
Eighth ,,	JOHN WILLIAMS.	1845	178
Ninth ,,	ROBERT CAMPBELL.	1850	179
VENI SANCTE SPIRITUS	ROBERT II. OF FRANCE.	d. 1031	181
First Version	JOHN AUSTIN.	1668	183
Second Version	EDWARD CASWALL.	1848	184
Third ,,	FREDERIC W. FABER.	1849	186
Fourth ,,	R. CAMPBELL.	1850	187
Fifth ,,	JOHN MASON NEALE.	1851	188
Sixth ,,	RAY PALMER.	1858	189

TABLE OF CONTENTS.

	Author.	Date.	Page.
VENI SUPERNE SPIRITUS	Unknown.		
First Version	ISAAC WILLIAMS.	1839	191
Second Version	WILLIAM J. BLEW.	1851	192
ADSIS SUPERNE SPIRITUS	Unknown.		
First Version	I. WILLIAMS.	1839	193
Second Version	JOSEPH F. THRUPP?	185–	194
Third ,,	HORATIUS BONAR.	1861	195
Fourth ,,	E. L. BLENKINSOPP.	1864	197
NUNC SANCTE NOBIS SPIRITUS	AMBROSE?		
First Version	J. H. NEWMAN.	1836	198
Second Version	JOHN CHANDLER.	1837	199
Third ,,	JANE CREWDSON.	1864	199
O FONS AMORIS SPIRITUS	Unknown.		
First Version	J. CHANDLER.	1837	200
Second Version	I. WILLIAMS.	1839	201
SANCTI SPIRITUS ADSIT NOBIS GRATIA	NOTKER.	d. 912	
First Version	J. M. NEALE.	1863	201
Second Version	E. C. BENEDICT.	1871	203
ALMUM FLAMEN, VITA MUNDI	Unknown, tr. KYNASTON.	1862	205
O IGNIS SPIRITUS PARACLITI	HILDEGARDE.	d. 1197	
First Version	R. F. LITTLEDALE.	1864	207
Second Version	T. G. CRIPPEN.	1868	208
AMOR PATRIS ET FILII	Unknown, tr. LITTLEDALE.	1864	210
VENI CREATOR SPIRITUS, SPIRITUS RECREATOR	ADAM OF ST. VICTOR. ab.	1172	211
VENI SUMME CONSOLATOR	,, ,, ,,	,,	213
SIMPLEX IN ESSENTIA	,, ,, ,,	,,	
First Version	E. A. WASHBURN.	1871	216
Second Version	S. W. DUFFIELD.	1871	218
O Inexhaustive Fount of Light!	E. CASWALL.	1858	220
SPIRITUS SANCTE, PIE PARACLITE	HILDEBERT.	d. 1133	222
	tr. E. A. WASHBURN.	1871	

ITALIAN HYMN.

| Come down, O Love divine! | BIANCO DA SIENA. | d. 1434 | **225** |

GERMAN HYMNS.

	Author.	Date.	Page.
Komm, Heiliger Geist	Martin Luther.	1524	230
First Version	Myles Coverdale.	153–	231
Second Version	J. C. Jacobi.	1722	232
Third "	A. T. Russell.	1851	234
Fourth "	C. Winkworth.	1855	235
Nun bitten wir den Heiligen Geist	Luther.	1524	236
First Version	M. Coverdale.	153–	237
Second Version	A. T. Russell.	1851	238
Third "	Richard Massie.	1854	239
Komm, Gott, Schöpfer, Heiliger Geist	Luther.	1524	240
First Version	R. Massie.	1854	240
Second Version	Anonymous.	1852	241
O du allersüszste Freude	Paul Gerhardt.	1653	242
First Version	J. C. Jacobi.	1725	242
Second Version	A. M. Toplady.	1776	245
Third "	C. Winkworth.	1863	247
Zeuch ein zu deinen Thoren	Paul Gerhardt.	1656	249
First Version	C. Winkworth.	1855	249
Second Version	"	1862	253
O Heil'ger Geist, kehr'bei uns ein	Michael Schirmer.	1650	256
Brunquell aller Güter	John Frank.	1660	258
Komm, o komm, du Geist des Lebens	J. Neander.	d. 1680	260
First Version	C. Winkworth.	1858	261
Second Version	C. W. Schaeffer.	1866	263
Schmückt das Fest mit Maien	Benjamin Schmolke.	1715	264
Hochgelobter Geist und Herr	Christian Gregor.	d. 1801	267
O Gott, O Geist, O Licht des Lebens	G. Tersteegen.	1731	269
First Version	C. Winkworth.	1855	269
Second Version	B. H. Kennedy?	1863	270

TABLE OF CONTENTS.

	Author.	Date.	Page.
Thou Who lovest us as a Father	DAVID BRUHN.	d. 1782	272
O Geist des Herrn	J. C. Lavater.	d. 1801	274
Geist des Glaubens	C. J. P. Spitta.	1833	275
O komm, du Geist der Wahrheit	,,	1833	278

DANISH HYMNS.

Thou Holy Spirit, Comforter	Christensen.	tr. 1868	280
Returned is sacred Pentecost	Anonymous.	tr. 1850	281
Be our support, O Holy Ghost	,,	,,	283
God Holy Ghost, teach us in faith	,,	,,	284

FRENCH HYMNS.

Spirit of Charity	Mme. Guion.	d. 1717	285
O Holy Spirit, blessed Comforter	César Malan.	tr. 1866	286
Spirit of Truth, Thy gracious beams	,,	,,	287

OLD ENGLISH HYMNS.
1530–1700.

O Holy Spirite, our Comfortoure	Myles Coverdale.	153–	291
Come, Holy Spirit, God of might	Old Version Psalms.		292
Come, Holy Ghost, eternall God	Francis Kinwelmersh.	1576	294
O heavenly Spirit of especiall power	Richard Vennard.	1601	295
O Holy Spirit, assist me	Anonymous.	ab. 1600	297
Fragments	Edmund Spenser.	1596	298
Listen, sweet Dove, unto my song	George Herbert.	d. 1632	299
Providence	,,	,,	300
And art Thou grieved	,,	,,	302
The same rewritten	John Wesley.	1739	303
Fountain of sweets! Eternal Dove	Joseph Beaumont.	1652	304
In the houre of my distress	Robert Herrick.	1647	305
O Thou eternal Spright!	Henry More.	1640	307
The Lord's Garden	John Austin.	1668	307
Come, mild and holy Dove	,,	,,	309
O sacred Spirit, within my soul	John Rawlet.	1687	311
Come, blessed Spirit, descend	Lancelot Addison.	1699	312

b

TABLE OF CONTENTS.

ENGLISH HYMNS OF THE EIGHTEENTH CENTURY.

	Author.	Date.	Page.
Why should the children of a King	ISAAC WATTS.	1707	315
Eternal Spirit, we confess	,,	1709	316
Come, Holy Spirit, heavenly Dove	,,	1707	317
Come, Holy Spirit, heavenly Dove	SIMON BROWNE.	1720	318
He's come! let every knee be bent	ANONYMOUS.	1733	319
O Thou propitious Paraclete	THOMAS CONEY.	1722	321
Come, Holy Ghost, celestial Dove	THOMAS HARRISON.	1721	323
Dear Comforter of pious souls	JAMES CRAIG.	1727	324
Awake, awake, Thou Spirit sweet	JOHN WRIGHT.	1727	325
Hail, Holy Ghost, Jehovah	SAMUEL WESLEY, Jr.	1736	327
Hear, Holy Spirit, hear	CHARLES WESLEY.	1739	328
Come, Holy Ghost	,,	,,	331
Come, Holy Ghost	,,	1740	332
Come, Holy Ghost, our hearts	,,	,,	334
Hymns on the Lord's Supper	,,	1745	335-6
Spirit of Faith, come down	,,	1746	337
Come, holy, celestial Dove	,,	,,	338
Author of every work divine	,,	,,	340
Spirit of Truth, descend	,,	,,	346
Eternal Spirit, come	,,	,,	349
Holy, sanctifying Dove	,,	1749	350
Stay, Thou insulted Spirit, stay	,,	,,	351
O Thou meek and injured Dove	,,	,,	352
In National Danger	,,	1756	353
Short Scripture Hymns	,,	1762	354-8
The Fruit of the Spirit	,,	,,	358
Inspirer of the ancient Seers	,,	,,	359
Spirit of truth, essential God	,,	1767	361
"Hymns on the Trinity"	,,	,,	362-3
Kindler of seraphic fire	,,	,,	364
Come, Thou all-inspiring Spirit	,,	,,	365
Spirit of supplication	,,	,,	366
Spirit of Love, return	,,	,,	368
Spirit of revelation	,,		369
Awake and blow, Thou purest Wind	JOHN CENNICK.	1742	370
Holy Ghost, anointing Dove	,,	1741	371

TABLE OF CONTENTS.

	Author.	Date.	Page.
After a Dispute	John Cennick.	1741	371
At Adult Baptism	"	1742	372
Now may the Spirit's holy Fire	Robert Seagrave.	1742	373
For an Awakening	"	"	375
Holy Spirit, gently come	William Hammond.	1745	376
Descend, immortal Dove	Philip Doddridge.	d. 1751	378
Great Spirit of Immortal Love	"	"	379
Hear, gracious Sovereign	"	"	380
Come, descend, O heavenly Spirit	Thomas Rawson.	1757	380
Come, Holy Spirit, come	Joseph Hart.	1759	382
Blest God, that once in fiery tongues	"	"	383
Blest Spirit of Truth, eternal God	"	"	384
Descend from Heaven	"	"	385
Come, Holy Spirit, now descend	William Williams.	1759	387
Earnest of future bliss	Augustus M. Toplady.	1759	388
Fain would I mount	"	1771	390
Eternal Spirit, Source of light	Samuel Davies.	d. 1761	390
Eternal Spirit! 'twas Thy Breath	Elizabeth Scott.		392
Come, Holy Ghost	John Willison.	1767	393
Breathe, descending Holy Spirit	James Neale.	1763	394
Gentle Spirit, waft me over	Richard Kempenfelt.	1767	395
The Rapture	"	"	396
Adult Baptism	John Fellows.	1773	399
Blest Harbinger of future joys	"	"	401
Spirit of mercy, truth, and love	Anonymous.	1775	402
Gracious Spirit, Dove divine	John Stocker.	1777	403
Come, Thou soul-transforming	Jonathan Evans.	1784	404
Thou Source of all vigor divine	John Ryland.	1786	405
Eternal Spirit, mighty Lord	Samuel Medley.	1789	406
Great Spirit, by Whose mighty power	Thomas Haweis.	1792	407
Spirit of God and glory, send	"	"	408
Spirit of power, descend	"	"	409
Thou Spirit of eternal Truth	Maria F. Cowper.	1792	409
The Retrospect	"	"	411
Come, Holy Spirit, come	Benjamin Beddome.	d. 1795	413
Come, blessed Spirit, Source	"	"	414
Eternal Spirit, Source of good	"	"	414
My faith is weak, my foes are strong	"	"	415
Ere Nature, lovely child, arose	Samuel Pattison.	1792	416

TABLE OF CONTENTS.

	Author.	Date.	Page.
Holy Ghost, the Comforter	SAMUEL PATTISON.	1792	417
Holy Spirit, now descend	RICHARD BURNHAM.	1796	419
Come, Holy Ghost, and warm	ANONYMOUS.	1798	419
Hail, Holy Spirit	SIMON BROWNE.	1720	421

ENGLISH HYMNS OF THE NINETEENTH CENTURY.

	Author.	Date.	Page.
Holy Ghost, inspire our praises	BASIL WOODD.	1800	425
Come, Thou almighty Comforter	DANIEL HERBERT.	1801	426
Come, Holy Spirit! calm my mind	JOHN STEWART.	1803	427
Spirit of God, on Thee we call	JOHN KEMPTHORNE.	1810	428
Eternal Spirit, Source of Truth!	THOMAS COTTERILL.	1811	429
Spirit of truth, Thy grace impart			430
Holy Ghost, Whose fire celestial	ANONYMOUS.	1815	431
Spirit of Truth, O Holy Ghost	,,	,,	431
Holy Ghost, we look to Thee	WILLIAM GADSBY.	1814	432
Holy Spirit, heavenly Dove	JOSEPH IRONS.	1816	433
Holy Spirit, heavenly Witness	,,	,,	434
Eternal Spirit, let me know	,,	,,	435
Almighty Spirit, we	THOMAS ROW.		436
Spirit Jehovah! glorious Lord!	ROBERT HAWKER.		437
Holy Ghost, with light divine	ANDREW REED.	1817	439
Spirit Divine! attend our prayers	,,	1842	440
Lord God, the Holy Ghost	JAMES MONTGOMERY.	1819	442
Spirit of power and might, behold	,,	1825	443
O Spirit of the living God	,,	,,	444
Thee will we praise	HENRY LOWE.	1820	445
Inspired by Thee	S. B. HASLAM.	1833	446
Spirit of Truth! on this Thy day	REGINALD HEBER.	1827	446
Confirmation	JOHN KEBLE.	1827	447
Ordination	,,	,,	448
How dare we pray Thee dwell within	,,		450
For Help in the Fight	ANONYMOUS.	1828	450
O turn, most Holy Spirit! turn	,,	,,	451
Prayer for Simplicity	R. DUNDERDALE.	1829	452
Eternal Spirit, by Whose power	W. H. BATHURST.	1831	453
Spirit of Life, Thy influence shed	,,	,,	454

TABLE OF CONTENTS.

	Author.	Date	Page.
Spirit of holiness, look down	W. H. Bathurst.	1831	455
Holy Spirit, from on high	,,	,,	456
Holiest Source of consolation	Baptist W. Noel?	1832	457
Spirit of God, Whose sacred fire	Anonymous.	,,	457
Once more the Christian Pentecost	,,	,,	458
Holy Spirit, Fount of blessing	Thomas J. Judkin.	1831	459
O Holy Spirit, Who didst shed	,,	,,	460
Spirit of Mercy, dwell	William W. Hull.	1833	461
Eternal Spirit, Lord of Light	Eliza J. Fallow.	,,	461
Prayer for a Minister	C E. Tonna.	1834	462
Gracious Spirit, Source of bliss	S. C. E. Neville.	1836	463
Holy Ghost, Thy power impart	,,	,,	464
O breathe upon this languid frame	Josiah Conder.	,,	465
Blessed Spirit! Thou Who deignest	Charlotte Elliott.	1836	466
God of peace and consolation	,,	1854	467
Holy Comforter! Who guidest	,,	1841	468
For Faith, Hope, and Charity	Richard Mant.	1837	469
Sunday Morning	James Edmeston.		470
Holy Spirit, come renew me	,,		471
Spirit of Life, go forth!	Anonymous.	1837	472
O Holy Spirit, come	William Allen?	1835	472
Spirit of Truth and Holiness	Anonymous.	1838	473
Spirit of Power! to Thee I cry	,,	,,	474
Breathe, Holy Spirit, from above	,,	1829	475
For a Child	Diana A. Thrupp.	1840	476
For Ember Week	Henry O'Neile.	,,	477
Gracious, free, and sovereign Spirit	J. C. H.	1842	478
Fountain of Life most pure	William P. Sparks.	,,	479
Holy Spirit, mystic Dove	Joseph Jones.	,,	481
Spirit of Truth! my mind illume	,,	,,	483
Saviour, Thy Father's Promise send	Henry Alford.	1844	484
Spirit of Life and Light, descend	Nathaniel Meeres.	1845	484
For a Blessing on Preaching	John Leifchild.	1842	485
Blest Spirit, from the Eternal Sire	William M. Bunting.	,,	487
O Holy Ghost, Who didst descend	Isaac Williams.	1843	488
The Communion of Saints	,,	,,	490
Glory, Holy Ghost, to Thee	,,	,,	490
Thou Who camest from above	John Mason Neale.	1844	491
Blest Comforter, Balm of the mind	Anonymous.	,,	492

xxii   TABLE OF CONTENTS.

	Author.	Date.	Page
O Spirit of Love	John Harding.	1847	493
Spirit that dwellest where	Julia C. Grimani.	1849	494
O Holy Ghost, the Comforter	J. E. Browne.	,,	495
Eternal Former of the holy mind	Robert Montgomery.	1851	497
Single Verses	,,	,,	498
Spirit of Truth, be Thou my Guide	Anne Bronte.	d. 1849	498
Great Spirit, like a rushing wind	Benjamin S. Hollis.	1849	499
O Holy Ghost, we praise Thy Name	,, ?	,,	500
Holy Ghost, Whose potent word	,, ?	,,	501
Spirit of God, I cannot rest	,, ?	,,	502
Fountain of Love! Thyself true God	Frederick W. Faber.	,,	503
Holy Ghost, come down	,,		505
O for those solitary hours	Matthew Bridges.	1848	507
Grace Increate!	Edward Caswall.	1858	508
Holy Spirit, given	Arthur T. Russell.	1851	510
O Thou Who by the Lord	,,	,,	511
Now is the Church's joyous feast	,,	,,	512
Blest Comforter, Who didst inspire	,,	,,	513
Holy Ghost, Who us instructest	,,	,,	513
Come, O promised Comforter	,,	1848	514
Come, Holy Ghost, on us descend	,,	,,	515
Come to our poor nature's night	George Rawson.	1853	516
And will the mighty God	,,	1862	518
O Holy Spirit, send	John Flesher.	1853	519
O Spirit of the living God	Anonymous.	,,	520
Gracious Spirit, from on high	Margaret Mackay.	1854	521
Spirit of God! descend	George Croly.	,,	522
When across the inward thought	Henry G. Tomkins.	1855	523
Gracious Spirit, dwell with me	Thomas T. Lynch.	1855	524
Spirit! Whose various energies	,,	,,	526
Spirit of sacred happiness	,,	,,	527
Spirit of Beauty!	,,	,,	528
Holy Communion	,,	1868	529
God the Spirit, we aspire	Eliza Humphreys.	1856	529
Confirmation	J. H. Butterworth.	1857	531
O Holy Spirit, now descend on me	Christina Forsyth.	1861	532
O Holy Spirit! Comforter divine	,,	,,	534
Holy Spirit, Source of Light	C. Newman Hall.	1857	535
Wind of the North! awake	Charles B. Tayler.		535

TABLE OF CONTENTS.

	Author.	Date.	Page.
Till the day dawn	Horatius Bonar.	1857	537
Spirit of everlasting Grace	,,	,,	537
Come, mighty Spirit, penetrate	,,	1861	538
Mighty Comforter, to Thee	,,	,,	539
Almighty Comforter and Friend	,,	1866	540
When the leaves of life are falling	,,	,,	541
Holy Ghost, Thou satest brooding	Robert W. Evans.	1860	543
The Body's Temple	,,	,,	545
Meekness of Spirit	,,	,,	548
O Holy Ghost Who down dost come	Thomas H. Gill.	1863	550
Holy Spirit! dwell with me	,,	1848	551
The Divine Renewer	,,	1867	552
The Unchanging Renewer	,,	1869	554
The Spirit's Dealings	,,	1854	555
Lord, when we come	,,	,,	557
O Spirit sweet and pure	,,	1868	558
O Spirit of our spirit	Charlotte M. Noel.	1862	560
Spirit of Bondage unto fear	Samuel Dunn.	,,	561
Spirit of Christ, descend	,,	,,	562
Hear, Holy Spirit	Francis Pott.	tr. 1861	563
The Lord is gone	Anonymous.	1861	564
When the Lord of Hosts ascended	C. Wordsworth.	1862	565
Holy Ghost, Illuminator	,,	,,	568
Gracious Spirit, Holy Ghost	,,	,,	570
Confirmation	,,	,,	571
Spirit of God, that moved of old	Cecil F. Alexander.	1858	572
O Holy Spirit, come	Oswald Allen.	1862	573
Spirit of Power and Truth and Love	W. L. Alexander.	1849	574
Praise be Thine, most Holy Spirit	Thomas Burbidge.		576
Sonnets	Anonymous.		578–580
Silence in Heaven	Herbert Kynaston.	1862	580
Holy Spirit! long expected	John S. B. Monsell.	1863	581
Gift of the Father's living Love	,,	,,	583
Come, Holy Spirit, come	Thomas Davis.	1864	584
We give Thee thanks, Good Spirit	B. E. Bishop.	1863	585
Eternal Spirit, Thee we praise	Anonymous.	1862	585
O Lord, Thy Holy Spirit send	,,	1864	586
Thou blessed Spirit, by Whose aid	,,	1863	587
O Spirit, Lord and God	,,	1864	588

	Author.	Date.	Page.
O Spirit, descend	D vid Thomas.	1866	590
Unseen Spirit, Lord of Life	W. R. Percival.	,,	590
Spirit of Life and Light	,,	,,	592
Let Thy wondrous way be known	A. Jackson.	,,	593
Opening a Place of Worship	Joseph Tritton.	1867	594
God the Spirit, we adore Thee	Samuel J. Stone.	1866	595
Confirmation	James G. Faithfull.	1867	596
Come Thou, O come	Gerard Moultrie.	tr. 1867	598
Litany of the Holy Ghost	R. F. Littledale.	1867	599
Another	Thomas B. Pollock.	1870	601
Twelve Fruits of the Spirit	,,	,,	605
Spirit of Christ, Thou speakest	Edward W. Eddis.	1868	606
Holy Ghost, this day descending	James Gabb.	1871	607
Who but Thou, almighty Spirit	"Eriphas."	1821	609

AMERICAN HYMNS.

Eternal Spirit, wilt Thou dwell	Anonymous.	1821	611
Blest Comforter Divine	Lydia H. Sigourney.	1824	612
Spirit of Holiness, descend	Samuel F. Smith.	1843	613
O Spirit of Holiness, breathe	Thomas Hastings.	1850	614
Creator Spirit! come and bless us	William Croswell.	d. 1851	615
O Holy Comforter	Ray Palmer.	1865	616
O Thou Whose influence wakes	Anonymous.	1856	617
Holy Ghost, Thou Source of Light	,,	1858	618
Spirit, poured on Pentecost	,,	1859	619
O for a heart of calm repose	,,	1864	620
O Spirit of the Lord of Hosts	William Pinkney.	1865	621
Blow on, Thou mighty Wind	John Henry Hopkins.	1860	624
For Reunion	,,	186-	626

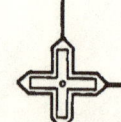
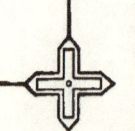

Introductory.

———•———

PART I.

PRAYERS FOR THE HOLY GHOST.

The Promise of the Father.

Proverbs i. 23. I will pour out my SPIRIT unto you.
Isaiah xliv. 3. I will pour my SPIRIT upon thy seed.
Ezekiel xxxvi. 27. I will put my SPIRIT within you.
Joel ii. 28. It shall come to pass afterward, that I will pour out my SPIRIT upon all flesh.

The Promise of Christ.

St. John xiv. 16–18. I will pray the FATHER, and He shall give you another COMFORTER, that He may abide with you for ever; even the SPIRIT of Truth; whom the world cannot receive, because it seeth Him not, neither knoweth Him: but ye know Him; for He dwelleth with you, and shall be in you. I will not leave you comfortless: I will come to you.

xiv. 26. The COMFORTER, which is the HOLY GHOST, whom the FATHER will send in my name, He shall teach you all things, and bring all things to your remembrance, whatsoever I have said unto you.

xv. 26. When the COMFORTER is come, whom I will send unto you from the FATHER, even the SPIRIT of Truth, which proceedeth from the FATHER, He shall testify of Me.

xvi. 7. It is expedient for you that I go away: for if I go not away, the COMFORTER will not come unto you; but if I depart, I will send Him unto you.

xvi. 13, 14. When He, the SPIRIT of Truth, is come, He will guide you into all Truth: for He shall not speak of Himself; but whatsoever He shall hear, that shall He speak: and He will show you things to come. He shall glorify Me: for He shall receive of mine, and shall show it unto you.

[And just before His Ascension:]

Luke xxiv. 49. Behold, I send the Promise of my FATHER upon you.

M AKE me a clean heart, O GOD, and renew a right spirit within me.

Cast me not away from Thy presence, and take not Thy HOLY SPIRIT from me.

O give me the cómfort of Thy help again, and stablish me with Thy free SPIRIT.

O GOD the King of glory, who hast exalted Thine only Son JESUS CHRIST with great triumph unto Thy Kingdom in Heaven: we beseech Thee, leave us not comfortless, but send to us Thine HOLY GHOST to comfort us, and exalt us unto the same place whither our Saviour CHRIST is gone before: who liveth and reigneth with Thee and the HOLY GHOST, one GOD, world without end.

SEND, we beseech Thee, almighty GOD, Thy HOLY SPIRIT into our hearts, that He may rule and direct us according to Thy will, comfort us in all our temptations and afflictions, defend us from all error, and lead us into all Truth; that we, being steadfast in the faith, may increase in love and in all good works, and in the end obtain everlasting life: through JESUS CHRIST Thy Son our Lord.

L AMB of GOD, that takest away the sins of the world,
Pour on us the HOLY SPIRIT.

LAMB of GOD, that takest away the sins of the world,
Send forth on us the promised SPIRIT of the FATHER.

LAMB of GOD, that takest away the sins of the world,
Give unto us the SPIRIT of Peace.

PRAYERS FOR THE HOLY GHOST.

O LORD, THY WING OUTSPREAD!

WILLIAM JOHN BLEW. From his *Church Hymn and Tune Book*. 1851-5.
There is a doxology, here omitted.

O LORD, Thy wing outspread,
    And us Thy flock enfold;
Thy broad wing spread, that covered
    Thy mercy-seat of old:
And o'er our nightly roof,
    And round our daily path,
Keep watch and ward, and hold aloof
    The devil and his wrath.

For thou dost fence our head,
    And shield — yea, Thou alone —
The peasant on his pallet-bed,
    The prince upon his throne.
Make then our heart Thine ark,
    Whereon Thy Mystic Dove
May brood, and lighten it, when dark,
    With beams of peace and love;

That dearer far to Thee
    Than gold or cedar-shrine
The bodies of Thy saints may be,
    The souls by Thee made Thine:

So never more be stirred
    That voice within our heart,
The fearful word that once was heard, —
    Up! let us hence depart.[1]

O THOU THAT HEAREST PRAYER!

JOHN BURTON: born 1803; a cooper at Stratford in Essex: author of several books in verse and prose. This popular hymn, which was long anonymous, first appeared in the *Baptist Magazine*, 1824.

O THOU that hearest prayer,
    Attend our humble cry;
And let Thy servants share
    Thy blessing from on high:
We plead the promise of Thy Word;
Grant us Thy Holy Spirit, Lord!

If earthly parents hear
    Their children when they cry;
If they, with love sincere,
    Their children's wants supply;
Much more wilt Thou Thy Love display,
And answer when Thy children pray.

Our heavenly Father Thou;
    We, children of Thy Grace:

---

[1] In allusion to the story, that just before the siege and destruction of Jerusalem voices were heard in the Temple, saying, "Let us go hence."

O let Thy Spirit now
    Descend and fill the place,
That all may feel the heavenly flame,
And all unite to praise Thy Name.

O may that sacred Fire,
    Descending from above,
Our frozen hearts inspire
    With fervent zeal and love;
Enlighten our beclouded eyes,
And teach our grovelling souls to rise.

And send Thy Spirit down
    On all the nations, Lord,
With great success to crown
    The preaching of Thy Word;
That heathen lands may own Thy sway,
And cast their idol-gods away.

Then shall Thy kingdom come
    Among our fallen race,
And the whole earth become
    The temple of Thy Grace;
Whence pure devotion shall ascend,
And songs of praise, till time shall end.

O GOD OF LOVE AND POWER!

JOHN MASON NEALE, D.D., 1818-1866: the greatest hymnist of our day, though he is more eminent in translations than in originals. This piece is from his *Hymns for Children*, 1844.

FOR THE THIRD HOUR.

O GOD of love and power,
    Behold us drawing near,
And choosing Thine appointed hour
    To worship in Thy fear.

The very hour of old
    Wherein Thy Spirit came
Upon the apostles of Thy fold,
    Like cloven tongues of flame.

O gracious Lord, do Thou
    That Holy Spirit send
To dwell with us and guide us now,
    And teach us to the end.

From men below the skies,
    And all the heavenly host,
To God the Father praise arise,
    To Son and Holy Ghost.

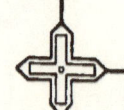

ERE THE WORLD, WITH LIGHT INVESTED.

WILLIAM HILEY BATHURST: born 1796; from 1820 to 1852 Rector of Barwick-in-Elmet. His *Psalms and Hymns* (1831; second edition, 1842) have afforded several pieces to general use; they include a nearly entire version of the Psalms, and 206 Hymns, no less than fourteen of which invoke or celebrate the Holy Spirit. The four next given are his.

GENESIS i. 2.

ERE the world, with light invested,
    Rose from its primeval sleep,
Gloom and desolation rested
    On the surface of the deep:
        Earth and ocean
Formed one rude and shapeless heap.

There the Holy Spirit moving,
    Wide His fostering pinions spread,
Till, beneath His power improving,
    Nature seemed no longer dead:
        Light and beauty
Rose to crown her radiant head.

Blessed Spirit, we implore Thee,
    Yet once more Thy succor lend;
Scatter the thick clouds before Thee
    Which through all the earth extend;
        On all nations
Bid the Light of Life descend.

See what sin and what delusion
    In this wretched world are found!

Stay the torrent of confusion,
    Ere it spreads destruction round:
      Where sin triumphed,
    Now let Grace and Truth abound.

II.

THE SPIRIT OF THE FATHERS.

O FOR that flame of living fire
    Which shone so bright in saints of old;
Which bade their souls to heaven aspire,
    Calm in distress, in danger bold!

Where is that Spirit, Lord, which dwelt
    In Abraham's breast, and sealed him Thine.
Which made Paul's heart with sorrow melt,
    And glow with energy divine?

That Spirit which from age to age
    Proclaimed Thy Love and taught Thy ways:
Brightened Isaiah's vivid page,
    And breathed in David's hallowed lays?

Is not Thy Grace as mighty now
    As when Elijah felt its power;
When glory beamed from Moses' brow,
    Or Job endured the trying hour?

Remember, Lord, the ancient days;
    Renew Thy work, Thy Grace restore;
Warm our cold hearts to prayer and praise,
    And teach us how to love Thee more.

III.

LORD, SHOW THY GLORY AS OF OLD.

LORD, show Thy glory, as of old,
   The work of heavenly Love display,
And let our longing eyes behold
   Another Pentecostal day:
Our fervent wishes deign to crown,
And send Thy quickening Spirit down.

Thou seest, Lord, how far we stray,
   Opprest with ills we cannot flee;
How sin hath drawn our hearts away
   From peace, from happiness, and Thee:
Thy gracious Spirit, Lord, bestow,
And snatch us from the depth of woe.

Encompast with a host of foes,
   Our strength is small, our danger nigh:
Where can we find some brief repose,
   Or whither for protection fly?
O Lord, Thy mighty Spirit send,
Our hearts to strengthen and defend.

Now let a brighter day begin
   Than ever yet was witnessed here:
Bid the dark-gathering clouds of sin
   Before Thy presence disappear;
Reign in each heart; in every place
Set up the empire of Thy grace.

IV.

FULL OF WEAKNESS AND OF SIN.

ROMANS viii. 26.

FULL of weakness and of sin,
    We look to Thee for life:
Lord, Thy gracious work begin,
    And calm the inward strife.

Though our hearts are prone to stray,
    Be Thou a constant Friend:
Though we know not how to pray,
    Thy saving mercy send.

Let Thy Spirit, gracious Lord,
    Our souls with love inspire;
Strength and confidence afford,
    And breathe celestial fire.

Teach us first to feel our need,
    Then all that need supply;
When we hunger, deign to feed,
    And hear us when we cry.

When we cleave to earthly things,
    Send Thy reviving Grace:
Raise our souls, and give them wings
    To reach Thy holy place.

FOR ANOTHER PENTECOST.

BENJAMIN GOUGH: born 1805; a retired merchant, residing at Mountfield, near Faversham. Author of *Lyra Sabbatica*, 1865, and *Kentish Lyrics*, 1867. From the former of these, a work of considerable merit, the three following pieces are taken.

JOEL ii. 28.

QUICKEN, Lord, Thy Church and me;
   Send the promised Spirit down;
Holy One, Eternal Three,
   All Thy former mercies crown:
Father, Son, and Holy Ghost,
Send another Pentecost!

Let the living fire descend,
   Cloven tongues on every head,
Tongues which all may comprehend, —
   Speak Thy Life into the dead!
Suddenly the power of Grace
Send from Heaven, and fill the place.

Send the rushing mighty wind,
   Give the utterance divine;
Let us know the Spirit's mind;
   Let us speak in words of Thine:
Send a pure baptismal shower, —
Tongues of fire, and words of power.

As of old, so be it now,
   Now the glorious scene repeat;

See Thy humbled people bow,
    Waiting lowly at Thy feet,
Crying all, with one accord,
Send the promised Spirit, Lord!

First on the believing few,
    Then in widening power unfurled;
Gathering, as the deluge grew,
    Pour Thy Spirit on the world:
Bright in panoply divine
Bid Thy Church arise and shine.

Jesus, glorious Victor, come!
    Thou whose right it is to reign;
Call Thine ancient people home,
    Paradise restore again:
Father, Son, and Holy Ghost,
Send another Pentecost!

COME FROM THE FOUR WINDS, O BREATH!

EZEKIEL xxvii. 9.

COME from the four winds, O Breath,
    And breathe upon these slain!
All the earth is full of death,
    And sin and sorrow reign.
Father, Son, and Holy Ghost,
    Hear the universal cry
Of Thy sacramental host,
    Who at Thy footstool lie.

Now in humble faith we plead
  The promise and the oath,
Waiting in this hour of need
  Till Thou fulfil them both.
Honor now the precious Blood;
  O make good Thy royal word!
Send the Spirit like a flood,
  The Spirit of the Lord.

Never will we cease to pray
  Till Thou Thy Spirit give,
Turn our darkness into day,
  And cause the dead to live;
Till Thy glorious Church arise,
  And all the earth for Christ enfold,
Pure as heaven's o'er-arching skies,
  Or Paradise of old.

Never will we cease to pray
  Till every sinful soul
Unto Jesus finds his way,
  And is by faith made whole.
Until all shall know the Lord,
  Still we cry, and cry again, —
Conquer with Thy Spirit's sword,
  And hasten Jesu's reign.

COME, YE WHO DESIRE AN ANSWER BY FIRE.

COME, ye who desire an answer by fire,
    And long for the day
When Jesus His sceptre o'er all men shall sway,

Join the catholic cry for the power from on high,
    The Spirit divine,
And pray till you get the life-giving sign.

With importunate prayer your petitions declare,
    And mightily cry,
Expecting just now a gracious reply.

Through the covenant Blood which on Calvary flowed,
    The Spirit is ours;
And the blessing is promised in plentiful showers.

For the Spirit we pray: no longer delay,
    O Fire from on high!
Descend, Lord and Giver of Life, while we cry.

In shaking and might, in glory and light,
    On every brow,
Thou Spirit of burning, come, visit us now!

Every heart cries, "Come in, and cleanse me from sin
    In Jesus's blood,
And fill with the Spirit and glory of God.".

SAVIOUR, I THY WORD BELIEVE.

O let the heavens rend! Holy Spirit, descend
    In Pentecost power,
Till the heathen are gathered to Christ as His
    dower.

O Jesus, all hail! Let Thy Gospel prevail
    Till the world is o'erspread,
And Paradise blooms with life from the dead.

SAVIOUR, I THY WORD BELIEVE.

AUGUSTUS MONTAGUE TOPLADY, 1740-1778: Vicar of Broad Hembury, Devon, and author of "Rock of Ages." From his Juvenile Poems, 1759.

SAVIOUR, I Thy word believe;
    My unbelief remove:
Now Thy quickening Spirit give,
    The unction from above.
Show me, Lord, how good Thou art;
    My soul with all Thy fulness fill:
Send the Witness, in my heart
    The Holy Ghost reveal.

Dead in sin till then I lie,
    Bereft of power to rise,
Till Thy Spirit inwardly
    Thy saving Blood applies.
Now thy mighty Gift impart,
    My sin erase, my pardon seal:
Send the Witness, in my heart
    The Holy Ghost reveal.

Blessed Comforter, come down,
    And live and move in me;
Make my every deed Thy own,
    In all things led by Thee;
Bid my every lust depart,
    And with me O vouchsafe to dwell:
Faithful Witness, in my heart
    Thy perfect Light reveal.

Let me in Thy Love rejoice,
    Thy shrine, Thy pure abode:
Tell me, by Thine inward voice,
    That I'm a child of God.
Lord, I choose the better part;
    Jesus, I wait Thy peace to feel:
Send the Witness, in my heart
    The Holy Ghost reveal.

Whom the world cannot receive,
    O manifest in me:
Son of God, I cease to live
    When I am not in Thee.
Now impute Thy whole desert,
    Restore the joy from whence I fell:
Breathe the Witness, in my heart
    The Holy Ghost reveal.

Hast Thou not for sinners groaned,
    And all men dearly bought?
Saviour, be in mercy found
    Of those that seek thee not:

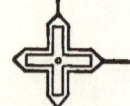 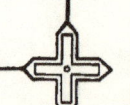

Scatter round Thy keenest darts,
  And sin from every soul expel:
Send the Witness, in their hearts
  The Holy Ghost reveal.

JESUS IS GONE UP ON HIGH.

THOMAS KELLY, 1769-1855: an Irish dissenter of wealth and family, and a man of learning and benevolence. His hymns, reprinted and enlarged in eight successive editions between 1804 and 1853, number in the last one 765, of which this (of the date 1806) is almost the only one that has more than a passing allusion to the Holy Spirit. I am glad to be able by its means to give the good man some place, though but an humble one, in this collection. Many of Mr. Kelly's lyrics have attained more or less popularity: their chief merit, however, lies in a certain earnest simplicity, not common in this age; for his pen seldom shows much either of grace or vigor.

JOHN xiv. 16.

JESUS is gone up on high,
  But His promise still is here:
He will all our wants supply;
  He will send the Comforter.

Let us now His promise plead,
  Let us to His throne draw nigh:
Jesus knows His people's need,
  Jesus hears His people's cry.

Who can boast a lot like theirs
  Whom the Lord vouchsafes to own?
Jesus listens to their prayers;
  What they ask in faith is done.

Saviour, this is our request:
  "On us make Thy face to shine;"
Grant us this; and for the rest,
  All is ours when we are Thine.

Send us, Lord, the Comforter,
   Pledge and Witness of Thy Love,
Dwelling with Thy people here,
   Leading them to joys above.

Till we reach the promised rest,
   Till Thy face unveiled we see,
Of this blessed hope possest,
   Teach us, Lord, to live to Thee.

ENTHRONED ON HIGH, ALMIGHTY LORD.

THOMAS HAWEIS, LL.B., M.D., 1732-1820; chaplain to the Countess of Huntingdon, and Rector of Aldwink'e, in Northamptonshire. His hymns appeared in 1792.

ENTHRONED on high, Almighty Lord,
   The Holy Ghost send down;
Fulfil in us Thy faithful word,
   And all Thy mercies crown.

Though on our heads no tongues of fire
   Their wondrous powers impart,
Grant, Saviour, what we most desire,
   Thy Spirit in our heart.

Spirit of life and light and love,
   Thy heavenly influence give;
Quicken our souls, born from above,
   In Christ that we may live.

To our benighted minds reveal
   The glories of His Grace,
And bring us where no clouds conceal
   The brightness of His face.

His Love within us shed abroad,
 Life's ever-springing well;
Till God in us, and we in God,
 In love eternal dwell.

FATHER, IF JUSTLY STILL WE CLAIM.

JOHN WESLEY, 1739: rewritten (the first five verses being here omitted) from HENRY MORE, 1614–1687. For More's original poem, see p. 73.

FATHER, if justly still we claim
 To us and ours the promise made,
To us be graciously the same,
 And crown with living fire our head.

Our claim admit, and from above
 Of holiness the Spirit shower;
Of wise discernment, humble love,
 And zeal and unity and power.

The Spirit of convincing speech,
 Of power demonstrative, impart;
Such as may every conscience reach,
 And sound the unbelieving heart:

The Spirit of refining fire,
 Searching the inmost of the mind,
To purge all fierce and foul desire,
 And kindle life more pure and kind:

The Spirit of faith, in this Thy day,
 To break the power of cancelled sin,
Tread down its strength, o'erturn its sway,
 And still the conquest more than win.

The Spirit breathe of inward life,
    Which in our hearts Thy laws may write;
Then grief expires, and pain and strife:
    'Tis nature all, and all delight.

On all the earth Thy Spirit shower,
    The earth in righteousness renew;
Thy kingdom come, and hell's o'erpower,
    And to Thy sceptre all subdue.

Like mighty wind, or torrent fierce,
    Let it opposers all o'errun,
And every law of sin reverse,
    That faith and love may make all one.

Yea, let Thy Spirit in every place
    Its richer energy declare;
While lovely tempers, fruits of grace,
    The kingdom of Thy Christ prepare.

Grant this, O holy God and true!
    The ancient seers Thou didst inspire:
To us perform the promise due,
    Descend and crown us now with fire.

LEAVE US NOT COMFORTLESS.

Josiah Conder, 1836.

LEAVE us not comfortless,
   O Thou our risen Lord!
But send Thy Spirit down, to bless
   And guide us with Thy Word.

By Him Thy gifts impart,
   Light, peace, and joy, and love;
Seal of adoption in our heart,
   Earnest of heaven above.

FATHER, IF THOU MY FATHER ART.

Charles Wesley, 1708-1788: by far the most voluminous, as he is the most brilliant, of English hymnists A complete list of his poetical publications would occupy forty or fifty lines: they are being reprinted now, by the British Wesleyan Methodist Conference, in twelve good-sized volumes. The number of his separate hymns is at least five thousand, perhaps considerably more. He alone, among all the versifiers of the last century, gave due place to the praises of the Holy Ghost: or rather to invocations of the same, for his voice was much oftener raised in prayer than in praise. Many of his compositions are given in this volume; there will be found in them, as in nearly every thing that he wrote, a vehemence of feeling and expression which was natural to his temperament, and inseparable from his religious system. The hymn immediately subjoined is from his second original volume, *Hymns and Sacred Poems*, 1740, and is there entitled, "Groaning for the Spirit of Adoption."

FATHER, if Thou my Father art,
   Send forth the Spirit of Thy Son;
Breathe Him into my panting heart,
   And make me know as I am known:
Make me Thy conscious child, that I
May "Father, Abba, Father," cry.

I want the Spirit of power within,
   Of love, and of an healthful mind;
Of power to conquer inbred sin,
   Of love to Thee and all mankind;
Of health, that pain and death defies,
Most vigorous when the body dies.

When shall I hear the inward voice,
   Which only faithful souls can hear?
Pardon and peace and heavenly joys
   Attend the promised Comforter.
He comes! and Righteousness divine,
And Christ, and all with Christ, is mine!

O that the Comforter would come!
   Nor visit as a transient guest,
But fix in me His constant home,
   And take possession of my breast,
And make my soul His loved abode,
The temple of indwelling God!

Come, Holy Ghost, my heart inspire,
   Attest that I am born again;
Come, and baptize me now with fire,
   Or all Thy former gifts are vain.
I cannot rest in sin forgiven:
Where is the earnest of my heaven?

Where the indubitable seal
   That ascertains the kingdom mine?

The powerful stamp I long to feel,
　　The signature of Love divine:
O shed it in my heart abroad,
　　Fulness of love, of heaven, of God!

FATHER OF OUR DYING LORD.

C. WESLEY.　From *Hymns and Sacred Poems*, 1742.

FATHER of our dying Lord,
　　Remember us for good;
O fulfil His faithful word,
　　And hear His speaking Blood.
Give us that for which He prays:
　　Father, glorify Thy Son!
Show His truth and power and grace,
　　And send the Promise down.

True and faithful Witness Thou,
　　O Christ, the Spirit give;
Hast Thou not received Him now
　　That we might now receive?
Art Thou not our living Head?
　　Life to all Thy limbs impart;
Shed Thy Love, Thy Spirit shed,
　　In every waiting heart.

Holy Ghost, the Comforter,
　　The Gift of Jesus, come!
Glows our heart to find Thee near,
　　And swells to make Thee room.

Present with us Thee we feel;
  Come, O come, and in us be;
With us, in us, live and dwell
  To all eternity.

FATHER, GLORIFY THY SON.

C WESLEY. From *Hymns of Petition and Thanksgiving for the Promise of the Father; or Hymns for Whit-Sunday,* 1746. The eleven following pieces are taken from this important tract.

JOHN xiv. 16, 17.

FATHER, glorify Thy Son;
  Answer His prevailing prayer;
Send that Intercessor down,
  Send that other Comforter,
Whom believingly we claim,
Whom we ask in Jesus' name.

Him the world cannot receive,
  Him they neither see nor know;
Blind in unbelief they live;
  All His inward work below,
All His inspirations, deem
Foolish as a madman's dream.

But we know by faith, and feel
  Him the Spirit of Truth and Grace.
With us He vouchsafes to dwell;
  With us, when unseen, He stays:
All our help and good, we own,
Freely flows from Him alone.

Yet, alas! we cannot rest
  Helped with an *external* Guide,
Till the transitory Guest
  Enter, and *in* us abide:
Give Him, Lord, Thy Spirit give,
In us constantly to live.

Wilt Thou not the promise seal,
  True and gracious as Thou art,
Send the Comforter to dwell
  Every moment in our heart?
Yes, Thou must the grace bestow:
Jesus said, It shall be so.

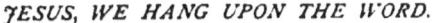

JESUS, WE HANG UPON THE WORD.

John xiv. 16.

JESUS, we hang upon the word
  Our faithful souls have heard from Thee;
Be mindful of Thy promise, Lord,
  Thy promise made to all, and me,
Thy followers who Thy steps pursue,
And dare believe that God is true.

Thou saidst, I will the Father pray,
  And He the Paraclete shall give,
Shall give Him in your hearts to stay,
  And never more His temples leave:
Myself will to My orphans come,
And make you My eternal home.

Come, then, dear Lord, Thyself reveal,
   And let the promise now take place;
Be it according to Thy will,
   According to Thy word of grace:
Thy sorrowful disciples cheer,
And send us down the Comforter.

He visits now the troubled breast,
   And oft relieves our sad complaint;
But soon we lose the transient Guest.
   But soon we droop again and faint,
Repeat the melancholy moan,
"Our joy is fled, our comfort gone."

Hasten Him, Lord, into our heart,
   Our sure inseparable Guide:
O might we meet, and never part!
   O might He in our heart abide,
And keep His house of praise and prayer,
And rest and reign for ever there!

SAVIOUR AND PRINCE OF PEACE.

JOHN xiv. 18-21.

SAVIOUR and Prince of Peace,
   Thy saying we receive:
Thou wilt not leave us comfortless,
   Thine own Thou wilt not leave.
Poor helpless orphans, we
   Awhile Thine absence mourn,

But we Thy face again shall see,
 But Thou wilt soon return.

No longer visible
 To eyes of flesh and blood,
Come, Lord, to us Thyself reveal,
 O come, and show us God.
Because Thou livest above,
 Let us Thy Spirit know,
And in the glorious knowledge prove
 Eternal Life below.

Hasten the day when we
 Shall surely know and feel
Thou art in God, and God in Thee,
 And Thou in us dost dwell.
To us who keep Thy word
 Thou with Thy Father come,
And love, and make us, gracious Lord,
 Thine everlasting home.

JESUS, OUR EXALTED HEAD.

JOHN xv. 26, 27.

JESUS, our exalted Head,
 Regard Thy people's prayer;
Send us, in Thy body's stead,
 The abiding Comforter.
From Thy dazzling throne above,
 From Thy Father's glorious seat,
Send the Spirit of Truth and Love,
 The eternal Paraclete.

Issuing forth from Him and Thee,
   O let the Blessing flow!
Pour the streaming Deity
   On all Thy Church below.
Him to testify Thy Grace,
   Him to teach how good Thou art,
Him to vouch Thy Godhead, place
   In every faithful heart.

God of God, and Light of Light,
   Thee let Him now reveal;
Justify us by Thy right,
   And stamp us with Thy seal:
Fill our souls with joy and peace;
   Wisdom, grace, and utterance give;
Constitute Thy witnesses,
   And in Thy members live.

By the Holy Ghost we wait
   To say, Thou art the Lord,
Saved, and to our first estate
   In perfect love restored.
Then we shall in every breath
   Testify the power we prove,
Publish Thee, in life and death,
   The God of Truth and Love.

JESUS, WE ON THE WORD DEPEND.

John xiv. 25-27.

JESUS, we on the word depend
   Spoken by Thee while present here;
"The Father in My name shall send
   The Holy Ghost, the Comforter."

That promise made to Adam's race,
   Now, Lord, in us, even us, fulfil;
And give the Spirit of Thy Grace,
   To teach us all Thy perfect will.

That heavenly Teacher of mankind,
   That Guide infallible impart,
To bring Thy sayings to our mind,
   And write them on our faithful heart.

He only can the words apply
   Through which we endless life possess,
And deal to each his legacy,
   His Lord's unutterable peace.

That peace of God, that peace of Thine,
   O might He now to us bring in,
And fill our souls with power divine,
   And make an end of fear and sin:

The length and breadth of love reveal,
   The height and depth of Deity,
And all the sons of glory seal,
   And change, and make us all like Thee.

SAVIOUR, LORD, WHO AT THY DEATH.

John xvi. 1-4.

SAVIOUR, Lord, who at Thy Death
    Peace didst to Thy Church bequeath,
Now confer the peace on me,
Bring me now *my* legacy.

Grant me (not as mortals give,
Hoping better to receive)
That for which I sigh and mourn:
Give, and look for no return.

Grant me for Thy mercy sake,
Me, who no return can make,
That which I can never buy:
Save, and freely justify.

Grant me (not as childish men
Grant, and ask their gifts again)
Peace, which none can take away,
Peace which shall for ever stay.

Now the benefit impart,
Speak it to my troubled heart;
Comfort and Thyself restore,
Come, and bid me sin no more.

Come, and wipe away my tears;
Come, and scatter all my fears;
Come, and take me to Thy breast,
Lull me to eternal rest.

FATHER, ADMIT OUR LAWFUL CLAIM.

LUKE xi. 13.

FATHER, admit our lawful claim,
  Let us that ask receive:
To us that ask in Jesus' name
  Thou shalt Thy Spirit give.

Jesus hath spoke the faithful word
  On them that ask Him here.
Thou shalt, in honor of our Lord,
  The Holy Ghost confer.

If evil we by nature know
  To give our children food,
Much more Thou wilt on us bestow
  The soul-sustaining good.

Our holy heavenly Father, Thou
  Regardest Thy children's prayer:
Answer, and send, O send us now,
  The promised Comforter.

We seek, Thou knowest, we seek Thy face:
  Let us the blessing find:
Open the door of faith and grace
  To us and all mankind.

Surely Thou wilt, we dare believe,
  For Jesus' sake alone,
Thou wilt to us the Spirit give,
  Give all good gifts in One.

HEAR ALL THE SAVIOUR'S CRY.

John vii. 37-39.

HEAR all the Saviour's cry
    On this great festal day:
"The man that would on Me rely,
    That *would* be happy, may.
If any of all mankind
    Is now athirst for God,
Now let him come to Me, and find
    And drink the living flood.

"He that believes on Me,
    The word of Truth shall feel:
The wilderness a pool shall be,
    The heath a springing well.
Forth from that faithful soul
    Rivers of Life shall flow,
And streams of Grace eternal roll
    O'er all the earth below."

Lord, we with joy embrace
    (What all may find fulfilled)
The promise made to all our race,
    And to believers sealed.
Who in Thy merit trust,
    Thy Spirit still receive;
And temples of the Holy Ghost
    And filled with God they live.

The Spirit of their God
    Doth in the saints abide:
He is, He is by Thee bestowed,
    For Thou art glorified.
Thy Blood's unceasing prayer
    And strong prevailing plea
Hath now obtained the Comforter
    For all mankind and me.

Lord, I believe the sure
    Irrevocable word,
And come to Thee distrest and poor,
    To Thee my faithful Lord.
I come athirst and faint
    Thy Spirit to receive:
Give me the Gift for which I pant,
    Thyself the Giver give!

In this accepted hour,
    The promised God impart;
Open a spring of life and power
    Eternal in my heart:
To all the world below
    So shall my bowels move,
So shall my heart like Thine o'erflow
    With everlasting love.

JESUS, LORD, IN PITY HEAR US.

JESUS, Lord, in pity hear us;
  O return, while we mourn,
    By Thy Spirit cheer us.

Swallowed up in sin and sadness,
  O relieve us that grieve,
    Turn our grief to gladness.

Send the Comforter to raise us;
  Let us see God in Thee
    Merciful and gracious.

Him, the Purchase of Thy Passion,
  O impart! cleanse our heart
    By His inspiration.

By the earnest of Thy Spirit,
  Let us know heaven below,
    Heaven above inherit.

Perfect when we walk before Thee,
  Filled with love then remove
    To our thrones of glory.

O THOU WHO BY THY BLOOD.

John xvi. 7.

O THOU who by Thy Blood
    Hast brought a world to God,
Thou who, to Thy Father gone,
    Dost in our behalf appear!
Hear Thy desolate servants groan,
    Send us down the Comforter.

    Hadst Thou not purged our stain,
        And gone to God again,
None of Adam's helpless race
    Could that blessed Spirit find;
But Thou hast obtained the Grace,
    Purchased Him for all mankind.

    Didst Thou not plead above
        For us Thy dying Love,
Never could we hope Thine aid,
    Never for Thy Spirit call;
But Thou hast the Father prayed,
    Hast received the Gift for all.

    "And if I go away,"
        (By faith we hear Thee say)
"I the Comforter will send,
    Comforter of you that grieve,
All your goings to attend,
    Ever in your hearts to live."

Amen, our hearts reply,
Uplifted to the sky;
Pant to be Thy blest abode,
Swell to be possessed by Thee,
Filled with the indwelling God,
Filled to all eternity.

SON OF GOD, FOR THEE WE LANGUISH.

JOHN xvi. 6, 7.

SON of God, for Thee we languish;
Still Thy absence we bemoan,
Overwhelmed with grief and anguish,
Poor, forsaken, and alone.
Thou art to Thy Heaven departed:
See us thence, with pity see,
Comfortless and broken-hearted,
Drooping, dead for want of Thee.

Once Thy blissful Love we tasted,
Cheered by Thee with Living Bread.
O how short a time it lasted!
O how soon the joy is fled!
Where is now our boasted Saviour,
Where our rapture of delight?
Thou hast, Lord, withdrawn Thy favor,
Thou art vanished from our sight.

Yet Thou hast the cause unfolded,
   Could we but the truth receive;
Thou in humbling Love hast told it,
   Needful 'tis for us to grieve.[1]
Stript of that excessive pleasure,
   Fondly we the loss deplore,
Till we find again our Treasure,
   Find, and never lose Thee more.

That we may Thyself inherit,
   Us Thou dost awhile forsake;
That we may receive Thy Spirit,
   Thou hast took His comforts back.
After a short night of mourning,
   We again shall see Thy face,
Triumph in Thy full returning,
   Glory in Thy perfect Grace.

For Thy transient outward presence
   We Thine endless Love shall feel;
Seated in our inmost essence
   Thou shalt by Thy Spirit dwell.
Jesus, come! Thyself the Giver
   Let us for the Gift receive;
Let us live in God for ever,
   God in us for ever live.

---

[1] "Compare Wesley's Works, vol. vi. pp. 84-91." This is Dr. Osborn's note, in his reprint of the Wesley poetry. The brothers (John and Charles) held some rather peculiar notions on this subject. In a foot-note to one of their hymns, — I quote from memory, — they say, "It may please God to remove our *Isaac*, our Joy in Himself."

PART II.

THE STORY OF PENTECOST.

The Story of Pentecost.

Acts ii. 1–16.

When the day of Pentecost was fully come, they were all with one accord in one place. And suddenly there came a sound from heaven, as of a rushing mighty wind, and it filled all the house where they were sitting. And there appeared unto them cloven tongues like as of fire, and it sat upon each of them. And they were all filled with the Holy Ghost, and began to speak with other tongues, as the Spirit gave them utterance. And there were dwelling at Jerusalem Jews, devout men, out of every nation under heaven. Now when this was noised abroad, the multitude came together, and were confounded, because that every man heard them speak in his own language. And they were all amazed, and marvelled, saying one to another, Behold, are not all these which speak, Galileans? And how hear we every man in our own tongue, wherein we were born? Parthians, and Medes, and Elamites, and the dwellers in Mesopotamia, and in Judea, and Cappadocia, in Pontus, and Asia, Phrygia, and Pamphylia, in Egypt, and in the parts of Libya about Cyrene, and strangers of Rome, Jews and Proselytes, Cretes and Arabians, we do hear them speak in our tongues the wonderful works of God. And they were all amazed, and were in doubt, saying one to another, What meaneth this? Others mocking said, These men are full of new wine. But Peter, standing up with the eleven, lifted up his voice, and said unto them, Ye men of Judea, and all ye that dwell at Jerusalem, be this known unto you, and hearken to my words: for these are not drunken as ye suppose, seeing it is but the third hour of the day. But this is that which was spoken by the prophet Joel.

O GOD, who as at this time didst teach the hearts of Thy faithful people, by sending to them the light of Thy HOLY SPIRIT: grant us by the same SPIRIT to have a right judgment in all things, and evermore to rejoice in His holy comfort: through the merits of JESUS CHRIST our Saviour, who liveth and reigneth with Thee, in the unity of the same SPIRIT, one GOD, world without end.

O GOD, who didst give The HOLY SPIRIT to Thine Apostles, grant unto Thy people the performance of their petitions, so that on us, to whom Thou hast given faith, Thou mayest also bestow peace by the same SPIRIT: through JESUS CHRIST our Lord.

THE STORY OF PENTECOST.

JAM CHRISTUS ASTRA ASCENDERAT.

Thomasius, Mone, and Wackernagel ascribe this to AMBROSE (d. 397), though Mone thinks the text has been corrupted. Daniel places it later. The Roman Breviary of Urban VIII., 1631, gives a greatly varied form: both this and the original are given in Daniel, I. 64. It was used at Matins at Pentecost. Translated by EDWARD CASWALL, in *Lyra Catholica*, 1848.

ABOVE the starry spheres,
To where He was before,
Christ had gone up, soon from on high
The Father's Gift to pour:

And now had fully come,
On mystic circle borne
Of seven times seven revolving days,
The Pentecostal morn.

When, as the Apostles knelt
At the third hour in prayer,
A sudden rushing sound proclaimed
The God of glory near.

Forthwith a tongue of fire
Alights on every brow:
Each breast receives the Father's light,
The Word's enkindling glow.

The Holy Ghost on all
    Is mightily outpoured;
Who straight in divers tongues declare
    The wonders of the Lord;

While strangers of all climes
    Flock round from far and near,
And with amazement each at once
    Their native accents hear.

But Judah, faithless still,
    Denies the hand divine,
And madly jeers the saints of Christ
    As drunk with new-made wine.

Till Peter in the midst
    Stood up and spake aloud,
And their perfidious falsity
    By Joel's witness showed.

Praise to the Father be!
    Praise to the Son who rose!
Praise, Holy Paraclete, to Thee,
    While age on ages flows!

CHRIST HAD REGAINED THE SKY.

ANOTHER VERSION.

CHRIST HAD REGAINED THE SKY.

By EDWARD ARTHUR DAYMAN, B.D., prebendary of Britton, and co-editor. with Lord Nelson and J. R. Woodford, of the *Sarum Hymnal*, 1868. From that collection it is taken.

CHRIST had regained the sky,
    To send down whence He came
The promise from on high,
    Made in the Father's Name:
His own await the hour
That seals their coming power.

The mystic destined day
    Of sevenfold circling years
Speeds onward on its way
    To herald hopes and fears,
To set the bondmen free:
Great year of Jubilee!

Within the temple there
    In silence all lay hushed —
Down, at that hour of prayer,
    Sudden the whirlwind rushed!
Not voiceless as of old,
God's presence now it told.

And cloven tongues of flame
    The Word's full warmth inspire;
And from the Father came
    The lamp of living fire,

To fill the faithful heart,
And light and life impart.

The Holy Ghost on each
  The gift of tongues hath poured,
To tell in varied speech
  The wonders of the Lord!
And Babel's work undone,
He binds the Church in one.

Parthian and Elamite,
  And strangers far and near,
Greek, Arab, Proselyte,
  Their own loved language hear.
All lands where man hath trod
Shall hear the voice of God.

Though Israelites combine
  With infidels to mock,
Nor drunkenness nor wine
  The faltering lips unlock,
But different tongues confess
God's Truth in soberness.

Outspake the Apostle bold,
  How God fulfilled His word,
And prophets had foretold
  The coming of the Lord:
By dream and vision known,
The Spirit seals His own.

Christ, may the Comforter
 From God the Father come,
And grace and power confer,
 And guide us to Thy home!
Renew the face of earth,
And give the world new birth.
     Amen.

AUDIMUR; ALMA SPIRITUS.

From the Parisian Breviary. Translation by Isaac Williams, 1839.

NOW our prayers are heard on high,
 And 'mid mortal men unblest
The good Comforter is nigh,
 Coming from the Father's breast.

What mysterious sight and sound
 Of our God the coming speaks?
Like a rushing wind profound,
 All the house His presence shakes.

Like a fiery shower it falls
 All the hallowed guests among,
Upon each within the walls
 Sitting like a flaming tongue.

While the bright and lambent blaze
 Plays their unharmed heads around,
It hath gone with piercing rays
 To their deepest hearts profound.

THE STORY OF PENTECOST.

All aghast the nations throng,
  While with other tongues they name
Things that unto Heaven belong,
  And whate'er they speak is flame.

Lo again, O sight of fear!
  For the hearer hath a tongue:
Of new prophets, while they hear,
  Hath another harvest sprung.

Praise to Father and to Son,
And to Thee, the Holy One,
By whose awful breath divine
Our dull spirits burn and shine.

BEATA NOBIS GAUDIA.

<small>Daniel and Fabricius ascribe this hymn to St. Hilary, Bishop of Poictiers from 355 to 368, the earliest of the Latin hymnists. Mone is persuaded that it is much later, and Wackernagel refers it to the 5th century. It was sung at compline or lauds at Pentecost. Translated by William John Blew, *Church Hymn and Tune Book*, 1851; reprinted in *Lyra Mystica* and in *The People's Hymnal*.</small>

R OUND roll the weeks our hearts to greet,
   With blissful joys returning;
For lo! the Holy Paraclete
  On twelve bright brows sits burning.
With quivering flame He lights on each
In fashion like a tongue, to teach
That eloquent they are of speech,
  Their hearts with true love yearning.

BEATA NOBIS GAUDIA.

While with all tongues they speak to all,
  The nations deem them maddened;
And drunk with wine the prophets call
  Whom God's good Spirit gladdened:
A marvel this, in mystery done;
The holy Paschal-tide outrun,
The duly numbered days have won
  Remission for the saddened.

O God most holy, Thee we pray
  With reverent brow low bending,
Grant us the Spirit's gifts to-day,
  The gifts from Heaven descending;
And since Thy Grace hath deigned to bide
Within our breasts once sanctified,
Deign, Lord, to cast our sins aside,
  Henceforth calm seasons sending.

To God the Father laud and praise,
  Praise to the Son be given;
Praise to the Spirit of all grace,
  The Fount of graces seven;
As was of old, all worlds before,
Is now, and shall be evermore,
When time and change are spent and o'er, —
  All praise in earth and Heaven.

GLADSOME FEAST!

Another Version, by the Rev. E. A. Washburn, D.D., of New York. Contributed. The allusion to the Jubilee is in accordance with a German note of Königsfeld.

GLADSOME feast! each rolling year
   Brings anew the season dear,
When upon the waiting host
Burning fell the Holy Ghost.

Quivering like a cloven tongue,
Heavenly light above them hung;
On their lips a word it came,
In their hearts a living flame.

Now in every voice they spake,
Awed the listening heathen shake:
'Twas no fire of maddening wine,
Theirs the Spirit's draught divine.

Mystic birth! revealed of old,
When the Paschal days were told,
And the circling Jubilee
Set the happy bondman free.

God of boundless mercy! now
With a lowly face we bow;
Give Thy Spirit from above,
Grant the largess of Thy Love.

Thou, whose tides of Grace could pour
On those hallowed hearts before,
Let our sinful bondage cease,
Bring our Jubilee of peace!

EYA MUSA DIC QUÆSO PRÆCLARA CHOREA.

From *The Sarum Missal in English*, 1868. The hymns in this are translated by CHARLES BUCHANAN PEARSON, Prebendary of Sarum. He has recently published these sequences in a volume; his renderings of them, says an English critic, are "always scholarly, and sometimes poetical."

NOW prompt, O Muse, the fitting strain,
And let the organ lend its tempered might;
Swell, pipe and string, the joyous note of praise;
Whilst we, with lifted heart and voice,
Devoutly sing the honor of this day.
For on this day descends the Paraclete
Upon Christ's faithful ones, filling their souls with grace,
A sudden sound is heard, and tongues of fire are seen,
And, lo! with accents not their own,
Untaught of man, they speak the wondrous works of God.
Yet carnal unbelief cries scornfully,
"Full of new wine are these:" misdeeming them
Whose hearts the Blessed Spirit with love inflames.
It is the fiftieth day
From the great Resurrection morn.

THE STORY OF PENTECOST.

Into their heart of hearts down glides the mystic
        fire;
  While to the city a clear sign is given.
Then forth they go, a light amid the gloom,
Dropping the Word's good seed in every land
      With many a sign of power,
      While the supernal dew
  Blesses the thirsty new-sown field.
And now, O Christ, Thy servants waiting on Thee
Here in Thine house, would fain their voice attune
To that new song which saints in glory sing.
To Him be endless glory, honor, power,
Who to all men that serve Him faithfully
In every clime the Spirit's aid vouchsafes!
Meekly, with one accord, the wondrous Gift we
        seek,
That He, the Holy Ghost, our inmost hearts
First cleansing, with all wisdom may enlighten.
                Alleluia!

LUX JUCUNDA, LUX INSIGNIS.

ADAM OF ST. VICTOR, twelfth century. Daniel esteems it "a Prose of the highest merit, inferior to none and superior to most, full of the flowers and fragrance of the Holy Scriptures." Translated by C. B. PEARSON, from the *Sarum Missal*, 1868. There is a partial version of this by Dr. HERBERT KYNASTON, in his *Occasional Hymns*, 1862.

THE illustrious day, when from the throne
    The fiery tongues came rushing down
On Christ's assembled band,

To enrich their tongues, their hearts to fill,
To kindred praise invites us still,
  With heart and tongue and hand.
Christ on this Pentecostal Day,
Revisiting without delay
  The Bride, His promise sent:
After the honey's treasured worth
The Rock a store of oil gave forth,
  The Rock now permanent.
From Sinai's Mount proclaimed the Law
Graven on stone the people saw,
  Not sent in tongues of fire:
Newness of heart and quickened mind,
With unity of tongue combined,
  The chosen few inspire.
O happy, O most festive day!
Whereon the early founders lay
  The Church's basis sure.
The rising Church's first-fruits born
To life anew this holy morn,
  Three thousand souls figúre.
The two loaves by the Law ordained
Two peoples represent, retained
  By faith's adopting tie.
The Head Stone of the corner, set
Between the two, together met,
  Hath wrought out unity.
New bottles, not the worn and old,
New wine are suitable to hold:
  With oil Elisha fills
The widow's vessels not a few:

So on fit hearts His holy dew
   God graciously distils.
We are not worthy of this wine,
Or oil, or of this dew divine,
   If discord reigns within:
His consolation cannot find
A place in a divided mind
   Or heart obscured by sin.
Come, Holy Comforter benign!
Our tongues control, our hearts incline!
If on us Thy blest Presence shine,
   No poison harms, no gall:
There is no joy, no pure content,
No health, no calm stabiliment,
Sweetness hath no constituent,
   Except Thy Grace do all.
Thou art the Light, the Oil to cure;
Thou working in the water pure,
Mysterious virtue dost assure
   To bless Thy chosen race.
By new creation born again,
To praise Thee now our hearts are fain;
By nature sons of wrath, we gain
   The privilege of Grace.
Thou art the Gift and Giver too,
All good on earth to Thee is due:
With gratitude our hearts endue,
To praise Thy Name with accents true
   Do Thou our lips ordain:
Cleanse us, we pray, from all our sin,
Of purity Thou Origin!

Grant we, in Christ renewed, may win
  A perfect life, and bring us in
    Where joys in fulness reign.

ANNI PERACTIS MENSIBUS.

From the Anglo-Saxon Hymnaries, where it was set for the Vigil of Pentecost. Translation by JOHN DAVID CHAMBERS: from his Lauda Syon, 1857.

A YEAR'S swift months have passed away,
    The joys of Pentecost are here;
At length returns the wished-for day,
  Again believing hearts to cheer.

'Twas then the Spirit of the Lord
  Filled with celestial joys the earth;
His radiant glories all abroad
  From Heaven throughout the world go forth.

For thus the Son of God Most High
  His promise to the Apostles made,
Ascending o'er the lofty sky,
  To send His Holy Spirit's aid.

Now He by surest proofs is here;
  Apostles' voices witness bear,
And various nations far and near
  In divers tongues His power declare.

Saved by the Spirit's wondrous Grace
  Of Father and of Son bestowed,
May we pour forth continual praise
  Throughout eternity to God.

LAUDES DEO DEVOTAS.

<small>A Compline Hymn ascribed to St. Notker; from the York Breviary, A.D. 912. Translation by J. D. Chambers, from his *Sarum Hours*, 1852. Revised in the Rev. James Skinner's *Daily Service Hymnal*, 1864. There are two other versions, one in *Lyra Mystica*, by W. J. Blew, and one in the *Sarum Missal*, by C. B. Pearson.</small>

ALL laud and worship o'er the earth
    Let Universal Church pour forth
      With sweet and solemn voice to God:
This day, to the Apostles given,
The Holy Spirit's Grace from Heaven
      In tongues of fire was shed abroad.

To cleanse our souls from stain of sin,
That He may come and dwell within,
      Now present be the Paraclete!
That we may please Him evermore,
May He into our bosoms pour
      His gifts and graces ever meet.

Now for eternal ages long,
Let Alleluia be our song
      To God, the Blessed Three in One:
All praise and power and majesty,
With honor, might, and glory, be
      In earth and Heaven forever done.

PENTECOSTAL ODES.

From the Service Books of the Holy Eastern Church. Translated by WILLIAM CHATTERTON DIX, in *Lyra Mystica*, 1865.

I.

AN ODE OF AN UNKNOWN AUTHOR.

WE keep the Feast of Pentecost,
  The Coming of the Holy Ghost;
Our hope is now fulfilled, and we
Receive the mighty mystery.

The day of promise long foretold,
The time appointed we behold,
And therefore gladly now we sing,
To Thee be praise, Creator, King.

O wondrous Gift of Christ the Lord
On His disciples newly poured,
That they to all might Grace proclaim,
And publish far the Saving Name.

Thy Love immortal, Word of God,
In foreign tongues they sound abroad,
And all the wounds of sin to heal
Thy signal mercy they reveal.

The Holy Spirit all things leads,
From Him all Prophecy proceeds,
His Priests He ever sanctifies,
He makes the poor and lowly wise.

On fishers He hath poured His Grace;
He rules the Church, His dwelling-place;
He welds her order, and His might
Protects her children in the fight.

Thee, One in Nature, One in throne,
Eternal Comforter, we own,
With God the Father and the Son,
The ever-blessed Three in One.

II.

AN ODE OF S. JOHN DAMASCENE.

[The greatest of the Greek sacred poets. Little is known of his life: he died about A.D. 780. Several of his lyrics have been nobly translated by Dr. J. M. NEALE, in his *Hymns of the Eastern Church*, 1862.]

THE tuneful sound of music
    Burst sweetly forth of old
In honor of the idol,
    The lifeless form of gold:[1]
We cry, with awe adoring
    The Spirit's radiant flame,
Sole Trinity, we bless Thee,
    For evermore the same.

They who the Voice Prophetic
    Knew not as Word of Thine,
The unknown tongues regarded
    As drunkenness of wine:

---

[1] Exodus xxxii. 18, 19.

But we in faith devoutly
    Give God the honor due:
Sole Trinity, we bless Thee,
    Who makest all things new.

The prophet Joel looking
    Upon the face of God,
Astonied heard Him speaking,
    And told His words abroad:
They whom I give My Spirit
    Shall cry, thus filled with might,
Sole Trinity, we bless Thee,
    O everlasting Light.

The third day-hour abounded
    With Grace, that we might know
The Source of blessing, Threefold,
    Whence benedictions flow.
And now, on this glad morning,
    The best and chief of days,
Sole Trinity, we bless Thee
    In hymns of grateful praise.

III.

AN ODE OF S. COSMAS THE MELODIST.

Foster-brother to S JOHN DAMASCENE, and next to him among the Greek ecclesiastical poets. He was a monk of S. Sabbas, and Bishop of Maiuma, near Gaza; he died about A.D. 760. Like DAMASCENE, he was extremely fond of types and Scripture figures.

HE who with His mighty hand
    Breaks the battle and the brand,
Now hath buried in the tide
Egypt's chariots and her pride.

Songs of victory we sing:
Perished are her host and king.
Tell the triumph far and wide;
God the Lord is glorified.

Thou a Light on earth hast shined,
Christ, the Lover of mankind:
Thou the Comforter hast sent:
All hath found accomplishment
Which the Law and Prophets old
In the ages past foretold;
Every promise, every word
Which Thy dear disciples heard.

For the Holy Spirit's Grace
On the true and faithful race
Freely hath to-day been poured,
From the world's foundation stored:
Gladly then these hymns we lift,
Thankful for the wondrous Gift,
Praising, as is right and meet,
God the blessed Paraclete.

IV.

AN ODE OF S. JOSEPH OF THE STUDIUM.

The most voluminous of the Greek poets: he lived about A.D. 830. This is but a fragment of his great "Canon for Ascension," translated by Dr. JOHN MASON NEALE, in his most exquisite and invaluable little book, *Hymns of the Eastern Church*, 1862.

HOLY Gift, surpassing comprehension!
    Wondrous mystery of each fiery tongue!
Christ made good His promise in Ascension:
O'er the Twelve the cloven flames have hung!

Spake the Lord, or ere He left the Eleven:
" Here in Salem wait the Gift I send:
Till the Paraclete come down from Heaven,
Everlasting Guide and Guard and Friend."

O that shame, now ended in His glory!
O that pain, now lost in joy unknown!
Tell it out with praise, the whole glad story,
Human nature at the Father's throne!

I WILL NOT LEAVE YOU COMFORTLESS.

GEORGE V. COX: *Hymns for the Black Letter Saints' Days*, 1845.

I WILL not leave you comfortless —
  The promised Spirit comes to bless:
The Pentecostal Day is come,
And with one mind, in common home,
The sad disciples of the Lord
Waiting, obey His solemn word.
  O let His word with us abide,
  While thus we keep our Whitsuntide!

Sudden, above, and all around
A mighty Wind, a rushing Sound
Comes from the clouds asunder riven;
Resistless comes — it comes from Heaven.
Its power expansive makes its way,
And fills the chamber where they pray.
  O may that power with us abide
  To cheer us in our Whitsuntide!

Not sounds alone, but sights are there,
For cloven tongues of fire appear;
Brighter than jewelled diadem,
They rest on each and all of them:
The heavenly influence spreads: and they
Exulting hail the glorious day.
    And O, may we with thankful pride
    Thus hail our glorious Whitsuntide!

Filled from one Source, the Holy Ghost,
(Jesus their theme, His Cross their boast)
No other teaching they require,
Kindled, inspired by Heaven's own Fire.
In tongues ne'er learnt they Jesus preach,
E'en as the Spirit's breathings teach.
    O help us, teach us, heavenly Guide,
    To keep aright our Whitsuntide!

The tidings soon were noised abroad
Of powers that spoke the present God;
And numbers vast of pious men
From every clime 'neath Heaven's ken,
Each in his native language heard
From men untaught the sacred word.
    O spread those tidings far and wide,
    Blest Founder of our Whitsuntide!

Well might those listeners cry, O see!
Are they not all from Galilee?
How in our proper tongue doth each
Catch words of wisdom from their speech?

To keep a Feast from far we came,
A holier Feast we now proclaim.
　　And O, what they far off descried,
　　May we enjoy each Whitsuntide!

HAIL THE JOYFUL DAY'S RETURN.

ROBERT CAMPBELL, solicitor in Edinburgh: died 1868. He was the compiler, and chief author, of a small collection of *Hymns and Anthems for use in the Holy Services of the Church, within the United Diocese of St. Andrew's, Dunkeld, and Dunblane*, put forth with the approval of Bishop Torry, in 1850. He dealt chiefly in translations from the Latin; but this vigorous lyric seems to be original.

HAIL the joyful day's return,
　　Hail the Pentecostal morn,
Morn when our Ascended Head
On His Church His Spirit shed.
Like to cloven tongues of flame
On the Twelve the Spirit came;
Tongues, that earth may hear the call;
Fire, that Love may burn in all.

Hear the speech before unknown;
Trembling crowds the wonder own:
What though hardened some abide,
And the holy work deride?
Lord, to Thee Thy people bend,
Unto us Thy Spirit send:
Blessings of this sacred day
Grant us, dearest Lord, we pray.

Thou who didst our fathers guide,
With their children still abide;
Grant us pardon, grant us peace,
Till our earthly wanderings cease.
To the Father praises sing,
Praise to Christ our risen King,
Praise to Thee, the Lord of Love,
Blessed Spirit, Holy Dove.

MIDNIGHT CLOUDS ARE ROLLED AWAY.

CHARLES LAURENCE FORD: from *Hymns for the Public Worship of the Church*, 1858, by the Rev. ROBERT H. BAYNES, now Vicar of St. Michael's, Coventry.

MIDNIGHT clouds are rolled away,
    Dawns the Pentecostal Day:
Struggling through the twilight gloom
Sunshine seeks the upper room,
Softly entering, as it sees
Waiting saints upon their knees.

Waiting long with one accord
For the Promise of their Lord;
Pouring forth the heart's full prayer
For His glorious presence there:
Glad the morning light they spy—
Surely now their Sun is nigh!

Hark! a rushing sound is given,
As a mighty wind from Heaven!

Hearts exclaim, while lips are dumb,
Lo, the Comforter is come!
See where every cloven spire
Crowns with pure baptismal fire!

Now the night of fear is o'er,
Silence seals their lips no more.
Lord! to us like gift impart;
Fill with fire each waiting heart;
Then, Thy wondrous Love to show,
Burning words, like flame, shall flow.

EXCEEDING FAITHFUL IN THY WORD.

GEORGE WITHER, 1588-1667, was a Puritan through the Civil War, though before that he had stood so well at court as to receive from James I. an exclusive patent for his *Hymns and Songs of the Church*, 1623. In that volume this is set for Pentecost. He afterward rewrote (without improving) it, for his *Hallelujah*, 1641.

EXCEEDING faithful in Thy word,
  And just in all Thy ways,
We do acknowledge Thee, O Lord,
  And therefore give Thee praise:
For as Thy promise Thou didst pass
  Before Thou went'st away,
Sent down Thy Holy Spirit was
  At His appointed day.

While Thy disciples in Thy name
  Together did retire,
The Holy Ghost upon them came
  In cloven tongues of fire;

That in their calling they might be
    Confirmèd from above,
As Thou wert, when He came on Thee,
    Descending like a dove.

Whereby those men, that simple were
    And fearful till that hour,
Had knowledge at an instant there,
    And boldness armed with power;
Receiving gifts so manifold
    That since the world begun
A wonder seldom hath been told
    That could exceed this one.

Now also, blessed Spirit, come,
    Unto our souls appear,
And of Thy graces shower Thou some
    On this assembly here:
To us Thy dove-like meekness lend,
    That humble we may be,
And on Thy silver wings ascend,
    Our Saviour Christ to see.

O let Thy cloven tongues, we pray,
    So rest on us again,
That both the Truth confess we may,
    And teach it other men.
Moreover let Thy heavenly fire,
    Enflamèd from above,
Burn up in us each vain desire,
    And warm our hearts with love.

Vouchsafe Thou likewise to bestow
  On us Thy sacred peace,
We stronger may in union grow
  And in debates decrease:
Which peace though many yet contemn,
  Reformèd let them be,
That we may, Lord, have part in them,
  And they have part in Thee.

NAY, STARTLE NOT.

CHRISTOPHER HARVIE, author of *The Synagogue: Sacred Poems in Imitation of Mr. George Herbert,* 1640. This work went through many editions, and was long bound with Herbert's *Temple.*

NAY, startle not to hear the rushing wind
    Wherewith this place is shaken:
Attend awhile, and thou shalt quickly find
      How much thou art mistaken,
        If thou think here
        Is any cause to fear.

Seest thou not how on those twelve reverend heads
      Sit cloven tongues of fire?
And as the rumor of that wonder spreads,
      The multitude admire
        To see it, and
        Yet more amazèd stand,

To hear at once so great variety
      Of language from them come,
Of whom they dare be bold to say they be

Bred nowhere but at home,
    And never were
In place such words to hear.

Mock not, profane despisers of the Spirit,
    At what's to you unknown:
This Earnest He hath sent, who must inherit
    All nations as His own;
      That they may know
How much to Him they owe.

Now that He is ascended up on high
    To His celestial throne,
And hath led captive all captivity,
    He'll not receive alone,
      But likewise give
Gifts unto all that live:

To all that live by Him, that they may be
    In His due time, each one,
Partakers with Him, in His victory;
    Nor He triumph alone,
      But take all His
Unto Him where He is.

To fit them for which blessed state of glory
    This is His Agent here:
To publish to the world that happy story,
    Always and everywhere
      This resident
Embassador is sent.

Heaven's Lieger upon earth to counterwork
    The mines that Satan made,
And bring to light those enemies, that lurk
    Under sin's gloomy shade:
        That hell may not
        Still boast what it hath got.

Thus Babel's curse, confusion, is retrieved;
    Diversity of tongues
By this division of the Spirit relieved:
    And,. to prevent all wrongs,
        One Faith unites
        People of different rites.

O let His entertainment then be such
    As doth Him best befit:
Whatever He requireth think not much
    Freely to yield Him it:
        For who doth this
        Reaps the first-fruits of bliss.

THY HEAVENLY KINGDOM HERE BELOW.

JOSEPH BEAUMONT, D.D., 1615-1699: Master of Peter-House, and King's Professor of Divinity at Cambridge: author of *Psyche*, the longest poem in the English language, and of some minor pieces which, written in 1652, were not printed till 1749.

THY heavenly kingdom here below
    Now like itself, dear Lord, doth show,
And needs no metaphor to tell
How lofty things beneath can dwell:
Now Thy celestial flames are hither sent
To light the stars of earth's new firmament.

How bright they shine! brave stars, whose light
Spreads day upon the face of night!
And gilds the farthest shades, which lie
Hid from the upper heaven's great eye;
Coasts to the glaring sun unknown shall say,
Welcome, sweet beams of bright religious day.

These heavens Thy glory shall declare,
And with Thy praises fill the air.
The tongues of this great day shall send
Thy name unto the world's vast end.
Where'er it lists this Spirit shall blow, and find
Its chariot on the wings of every wind.

TONGUES OF FIRE FROM HEAVEN DESCEND.

Bishop JEREMY TAYLOR, 1613-1667. His *Festival Hymns* were attached to *The Golden Grove*, 1655.

TONGUES of fire from Heaven descend,
    With a mighty rushing wind,
    To blow it up, and make
      A living fire
Of heavenly charity, and pure desire,
Where they their residence should take.
On the Apostles' sacred heads they sit;
Who now, like beacons, do proclaim and tell
The invasion of the host of hell;
    And give men warning to defend
Themselves from the enraging brunt of it.

Lord, let the flames of holy Charity,
   And all her gifts and graces, slide
Into our hearts, and there abide;
That, thus refinèd, we may soar above
With it, unto the element of Love,
   Even unto Thee, dear Spirit;
And there eternal peace and rest inherit.

WHEN CHRIST HIS BODY UP HAD BORNE.

HENRY MORE, 1614–1687; the celebrated Cambridge Platonist. His few hymns, whose poetical merit is but small, were printed with his *Theological Works*, in 1668.

WHEN Christ His body up had borne
   To Heaven, from His Disciples' sight,
Then they like orphans all forlorn
   Spent their sad days in mournful plight.

But He ascended up on high,
   More sacred gifts for to receive
And freely shower them from the sky
   On those which He behind did leave.

He for the presence of His flesh
   To them the Holy Spirit imparts,
And doth with living springs refresh
   Their thirsty souls and fainting hearts.

While with one mind, and in one place,
   Devoutly they themselves retire,
In rushing wind the promised Grace
   Descends, and cloven tongues of fire.

The house th' Almighty's Spirit fills,
    Which doth the feeble fabric shake;
But on their tongue such power instils,
    That makes the amazed hearer quake.

The Spirit of holy zeal and love,
    And of discerning, give us, Lord;
The Spirit of power from above,
    Of unity and good accord.

The Spirit of convincing speech,
    Such as will every conscience smite.
And to the heart of each man reach,
    And sin and error put to flight:

The Spirit of refining fire
    Searching the inmost of the mind.
To purge all foul and fell desire,
    And kindle Life more pure and kind.

The Spirit of faith, in this thy day,
    Of power against the force of sin,
That through this faith we ever may
    Against our lusts the conquests win.

Pour down Thy Spirit of inward Life,
    Which in our hearts Thy Laws may write,
That without any pain or strife
    We naturally may do what's right.

On all the earth Thy Spirit pour,
   In righteousness it to renew:
That Satan's kingdom 't may o'erpower,
   And to Christ's sceptre may subdue.

Like mighty wind or torrent fierce,
   Let it withstanders all o'errun,
And every wicked law reverse,
   That Faith and Love may make all one.

Let peace and joy in each place spring,
   And righteousness, the Spirit's fruits,
With meekness, friendship, and each thing
   That with the christian spirit suits.

Grant this, O holy God and true,
   Who th' ancient Prophets did inspire:
Haste to perform Thy Promise due,
   As all Thy Servants Thee desire.

[The ideas of this are better than the expression. John Wesley rewrote the whole piece, in his *Hymns and Sacred Poems*, 1739, and part of that version has already been given, on p. 21.]

WHITE SUNDAY.

HENRY VAUGHAN, 1621-1695, next in rank to George Herbert among the poets of that age and school. From his *Silex Scintillans*, Part II., 1654. As is usual with Vaughan and his fellows, this piece is crowded with ideas and somewhat obscure in style.

WELCOME, white day! a thousand suns,
   Though seen at once, were black to thee!
For after their light, darkness comes;
But thine shines to eternity.

Those flames which on the Apostles rushed
At this great Feast, and in a tyre
Of cloven tongues their heads all brushed
And crowned them with prophetic fire, —

Can these new lights be like to those,
These lights of serpents like the Dove?
Thou hadst no gall even for Thy foes,
And Thy two wings were grief and love.

Though then some boast that fire each day,
And to Christ's coat pin all their shreds,
Not sparing openly to say,
His candle shines upon their heads;

Yet while some rays of that great Light
Shine here below within Thy Book,
They never shall so blind my sight
But I will know which way to look.

For though Thou dost that great light lock,
And by this lesser commerce keep,
Yet by these glances of the flock
I can discern wolves from the sheep.

Not but that I have wishes too,
And pray, "These last may be as first,
Or better;" but Thou long ago
Hast said, "These last should be the worst."

Besides, Thy method with Thy own,
Thy own dear people, pens our times;
Our stories are in theirs set down,
And penalties spread to our crimes.

Again, if worst and worst implies
A state that no redress admits,
Then, from Thy Cross unto these days
The rule without exception fits.

And yet, as in night's gloomy page
One silent star may interline;
So in this last and lewdest age
Thy ancient Love on some may shine.

For though we hourly breathe decays,
And our best note and highest ease
Is but mere changing of the keys,
And a consumption that doth please:

Yet Thou, the great eternal Rock,
Whose height above all ages shines,
Art still the same, and canst unlock
Thy waters to a soul that pines.

Since then Thou art the same this day
And ever as Thou wert of old,
And nothing doth Thy Love allay
But our heart's dead and sinful cold;

As Thou long since wert pleased to buy
Our drowned estate, taking the curse
Upon Thyself, so to destroy
The knots we tied upon Thy purse, —

So let Thy Grace now make the way
Even for Thy Love; for by that means
We, who are nothing but foul clay,
Shall be fine gold which Thou didst cleanse.

O come! refine us with Thy fire!
Refine us! we are at a loss:
Let not Thy stars for Balaam's hire
Dissolve into the common dross!

AT PENTECOST, ILLUSTRIOUS DAY!

Simon Browne, 1680–1732: Independent minister at Portsmouth and in London. His *Hymns and Spiritual Songs, designed as a Supplement to Dr. Watts' Hymns*, appeared in 1720, and were reprinted in 1741 and 1760.

AT Pentecost, illustrious day!
   With one accord the Apostles met
There where their Master bid them stay
   And for the Father's promise wait.

Nor did they sit in long suspense;
   From Heaven a sudden sound was heard,
Like wind impetuous rushing thence,
   And cloven tongues of fire appeared.

The heavenly blast filled all the room,
    A tongue descends on every head:
And now the Paraclete is come,
    To make them glad, and help them plead.

With flowing speech in foreign tongues
    God's wondrous works they now proclaim:
Whilst of all nations numerous throngs
    To witness to the wonder came.

Surprised they heard illiterate Jews
    The language of each country speak:
The tongue of Medes, of Libyans, use,
    Arabic, Persian, Roman, Greek.

Thus did the Holy Ghost inspire
    And fit them Christian truths to spread,
Fill every heart with light and fire,
    Teach every tongue to preach and plead.

Thus did He open witness bear
    To their authority divine;
Make stupid lands attentive hear,
    And all their gods and lusts resign.

Thus tidings of salvation run
    Through every nation far and near,
And everywhere beneath the sun
    The triumphs of the Cross appear.

NOW CHRIST ASCENDS ABOVE THE SKIES.

WILLIAM HAMMOND (died 1783) was first a Churchman, then a Calvinistic Methodist, and finally a Moravian. His Psalms, Hymns, and Spiritual Songs appeared in 1745. He was a fair scholar, and this is doubtless founded on Jam Christus astra ascenderat.

NOW Christ ascends above the skies;
  He now returns to Paradise,
From whence He lately kindly came:
The promised Spirit He sends down,
To make His great salvation known
  And spread the savor of His Name.
When Pentecost was fully come,
They all assembled in one room,
  And joined in mutual prayer and praise:
Then suddenly a sound was heard,
Twelve cloven tongues of fire appeared,
  And on the Apostles' heads took place.

The rushing wind that went before
Declares our Lord's almighty power,
  His power to cast opposers down:
The efficacy of His Love
Like a refiner's fire doth prove,
  And warm and melt even hearts of stone.
With joy and gladness they proclaim
The wonders of the bleeding Lamb;
  They boldly publish Jesu's Word:
Their hearts with heavenly ardor fired,
Their lips with diverse tongues inspired,
  They preach the Gospel of our Lord.

'Tis madness to a carnal ear
To hear a child of God declare
   What Jesus for his soul hath done;
Freely to talk of sins forgiven,
To say that we are sure of Heaven,
   Is all a language quite unknown.
Worldlings deny the power divine,
Impute the work of Grace to wine,
   And say the saints are drunk or mad:
But they who taste our Saviour's Grace
In Him find solid happiness;
   In Christ they triumph, and are glad.

His Promise stands for ever sure,
My Spirit on all flesh I pour,
   All flesh shall My Salvation see.
A Christian heart is Christ's abode,
A living temple of his God,
   A temple of the sacred Three.
Christ dwells in him, and he in Christ;
He into Jesus is baptized,
   In spirit he with Christ is one.
Jesu, our souls are joined to Thee
In everlasting unity;
   We live by Christ, and Christ alone.

WHEN THE BLEST DAY OF PENTECOST.

Joseph Hart, 1712-1768; minister in Jewin Street, and author of various popular hymns. His first edition, containing this, appeared 1759.

WHEN the blest day of Pentecost
    Was fully come, the Holy Ghost
      Descended from above,
Sent by the Father and the Son
(The Sender and the Sent are one),
      The Lord of Life and Love.

Within one house, with one accord,
The faithful followers of our Lord,
      Waiting his Promise, sit;
That, vested with supernal power,
They might be then, and not before,
      To preach the Gospel fit.

Sudden a rushing wind they hear,
And fiery cloven tongues appear
      And sat on every one.
Cloven, perhaps to be the sign
That God no longer would confine
      His Word to Jews alone.

To every nation under heaven
To hear the Gospel-sound is given;
      The call to all extends.
As ours was parted long ago,
So God divides His language too,
      And after sinners sends.

And were these first disciples blest
With heavenly gifts, and shall the rest
   Be passed unheeded by?
What, has the Holy Ghost forgot
To quicken souls that Christ has bought,
   And let them lifeless lie?

No, Thou almighty Paraclete,
Thou shedd'st Thy heavenly influence yet,
   Thou visit'st sinners still:
Thy breath of Life, Thy quickening flame,
Thy power, Thy Godhead, still the same,
   We own, because we feel.

GRANTED IS THE SAVIOUR'S PRAYER.

CHARLES WESLEY: from *Hymns and Sacred Poems*, 1739. The last of a series of five hymns for the great Festivals.

GRANTED is the Saviour's prayer,
   Sent the gracious Comforter;
Promise of our parting Lord,
Jesus, to His heaven restored:

Christ, who now gone up on high,
Captive leads captivity,
While His foes from Him receive
Grace, that God with man may live.

God, the everlasting God,
Makes with mortals His abode;
Whom the heavens cannot contain,
He vouchsafes to dwell in man.

Never will He thence depart,
Inmate of an humble heart;
Carrying on His work within,
Striving till He cast out sin.

There He helps our feeble moans,
Deepens our imperfect groans;
Intercedes in silence there,
Sighs the unutterable prayer.

Come, divine and peaceful Guest,
Enter our devoted breast:
Holy Ghost, our hearts inspire,
Kindle there the gospel fire.

Crown the agonizing strife,
Principle and Lord of life:
Life divine in us renew,
Thou the Gift and Giver too!

Now descend and shake the earth,
Wake us into second birth;
Now Thy quickening influence give,
Blow, and these dry bones shall live.

Brood Thou o'er our nature's night, —
Darkness kindles into light;
Spread Thy overshadowing wings, —
Order from confusion springs.

Pain and sin and sorrow cease,
Thee we taste, and all is peace;
Joy divine in Thee we prove,
Light of truth, and fire of love.

FATHER OF EVERLASTING GRACE.

CHARLES WESLEY: from *Hymns for Whit-Sunday*, 1746

FATHER of everlasting grace,
   Thy goodness and Thy truth we praise;
Thy goodness and Thy truth we prove;
Thou hast, in honor of Thy Son,
The Gift unspeakable sent down,
   The Spirit of life, and power, and love.

Thou hast the prophecy fulfilled,
The grand original compact sealed,
   For which Thy word and oath were joined:
The Promise to our fallen head,
To every child of Adam made,
   Is now poured out on all mankind.

The purchased Comforter is given,
For Jesus is returned to Heaven,
   To claim, and then the Grace impart:
Our day of Pentecost is come,
And God vouchsafes to fix His home
   In every poor expecting heart.

Father, on Thee whoever call
Confess Thy promise is for all,
   While every one that asks receives,
Receives the Gift and Giver too,
And witnesses that Thou art true,
   And in Thy Spirit walks and lives.

Not to a single age confined,
For every soul of man designed,
  O God, we now that Spirit claim:
To us the Holy Ghost impart,
Breathe Him into our panting heart;
  Thou hear'st us ask in Jesu's name.

Send us the Spirit of Thy Son,
To make the depths of Godhead known,
  To make us share the life divine:
Send Him the sprinkled blood to apply;
Send Him our souls to sanctify,
  And show and seal us ever Thine.

So shall we pray, and never cease;
So shall we thankfully confess
  Thy wisdom, truth, and power, and love;
With joy unspeakable adore,
And bless and praise Thee evermore,
  And serve Thee like Thy hosts above:

Till, added to that heavenly choir,
We raise our songs of triumph higher,
  And praise Thee in a bolder strain;
Outsoar the first-born seraph's flight,
And sing, with all our friends in light,
  Thine everlasting Love to man.

REJOICE, REJOICE. YE FALLEN RACE.

CHARLES WESLEY: from *Hymns and Sacred Poems*, 1742.

REJOICE, rejoice, ye fallen race,
  The Day of Pentecost is come!
Expect the sure descending Grace,
  Open your hearts to make Him room.

Our Jesus is gone up on high,
  For us the blessing to receive;
It now comes streaming from the sky,
  The Spirit comes, and sinners live.

To every one whom God shall call
  The promise is securely made;
To you far off; He calls you all;
  Believe the word that Christ hath said:

"The Holy Ghost, if I depart,
  The Comforter shall surely come,
Shall make the contrite sinner's heart
  His loved, His everlasting home."

Lord, we believe to us and ours
  The apostolic promise given;
We wait to taste the heavenly powers,
  The Holy Ghost sent down from Heaven.

Ah, leave us not to mourn below,
  Or long for Thy return to pine;
Now, Lord, the Comforter bestow,
  And fix in us the Guest divine.

Assembled here with one accord,
    Calmly we wait the promised grace,
The purchase of our dying Lord;
    Come, Holy Ghost, and fill the place.

If every one that asks may find,
    If still Thou art to sinners given,
Come as a mighty rushing wind,
    To shake our earth come down from Heaven.

Behold, to Thee our souls aspire,
    And languish Thy descent to meet;
Kindle in each Thy living fire,
    And fix in every heart Thy seat.

Wisdom and strength to Thee belongs:
    Sweetly within our bosoms move;
Now let us speak with other tongues
    The new strange language of Thy Love.

Spirit of faith, within us live,
    And strike the crowd with fixt amaze;
Open our mouths, and utterance give
    To publish our Redeemer's praise:

To testify the Grace of God,
    To-day as yesterday the same,
And spread through all the earth abroad
    The wonders wrought by Jesu's Name.

SINNERS, YOUR HEARTS LIFT UP.

Another from the same source.

SINNERS, your hearts lift up,
    Partakers of your hope!
This the Day of Pentecost:
    Ask, and ye shall all receive:
Surely now the Holy Ghost
    God to all that ask shall give.

    Ye all may freely take
        The Grace for Jesu's sake:
He for every man hath died,
    He for all hath rose again;
Jesus now is glorified,
    Gifts He hath received for men.

    He sends them from the skies
        On all His enemies:
By His Cross He now hath led
    Captive our captivity:
We shall all be free indeed,
    Christ the Son shall make us free.

    Blessings on all He pours
        In never-ceasing showers;
All He waters from above,
    Offers all His joy and peace,
Settled comfort, perfect love,
    Everlasting righteousness.

    All may from Him receive
      A power to turn and live;
Grace for every soul is free;
    All may hear the effectual call:
All the Light of Life may see;
    All may feel He died for all.

    Drop down in showers of love,
      Ye heavens from above!
Righteousness, ye skies, pour down!
    Open, earth, and take it in;
Claim the Spirit for your own,
    Sinners, and be saved from sin!

    Father, behold we claim
    . The Gift in Jesu's name!
Him, the promised Comforter,
    Into all our spirits pour;
Let Him fix His mansion here,
    Come, and never leave us more.

LET SONGS OF PRAISES FILL THE SKY.

THOMAS COTTERILL, 1779-1823; perpetual curate of St. Paul's, Sheffield. He published a *Selection of Psalms and Hymns*, the chief edition of which, 1819, contains this.

LET songs of praises fill the sky:
    Christ, our ascended Lord,
Sends down His Spirit from on high,
    According to His word:
All hail the day of Pentecost,
The coming of the Holy Ghost!

The Spirit, by His heavenly breath,
  New life creates within;
He quickens sinners from the death
  Of trespasses and sin:
All hail the day of Pentecost,
The coming of the Holy Ghost!

The things of Christ the Spirit takes,
  And shows them unto men;
The fallen soul His temple makes;
  God's image stamps again:
All hail the day of Pentecost,
The coming of the Holy Ghost!

Come, Holy Spirit, from above,
  With Thy celestial fire;
Come, and with flames of zeal and love
  Our hearts and tongues inspire!
Be this our day of Pentecost,
The coming of the Holy Ghost!

THERE WAS A LOWLY UPPER ROOM.

CECIL FRANCES ALEXANDER, wife of the present Bishop of Derry. From her *Verses for Holy Seasons*, 1840 (?).

THERE was a little lowly upper room
  Within the walls of proud Jerusalem,
Where met a few poor men in grief and gloom,
  Talking of Him who once had walked with them.

THE STORY OF PENTECOST.

There came a sound as of a rushing wind,
   And filled up all the place where they were met,
And flaming figures of unwonted kind,
   Like tongues of fire, upon each brow were set.

That was the Promise of the Father, come
   To them who waited, mourning for their Lord;
And the closed lips, that were so dead and dumb,
   Are loosed at once to speak His precious Word.

Then all the strangers from afar, who came
   From Asian shores, from Europe's fairer strands,
From Afric's deserts, wondering heard His Name
   In the dear language of their native lands.

Not now in form distinct of flaming light
   Comes that great Spirit on our earth to dwell,
But, like the strong wind whispering at night,
   Its mighty impulse is invisible.

Yet to the lowly and obedient heart
   In gentleness and might its breath shall come,
Bidding the Christian choose the better part,
   Stirring with thought of his eternal Home.

O Lord ascended! from Thy glory's throne,
   On Thy baptizèd children kneeling lowly,
Look down in mercy! we were made Thine own;
   Give our poor hearts Thy Spirit strong and holy.

THE DAY OF PENTECOST.

Archer Thompson Gurney: born 1820: chaplain in Paris, and author of many works, poetical and other. From *Lyra Messianica*, 1864.

THE Day of Pentecost,
   When down the Holy Spirit came,
And sat like cloven tongues of flame
   On the Apostles' host:

The Day of Pentecost,
When first in all His wondrous power
Himself, as everlasting Dower,
   Bestowed the Holy Ghost:

The Day of Pentecost,
When that amazing boon was given
By which on earth we dwell in Heaven,
   And joy when stricken most:

The Day of Pentecost,
When that celestial Grace was won
By which alone we reach the Son,
   And count His Cross our boast:

The Day of Pentecost
Has dawned again our souls to cheer:
Then bring us all to Jesus near,
   O God the Holy Ghost!

ONCE THE DEWS OF NIGHT HAVE SHED.

Eliza Humphreys. Metrical Collects, 1856.

ONCE the soft dews of night have shed
    Their influence on earth's fertile bed,
  Since the Pentecostal Light,
  With its fiery glory bright,
Descended on the souls who with such glad accord
Waited in faith the promise of their Lord.

  Day of joy, of high remembrance,
  In our souls renew thy fragrance;
    Thoughts of Thee, O Paraclete!
    Exalted meditations sweet,
Be like the holy oil on Aaron's garments poured,
Like choicest perfume in frail vessels stored.

  With conscious life our souls surround,
  Plead in us with Thy sacred sound;
    Evermore may we rejoice
    In that still sweet inward voice,
Calling our souls to God, by every outward sign,
All earthly things wearing a hue divine.

  Gilding all duties with Thy light,
  Like floating clouds at sunset bright,
    Earthly burdens lose their weight,
    Mourners dwell not desolate,
Sinners all penitent the coming radiance own,
The rainbow light divine from Jesu's throne!

Ascended Saviour! great Thy Love,
Sending the Spirit from above:
 Thou livest, reignest glorious,
 O'er every foe victorious,
Thou ever good and gracious promise-keeping Lord,
With Father, Spirit, Trinity adored!

CHRIST OUR SUN ON US AROSE.

Dr. RICHARD F. LITTLEDALE. From *The People's Hymnal*, 1867. There it has an *Alleluia* after each line.

CHRIST our Sun on us arose,
 From His glory fled our foes.
Christ our Sun from us is gone,
And our hearts were faint and wan.
Thirsty yearned we for His Grace,
Weary watched we for His face,
While the bare and lonely shrine
Waited for the Guest divine.

Joy hath come to earth again;
Downward poured the Spirit's rain;
And the rushing Wind of might
Swept away the clouds of night.
She whom weary years before
In His Love He hovered o'er,
Mother, Daughter, Spouse of God,
Chants anew her song of laud:

And the Apostolic choir,
Glowing with the tongues of fire,
Clearer now and joyous raise
Christ their Monarch's endless praise.
He hath let His Breath go forth
And renewed the face of earth,
Bid the brook a river be,
And the river made a sea.

From the snows where Scythians toil
To Cyrene's thirsty soil,
From the Indian's distant home
To the gates of mighty Rome,
Alleluia! raise the song,
Raise it high, and raise it long,
To the Father and the Word
And the Spirit, God adored.
     Alleluia!

ONE THE DESCENDING FLAME.

JOHN KEBLE: 1792–1866: Vicar of Hursley. From *Lyra Innocentium*, 1846.

"The promise is unto you and to your children."

ONE the descending Flame,
 But many were the tongues of fire;
From one bright Heaven they came,
But here and there in many a spire;
 In many a living line they sped
 To rest on each anointed head.
There, as yon stars in clearest deep of night,
The glory-crowns shone out in many-colored light.

One the dread rushing Wind,
But many were the tones of praise,
  Love guiding each to find
His way in Music's awful maze.
Many the tongues, the theme was one,
The glory of the Incarnate Son,
How He was born, how died, how reigns in Heaven,
And how His Spirit now to His new-born is given.

  Joined in that choral cry
Were all estates, all tribes of earth:
  Only sweet infancy
Seemed silent in the adoring mirth.
Mothers and maiden there behold
The Maiden Mother: young and old
On apostolic thrones with joy discern
Both fresh and faded forms, skilled for all hearts to
      yearn.

  Widows from Galilee,
Levites are there, and elders sage
  Of high and low degree;
But naught we read of that sweet age
Which in His strong embrace He took,
And sealed it safe, by word and look,
From earth's foul dews, and withering airs of hell:
The Pentecostal chant no infant warblings swell.

  Nay, but she worships here,
Whom still the Church in memory sees
  (O thought to mothers dear)
Before her Babe on bended knees,

Or rapt, with fond adoring eye,
  In her sweet nursing ministry.—
How in Christ's anthem fails the children's part,
While Mary bears Him throned in her maternal
    heart?

  Hear too that shepherd's voice,
    Whom o'er His lambs the Saviour set
  By words of awful choice,
When on the shore His saints He met.
Blest Peter shows the key of Heaven,
And speaks the grace to infants given:
"Yours is the promise, and your babes', and all,
Whom from all lands afar the Lord our God shall
    call."

WHEN GOD OF OLD CAME DOWN.

JOHN KEBLE. From *The Christian Year*, 1827.

WHEN God of old came down from Heaven,
    In power and wrath He came;
Before His feet the clouds were riven,
    Half darkness and half flame:

Around the trembling mountain's base
    The prostrate people lay:
A day of wrath, and not of grace;
    A dim and dreadful day.

But when He came the second time,
   He came in power and love;
Softer than gale at morning prime
   Hovered His holy Dove.

The fires, that rushed on Sinai down
   In sudden torrents dread,
Now gently light, a glorious crown,
   On every sainted head.

Like arrows went those lightnings forth
   Winged with the sinner's doom,
But these, like tongues, o'er all the earth
   Proclaiming life to come.

And as on Israel's awe-struck ear
   The voice exceeding loud,
The trump, that angels quake to hear,
   Thrilled from the deep, dark cloud:

So, when the SPIRIT of our GOD
   Came down His flock to find,
A voice from Heaven was heard abroad,
   A rushing, mighty wind.

Nor doth the outward ear alone
   At that high warning start:
Conscience gives back the appalling tone;
   'Tis echoed in the heart.

It fills the Church of GOD; It fills
    The sinful world around;
Only in stubborn hearts and wills
    No place for It is found.

To other strains our souls are set:
    A giddy whirl of sin
Fills ear and brain, and will not let
    Heaven's harmonies come in.

Come LORD, come Wisdom, Love, and Power;
    Open our ears to hear;
Let us not miss the accepted hour;
    Save, LORD, by love or fear.

DAY DIVINE! WHEN SUDDEN STREAMING.

THOMAS H. GILL; a living English layman. This double hymn was written in 1850, and printed in 1853, and again in his *Golden Chain of Praise*, 1869.

DAY divine! when sudden streaming
    To the Lord's first lovers came
Glory new and treasure teeming,
    Mighty gifts and tongues of flame!
Day to happy souls commended,
    When the Holy Ghost was given,
When the Comforter descended,
    And brought down the joy of Heaven!

Lord, to-day Thy people learneth
  No past wonder, no strange tale;
Lord, to-day Thy people yearneth
  Here the Holy Ghost to hail!
O'er again to write this story
  Our weak trembling souls aspire:
Unto us may come the glory,
  Full on us may fall the fire!

Hath the Holy Ghost been holden
  By those ancient saints alone?
Only may the ages olden
  Call the Comforter their own?
Ah, their portion we inherit,
  Ours the sorrow, ours the sin:
We beseech the Holy Spirit;
  We the Comforter would win.

II.

THE SPIRIT'S BEST GIFTS.

WOULD the Spirit more completely
  Make abode with saints of old?
Would the Comforter more sweetly
  Thy first lovers, Lord, enfold?
Wonders we may not inherit;
  Signs and tongues we do not crave;
Yet we still receive the Spirit,
  Still the Comforter we have.

Still are given His gifts most precious;
  Open lies His richest store:
We may win His Grace most gracious,
  We His deepest deep explore!
Signs most glorious, all excelling,
  Witness brightest we may show;
Sure the Holy Ghost is dwelling
  With the souls that holier grow.

Hope that makes ashamèd never,
  Perfect peace that passeth thought,
Mighty joy that stayeth ever,
  Love divine that changeth not;
Such the gifts that still are given,
  Such the glory we may boast:
Help us, Lord, to this pure Heaven
  Breathe on us the Holy Ghost.

PART III.

THE FRUITS OF THE SPIRIT

AND Thou Thy Spirit dost bestow
  To hallow all our life to Thee,
To pour clear light on all below,
  And give the blinded power to see.
Thou Comforter from age to age
  Of all the weary, all who weep;
  Whose peace within us true and deep
Is earnest of our heritage:
  Hearken, my spirit cries to Thee,
  Spirit of Love, O love Thou me!
PHILIP FREDERIC HILLER (1699–1769).

To God the Spirit's Name
  Immortal worship give,
Whose new-creating power
  Makes the dead sinner live:
His work completes the great design,
And fills the soul with joy divine.
WATTS, 1709.

WONDER-WORKING Spirit! Thine
  The efficacious Grace we sing:
Set on us Thy seal divine,
  Safely to Thy kingdom bring:
Mortify each sinful deed,
  Daily strengthen every grace;
Lead us, urge us on with speed,
  And let glory crown the race!
JOHN RYLAND, 1796.

O Thou Author of sanctification, Spirit of love and truth, I adore Thee as the Origin of my eternal welfare, I thank Thee as the Sovereign Dispenser of the benefits that I receive from on high; and I invoke Thee as the source of the light and strength which is necessary to me to know good and to practise it. O Spirit of light and strength, enlighten my understanding, strengthen my will, purify my heart, rule all the movements thereof, and make me docile to all Thy inspirations. Pardon me, Spirit of grace and mercy: pardon my continual unfaithfulness, and the wretched blindness with which I have so repulsed the gentlest, and the most powerful impulses of Thy Grace. I desire by the aid of this same Grace to cease from being rebellious to it, and henceforth to follow its movements with such docility, that I may taste the fruits and enjoy the blessings which Thy sacred gifts produce in the soul. To Thee, with the Father and the Son, be all glory forever. Amen.

COME, then, O Holy Spirit, come; come, O come, most merciful Comforter; come, Thou blessed Paraclete; come, Thou celestial Fire; come, Thou Purifier of sins, Thou Healer of wounds; come, Thou Upholder of the falling, Thou Lifter-up of the fallen; come, Thou Teacher of the humble, Thou Destroyer of the proud; come, Thou Friend of the friendless, Hope of the hopeless, Consoler of the sorrowful, Haven of the weary, Physician of the sick; come, Thou Glory of the living, Only Salvation of the dying! Come, O most holy, thrice holy, Holy Ghost, come, and have pity on me; anoint and bless me; direct me and defend me; strengthen me, and comfort me; confirm me, and gladden me; fit me for Thyself; and having made me fit, dwell in me forever; and grant that my littleness may be acceptable to Thy Greatness, my weakness to Thy Strength, according to the multitude of Thy compassion; through Jesus Christ our Saviour, Who with the Father liveth and reigneth in Thy Unity for ever and ever. Amen.

THE FRUITS OF THE SPIRIT.

BUT WHO SHALL COMFORT?

From The Name of Jesus, and other Verses, for the Sick and Lowly, 2d edition, 1862: CHARLOTTE M. NOEL. But part of the poem is given here: the first three verses are omitted, and the last six appear elsewhere in this volume. It has this heading, 1 Cor. xii. 3: "No man can say that Jesus is the Lord but by the Holy Ghost."

"BUT who shall comfort now that He is gone,
   And keep in our remembrance what He taught?
Moulding our acts as He would have them done,
   Cleansing the springs of action and of thought?"

Ten days past on before the answer came,
   Ten slow expectant days of ceaseless prayer;
Then a swift rushing wind and tongues of flame
   The Presence of an unseen Power declare.

He Who of old within the triple Life
   Of the Eternal Godhead moved and wrought,
And from Earth's darkness and chaotic strife
   A world of perfect good and order brought;

He Who by perfect fellowship abode
   In the Humanity of God's own Son,
From thence descends mysteriously endowed
   With power to help and heal us one by one.

He is the Spirit of the Son indeed,
    Co-equal in humility and Love,
In that strong patience that can mourn and bleed,
    But never from the soul it loves remove.

For eighteen hundred years has He remained
    Quickening, transforming, working as He will;
Quenched, scorned, forgotten, limited, and pained,
    He in His meekness lingers with us still.

All growth in wisdom, all pure Love's increase,
    All noble daring and endurance meek,
All battles for the Truth, all sighs for Peace,
    The Presence of the Comforter bespeak.

We seem divided, scattered, and alone,
    With sounds of strife the tranquil Heavens ring:
Meanwhile He binds us all and every one
    In bonds of growing union to our King.

We pray for holiness, then deeply sin;
    Now we presume, then angrily despair;
He bears our wilfulness, He pleads within
    Unuttered moans that never thrill the air.

His Breath too stirs all prayer that doth rejoice
    To rise like incense to the Central Sun;
All praise is the intoning of His Voice,
    Swelling from whispers in the heart begun.

DIR, DIR, JEHOVAH, WILL ICH SINGEN.

BARTHOLOMEW CRASSELIUS, 1677–1724: a pupil of Franke, afterwards pastor at Nidden and Dusseldorf. He wrote but nine hymns. The date of this is 1697. Translation by CATHARINE WINKWORTH, *Chorale Book*, 1862.

JEHOVAH, let me now adore Thee,
    For where is there a God such, Lord, as Thou?
With songs I fain would come before Thee;
O let Thy Spirit deign to teach me now
To praise Thee in His Name, through Whom alone
Our songs can please Thee, through Thy blessed Son.

Yes, draw me to the Son, O Father,
That so the Son may draw me up to Thee.
    Let every power within me gather,
To own Thy sway, O Spirit; rule in me,
That so the peace of God may in me dwell,
And I may sing for joy and praise Thee well.

Grant me Thy Spirit: then my praises
Will sound aright, no jarring tone or word:
    Sweet are the songs the heart then raises,
Then I can pray in truth and spirit, Lord:
Thy Spirit bears mine up on eagle's wing,
To join the psalms the heavenly choirs now sing.

For He can plead for me with sighings
That are unutterable to lips like mine;
    He bids me pray with earnest cryings,
Bears witness with my soul that I am Thine,

Co-heir with Christ, and thus may dare to say,
O Abba Father, hear me when I pray.

   When thus Thy Spirit in me burneth,
And makes this cry to break from out my heart,
   Thy heart, O Father, toward me yearneth,
And longs all precious blessings to impart;
Thy ready Love rejoiceth to fulfil
The prayer breathed out according to Thy will.

   And what Thy Spirit thus hath taught me
To seek from Thee, must needs be such a prayer
   As Thou wilt grant, through Him who bought me
And raised me up to be Thy child and heir:
In Jesu's name fearless I seek Thy face,
And take from Thee, my Father, grace for grace.

   O joy! our hope and trust are founded
On His sure Word and witness in the heart:
   I know Thy mercies are unbounded,
And all good gifts Thou freely wilt impart.
Nay, more is lavished by Thy bounteous Hand
Than we can ask or seek or understand.

   O joy! in His Name we draw near Thee,
Who ever pleadeth for the sons of men:
   I ask in faith, and Thou wilt hear me,
In Him Thy promises are all Amen.
O joy for me! and praise be ever Thine,
Whose wondrous Love has made such blessings
      mine!

HIS HOLY SPIRIT DWELLETH.

PAUL GERHARDT, 1606-1676: part of a hymn of fifteen verses (*Ist Gott für mich, so treie*). Translation by RICHARD MASSIE, 1856. These verses are the 7th, 8th, and 9th of Gerhardt, and the 4th, 5th, and 6th of Massie's version.

HIS Holy Spirit dwelleth
  Within my willing heart,
Tames it when it rebelleth,
  And soothes the keenest smart.
He crowns His work with blessing,
  And helpeth me to cry
"My Father!" without ceasing
  To Him who dwells on high.

And when my soul is lying
  Weak, trembling, and opprest,
He pleads with groans and sighing
  That cannot be exprest;
But God's quick eye discerns them,
  Although they give no sound,
And into language turns them,
  Even in the heart's deep ground.

To mine His Spirit speaketh
  Sweet words of soothing power,
How God to him that seeketh
  For rest, hath rest in store.
There God Himself prepareth
  My heritage and lot,
And though my body weareth,
  My heaven shall fail me not.

WACH AUF, DU GEIST DER ERSTEN ZEUGEN.

CHARLES HENRY VON BOGATZKY, 1690-1774: author of 411 hymns, and of the famous *Golden Treasury*. This one, which has in the original fourteen verses, was published in 1749, with the title, "A Prayer to the Lord to send faithful laborers into His harvest, that His Word may be spread all over the world." "It was composed," says the author, "at a time when the Lord especially stirred him up to pray for the extension of His kingdom through faithful laborers." It is "much sung at missionary meetings in Germany." Translated by Miss WINKWORTH, 1855.

AWAKE, Thou Spirit, who of old
   Didst fire the watchmen of the Church's youth,
Who faced the foe, unshrinking, bold,
Who witnessed day and night the eternal Truth,
Whose voices through the world are ringing still,
And bringing hosts to know and do Thy Will!

O that Thy fire were kindled soon,
That swift from land to land its flame might leap!
   Lord, give us but this priceless boon
Of faithful servants, fit for Thee to reap
The harvest of the soul: look down and view
How great the harvest, yet the laborers few.

Lord, let our earnest prayer be heard,
The prayer Thy Son Himself hath bid us pray;
   For lo! Thy children's hearts are stirred
In every land in this our darkening day,
To cry for help with fervent soul to Thee;
O hear us, Lord, and speak, Thus let it be!

O haste to help ere we are lost!
Send forth evangelists, in spirit strong,
   Armed with Thy Word, a dauntless host,
Bold to attack the rule of ancient wrong;

And let them all the earth for Thee reclaim,
To be Thy kingdom, and to know Thy Name.

Would there were help within our walls!
O let Thy promised Spirit come again,
  Before whom every barrier falls,
And ere the night once more shine forth as then!
O rend the heavens and make Thy presence felt!
The chains that bind us at Thy touch would melt.

And let Thy Word have speedy course,
Through every land the Truth be glorified,
  Till all the heathen know its force,
And gather to Thy churches far and wide.
And waken Israel from her sleep, O Lord!
Thus bless and spread the conquests of Thy Word!

The Church's desert paths restore,
That stumbling blocks which long in them have
      lain
  May hinder now Thy Word no more;
Destroy false doctrine, root out notions vain:
Set free from hirelings, let the Church and school
Bloom as a garden 'neath Thy prospering rule.

DEAR DOVE, THY PRISONER MAY I BE!

FAITHFUL TEATE. *Ter Tria, or the Doctrine of the Three Sacred Persons, Father, Son, and Spirit;* 1669. I take this through the great Moravian Collection of 1754. Rude as the verses are, they contain ideas enough to furnish a dozen modern hymns.

DEAR Dove, Thy prisoner may I be!
    Bondage is like to be my state,
If to myself Thou leav'st me free:
    He's free, whom Thou dost captivate.

With the Lord's Spirit is liberty:
    No man can say, *Jesus the Lord*,
But by the Spirit, or can cry
    Abba, till Thou teach him that word.

I long had been a stammerer,
    Could not pronounce the Shibboleth
That might my prayer to God endear,
    Till the free Spirit gave speech and breath.

I was in suit, nor could make good
    My title: but said this free Spirit,
"Soul, take this seal, the seal of blood;
    I'm Witness that thou shalt inherit."

Ere now I read, but what was next
    I always stupidly forgot:
I found a riddle in each text;
    But this good Spirit loosed the knot.

Surely this Spirit of spirits framed
    That Book of books, my Bible dear;
A thing that all things can be named;
    Food, physic, pleasure, wealth are here.

A Book that makes the simple wise;
    A Book that proves the wisest fools;
A Book that helps the reader's eyes;
    A Book that baffles all the schools.

It told my story ere I was;
    It tells me also what shall be
When I'm no more; what doom shall pass
    On persons, churches, states, and me.

My barren ground oft called for rain,
    Gasping to Heaven for a flood;
This Spirit but flowed in amain,
    And I was filled with all that's good.

He in mine heart doth shed abroad
    God's dear and never-dying Love;
Yet scarce a day, but His sharp rod
    Doth me in faithfulness reprove.

This tender Spirit who would grieve?
    If I my Comforter make sad,
Who only can sad hearts relieve,
    Alas, my God, who'll make me glad?

THE FRUITS OF THE SPIRIT.

"Man, follow thy own native light,"
  Say some, "And thou shalt perfect be!"
Perfect, indeed, like noon of night!
  Lord, in Thy Spirit's Light lead me.

A SONG OF PRAISE FOR JOY IN THE HOLY GHOST.

JOHN MASON: died 1694: rector of Water-Stratford, Bucks, and one of the most delightful of our early poets, remarkable for intense devotion and an agreeable antique simplicity of style. His 33 *Songs of Praise*, with a few others, appeared 1683, passed through several editions, were then forgotten, revived within the last half-century, and reprinted by Mr. Daniel Sedgwick, the London hymnologist, in 1859.

MY soul doth magnify the Lord,
  My spirit doth rejoice
In God, my Saviour and my God;
  I hear His joyful voice.
I need not go abroad for joy,
  Who have a feast at home;
My sighs are turnèd into songs;
  The Comforter is come.

Down from above the blessed Dove
  Is come into my breast,
To witness God's eternal Love;
  This is my heavenly Feast.
This makes me *Abba*, *Father*, cry
  With confidence of soul;
It makes me cry, *My Lord, my God*,
  And that without control.

There is a Stream which issues forth
　　From God's eternal throne
And from the Lamb; a living Stream,
　　Clear as the crystal stone.
The Stream doth water Paradise,
　　It makes the angels sing:
One cordial drop revives my heart;
　　Hence all my joys do spring.

Such joys as are unspeakable,
　　And full of glory too;
Such hidden manna, hidden pearls,
　　As worldlings do not know.
Eye hath not seen, nor ear hath heard,
　　From fancy 'tis concealed,
What Thou, Lord, hast laid up for Thine,
　　And hast to me revealed.

I see Thy face, I hear Thy voice,
　　I taste Thy sweetest Love:
My soul doth leap: but O for wings,
　　The wings of Noah's dove!
Then should I flee far hence away,
　　Leaving this world of sin:
Then should my Lord put forth His Hand,
　　And kindly take me in.

Then should my soul with angels feast
　　On joys that always last:
Blest be my God, the God of joy,
　　That gives me here a taste.

THE LOVE OF THE SPIRIT I SING.

ROMANS xv. 30.

John Ryland, D.D., 1753–1825: a distinguished Baptist minister, and author of 99 hymns. This was written in 1796.

THE Love of the Spirit I sing,
   By whom is redemption applied;
Who sinners to Jesus can bring,
   And make them His mystical bride.

'Tis He circumcises their hearts,
   Their callousness kindly removes,
Light, life, and affection imparts
   To those that so freely He loves.

He opens the eyes of the blind,
   The beauties of Jesus to view;
He changes the bent of the mind,
   The glory of God to pursue.

The stubbornest will He can bow,
   The foes that dwell in us restrain;
And none can be trodden so low,
   But He can revive them again.

His blest renovation begun,
   He dwells in the hearts of His saints;
Abandons His temple to none,
   Nor e'er of His calling repents.

Imprest with the image divine,
   The souls to redemption He seals;
And each with the Saviour shall shine,
   With glory complete He reveals.

How constant Thy Love I believe,
   Which steadfast endures to the end:
Then never, my soul, may I grieve
   So loving, so holy a Friend.

THE INFLUENCE OF THE SPIRIT OF GOD IN THE HEART.

JOHN xiv. 16, 17.

ANNE STEELE, 1716–1778: daughter of a Baptist minister at Broughton, in Hampshire, and an invalid throughout life. She was a thoroughly devout and excellent woman, and after a mild fashion a graceful and pleasing poetess: many of her hymns are still popular. They, with some other verses and a few prose essays, appeared under the signature of "Theodosia" in 1760, and were reprinted in three volumes, Bristol, 1780; in two volumes, Boston, 1808; and in one by Mr. Sedgwick, 1863.

DEAR Lord, and shall Thy Spirit rest
   In such a wretched heart as mine?
Unworthy dwelling! glorious Guest!
   Favor astonishing, divine!

When sin prevails and gloomy fear,
   And hope almost expires in night,
Lord, can Thy Spirit then be here,
   Great Spring of comfort, life, and light?

Sure the blest Comforter is nigh,
  'Tis He sustains my fainting heart;
Else would my hopes for ever die,
  And every cheering ray depart.

When some kind promise glads my soul,
  Do I not find His healing voice
The tempest of my fears control,
  And bid my drooping powers rejoice?

Whene'er to call the Saviour mine
  With ardent wish my heart aspires,
Can it be less than Power divine
  Which animates these strong desires?

What less than Thy almighty word
  Can raise my heart from earth and dust,
And bid me cleave to Thee, my Lord,
  My Life, my Treasure, and my Trust?

And when my cheerful hope can say,
  "I love my God and taste His Grace,"
Lord, is it not Thy blissful ray
  Which brings this dawn of sacred peace?

Let Thy kind Spirit in my heart
  For ever dwell, O God of Love;
And light and heavenly peace impart,
  Sweet earnest of the joys above.

TAKE NOT THY HOLY SPIRIT FROM ME.

PSALM li. 11.

John Fawcett, D.D., 1739-1817: a Baptist minister at Wainsgate, and author of 166 hymns, which appeared 1782, and again in 1817. Some of them have been popular. He was a good man and a laborious pastor.

THE God of grace will never leave
  Or cast away His own;
Yet when we do His Spirit grieve,
  His comforts are withdrawn.

If we His sacred motions slight
  Or disobey His voice,
He will suspend His cheering light
  And soul-transporting joys.

When pride and self begin to swell,
  The Comforter departs:
The high and lofty One will dwell
  In humble broken hearts.

When noisy war and strife abound
  We grieve the peaceful Dove;
His gracious influence is found
  In paths of truth and love.

If we indulge some darling sin
  Or disregard His laws,
His succor and support divine
  The heavenly Guest withdraws.

THE FRUITS OF THE SPIRIT.

And then, alas! how cold and dead
   Will our devotions be!
But, Lord, our spirits ever dread
   To be forsook by Thee.

O leave us not to sin a prey,
   Nor yet to Satan's wiles;
But guide us in Thy heavenly way
   And cheer us with Thy smiles.

LEADINGS OF THE SPIRIT.

BENJAMIN BEDDOME, 1717-1795: Baptist minister at Bourton, Gloucestershire, for 52 years. His hymns were published, long after his death, by Robert Hall, in 1818. This is the origin of Hymn 210, in the Prayer-Book Collection.

THAT we might walk with God
   He forms our hearts anew;
Takes us, like Ephraim, by the hand,
   And teaches us to go.

He by His Spirit leads
   In paths before unknown;
The work to be performed is ours,
   The strength is all His own.

Assisted by His Grace
   We still pursue our way,
And hope at last to reach the prize,
   Secure in endless day.

'Tis He that works to will,
'Tis He that works to do:
His is the power by which we act,
His be the glory too.

AWAY WITH OUR FEARS!

CHARLES WESLEY: from his *Hymns for Whit-Sunday*, 1746.

AWAY with our fears,
Our troubles and tears!
The Spirit is come,
The Witness of Jesus returned to His Home:
The pledge of our Lord,
To His Heaven restored,
Is sent from the sky,
And tells us our Head is exalted on high.

Our Advocate there
By His Blood and His Prayer
The Gift hath obtained,
For us He hath prayed, and the Comforter gained:
Our glorified Head
His Spirit hath shed,
With His people to stay,
And never again will He take Him away.

Our heavenly Guide
With us shall abide;
His comfort impart,
And set up His kingdom of love in the heart:

THE FRUITS OF THE SPIRIT.

   The heart that believes
   His kingdom receives,
   His power and His peace,
His life, and His joy's everlasting increase.

   The Presence divine
   Doth inwardly shine,
   The Shéchinah rests
On all our assemblies, and glows in our breasts.
   By day and by night
   The pillar of light
   Our steps shall attend,
And convoy us safe to our prosperous end.

   Then let us rejoice
   In heart and in voice,
   Our Leader pursue,
And shout as we travel the wilderness through;
   With the Spirit remove
   To Sion above,
   Triumphant arise,
And walk in our God, till we fly to the skies.

SINNERS, LIFT UP YOUR HEARTS.

Charles Wesley: from the same tract.

SINNERS, lift up your hearts,
  The Promise to receive;
Jesus Himself imparts,
  He comes in man to live:

The Holy Ghost to man is given;
Rejoice in God sent down from Heaven.

   Jesus is glorified,
      And gives the Comforter,
   His Spirit, to reside
      In all His members here:
The Holy Ghost to man is given;
Rejoice in God sent down from Heaven.

   To make an end of sin,
      And Satan's works destroy,
   He brings His kingdom in,
      Peace, righteousness, and joy:
The Holy Ghost to man is given;
Rejoice in God sent down from Heaven.

   The cleansing Blood to apply,
      The heavenly Life display,
   And wholly sanctify
      And seal us to that Day,
The Holy Ghost to man is given;
Rejoice in God sent down from Heaven.

   Sent down to make us meet
      To see His glorious face,
   And grant us each a seat
      In that thrice happy place,
The Holy Ghost to man is given;
Rejoice in God sent down from Heaven.

From Heaven He shall once more
Triumphantly descend,
And all His saints restore
To joys that never end:
Then, then, when all our joys are given,
Rejoice in God, rejoice in Heaven.

WHITHER SHALL A CREATURE RUN?

PSALM cxxxix. 7–12.

CHARLES WESLEY: from his *Hymns on the Trinity*, 1767. Perhaps this splendid paraphrase does not strictly belong here: but being little known, I am unwilling to omit it. It is one of the finest samples of this author's objective writing; a style in which, though he seldom exercised it, he was as much a master as in the delineation of "frames and feelings."

WHITHER shall a creature run,
   From Jehovah's Spirit fly?
How Jehovah's presence shun,
   Screened from His all-seeing eye?
Holy Ghost, before Thy face
   Where shall I myself conceal?
Thou art God in every place,
   God incomprehensible.

If to Heaven I take my flight,
   With beatitude unknown
Filling all the realms of light,
   There Thou sittest on Thy throne!
If to Hell I could retire,
   Gloomy pit of endless pains,
There is the consuming fire,
   There almighty Vengeance reigns.

If the morning's wings I gain,
    Fly to earth's remotest bound,
Could I hid from Thee remain,
    In a world of waters drowned?
Leaving lands and seas behind,
    Could I the Omniscient leave?
There Thy quicker hand would find,
    There arrest, Thy fugitive.

Covered by the darkest shade,
    Should I hope to lurk unknown,
By a sudden light bewrayed,
    By an uncreated Sun,
Naked at the noon of night
    Should I not to Thee appear?
Forced to acknowledge in Thy sight,
    God is Light, and God is here!

BE FILLED WITH THE SPIRIT.

JOHN BARCLAY, 1734-1798, was the founder of a Scotch sect known as Bereans or Barclayans. He published various theological and poetical works, the latter in 1767 and 1776. None of his hymns have come into use, but they are distinguished by great vigor of style and the occasional presence of striking and sometimes just ideas. Barclay seems to have been an able, honest, and somewhat eccentric man. He had a way of adapting his "Spiritual Songs" to popular Scottish melodies, and secularizing as far as might be the treatment of sacred themes.

DRINK deep of the Spirit, and thou shalt be filled,
    Be filled with the sweetest enjoyment:
Attend to the Spirit, and thou shalt be skilled,
    Be skilled in the best of employment.

THE FRUITS OF THE SPIRIT.

Be led of the Spirit, and thou shalt rejoice,
    Rejoice in the happiest ending:
The Spirit will lead thee to heavenly joys;
    To Heaven O then be thou bending.

Give ear to the Spirit; He'll perfectly teach,
    He'll teach you celestial lessons:
He'll build up your walls, yea, and heal every breach,
    Adorning you round with His blessings.
Be friends with the Spirit, and laugh at your foes;
    With Him you may boldly defy them:
He'll guard you from every temptation that blows,
    And give you the power to deny them.

Revere thou the Spirit, who dwells in thy breast;
    Revere Him in humble submission:
Wherever He dwelleth a welcomèd Guest,
    He giveth a sealèd remission.
Exult in the Spirit, exult evermore,
    Exult in His high consolations;
In raptures of gladness before Him adore,
    Triumphing o'er all tribulations.

Amen to the Spirit in all that He says;
    Amen, and Amen to His doing!
Amen to the Spirit in all of His ways!
    The Spirit preserves me from ruin.
I'm filled with the Spirit, and led by the hand,
    In all of my workings directed:
The Spirit, He gives me the word of command,
    In all my behavior respected.

I'm taught of the Spirit, and built like a wall
  By Him the infallible Teacher:
I laugh now at Satan and stratagems all,
  Since the Spirit alone was my Preacher.[1]
The Spirit, He loves me, and gives me His joys,
  My spirit to Him being subject:
He defendeth His darlings; their foes He destroys;
  My foes of His wrath are the object.

My spirit is turnèd as wax to the seal
  Beneath His sweet holy impression:
I cannot express what already I feel;
  Yet Heaven remains in reversion.
Begone, idle toyings, begone ye from me!
  I am otherwise fully employed;
Possest of the Spirit: the Spirit is He,
  With a rival who can't be enjoyed.[2]

THE INDWELLING SPIRIT.

John Barclay: 1767 or 1776.

O LOVE ye the Spirit indwelling;
  In humble submission adore;
No passion, no motion, rebelling,
  From henceforth, Amen, evermore.
He floweth with tender compassion,
  Demanding reciprocal fires;

---

[1] 1 John iv. 6.
[2] He refers to Montrose's famous song:
  "As Alexander I will reign, and I will reign alone:
  My thoughts did evermore disdain a rival on my throne."

THE FRUITS OF THE SPIRIT.

To purpose of love let Him fashion
   Your spirit with all your desires.

Beholding the moving example
   Of Jesus who died in your stead,
Your body, becoming His temple,
   Keep holy for Jesus your Head.
If the flesh should advise you to sinning,
   The Spirit well knoweth the plot,
Your doing, with all your designing,
   Remarking the time and the spot.

Beware then of grieving the Spirit
   With curst Babylonian stuff:
Fly, fly ye before ye come near it,
   Lest He blow ye away with a puff.
Thus Achan receivèd damnation
   For the coveted garment and gold:
Rejecting both God and salvation,
   Who resisteth the Spirit is bold.

THE SPIRIT IN THE WORD.

REV. xxii. 17.

Thomas Gibbons, D.D., 1720-1785: an eminent Independent minister in London: author of various works, including two volumes of Hymns, 1769 and 1784. In the former is found this piece, headed "The Sinner's Welcome to the Waters of Life," which may have suggested the popular and more recent lyric of Bishop Onderdonk, given below.

THE Spirit in the Word
   And in His motions cries,
"Come to the Fountain-Head of Life,
   And come for large supplies."

THE SPIRIT'S WHISPER.

The Bride, the Church on Earth,
    And Church in Heaven combine
To bid unworthy sinners come
    And drink the joys divine.

Let him that hears the call
    Spring from his long delay,
And charge his soul to run, to fly,
    And seize the bliss to-day.

Let him who feels his thirst,
    Nor can endure its rage,
Come to Salvation's copious springs
    And all his pains assuage.

And whosoever will
    Is welcome to receive
The streams of everlasting Life
    That Heaven will freely give.

Jesus, is this Thy voice?
    We bless the gracious call,
And fly with joyful haste to Thee,
    Our Saviour and our all.

THE SPIRIT'S WHISPER.

HENRY USTIC ONDERDONK, D.D., rector of St. Ann's, Brooklyn, afterwards (1827) Bishop of Pennsylvania. It appeared in the Prayer-Book Collection, 1826.

THE Spirit, in our hearts,
    Is whispering, "Sinner, come:"
The Bride, the Church of Christ, proclaims
    To all His children, "Come!"

Let him that heareth say
  To all about him, "Come!"
Let him that thirsts for righteousness,
  To Christ, the Fountain, come!

Yes, whosoever will,
  O let him freely come,
And freely drink the stream of Life:
  'Tis Jesus bids him come.

Lo! Jesus, who invites,
  Declares, "I quickly come;"
Lord, even so! I wait Thy hour;
  Jesus, my Saviour, come!

"THE LETTER KILLETH, BUT THE SPIRIT GIVETH LIFE."

2 Cor. iii. 6.

S. B. HASLAM, "minister of Zion Chapel, Waterloo Road, London;" from his *Divine Aspirations: a Compilation of Spiritual Hymns upon the Glorious Doctrines, Experience, and Practice of True Religion*, 1824: a curious book, containing many originals. This has eleven verses: we take the first two and the last four.

BLEST be the God who men inspired
  To speak and write Heaven's laws abroad!
But not the threatening nor reward
  Can drive or draw one soul to God.

Blest be the Lord who precept gives,
  Instructing how to do His Will!
Yet none by letter-precept lives,
  But dead to God remaineth still.

. . . . .

'Tis not on signs God's saints are fed;
   'Tis substance they must live upon:
That sacred, mystic "Flesh and Blood"—
   The living Spirit of God's Son.

Nor prophets' word nor prophets' pen
   Can move, or vital spirit give;
The living God who moved the men
   Must live in us, and then we live.

But so the sacred Scripture tells—
   Then cease, vain struggling, cease thy strife—
That even inspired letter kills:
   'Tis the INSPIRER giveth Life.

Then, O Thou vital Spirit, give
   The Life Divine to live upon;
Or rather *in* the Life to live,
   And *by* it live upon the Son.

"GRIEVE NOT THE SPIRIT."

S. B. HASLAM, 1833: from the second edition of his collection.

I WOULD not grieve my dearest Lord
   In action, feeling, thought, or word;
   But I would live to prove
The fulness of redeeming Grace,
The heights of perfect righteousness,
   The depths of humble love.

THE FRUITS OF THE SPIRIT.

Thy heavenly Spirit, Lord, impart,
Through all my head, through all my heart,
   That I may think and feel
Far, far above earth's narrow bounds,
Its sordid movements, giddy rounds,
   And breathe celestial weal.

Essential, pure, eternal Life!
Thou art the death of mortal strife,
   The end of death and sin:
Now let Thy blest salvation flow
To every friend, to every foe,
   And full salvation reign!

"THE LOVE OF THE SPIRIT."

ROM. xv. 30.

Rippon's *Selection*, tenth edition, 1800: altered from BENJAMIN BEDDOME.

LORD, 'twas a time of wondrous Love
   When Thou didst first draw near my soul,
And by Thy Spirit from above
   My raging passions didst control.

Guilty and self-condemned I stood,
   Nor dreamt of Life and bliss so near;
But He my evil heart renewed,
   And all His graces planted there.

He will complete the work begun,
By leading me in all His ways:
To God the Father, God the Son,
And God the Spirit, equal praise.

"THE WIND BLOWETH WHERE IT LISTETH."

JOHN iii. 8.

INGRAM COBBIN, 1777–1851: known by his Commentaries, &c. The date of this is probably 1820 or 1828: I find it in later Collections.

AS blows the wind, and in its flight
Escapes the glance of keenest sight;
So are the wonder-working ways
Of God's regenerating Grace.

As nothing can its power withstand
But Him who holds it in His hand,
So are the soul's corruptions slain
When once that soul is born again.

As o'er our frames we feel the gale
Gently or mightily prevail,
So some are softly drawn to heaven,
And others as by tempests driven.

And as the herbs, the flowers, the trees,
Are seen to bend beneath the breeze,
So visible the change we view
When Grace doth thus the heart renew.

THE FRUITS OF THE SPIRIT.

Come, Holy Spirit, and impart
Thy secret virtue to each heart;
And let this be the happy hour
To show Thy mighty quickening power.

THE SOVEREIGN SPIRIT.

CHRISTOPHER WORDSWORTH, D.D., Bishop of Lincoln: from *The Holy Year*, 1862. It is there set for Tuesday in Whitsun Week.

NOT bound by chains, nor pent in cells
   Of person or of place,
But like the air untrammelled, blow
   The breezes of Thy Grace.

Not only Moses in the cloud
   With heavenly flame is fired;
Eldad and Medad in the camp
   Are, Lord, by Thee inspired.

A Balaam and a Caiaphas
   May prophesy of Thee;
Saul also may, though David's foe,
   Among the prophets be.

Not prophecy, nor tongues, nor faith
   That mountains could remove,
Will profit him who has those gifts,
   Without the grace of love.

As beacons fade, though some may live
   Saved by their guiding ray,
So he who does to others preach
   May be a castaway.

The Spirit is not tied to means,
   But sovereign is and free;
But when Thou hast prescribed the means,
   Tied to those means are we.

No Abanas nor Pharpars, Lord,
   To Jordan we prefer;
But in Thy ordered means of Grace
   We seek the Comforter.

We love these means, for they are Thine,
   Which heavenly life impart;
They channels are, through which it flows;
   But Thou the Fountain art.

The vessel of our thirsting hearts
   To Thee in them we bring;
O grant us, Lord, in Heaven to drink
   Of Thine eternal Spring.

To Father, Son, and Holy Ghost,
   One God and Persons Three,
For gifts of Grace, and hopes of bliss,
   All praise and glory be.

THOU WHO FRAMEDST THIS GOODLY WORLD.

PSALM xxxiii.

JOHN HENRY ALEXANDER, born 1812, at Annapolis, Md., died 1866, has published several scientific works, and a volume of *Introits, or Ante-Communion Psalms*; Philadelphia, 1844. From this are taken the three following.

THOU who framedst this goodly world;
   Thou whose Spirit erst did move
     O'er the treasures of the deep;
Now when again, as once, unfurled
   Glows the banner of Thy Love,
     Help us in Thy host to keep!

Thou hast fashioned every heart;
   Thou canst fathom each device
     Of our idol-building here,
That rests, with but short-sighted art,
   On proud human power and price
     When the time of dearth is near.

If, for all our high desire,
   Lingering cowards in Thy camp,
     We should look to such as these;
Once more O let Thy tongues of fire,
   Whose strong flame earth cannot damp,
     On our recreant terrors seize:

And again from Heaven look down
   On the chamber of our hearts,

    (Where a few frail hopes yet wait
   For Thee Thy Pentecost to crown)
     Each to mould, in varied parts,
       Till Thy counsel sure is met!

O GOD, WHEN WILT THOU COME?

PSALM ci.

O GOD, when wilt Thou come?
     Lighting our life and home
And wilful hearts with Thy plain, near command;
     Showing the open door
     Seen but in types before,
Whereat, revealed and gracious, Christ doth stand.

     Thou hast the answer made,
     What time Thy Spirit said,
No wicked thing Thine helping hand should claim;
     No heavenly dews should bless
     Sins of unfaithfulness;
No angel write on high the slanderer's name.

     Nor is that answer lost
     Since the bright Pentecost
When Thou, O Spirit, cam'st down visibly:
     But all life-fruits below
     Must richer, riper grow,
Warmed by a ray more genial, pure, and high.

        And all the love and faith
        That blossomed in the path
Of olden saints, more need be in our part;
        Till here, one day, we bring
        Best, hardest offering,
The walking in our house with perfect heart.

BE JOYFUL IN THE LORD, YE LANDS!

PSALM C.

BE joyful in the Lord, ye lands!
    Serve Him with gladness and with song:
No more sad rites, or hard commands,
His statutes or your worship throng:

No difficult or distant shrine
A weary pilgrimage compels;
O'er the whole earth His altars shine;
Your hearts are courts wherein He dwells.

He calls you, wanderers, to His fold
With sweetest voice, by strongest spell;
'Twas His your earthly frames to mould;
His Spirit comes with yours to dwell.

And we would give Thee welcome, Lord!
O Holy Ghost, our hearts renew,
Till we have learned and proved this word —
God ever gracious is, and true.

WHIT-SUNDAY.

HARRIET AUBER, 1773–1862, of Hoddesdon, Herts: author of *The Spirit of the Psalms*, 1829, an important work, which must not be confounded with Lyte's production bearing the same title, 1834. An account of Miss Auber may be found in JOSIAH MILLER's *Singers and Songs of the Church*, 1869.

OUR blest Redeemer, ere He breathed
    His tender, last farewell,
A Guide, a Comforter, bequeathed
    With us to dwell.

He came in semblance of a dove,
    With sheltering wings outspread,
The holy balm of peace and love
    On earth to shed.

He came in tongues of living flame,
    To teach, convince, subdue;
All-powerful as the wind He came,
    As viewless too.

He came sweet influence to impart,
    A gracious, willing Guest,
While He can find one humble heart
    Wherein to rest.

And His that gentle voice we hear,
    Soft as the breath of even,
That checks each fault, that calms each fear,
    And speaks of Heaven.

And every virtue we possess,
   And every victory won,
And every thought of holiness,
   Are His alone.

Spirit of Purity and Grace,
   Our weakness pitying see;
O make our hearts Thy dwelling-place,
   And worthier Thee.

"WHOSE HEART THE LORD OPENED."

ACTS xvi. 14.

Mrs. THOMAS CREWDSON, 1809–1863, of Manchester, born Jane Fox: author of several volumes of poetry, written during a long illness. From *The Little While, and other Poems*, 1864.

WE cannot see the wondrous Hand
   That makes the budding flower expand:
One sunbeam's kiss, one dewdrop's fall,
May open wide its coronal,
And every folded petal part,
That noon's full tide may reach its heart.

And yet the Hand that drops the dew
Is shaded from our finite view;
And He who guides the ray of light
Is hidden from our mortal sight.
We see not, but we own the Power
That makes the bud become the flower.

THE SPIRIT'S QUICKENING.

O Lord! Thy Hand alone can part
The shadows that enfold man's heart;
Thy Holy Spirit's quickening Breath
Can vivify the germ of faith;
Thy Word can cause the bud to grow,
Thy touch can make the flower to blow.

To Thee our infant flowers we bring,
Our buds, so slow in opening:
Perchance, within the folded cup,
The germ of Life is treasured up:
We bring them, Lord, to crave Thy aid,
To that dear place where prayer is made.

One gracious drop of heavenly Dew
May bring the hidden Life to view;
One touch of Love the leaves unroll,
And shed Truth's noontide o'er the soul;
And thus, by sweet degrees, transmute
The open blossom into fruit.

FOR CONSISTENCY.

From *A Collection of Psalms and Hymns* by the Rev. R. Frost, Incumbent of St. Matthias' Church, Salford; 1832. Authorship unknown.

BRETHREN, let us join to raise
To the Spirit hymns of praise:
Thanks, eternal thanks, be given
For this precious Gift of Heaven.

THE FRUITS OF THE SPIRIT.

If we of the Spirit talk,
Let us in the Spirit walk:
If the Spirit reign within,
Let the Spirit's work be seen.

If we in the Spirit live
And the Spirit's Grace receive,
Let us in His ways be found,
And in holy fruits abound.

Thus shall we abroad proclaim
Honor to the Christian name:
Thus shall our religion shine,
And the work appear divine.

Thus shall we, while here below,
In the Saviour's likeness grow,
And be fitted by His Love
For His praise in Heaven above.

THE NINTH COMMANDMENT.

ADA CAMBRIDGE is a young lady in the parish of St. Michaels, Coventry: at least so one may suppose from the fact that her popular *Hymns on the Holy Communion*, 1866, were submitted to and introduced by the Vicar thereof, the Rev. R. H. Baynes. She has also published *Hymns on the Litany*. This is from the former work.

MAY Thy Spirit, bright and holy,
    With His tender, shielding wings,
With the pure celestial glory
    That His Presence only brings,

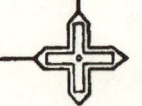

THE NINTH COMMANDMENT.

In our heart forever dwelling,
  Keep the evil one at bay.
By our Saviour's Cross and Passion,
By His willing intercession,
  Hear, and answer us, we pray!

He is watching, ever watching,
  In a silence dark and dread,
Round each fervent aspiration
  His ensnaring toils to spread;
On each thought to breathe pollution,
  Every word to taint with sin:
And how can we foil his power
In the dark and trying hour,
  With no Spirit-light within?

He is striving, ever striving
  To break down and to destroy,
With the finest gold to mingle
  What he can of base alloy;
In the garden fair and fragrant,
  Where Thy blessed Feet have been,
To crush all the tender beauty —
Flowers of love and truth and duty,
  And the buds that grow between.

He is trying, ever trying
  On Thy fairest work to breathe,
With its first celestial sweetness
  Some undying curse to wreathe;
But we fear not, gentle Spirit,

When Thy shielding wings are nigh!
Then he comes not, hearts assailing,
For he knows there's no prevailing
   'Gainst that wondrous Sanctity.

He may strive to sow them, vainly,
   Those accursed bitter seeds
That grow up to sinful anger
   And untruthful words and deeds:
Though our eyes are all unwatchful,
   Thine, so loving, never sleep,
And their clear and steady shining,
Every snare of his divining,
   Can the frail soul-fortress keep.

O! he knows our sinful weakness,
   That our love is mostly cold,
All too feeble and too selfish
   Thy great Name of Truth to hold.
Ah! he knows how oft 'tis hidden,
   This baptismal seal of Thine!
And he feels his strength increasing
When the Beacon-light is ceasing
   In our shadowed heart to shine.

But he knows Thy Love, O Spirit!
   That 'tis stronger than his hate,
That forever and forever
   It is kept inviolate.
And he dares not face Thy Presence,
   Brooding human passions o'er;

Though our weakness may assist him,
He knows Thy strength can resist him,
  Can resist him evermore!

So be with us, ever with us,
  In our daily toil and strife;
Purify Thou all the sources
  Of our erring daily life!
Do Thou guard it from the Tempter
  With Thy white wings, gentle Dove!
In that sure and safe protection
Bloom the flowers of sweet affection,
  And the fruits of truth and love.

THE WITNESS OF THE SPIRIT.

1849.

THOMAS H. GILL, Esq., of Lewisham, Kent: born 1819: author of *The Anniversaries*, 1858, *The Papal Drama*, 1866, and *The Golden Chain of Praise*, 1869: one of the most remarkable hymnists of the time, though he is only beginning to be known and used. His hymns, 165 in number, are collected in the last-named volume. The eight which follow here are his. His own title, and the date of composition, are given above each.

BRIGHT Presence! may my soul have part
  In those sweet beams of Thine?
Lord! soundeth in mine inmost heart
  Thy very Voice divine?
Yes, Lord, with Thee I may partake;
  To me Thou wilt repair,
This soul wilt cheer and warn and wake,
  The Spirit's witness there!

In holy tasks, in noble pain
   My soul this comfort hath:
The amazèd world exclaims in vain;
   The Spirit witnesseth.
To break my peace the tumult seeks:
   I have no ears to hear;
So mightily the Spirit speaks,
   So sweetly fills mine ear.

Alas, my Lord! that Sense and Sin
   To tempt this soul should dare,
That Thine own foes should audience win,
   The Spirit's witness there!
He speaketh oft, He warneth clear,
   He witnesseth in vain:
Repent, sad soul, if thou wouldst hear
   The Voice Divine again!

Glad soul! art thou ashamed to smile?
   Of gladness hast thou fear?
Thou mayst enjoy Thy golden while,
   Yes, boldly take thy cheer.
Each glorious hour thou mayst renew
   In thine own bower of bliss;
O sweet and strong the joy whereto
   The Spirit witnesses!

Alas! do subtle foes conspire
   To darken my soul's day,
To quench the bright celestial fire
   And take my Lord away?

I need not seek o'er all the earth
    Wherewith to guard my faith;
A Champion near and strong springs forth;
    The Spirit witnesseth.

My Father! when Thy child delights
    To feel himself Thine own,
And others would deny his rights
    And thrust him from Thy throne;
I still draw near, I still rejoice,
    Thy child doth nothing care,
If to his claim Thy Spirit's voice
    Its witness sweet doth bear.

O that this Voice my soul did stir
    Nor make it sadly start!
O that Thy Spirit oftener
    Bore witness with my heart!
O that His gracious, awful Voice
    More swiftly caught mine ear!
O that I always could rejoice
    His witness, Lord, to hear!

One day the joy may fully come,
    The music may be mine;
O ever in the Heavenly Home
    Sweet sounds the Voice Divine.
To each desire, to each delight,
    "Yes," "Yes," it sweetly saith:
Smile on, sing on, ye Angels bright!
    The Spirit witnesseth.

THE EARNEST OF THE SPIRIT.

1850: printed 1853.

WHY hasteth on this pilgrim throng
    As burthened with no cares?
These lowly souls, why swells their song
    As though the world was theirs?

What can their happy fulness crave?
    Where can their wishes rove?
Thy Holy Spirit, Lord, they have,
    The Earnest of Thy Love.

They needs must rest in glorious things
    With whom the Spirit dwells;
Sweet messages the Spirit brings,
    Great news the Spirit tells.

Lord, if Thy gracious Voice divine
    One whisper sweet lets fall,
They know that Thou hast made them Thine,
    That Thou hast given them all.

O if the Lord Himself hath given,
    All else, they know, must come —
The shining thrones, the blissful Heaven,
    The everlasting Home.

Lord, may not I these tidings hear,
    These messages receive?
Assure my soul that she is dear;
    To me the Spirit give.

Teach me no other prayer to lift,
  No other boon to crave;
Mine all Thy Grace, mine every gift,
  If I the Earnest have.

Take all Thine other gifts away,
  But do not Thou remove;
All things remain, if with me stay
  This Earnest of Thy Love.

"THE SPIRIT HELPETH OUR INFIRMITIES."

From *The Anniversaries*, 1858; written in 1854.

ALAS these pilgrims faint and worn!
  Alas this vale of tears!
These sinners sore who sink and mourn
  Through the long mortal years!

Behold this Garden of the Lord!
  These guests in raiment bright!
This beauty hath the Spirit poured,
  Hath made that darkness light.

Ah faithless souls that dwelt apart!
  Ah lonely, loveless throng!
No fire within each joyless heart —
  Dull, dull each formal tongue!

THE FRUITS OF THE SPIRIT.

Behold these brethren dear! inquire
   How hath this sweetness grown:
The Spirit sets their souls on fire,
   The Spirit makes them one.

Kneel with this prayerful company,
   Join, join these cheerful songs:
The Spirit makes this melody,
   The Spirit tunes these tongues.

Ah weaklings vain, who faintly wrought,
   Who soon the strife gave o'er,
Who no sweet gift the brethren brought,
   The Lord no tribute bore!

The Spirit pours the lavish love
   Of this gift-bearing throng;
These linkèd hands that mountains move,
   The Spirit makes them strong.

He leadeth forth His awful host,
   He mingleth in the fight:
O army of the Holy Ghost,
   What shall withstand your might?

Ah souls their veilèd Heaven that mourned!
   Ah glory faint and dim!
Ah tearful eyes that vainly yearned!
   Ah distant Seraphim!

THE HEAVENLY DOVE.   153

Blest souls, that now Heaven's glory greet,
    That here Heaven's rapture feel!
The Spirit brings this earnest sweet,
    The Spirit sets His seal.

Ne'er from His dwelling-place so dear,
    The Spirit will remove:
O Church of God, reveal Him here!
    Soar on His wings above!

"O THAT I HAD WINGS LIKE A DOVE."

PSALM lv. 6.

"The Spirit descending like a dove." — MAT. iii. 15.

1855.

O SMITTEN soul that cares and conflicts wring,
    O fainting heart that burdens sore oppress;
What glory gleameth from each gladsome wing!
What sweetness wrappeth the still wilderness!

Thou mournest o'er the radiant wings denied;
Thou yearnest for the Happy Isles afar;
Fain on the dove's soft pinion wouldst thou glide,
And win sweet peace from the calm desert air.

These yearnings bright, O vainly are they stirred?
These golden dreams, for nothing do they come?
Ah, woos thee mockingly each soaring bird?
Ah, vainly calleth thee some smiling home?

Unbounded heart! thou shapest bright desires,
Yet richlier hath thy Heavenly Lover wrought:
Yes, more than all each golden dream requires
Preventing Grace hath in sweet fulness brought.

What needs this envy of the swift-winged dove,
This quest of deserts that no cheer may make,
When the sweet Spirit leaves His Home above,
When I, bright Dove Divine, Thy wings may take?

Thou bringest me the branch of heavenly peace,
Midst winds that roar and waters that would whelm,
And steepest me, here on the stormy seas,
In the deep stillness of Thine own bright realm.

Thou comest not near, sweet Dove, with fleeting beam
And hasty wing to mock my sad estate:
Still over me those glorious pinions gleam;
Still, still for me those tender wings do wait.

O Dove Divine! no more the captive sighs,
The weary soul pours forth no bootless prayer:
I breathe the quiet of Thine own soft skies;
I drink the fragrance of Thine own sweet air.

THE DIVINE GLADDENER.

1849. This and the three following were printed in GEORGE DAWSON's *Psalms and Hymns*, 1853.

DO we only give Thee heed,
    Lord, when other help hath gone?
Doth the soreness of our need
    Send us to the Heavenly Throne?
Wherefore should our souls repair
Only to the Comforter?

Must not Thy glad creatures yearn
    Of their best their Lord to bring?
Must not happy spirits burn
    To their Gladdener to spring?
Hath our joy for Thee no place?
Art Thou not our God of Grace?

Should not each bright golden hour
    Lay its lustre at Thy feet?
May not, Lord, our blissful bower
    Rise beneath Thy mercy-seat?
Who like happy souls may call
For the wings celestial?

Maketh not Thy presence cheer?
    May Thy lovers, Lord, be sad?
Who are like the angels near,
    Who are like the angels glad?
Fullest joy our hearts doth stir
When we feel the Gladdener.

When our life is all delight
  On the happy Heavenly Hill,
'Tis because Thy presence bright
  All the Heavenly Life doth fill.
Heaven our Land of Joy we call,
For the Lord is all in all.

There our very bower of bliss
  Is Thine awful Holy Place;
There our only Paradise
  Is the shining of Thy face.
Still on us Thy face doth shine;
Still streams on our joy divine.

THY HAPPY ONES A STRAIN BEGIN.

Written 1846, rewritten 1868. The second verse is from the old reading, somewhat altered.

THY happy ones a strain begin;
  Dost Thou not, Lord, glad souls possess?
Thy cheerful Spirit reigns within:
  We feel Thee in our joyfulness.

Our mirth is not afraid of Thee;
  Our life rejoices to be bright:
We would not from our gladness flee,
  But show it in the Gladdener's sight.

Thou wilt not, Lord, our smiles deny;
  The Spirit loves the mirth He makes;
O sweet to the Taskmaster's eye
  The cheer that each true servant takes.

We turn to Thee a smiling face;
  Thou sendest us the smile again:
Our joy the fulness of Thy Grace;
  Thine own the cheer of this glad strain.

Thou God of joy! our souls do well
  The Life hereafter to forestall;
We go with happy ones to dwell,
  To help the joy celestial.

"GRIEVE NOT THE HOLY SPIRIT."

1849.

LORD, am I precious in Thy sight?
  Lord, wouldst Thou have me Thine?
What, may I grieve, may I delight
  The Majesty Divine?

Dost Thou so sweetly urge and press
  My soul Thy Heaven to win?
Lord, dost Thou love my faithfulness?
  Lord, dost Thou hate my sin?

O Holy Spirit! dost Thou mourn
  When I from Thee depart?
Dost Thou rejoice when I return,
  And give Thee back my heart?

O sweet, strange height of Grace Divine,
  My sin Thy grief to make,
And this poor faithfulness of mine
  For Thy delight to take!

Strange height of sin to spurn the Love
  That yearns to make me blest,
And drive away the Heavenly Dove
  That fain would be my Guest!

O happy Heaven, where Thine embrace
  I never more shall leave,
Nor ever cast away Thy Grace,
  Nor once Thy Spirit grieve!

Let me, dear Lord, each grace possess
  That makes Thy Heaven more bright,
And bring the humble holiness
  That gives my God delight.

THE GLORY OF THE LATTER DAYS.

"The power of Thy Grace is not passed away with the primitive times, as fond and faithless men imagine, but Thy kingdom is now at hand, and Thou standing at the door."—MILTON.

(Written 1846: rewritten 1866.)

OUR God, our God! Thou shinest here,
  Thine own this latter day:
To us Thy radiant steps appear;
  We watch Thy glorious way.

Thou tookest once our flesh: Thy face
  Once on our darkness shone:
Yet through each age new births of Grace
  Still make Thy glory known.

Not only olden ages felt
 The presence of the Lord;
Not only with the fathers dwelt
 Thy Spirit and Thy Word.

Doth not the Spirit still descend
 And bring the heavenly fire?
Doth He not still Thy Church extend
 And waiting souls inspire?

Come, Holy Ghost, in us arise,
 Be this Thy mighty hour!
And make Thy willing people wise
 To know Thy day of power!

Pour down Thy fire in us to glow,
 Thy might in us to dwell;
Again Thy works of wonder show,
 Thy blessed secrets tell!

Bear us aloft, more glad, more strong
 On Thy celestial wing,
And grant us grace to look and long
 For our returning King.

He draweth near, He standeth by,
 He fills our eyes, our ears;
Come, King of Grace, Thy people cry,
 And bring the glorious years!

ASCENSION AND PENTECOST.

<small>ARTHUR MIDDLEMORE MORGAN, 1856.   Through *Lyra Messianica*, 1864.</small>

O SON of God, who wentest up on high
    Only to come more nigh,
More nigh Thy orphaned Twelve, the first of us
    Thy sons innumerous,
Lo, at the break of Pentecostal Day
    We list what God will say;
In Sion, in the mountain of Thy choice
    We wait the still small Voice.

He speaks, He speaks! now he that hath an ear
    Let him the loved Voice hear:—
That where I am My own might be alway,
    On earth I would not stay:
A little while, and in My gracious rain
    To earth I came again,
That I with man might dwell, and be his Friend
    Even unto the end.

The Flesh which died, which nevermore shall die,
    'Twas that I bare on high;
My Death, my Life, to work 'mid sin and woe,
    'Twas that I sent below:
Summed in the mighty Wind and Tongues of fire
    Are all ye can desire,
That ye may work with this your God, and be
    Mine through eternity.

Amen, Amen! so be it, Lord, with all
    Who love Thy Festival!
Thou hast not left us orphans; to our need
    The Comforter indeed,
The eternal Father's Promise, Thy work's Crown,
    The Spirit hath come down;
The Father thus, and Son, in souls may dwell
    Forever. It is well.

SONGS OF PRAISE AND PRAYER

TO

GOD THE HOLY GHOST.

LATIN HYMNS.

The Latin Hymns were the chief ones of the Church at large for some 1200 years, from the beginnings of any thing like systematic Hymnody in the fourth century to the Protestant Reformation. They are therefore of the greatest importance, and must be considered at length in any Collection attempting, as this does, to be not only catholic in scope but historical in treatment. The large range of time and space which they cover — nearly the whole of civilized Europe, throughout the primitive and middle ages — gives them sufficient variety of matter and style, and a few of our readers may possibly be surprised at the freshness and breadth of thought, and warmth and depth of devotion, to be found in some of them.

It may be thought that too much space is occupied by the numerous versions of *Veni Creator* and *Veni Sancte Spiritus*. But the vast historical importance of those hymns is not greater than their intrinsic merit: whatever of this sort has been written since (in any language) is little more than a paraphrase on them. Let any reader compare the native English lyrics which will follow by and by, and judge for himself. Moreover, I had in the case of *Veni Creator* the rare advantage of versions running through three centuries, and coming from widely different schools and men: the translations thus resemble each other less than many independent originals will be found to do. With *Veni Sancte* there is more sameness, most of the versions closely approximating in date and coming from the same school : but something of the unparalleled loveliness of the original will appear in every rendering. This volume probably contains nothing grander than DRYDEN's paraphrase of *Veni Creator*, and nothing sweeter than CASWALL's *Veni Sancte*.

Of these and the other common Breviary pieces the versions might have been yet further multiplied. Of the later (and usually longer) Latin Spirit-hymns, many are yet untranslated.

The materials for the student of Latin sacred verse are well known: DANIEL, *Thesaurus Hymnologicus*; MONE, *Hymni Latini Medii Ævi* (the first volume has the same title in German) ; WACKERNAGEL, *Kirchenleider*, Vol. 1.: and of smaller but not less learned or reliable works, Dr. NEALE, *Hymni Ecclesiæ*, 1851, *and Sequentiæ*; and Archbishop TRENCH, *Sacred Latin Poetry*, 1849, 1864.

Our English translations have been almost entirely made in the last 35 years. A seventeenth-century poet here and there rendered a few well-known lyrics from the Breviaries: in the last century, and the first third of this, nothing of the sort was done, or near it. We owe our present comparative wealth in this department — altogether as to the impulse, and largely in the actual results — to the Oxford Tractarian movement. Dr. Newman began, in 1836, contenting himself with a dozen or two hymns for the Hours &c.: he was followed by several English Churchmen (not necessarily sharing fully his views), and one or two who followed him to Rome. Now, of course, the fruits of their labors are common property, as the field which they opened has become more or less familiar and interesting to all.

The noticeable books are by CHANDLER, 1837: Bishop MANT, 1837: ISAAC WILLIAMS, 1839: WILLIAM JOHN COPELAND (*Hymns for the Week and Hymns for the Seasons*), 1847: CASWALL, 1848: CAMPBELL, 1850: NEALE, 1851: BLEW, 1851-5: CHAMBERS, 1857, 1866: KYNASTON, 1862. All these, except MANT and COPELAND (whose work, though not without merit, is of limited extent, and the ground better covered by others), are extracted from and referred to in the following pages; as are several others, whose labors have been slighter, more desultory, or uncollected.

A Prayer of S. Nierses of Clajes.

SPIRIT of GOD, and true GOD, Who didst come down at the Jordan, and on the day of Pentecost, and Who didst enlighten me in Holy Baptism; I have sinned against heaven and before thee: but purify me again with Thy Divine fire, as Thou didst purify the Apostles with tongues of fire; And have mercy on all Thy creatures.

A Prayer of S. Cyprian.

OH Holy Spirit, be Thou present, and from heaven shed down Thy consolations on them that expect Thee: sanctify the temple of our body, and consecrate it a habitation to Thyself. Make the souls that desire Thee joyful with Thy presence. Make the house fit for Thee, the Inhabitant: adorn Thy chamber and surround the place of Thy rest with all virtues; strew the pavement with jewels; let Thy mansion shine with the brightness of carbuncles and precious stones; and let the odors of all Thy gifts inwardly discover themselves; let Thy fragrant balsam perfume Thy residence, and expel whatever is noisome and the spring of corruption; do Thou make this our joy stable and lasting: and this renovation of Thy creature do Thou continue forever in unfading beauty. Amen.

LATIN HYMNS.

VENI CREATOR SPIRITUS.

The authorship of this hymn is uncertain. DANIEL, *Thesaurus*, IV. 124, ascribes it to CHARLEMAGNE (died 814). The first distinct mention of it is in the *Historia Delationis S. Marculfi*, A.D. 898 (given by Mabillon in his edition of the *Annales Ord. S. Bened.* T. VI. p. 532). The Bollandists in the *Acta Sanctorum*, in the life of NOTKER, ascribe it to CHARLEMAGNE. DANIEL says that the action of the Synod, assembled by his authority at Aquisgranum in 809, on the doctrine proposed by him concerning the procession of the Holy Spirit from the Father and the Son, moved him to the preparation of this hymn, and that it was probably written by him.

Others have supposed that it was written for CHARLEMAGNE by ALCUIN. TRENCH says it "is certainly older."

MONE, *Lateinische Hymnen*, I. 242, affirms that it could not have been written by CHARLEMAGNE, who was not sufficiently master of the Latin language to write it. The accentuation in the 5th verse betrays an acquaintance with the Greek, of which CHARLEMAGNE was ignorant. He ascribes it to GREGORY THE GREAT, to the style of whose hymns it has much resemblance.

WACKERNAGEL, *Kirchenlieder*, I. 75, agrees with MONE in ascribing it to GREGORY THE GREAT. The Codex from which the Hymns of HRABANUS MAURUS were edited (Mayence, 1617) ascribes it to HRABANUS.

The 6th verse, *Da gaudiorum præmia*, is generally conceded to be a later insertion.

The Hymn at once took high rank among the Spirit-Hymns. It was appointed to be used, says DANIEL, at the creation of a Pope, the election of a Bishop, the coronation of Kings, the celebration of a Synod, the elevation and translation of saints, &c. In the Breviary it is appointed for the Vespers of Pentecost, and at Terce, in commemoration of the descent of the Spirit upon the Apostles at that hour. It was among the earliest of the translations at the Reformation in the German and Anglican Churches, and appointed for use both in the Ordination service, and on other important occasions.

VENI Creator Spiritus,
Mentes tuorum visita,
Imple supernâ gratiâ
Quæ tu creâsti pectora.

Qui Paraclitus diceris,
Altissimi donum Dei,
Fons vivus, ignis, caritas,
Et spiritalis unctio.

LATIN HYMNS.

Tu septiformis munere,
Dextræ Dei tu digitus,
Tu rite promissum Patris,
Sermone ditans guttura.

Accende lumen sensibus,
Infunde amorem cordibus,
Infirma nostri corporis
Virtute firmans perpeti.

Hostem repellas longius,
Pacemque dones protinus,
Ductore sic te prævio,
Vitemus omne noxium.

Da gaudiorum præmia,
Da gratiarum numera,
Dissolve litis vincula,
Adstringe pacis fœdera.

Per te sciamus da Patrem,
Noscamus atque Filium,
Te utriusque Spiritum
Credamus omni tempore.

Sit laus Patri cum Filio,
Sancto simul Paraclito,
Nobisque mittat Filius
Charisma Sancti Spiritûs.

FIRST VERSION.

GEORGE WITHER, 1588-1667: from his *Hymnes and Songs of the Church*, 1623. The hymn, he says, is "here translated syllable for syllable, and in the same kind of measure which it hath in the Latin."

COME, Holy Ghost, the Maker, come;
    Take in the souls of Thine Thy place;
Thou whom our hearts had being from,
    O fill them with Thy heavenly Grace.
Thou art that Comfort from above
    The Highest doth by gift impart;
Thou Spring of Life, a Fire of Love,
    And the anointing Spirit art.

Thou in Thy gifts art manifold;
    God's right-hand Finger thou art, Lord;
The Father's Promise made of old,
    Our tongues enriching by Thy Word.

O give our blinded senses light;
  Shed love into each heart of our,
And grant the body's feeble plight
  May be enabled by Thy power.

Far from us drive away the foe,
  And let a speedy peace ensue:
Our Leader also be, that so
  We every danger may eschew.
Let us be taught the blessed creed
  Of Father and of Son by Thee,
And how from Both Thou dost proceed,
  That our belief it still may be.

To Thee, the Father, and the Son,
  (Whom past and present times adore)
The One in Three, and Three in One,
  All glory be for evermore!

SECOND VERSION.

WILLIAM DRUMMOND, of Hawthornden, 1585-1649: a friend of BEN JONSON, and "the first Scottish poet who wrote well in English." His *Poems* appeared 1616, and *Flowers of Zion, or Spiritual Poems*, 1623.

CREATOR, Holy Ghost, descend;
  Visit our minds with Thy bright flame,
And Thy celestial Grace extend,
  To fill the hearts which Thou didst frame:

Who Paraclete art said to be,
   Gift which the highest God bestows,
Fountain of Life, Fire, Charity,
   Ointment whence ghostly blessing flows.

Thy sevenfold Grace Thou down dost send,
   Of God's right hand Thou Finger art;
Thou, by the Father promisèd,
   Unto our mouths dost speech impart.

In our dull senses kindle light:
   Infuse Thy Love into our hearts,
Reforming with perpetual might
   The infirmities of fleshly parts.

Far from our dwelling drive our foe,
   And quickly peace unto us bring;
Be Thou our Guide, before to go,
   That we may shun each hurtful thing.

Be pleasèd to instruct our mind
   To know the Father and the Son;
The Spirit who them Both doth bind
   Let us believe, while ages run.

To God the Father glory great,
   And to the Son, who from the dead
Arose, and to the Paraclete
   Beyond all time imaginèd.

VENI CREATOR.

THIRD VERSION.

Bishop JOHN COSIN, 1594-1672. A native of Norwich and scholar of Caius College, Cambridge; Prebend of Durham, 1624, rector of Branspeth, 1626; in 1660 Dean and then Bishop of Durham. His *Collection of Private Devotions for the Hours of Prayer*, 1627, much offended the Puritans, who styled it "a book of Cozening Devotions." This work contains ten short hymns (three of them from the Latin), which are supposed to be his. This one is found with " Prayers for the Third Hour." At the revision of the Book of Common Prayer and Offices in 1662, it was put into the Ordinal, whence it has come into nearly universal use. — Bishop COSIN wrote several other books, in English and in Latin.

COME, Holy Ghost, our souls inspire,
 And lighten with celestial fire.
Thou the anointing Spirit art,
Who dost Thy sevenfold gifts impart.
Thy blessed unction from above
Is comfort, life, and fire of Love.
Enable with perpetual light
The dulness of our blinded sight.
Anoint and cheer our soilèd face
With the abundance of Thy Grace.
Keep far our foes; give peace at home:
Where Thou art Guide, no ill can come.
Teach us to know the Father, Son,
And Thee, of Both, to be but One;
That through the ages all along
This may be our endless song;
 Praise to Thy eternal merit,
 FATHER, SON, *and* HOLY SPIRIT.

LATIN HYMNS.

FOURTH VERSION.

This voluminous paraphrase is one of the few hymns added to STERNHOLD *and* HOPKINS' *Old Version of the Psalms, and may be nearly or quite as old: but its date and authorship are uncertain. With Bishop* COSIN'S *version, it found a place in the Ordination and Consecration services. The text, here and there, is somewhat modernized, as it stands in the Prayer Book.*

COME, Holy Ghost, eternal God,
  Proceeding from above,
Both from the Father and the Son,
  The God of peace and Love.
Visit our minds, into our hearts
  Thy heavenly Grace inspire;
That truth and godliness we may
  Pursue with full desire.
Thou art the very Comforter
  In grief and all distress;
The heavenly Gift of God most High;
  No tongue can it express;
The fountain and the living spring
  Of joy celestial;
The fire so bright, the love so sweet,
  The Unction spiritual.
Thou in Thy gifts art manifold,
  By them Christ's Church doth stand:
In faithful hearts Thou writ'st Thy law,
  The finger of God's hand.
According to Thy promise, Lord,
  Thou givest speech with grace;
That, through Thy help, God's praises may
  Resound in every place.

VENI CREATOR.

O Holy Ghost, into our minds
    Send down Thy heavenly light,
Kindle our hearts with fervent zeal,
    To serve God day and night.
Our weakness strengthen and confirm,
    For, Lord, thou know'st us frail;
That neither devil, world, nor flesh,
    Against us may prevail.
Our enemies put far from us,
    And help us to obtain
Peace in our hearts with God and man,
    The best, the truest gain.
And grant that Thou being, O Lord,
    Our Leader and our Guide,
We may escape the snares of sin,
    And never from Thee slide.
Such measures of Thy powerful Grace
    Grant, Lord, to us, we pray;
That Thou may'st be our Comforter
    At the last dreadful day.
Of strife and of dissension
    Dissolve, O Lord, the bands:
Tie fast the knots of peace and love
    Throughout all Christian lands.
Grant us the grace that we may know
    The Father of all might,
That we of His beloved Son
    May gain the blissful sight,
And that we may with perfect faith
    Ever acknowledge Thee,

The Spirit of Father, and of Son,
   One God in Persons Three.
To God the Father laud and praise,
   And to His blessed Son,
And to the Holy Spirit of Grace,
   Co-equal Three in One.
And pray we, that our only Lord
   Would please His Spirit to send
On all that shall profess His name,
   From hence to the world's end. Amen.

FIFTH VERSION.

Probably by NAHUM TATE, 1652-1715: being from the *Supplement* (1703) to his *New Version* of the Psalms. Though never equally honored by the Church, it is better than the corresponding version from STERNHOLD and HOPKINS. He made another, in long metre.

COME, Holy Ghost, Creator, come,
   Inspire the souls of Thine,
Till every heart which Thou hast made
   Is filled with Grace divine.
Thou art the Comforter, the Gift
   Of God, and Fire of Love;
The everlasting Spring of joy,
   And Unction from above.

Thy gifts are manifold; Thou writ'st
   God's laws in each true heart:
The Promise of the Father, Thou
   Dost heavenly speech impart.

Enlighten our dark souls, till they
    Thy sacred Love embrace;
Assist our minds, by nature frail,
    With Thy celestial Grace.

Drive far from us the mortal foe,
    And give us peace within;
That by Thy guidance blest, we may
    Escape the snares of sin.
Teach us the Father to confess,
    And Son, from death revived;
And with them Both, Thee, Holy Ghost,
    Who art from Both derived.

With Thee, O Father, therefore may
    The Son, from death restored,
And sacred Comforter, One God,
    Devoutly be adored;
As in all ages heretofore
    Has constantly been done,
As now it is, and shall be so
    When time his course has run.

SIXTH VERSION.

JOHN DRYDEN, 1632-1700. JOSIAH MILLER (*Singers and Songs of the Church*, 1869) says that he is believed to have written this hymn "late in life, when he had become a Romanist." It is a free paraphrase of the original.

CREATOR Spirit, by whose aid
    The world's foundations first were laid,
Come, visit every pious mind;
Come, pour Thy joys on human kind:

From sin and sorrow set us free,
And make Thy temples worthy Thee.
  O Source of uncreated Light,
The Father's promised Paraclete!
Thrice holy Fount, thrice holy Fire,
Our hearts with heavenly love inspire;
Come, and Thy sacred unction bring
To sanctify us while we sing.
  Plenteous of Grace, descend from high,
Rich in Thy sevenfold energy!
Thou Strength of His almighty Hand,
Whose power does heaven and earth command.
Proceeding Spirit, our Defence,
Who dost the gifts of tongues dispense,
And crown'st Thy gift with eloquence!
Refine and purge our earthly parts;
But O, inflame and fire our hearts!
Our frailties help, our vice control,
Submit the senses to the soul;
And when rebellious they are grown,
Then lay Thy hand, and hold 'em down.
  Chase from our minds the infernal foe,
And peace, the fruit of love, bestow;
And lest our feet should step astray,
Protect and guide us in the way.
  Make us eternal truths receive,
And practise all that we believe:
Give us Thyself, that we may see
The Father and the Son by Thee.
  Immortal honor, endless fame,
Attend the Almighty Father's name:

VENI CREATOR.

The Saviour Son be glorified,
Who for lost man's redemption died;
And equal adoration be,
Eternal Paraclete, to Thee.

SEVENTH VERSION.

ISAAC WILLIAMS, 1802-1865. His *Hymns from the Parisian Breviary*, 1839, though seldom fitted for popular use, have much subtle beauty.

COME, Thou Creating Spirit blest,
    And be our Guest,
And fill the hearts which Thou hast made
    With Thy sweet shade.
Thou who art called the Paraclete,
    From Thy blest seat,
The living Fount of light and love,
    Come from above.
Thou that in sevenfold power dost stand
    At God's right hand,
And layest on the untutored tongue
    The Spirit's song,
Unto our senses light impart,
    Love to our heart;
And may our flesh's infirmity
    Be strong in Thee:
May the foe's assaultings cease,
    And grant Thy peace;

That treading in Thy footsteps blest,
    We may find rest.
May we by Thee the Father know,
    And Son below,
And Thee, the Spirit, come from Both,
    Trust, nothing loth!
To Father, Son, and Holy One,
    Praise aye be done,
From whose sweet effluence divine
    We too may shine.

EIGHTH VERSION.

The Right Rev. JOHN WILLIAMS, D.D., now Bishop of Connecticut. From a little volume now scarce, *Ancient Hymns of Holy Church*, Hartford, 1845.

CREATOR Spirit, come! Thy dwelling-place
    To make forever in the newborn heart,
        And Thy supernal Grace
        Freely to us impart.

Thou whom we honor as the Paraclete,
Thou Gift of God, Thou Fount and Fire of Love,
        Most holy and most sweet,
        And unction from above:

Thou who the sevenfold gifts dost bring from heaven,
Standing at God's right hand through ages long,
        Thou who new songs hast given,
        And loosed the silent tongue:

VENI CREATOR.

Pour on our senses all Thy holy light,
And to our hearts bid flow the stream of love;
   Our weakness turn to might,
     Shed on us from above.

Drive far the foes that seek our spirits' sway,
And bind once more the broken bonds of peace:
   Lead us upon our way,
     And make our wanderings cease.

Make us to own through all eternity
Thee, with the Father and the Only Son,
   The Holy Persons, Three,
     The glorious Godhead, One.

To God the Father be all glory given,
And to the Son uprisen from the sod;
   Who reign with Thee in heaven,
     One only living God.

NINTH VERSION.

ROBERT CAMPBELL, Esq., Solicitor: compiler and chief author of a small but important collection of *Hymns and Anthems for use in the Holy Services of the Church, within the United Diocese of St. Andrew's, Dunkeld, and Dunblane:* Edinburgh, 1850.

CREATOR Spirit, Lord of Grace,
  O make our hearts Thy dwelling-place,
And with Thy might celestial aid
The souls of those whom Thou hast made.

Come from the throne of God above,
O Paraclete, O Holy Dove,
Come, Oil of gladness, cleansing Fire,
And Living Spring of pure desire.

O Finger of the Hand Divine,
The sevenfold gifts of Grace are Thine;
And touched by Thee the lips proclaim
All praise to God's most holy Name.

Then to our souls Thy light impart,
And give Thy Love to every heart;
Turn all our weakness into might,
O Thou, the Source of Life and Light.

Protect us from the assailing foe,
And Peace, the fruit of Love, bestow;
Upheld by Thee, our Strength and Guide,
No evil can our steps betide.

Spirit of Faith, on us bestow
The Father and the Son to know;
And, of the Twain the Spirit, Thee:
Eternal One, Eternal Three.

To God the Father let us sing;
To God the Son, our risen King;
And equally with These adore
The Spirit, God for evermore.

VENI SANCTE SPIRITUS.

DANIEL, MONE, TRENCH, and WACKERNAGEL unite in ascribing this hymn to ROBERT II. OF FRANCE, who died A.D. 1031. DANIEL says: "All lovers of sacred song, of every rank, hold the royal poet worthy to be compared to David singing psalms to the Name of the Lord." He unites with TRENCH in quoting the words of CHLICHTOVÆUS: "This Hymn cannot, in my opinion, be too highly commended, for it is above all commendation. I can readily believe that the author, whoever he was, when he composed this Hymn, found his soul filled with a certain celestial sweetness, which, the Holy Spirit Himself being the Author, poured forth so much gentle elegance in so few words."

TRENCH says: "There exists no sufficient reason for calling in question the attribution which has commonly been made of it to KING ROBERT. The loveliest, — for however not the grandest, such we call it, — of all the hymns in the whole circle of Latin sacred poetry has a king for its author. ROBERT THE SECOND, son of Hugh Capet, succeeded his father on the throne of France in 997. He was singularly addicted to church-music, which he enriched, as well as hymnology, with compositions of his own, such as, I believe, to this day hold their place in the services of the Romish Church. — Even were the story of the writer's life unknown to us, we should guess that this Hymn could only have been composed by one who had acquaintance with many sorrows, and also with many consolations. Nor should we err herein ; for if the consolations are plain from the poem itself, the history of those times contains the record of the manifold sorrows, within his own family and without it, which were the portion of this meek and afflicted king."

DIESSENBROCK, at the close of his Pentecostal Sermon (*Sermons*, Ratisbon, 1841), says: "How can I more appropriately close than with that beautiful and tender Hymn which describes all the gifts and operations of the Holy Spirit in the soul, so minutely, fervently, and with such living power, that the Church has ever listened to it as to the gentle cooing of the dove, and in the whole of this solemn festival season uses it in her daily prayers."

FRANTZ says: "The Hymn consists of 5 six-line stanzas or 10 half stanzas, with a refrain in *ium*; each 3 line half-stanza has three rhythmic endings of 7 syllables each, of which two are leonine, and the third corresponds with the third of the following half stanza. It is therefore an attempt to attain a very artistic form, which with less warmth and skill would have been stiff."

The original is given by DANIEL and MONE from separate codices of the 13th century.

KING ROBERT, says the Rev. JAMES WHITE, in his brilliant sketch of *Eighteen Christian Centuries*, was a "saint according to the notions of the time, and even now deserves the respect of mankind for the simplicity and benevolence of his character." He "placed himself, robed and crowned, among the choristers of St. Denis, and led the musicians in singing hymns and psalms of his own composition." One may own to feeling no little kindness for a mediæval monarch of this exceptional sort. However far from being a sagacious and successful ruler, he deserves a nobler title : and Mr. GILL's appreciative lines may perhaps apply nearly as well to him as to his more famous successor, Saint Louis : —

O seldom doth Heaven's sweetest smile repose
　　Where Earth her utmost splendor doth impress;
We look not, where the kingly purple glows,
　　For the white, gleaming robes of righteousness.

Yet once the oil upon his head was poured
　　Whose heart had won the unction of God's Grace;
A sovereign once each humblest saint outsoared,
　　The heavenliest soul was in the highest place.

O lowliness of mortal majesty!
　　O sceptred hand, God's righteous will that wrought!
Yes, once a thronèd servant faithfully
　　His work to the Divine Taskmaster brought.

O once in the rough ways of holiness
　　A monarch walked as in the paths of pleasure;
And only yielded to the sweet excess
　　Of loving his dear Lord in over-measure.

O shining Ones! O People of the sky!
　　Ye lack not quite the company of Kings;
Death clothes one monarch in new majesty;
　　To a more glorious throne Saint Louis springs.

Here is ROBERT's own hymn:

Veni Sancte Spiritus,	Sine tuo numine
Et emitte cœlitus	Nihil est in homine,
Lucis tuæ radium.	Nihil est innoxium.
Veni pater pauperum,	Lava quod est sordidum,
Veni dator munerum,	Riga quod est aridum,
Veni lumen cordium:	Sana quod est saucium:
Consolator optime,	Flecte quod est rigidum,
Dulcis hospes animæ,	Fove quod est languidum,
Dulce refrigerium:	Rege quod est devium.
In labore requies,	Da tuis fidelibus
In æstu temperies,	In te confidentibus
In fletu solatium.	Sacrum septenarium;
O lux beatissima,	Da virtutis meritum,
Reple cordis intima	Da salutis exitum,
Tuorum fidelium.	Da perenne gaudium.

VENI SANCTE SPIRITUS.

FIRST VERSION.

JOHN AUSTIN; died 1669. From *Devotions in the Ancient Way of Offices*, 1668.

COME, Holy Spirit, send down those beams
Which gently flow in silent streams
From Thy bright throne in Heaven above:
Come, Thou Enricher of the poor
And bounteous Source of all our store,
Come, fill our souls with Thy pure Love.

Come Thou, our soul's delicious Guest,
The wearied pilgrim's sweetest Rest,
The injured sufferer's best Relief:
Come Thou, our passions cool, allay,
Whose comfort wipes all tears away,
And into joy turns all our grief.

Come, Thou bright Sun, shoot home Thy darts,
Pierce to the centre of our hearts,
And make our living faith love Thee.
Without Thy Grace, without Thy Light,
Our strength is weakness, our day night,
And we can neither move nor see.

Lord, wash our sinful stains away,
Water from Heaven our barren clay,
Our many mortal bruises heal;
To Thy sweet yoke our stiff necks bow,
Warm with Thy fire our hearts of snow,
And soon our wandering feet repeal.

O grant Thy faithful, dearest Lord,
Whose only hope is Thy sure word,
  The saving gifts of Thy good Spirit;
Grant us in life t' obey Thy Grace,
Grant us at death to see Thy face,
  And heaven's eternal joys inherit.

All glory to the sacred Three,
One ever living Deity,
  All power ascribe, and bliss, and praise;
As at the first when time begun,
May the same homage still be done,
  While time does last, when time decays.

SECOND VERSION.

EDWARD CASWALL; born 1814; once a priest of the English Church, now of the Romish He is the most extensive (except Mr. CHAMBERS) and one of the most successful, among translators from the Latin: his *Lyra Catholica*, 1848, is a book of value for all. This is generally allowed to be the best version of *Veni Sancte*, and is in itself a very lovely hymn.

HOLY Spirit, Lord of Light!
  From Thy clear celestial height
    Thy pure beaming radiance give:

Come, Thou Father of the poor!
Come with treasures which endure!
  Come, Thou Light of all that live.

Thou of all consolers best,
Visiting the troubled breast,
  Dost refreshing peace bestow:

Thou in toil art Comfort sweet,
Pleasant Coolness in the heat,
  Solace in the midst of woe.

Light immortal! Light divine!
Visit Thou these hearts of Thine,
  And our inmost being fill:

If Thou take Thy Grace away,
Nothing pure in man will stay,
  All his good is turned to ill.

Heal our wounds, our strength renew;
On our dryness pour Thy dew;
  Wash the stains of guilt away:

Bend the stubborn heart and will;
Melt the frozen, warm the chill;
  Guide the steps that go astray.

Thou on those who evermore
Thee confess and Thee adore,
  In Thy sevenfold gifts descend:

Give them comfort when they die;
Give them life with Thee on high;
  Give them joys which never end.

THIRD VERSION.

Frederic William Faber. From Jesus and Mary, 1849.

COME, Holy Spirit! from the height
  Of heaven send down Thy blessed light!
Come, Father of the friendless poor!
Giver of gifts, and Light of hearts,
Come with that unction which imparts
  Such consolations as endure.

The soul's Refreshment and her Guest,
Shelter in heat, in labor Rest,
  The sweetest Solace in our woe!
Come, blissful Light! O come and fill,
In all Thy faithful, heart and will,
  And make our inward fervor glow.

Where Thou art, Lord! there is no ill,
For evil's self Thy Light can kill.
  O let that Light upon us rise!
Lord, heal our wounds, and cleanse our stains,
Fountain of Grace! and with Thy rains
  Our barren spirits fertilize.

Bend with Thy fires our stubborn will,
And quicken what the world would chill,
  And homeward call the feet that stray:
Virtue's reward and final grace,
The Eternal Vision face to face,
  Spirit of Love! for these we pray.

Come, Holy Spirit! bid us live;
To those who trust Thy mercy give
  Joys that through endless ages flow:
Thy various gifts, foretastes of Heaven,
Those that are named Thy sacred Seven,
  On us, O God of Love, bestow!

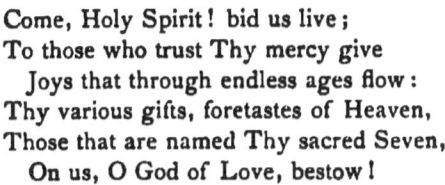

FOURTH VERSION.

Robert Campbell, 1850.

COME, O Spirit, Lord of Grace!
  From Thy heavenly dwelling-place
Bring pure light our gloom to chase.

Thine to wipe the bitter tear,
Thine the lonely heart to cheer:
Fainting spirits find Thee near.

Come, O Light most pure and blest,
Come, and fill each longing breast;
Be Thy people's constant Guest.

Come to cleanse the guilty stain,
On the hardened heart to rain,
Wounds of sin to heal again.

To Thy will the stubborn mould,
Warm and melt the bosom cold,
Bring the erring to the Fold.

Unto us who seek Thy face,
And in Thee reliance place,
Give Thy sevenfold gifts of Grace.

Pardon grant if we offend,
Grant us space till we amend,
Joy above that knows no end.

FIFTH VERSION.

Dr. JOHN MASON NEALE; from the *Hymnal Noted*, 1851. (The only rendering which follows the original in the double ending of each third line.)

COME, Thou Holy Paraclete,
   And from Thy celestial seat
  Send Thy light and brilliancy:

Father of the poor, draw near,
Giver of all gifts, be here;
  Come, the soul's true radiancy:

Come, of comforters the best,
Of the soul the sweetest guest, —
  Come in toil refreshingly:

Thou in labor rest most sweet,
Thou art shadow from the heat,
  Comfort in adversity.

O Thou Light most pure and blest,
Shine within the inmost breast
  Of Thy faithful company.

Where Thou art not, man hath nought;
Every holy deed and thought
  Comes from Thy Divinity.

What is soilèd, make Thou pure;
What is wounded, work its cure;
  What is parchèd, fructify:

What is rigid, gently bend;
What is frozen, warmly tend;
  Strengthen what goes erringly.

Fill Thy faithful, who confide
In Thy power to guard and guide,
  With Thy sevenfold Mystery:

Here Thy grace and virtue send;
Grant Salvation in the end,
  And in Heaven felicity.

SIXTH VERSION.

Dr. RAY PALMER of New York, 1858: perhaps the best of his translations.

COME, Holy Ghost, in love
  Shed on us from above
Thine own bright ray!
Divinely good Thou art;
Thy sacred gifts impart
To gladden each sad heart:
  O come to-day!

Come, tenderest Friend, and best,
Our most delightful Guest,
　With soothing power:
Rest, which the weary know,
Shade, 'mid the noontide glow,
Peace, when deep griefs o'erflow,
　Cheer us, this hour!

Come, Light serene, and still
Our inmost bosoms fill;
　Dwell in each breast:
We know no dawn but Thine;
Send forth Thy beams divine,
On our dark souls to shine,
　And make us blest!

Exalt our low desires;
Extinguish passion's fires;
　Heal every wound:
Our stubborn spirits bend;
Our icy coldness end;
Our devious steps attend,
　While heavenward bound.

Come, all the faithful bless;
Let all, who Christ confess,
　His praise employ:
Give virtue's rich reward;
Victorious death accord,
And, with our glorious Lord,
　Eternal joy!

VENI SUPERNE SPIRITUS.

Of the origin of this hymn little or nothing is known: it is found in recent Gallican Breviaries. Version by ISAAC WILLIAMS, 1839.

COME, Spirit from above!
    Earth, washed with blood of Him that died,
      With eyes of awe and love,
Awaits Thee, calm and purified.

    Come, in the holy name
Of Him who hath gone up on high:
      With Thy Baptism of flame
Cleanse Thou our hearts, and sanctify.

    A Father, gone from sight,
We mourn; pity our orphanhood,
      And with Thy gentle might
Heal us, and help us to be good.

    The lesson His sweet care
Forbore to teach the untutored heart,
      As yet unschooled to bear,
With Thy life-giving dew impart.

    The things by seer of old
Darkly and dim in shadow seen,
      Nations come to behold;
For Thou hast rent the veil between.

    Thy blest anointing give;
The letters, now on mute heart writ,
      Then shall come forth and live,
By Thy celestial brightness lit.

Throughout eternity
Unto the Father and the Son
And Spirit, glory be;
The Spirit, binding Three in One.

SECOND VERSION.

William John Blew. From his *Church Hymn and Tune Book*, 1851-2.

Come, heavenly Spirit, come:
  Cleansed by Christ's Blood, all lands
For Thee prepare a home,
  To Thee stretch forth their hands.

The Christ ascended hath:
  Thou then His promise pay,
And in Thy fiery bath
  Our bosoms wash this day.

Our missing One we mourn;
  Then pity our distress;
O comfort the forlorn
  And cheer the fatherless.

What Christ forbore to teach
  To hearts unfit to know,
Now in the mind of each
  Engraft, that it may grow.

Let Truth from ancient seers
   In shadow half concealed,
Now ring in all men's ears,
   Now lie to all revealed.

Let Thy sweet unction school
   All hearts, and on them write
The Law's now silent rule
   In characters of light.

To Sire and Son be praise;
   Praise, Holy Ghost, to Thee,
The Bond of Both always,
   Through all eternity.

ADSIS SUPERNE SPIRITUS.

Of obscure origin. Version by ISAAC WILLIAMS, 1839.

HAIL, Father of the poor, and Friend benign,
      Immortal Spirit Divine!
From out Thine own prolific bosom pour
Thy promised blessings on the barren earth,
      Which gladdeneth at Thy birth.
Here, where night comes from Heaven's alternate door
To muffle up the blooming eye of day,
     With uncreated ray
   Shine forth, cease not to shine;
Shine in our hearts, good Spirit, evermore.

Thou of the inner heart art Guest and Friend,
Thou of all labors art the sweet Repose;
    Thou op'st the fount of woes,
The cup of sorrow at Thy bidding flows.
But Thou dost Thy pure joys divinely blend,
And as the blended streams flow forth apace,
    Dost o'er them pitying bend.
        Thou art the Fount of Grace:
Grant us with holy hardness to contend,
To conquer and to win the immortal end,
    Which is to see Thy face,
And ever sing in the undefilèd place
The Father, Son and Thee, the Spirit benign,
    Bathed in whose fires divine,
Even our dull hearts may catch the light and shine.

SECOND VERSION.

Probably by JOSEPH FRANCIS THRUPP, Vicar of Barrington, Cambridgeshire: from his *Psalms and Hymns*, date not given.

  COME, Thou heavenly Spirit pure,
    Come, Enricher of the poor;
  Thou, of all good gifts the best,
  Come, our bosom's inmost Guest.

  Bid Thy beams of Truth divine
  Brightly on our darkness shine:
  Light to every mind impart,
  Strength to every fainting heart.

ADSIS SUPERNE SPIRITUS.

All the pomp and painted show
Of the luring world o'erthrow,
Lest its colors, falsely gay,
Tempt us from Thy paths to stray.

Let Thy lamp with splendor bright
Far outshine each earthly light,
That, from vanity set free,
We may seek to rise to Thee.

Distant far from Thee we roam;
Bring Thou then Thine exiles home:
Guide to Thee each wandering soul,
Thou our Road, and Thou our Goal.

Glory to the Father be,
Glory to the Son and Thee:
May our breasts, even here below,
With Thy glorious presence glow.

THIRD VERSION.

A paraphrase by Dr. HORATIUS BONAR, from his *Hymns of Faith and Hope*, Second Series, 1861.

COME, heavenly Spirit, come,
    Kind Father of the poor!
The Giver and the Gift,
    Enter my lowly door.
Be Guest within my heart,
Nor ever hence depart.

Thou the eternal Truth!
  Into dark hearts steal in;
True Light, give light to souls
  Sunk in the night of sin;
True Strength, put forth Thy power
For us in evil hour!

Ours is a world of wiles,
  Of beauteous vanities:
Come, and in us destroy
  Its fair impurities,
Lest, by its tempting arts,
From Thee it steal our hearts.

Unveil Thy glorious self
  To us, O Holy One,
That Thou into our hearts
  Mayst shine, Thyself alone!
Saved from earth's vanities,
To Thee we long to rise.

Renew us, Holy One!
  O purge us in Thy fire;
Refine us, heavenly Flame,
  Consume each low desire:
Prepare us as a sacrifice,
Well-pleasing in Thine eyes.

Far from Thee we have lived,
  Exiles from home and Thee:
O bring us back in love,

End our captivity.
Be Thou the Way we wend,
Be Thou that Way's blest End.

Glory to the Father be,
  Glory to the equal Son,
Glory to the Spirit be,
  Glory to the Three-in-One.
Spirit, 'tis Thy breath divine
Makes these hearts to burn and shine.

FOURTH VERSION.

By Edwin L. Blenkinsopp: from *Lyra Messianica*, 1864.

COME, O Spirit, graciously!
  Fount of Light, shine lucidly
    In the gloomiest night:
Be Thou Peace to weary souls;
When the turbid ocean rolls,
    Then let there be Light.

Scatter far vain fantasies:
Heal the wounded consciences
    Poisoned by their sin:
Fill each heart with charity
From Thy bounteous Deity
    Pouring Grace within.

Charity which flows from Thee,
Triple mail of charity,
    Gird around our heart;

Lest our great nocturnal foe
Slay us with a secret blow
　From his fiery dart.

Guard the trembling penitent,
Mingle peaceful heart-content
　With his anxious strife:
Make the stream of flowing tears
Lead on through the vale of years
　To eternal Life.

NUNC SANCTE NOBIS SPIRITUS.

Wackernagel ascribes this to St. Ambrose, who died A.D. 397. Daniel in his first volume calls it Ambrosian (a term applied to a mass of hymns resembling those of Ambrose in style and structure, though of later date); and in his fifth volume refers its first appearance to the 7th or 8th century. The earliest MS of it is at Darmstadt, and of the 8th century. It has always been used at Terce (the third hour). The doxology is a later addition. Translation by the famous Dr. John Henry Newman, 1836, from one of the *Tracts for the Times*. He has since rewritten it.

COME, Holy Ghost, who ever One
　　Art with the Father and the Son:
Come, Holy Ghost, our souls possess
With Thy full flood of holiness.

Let mouth and heart and flesh combine
To herald forth our creed divine;
And Love so wrap our mortal frame,
Others may catch the living flame.

Thou ever-blessed Three in One,
O Father and coequal Son,
O Holy Ghost the Comforter,
Thy Grace on Thy redeemed confer.

NUNC SANCTE NOBIS SPIRITUS.   199

SECOND VERSION.

JOHN CHANDLER, Vicar of Witley, Surrey, and Rural Dean. From his *Hymns of the Primitive Church*, 1837; a very meritorious and important work.

BLEST Spirit, one with God above,
Thou Source of life and holy love,
O cheer us with Thy sacred beams,
Refresh us with Thy plenteous streams.

O may our lips confess Thy Name,
Our holy lives Thy power proclaim:
With love divine our hearts inspire,
And fill us with Thy holy fire.

O holy Father, holy Son,
And Holy Spirit, Three in One,
Thy grace devoutly we implore;
Thy Name be praised for evermore.

THIRD VERSION.

A free paraphrase, by Mrs. JANE FOX CREWDSON, of Manchester: 1807–1863. From *The Little While, and other Poems*, 1864.

O HOLY Spirit, who art One
With God the Father, God the Son;
For the dear sake of Him who died,
Let not my prayer be turned aside,
But answer it, O Holy Dove,
By breathing o'er my soul His Love.

Oft as my feet approach Thy shrine,
Upon my heart's affections shine;
And as my lips Thy praises sing,
O consecrate the offering;
And let Thy sanctifying Grace
Make my whole soul Thy dwelling-place!

My Father, hallowed be Thy Name:
And glory be to Him who came
To take my flesh, and bear my load,
And lead the sinner back to God:
And be the psalm of praise to Thee,
Great Paraclete, eternally.

O FONS AMORIS SPIRITUS.

Of unknown origin. Version by John Chandler, 1837.

O HOLY Spirit, Lord of grace,
   Eternal Source of Love,
Inflame, we pray, our inmost hearts
   With fire from Heaven above.

As Thou dost join with holiest bonds
   The Father and the Son,
So fill Thy saints with mutual love
   And link their hearts in one.

To God the Father, God the Son,
   And God the Holy Ghost,
Eternal glory be from man,
   And from the angel-host.

SECOND VERSION.

Isaac Williams, 1839.

O SPIRIT, Fount of Love,
  Unlock Thy temple door,
  And on our spirits pour
Thy dayspring from above.

O Thou of the great Three
  Who art the Union,
  Unite us all in one
In bonds of charity.

Glory to God on high,
  And Him that cometh down
  Poor fallen man to own,
And Spirit ever nigh.

SANCTI SPIRITUS ADSIT NOBIS GRATIA.

By Notker, a monk of St. Gall: died about 912; author of the famous hymn, "In the midst of life we are in death," and introducer of a new style of sacred poetry. This sequence, says the translator, "was in use all over Europe, even in those countries, like Italy and Spain, which usually rejected sequences. In the Missal of Palencia the priest is ordered to hold a white dove in his hand while intoning the first syllables, and then to let it go." — Prose version by Dr. John Mason Neale, in his *Mediæval Hymns and Sequences*, second edition, 1863.

THE Grace of the Holy Ghost be present with us;
  And make our hearts a dwelling-place to Itself;
And expel from them all spiritual wickedness.
Merciful Spirit, Illuminator of men,

Purge the fearful shades of our mind.
O holy Lover of thoughts that are ever wise,
Of Thy mercy pour forth Thine Anointing into our senses.
Thou Purifier of all iniquities, O Spirit,
Purify the eye of our inner man,
To the end that the Father of all things may be seen by us,
He, whom the eyes of none save the pure in heart can behold.
Thou didst inspire the Prophets to chant aforehand their glorious heralding of Christ.
Thou didst confirm the Apostles, so that they shall bear Christ's glorious trophy through the whole world.
When, by His Word, God made the system of heaven, earth, seas,
Thou didst stretch out Thy Godhead over the waters, and didst cherish them, O Spirit!
Thou dost give virtue to the waters to quicken souls;
Thou, by Thine inspiration, grantest to men to be spiritual.
Thou didst unite the world, divided both in tongues and rites, O Lord!
Thou recallest idolaters to the worship of God, Best of masters!
Wherefore of Thy mercy hear us who call upon Thee, Holy Ghost,
Without Whom, as the faith teaches, all our prayers are in vain, and unworthy of the ears of God.

Thou, O Spirit, who by embracing the saints of all
   ages, dost teach them by the impulse of Thy
   Divinity;
Thyself, by bestowing on the Apostles of Christ a
   Gift immortal, and unheard of from all ages,
Hast made this day glorious.

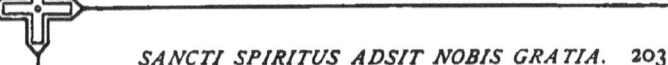

A METRICAL VERSION.

By ERASTUS C. BENEDICT, LL.D., of the New York Bar, translator of *The Hymn of Hildebert, and other Mediæval Hymns.* Contributed.

COME Holy Spirit, with Thy Grace,
   And make our hearts Thy dwelling-place,
  Our vices all expelling.
Thou only Source of light divine,
Come, chase away, with beams of Thine,
  The darkness in us dwelling.

Lover of thoughts forever wise,
Do Thou our senses exercise,
  Thine unction on them pouring.
Spirit that cleanseth every Sin,
Come purify our eye within,
  The soul to sight restoring.

For then, Almighty Maker, we
May face to face look up to Thee,
  The sacred precept showing,
That none, except the pure in heart,
Can ever see Thee as Thou art,
  Thy presence ever knowing.

When by His Word, God called to birth,
The frame of sea and skies and earth,
  Thou on the waters moving,
With gracious goodness didst incline
To cherish them with power divine,
  The Spirit's Godhead proving.

Thou dost the waters fructify,
And there the gift of life supply,
  Thy breath the gift bestowing.
Thou Spirit, breathing on the soul,
Dost bring it in Thine own control,
  Like Thee in spirit growing.

Thou, holy prophets didst impel
The coming Saviour to foretel,
  By inspiration teaching.
Thou strengthenedst His Apostles too,
To bear the cross the nations through,
  His blessed Gospel preaching.

And Thou this day hast glorious made;
And here, Thy wondrous power displayed
  The spread of truth presages.
The apostles' faith Thou didst restore,
By gifts to them unknown before,
  Unheard in all the ages.

And here in one Thy power unites
The world, which many tongues and rites
  In former times divided.

Thou Best of masters, by Thy Grace,
Idolaters in every place
  To worship God are guided.

Then, Holy Ghost, with willing ear
We pray Thee now our prayers to hear,
  Without Thee unavailing.
Thou who Thy saints hast always taught,
To Thy embrace they must be brought:
  Now make our prayers prevailing.

ALMUM FLAMEN, VITA MUNDI.

Authorship and date unknown. Partial version by Dr. HERBERT KYNASTON, a London Rector; born 1809. From his Occasional Hymns, 1862. There is another translation, in seven nine-line verses, in EDWARD CASWALL's Poems, 1858.

GENIAL Spirit, earth's Emotion,
  Pulsing with the gush of love,
Source of life to land and ocean,
  Sun and moon and stars above;
  Life of life, on all beneath
  Breathing joy and living breath,
Only rest and motion giving,
Spirit, to all creatures living!

Come, eternal God, Creator,
  With Thy sevenfold gifts endued,
Waning earth's Regenerator,
  Peaceful Giver of all good;

Comfort of the weary heart,
   Joy to all where'er Thou art;
Once the Babel tongues' delusion,
Now the living Word's diffusion!

O'er the darkling waters moving,
   Ere one ray was on the deep,
All its chaos clouds reproving,
   Stirring all its mighty sleep;
   Softly then the ruined earth
   Waking to its second birth,
O'er the fountain depths exuding
With Thy dove-like pinions brooding!

With Thy blasts the trumpets seven
   Widely through the earth were blown,
Where the angel stood, from heaven
   Thundered out before the throne;
   All the world beneath the skies
   Lighting to the Gospel-prize,
From the fiery arrows shielding
With Thy sevenfold buckler's wielding.

O IGNIS SPIRITUS PARACLITI.

This lovely sequence is ascribed to ST. HILDEGARDE, Abbess of the Cloister Rupertsburg near Bingen: died 1179 or 1197. It was printed by MONE, I. 234: here is his account of it. "A MS. of the 12th century at Wiesbaden, containing the letters of Hildegarde, gives this hymn with the music: the hymn was probably written by her. In the several parts, assonances and even rhymes are noticeable, but there is no regular division into correspondent verses, as in the tropes and sequences. Hildegarde appears no longer to have recognized the rules of Notker's sequences, and probably held them to be unmetrical hymns, like the Latin psalms." The original is also in DANIEL, V. 201. Translated by RICHARD FREDERIC LITTLEDALE, D.C.L., a voluminous author and eminent Churchman; and contributed by him to *Lyra Messianica*, 1864: afterwards inserted in *The People's Hymnal*, 1867.

O FIRE of God the Comforter, O Life of all that live,
Holy art Thou to quicken us, and holy, strength to give:
To heal the broken-hearted ones, their sorest wounds to bind,
O Spirit of all holiness, O Lover of mankind!
O sweetest taste within the breast, O Grace upon us poured,
That saintly hearts may give again their perfume to the Lord.
O purest Fountain! we can see, clear mirrored in Thy streams,
That God brings home the wanderers, that God the lost redeems.
O Breastplate strong to guard our life, O Bond of unity,
O Dwellingplace of Righteousness, save all who trust in Thee:
Defend those who in dungeon dark are prisoned by the foe,

And, for Thy will is aye to save, let Thou the captives go.
O surest Way, that through the height and through the lowest deep
And through the earth dost pass, and all in firmest union keep;
From Thee the clouds and ether move, from Thee the moisture flows,
From Thee the waters draw their rills, and earth with verdure glows,
And Thou dost ever teach the wise, and freely on them pour
The inspiration of Thy gifts, the gladness of Thy lore.
All praise to Thee, O Joy of life, O Hope and Strength, we raise,
Who givest us the prize of Light, who art Thyself all Praise.

ANOTHER VERSION.

By the Rev. T. G. CRIPPEN: from his *Ancient Hymns and Poems*, London, 1868. Of DR. LITTLEDALE's version, above given, he says: "It is thought that the following imitation, though somewhat diluted, will give a more correct idea of the character of the original."

O COMFORTER, Thou uncreated Fire,
　Who dost each living thing with life inspire!
Holy art Thou, to quicken all the creatures Thou hast made;
Holy art Thou, to sorely broken hearts affording aid;

Holy art Thou, to cleanse the wounds of souls by
    sin betrayed.
O Breath of Holiness, O Fire of Love,
Sweet Savor in our breasts, Who there dost move,
Infusing virtue's fragrant odors from above.
O Purest Fount, reflected in whose streams
We see, enlightened by Truth's radiant beams,
How God brings in the aliens, and the lost redeems.
Armor of life, and Hope of unity,
    Cheering each member in distress,
    Thou Corner-stone of righteousness,
O save the blessed souls that wait on Thee,
And rescue those who in a living grave
    Are prisoned by the ancient foe;
    Unloose their bonds, and let them go:
For godly might is Thine, and will to save.
O Thou sure Way, who passing up the steep
Of Heaven, o'er earth, and through the lowest
    deep,
Combinest each with each, and dost in union keep;
By Thee are clouds upborne, the breezes blow,
The rocks drink moisture, and the waters flow
In streams, and smiling earth with verdure is aglow.
And Thou dost teach the wise yet more and more,
Making them glad with Thy celestial lore.
Therefore to Thee be praise, who art the Music of
    all praise,
The Joy of life, and Hope, and Glory passing mor-
    tal gaze;
Giver of light that shines above through everlasting
    days.

AMOR PATRIS ET FILII.

From the Missal of Liege, 13th century: author unknown. Dr. NEALE calls it "A very admirable sequence: it seems as if the poet had the Veni Creator before his eyes when writing it. In some respects it resembles the Notkerian, in others the Victorine sequences." Translation by Dr. RICHARD F. LITTLEDALE, in Lyra Messianica, 1864.

LOVE of Father and of Son,
   True and glorious helping One,
  Comforter and Hope of all:
Of the saints unfading Light,
Prize of those that do aright,
  Lifter up of them that fall:
Giver of all holiness,
Fortitude and blessedness,
Lover of all righteousness,
Gracious, and of perfect might,
Merciful and infinite;
  Ever dearest, purest,
  Wisest, strongest, surest,
  Ever most unfailing Trust,
  Ever tender, ever just;
Lightener of hearts, through whom the Father and
  the Son we find,
Spirit of counsel, Balm for sin, Giver of joy, and
  Source of mind;
  Unchanging, gentle, lowly,
  Unconquered, noble, holy,
  Ever loving, ever swift,
  Most divine and chosen Gift;
  Understanding clear bestowing,

Giver of affection glowing,
Truth in Love forever showing;
   The Spirit of the Father,
   The Spirit of the Word,
   The Comforter who quickeneth,
   The Finger of the Lord;
Highest, sweetest, kindest, best,
Bountiful and lowliest;
Who as He wills, and when He wills,
And where He wills, His Grace instils,
   Teaches, fills, and lifts,
   Enriches with His gifts:
To gladden the Apostles, to take their grief away,
The Spirit of all knowledge, He comes to earth
   to-day:
He comes in all His fulness, the everlasting Lord,
And the Fount of perfect Wisdom upon their souls
   is poured.

VENI CREATOR SPIRITUS, SPIRITUS RECREATOR.

ADAM OF ST. VICTOR, the most prolific, and probably the greatest, of the mediæval hymnists Born either in England or Brittany, he studied at Paris, and about A.D. 1130 entered the monastery whence his name is taken, in the suburbs of that city. He died "somewhere between 1172 and 1192." The majority of his hymns, which had been lost, were discovered recently by M. GAUTIER, and the whole, amounting to 106, published at Paris in 1858.

ADAM's style is florid, heavily charged with metaphors, allusions and symbols, so as to be at times hardly intelligible to ordinary modern readers. Archbishop TRENCH says: "His most zealous admirers will hardly deny that he pushes too far, and plays overmuch with, his skill in the typical application of the Old Testament. So too they must own that sometimes he is unable to fuse with a perfect success his manifold learned allusion into the passion of his poetry. . . . His hymns have oftentimes as great a theological, as poetical or even devotional interest, the first indeed sometimes preponderating to the injury of the last." Because of this, in the hymns of his which follow, we have thought it necessary to omit a few unedifying verses. Spite of these faults and others, however, the same critic pronounces him "foremost among the Sacred Latin poets of the middle ages." Translation by Mrs. ELIZABETH CHARLES, author of *The Schönberg-Cotta Family* and other popular tales: from her very interesting and important work, *The Voice of Christian Life in Song*, 1858.

COME, Creator Spirit high,
   Recreating ever;
Given and giving from the sky,
   Thou the Gift and Giver.
Thou the Law within us writ,
Finger Thou that writest it,
   Inspired and Inspirer!

With Thy sevenfold graces good
   Sevenfold gifts be given,
For sevenfold beatitude
   And petitions seven.[1]
Thou the pure unstainèd Snow,
That shall never sullied flow;
Fire, that burns not though it glow;
Wrestler, ne'er defeat to know,
   Giving words of wisdom.

Kindle Thou Thyself in us,
   Thou both Light and Fire;
Thou Thyself still into us,
   Breath of Life, inspire!
Thou the Ray and Thou the Sun,
Sent and Sender, Thee we own:
Of the blessed Three in One,
Thee we suppliant call upon,
   Save us now and ever.

---

[1] The seven petitions in the Lord's Prayer.

VENI, SUMME CONSOLATOR.

Adam of St. Victor. Trench calls this "a very grand" hymn: it was first published by Gautier, 1858. The rendering (which we do not give entire) is by William John Blew, in Lyra Mystica, 1865. It is there headed, "After Adam of St. Victor," and is a paraphrase, or original poem founded on the Latin, rather than a translation. The ideas however are Adam's.

HEALTH of the helpless, Crown of consolation,
    Giver of Life, sweet Hope of man's salvation,
  Come with Thy Grace, O come,
Sun of the soul, and let Thy sunlight shine,
And warm with Love's soft glow the hearts of
      Thine;
And o'er the freshening field of Christendom
    Drop fatness, Dew divine;
  Till day by day, and hour by hour,
  Fed with the fulness of Thy power,
  Every woodland, every bower,
  Burst into leaf and fruit and flower,
    Filled with true Life's best food
  From Thee, the Fountain of all good.

Thou hearest the Dew fall on earth, where it lies,
From the River Thou hearest the Vapor arise,
And the scent of sweet Odor Thou knowest, whereby
Thy faith can the presence of Godhead descry:
    Dew, that from the Godhead bursts,
Whereof who deepest drinks the more he thirsts;
    Thirsting ever with a glow
    Quenchless as the Spirit's flow,
    Flowing alway, alway blessing:
    Thirst that knoweth no repressing.

By Him the wave is consecrate
Where for new birth the holy people wait,
    The water on whose face was borne
    God's Spirit at Creation's morn.
    Fount, of all holiness the Spring,
        Whence flows true love abroad,
    Clear Fount that cleanseth from all sin,
        Fount from the font of God;
    Great Fount, all fountains hallowing,
Without all blessing and all God within.

    Fire of flint, with naught of wood,
    Faring forth in mystic flood,
    Kid consuming, Fire of Heaven,
    Feeding on the dread unleaven,
    Fire, all earthly fire unlike,
        On the altar of our heart
    Strike the spark of light, O strike
The flame there still to burn and never thence
        depart.

    Shadow of the maidens seven,
        Seven that compassed the One;
    Type of the very Truth of Heaven
        That through all things dost run;
All-quickener, that with Life the world dost warm,
        O Spirit septiform:
    In several shape outlined,
    Yet varying not in kind,
    Forefend it ever, that we say
        Of Thee, the almighty Mind,

That Thou dost form obey,
  To form and shape confined.

Fire of Life, Life-giving Spring,
  Cleanse our hearts, and thither bring
Thy gifts of Grace, to enrich them and to bless;
  That kindled by the flame of charity,
    Meet offering we become to Thee
      Of love and holiness.
Breath of the Father and the Son, Thou best
  Leech of the sinful, Solace of the sad,
Strength of the weak, the worn wayfarer's Rest,
  Health of the sick, make Thou the mourner glad.
    Holy Love, like virgin's chaste,
      Fire of soul, yet maiden-pure,
    Those whom evil passions waste
      May Thine hallowed unction cure.

Voice of voices manifold,
Subtle Voice, by sound untold,
In the ear, and in the breast,
Voice to each that whisperest:
Voice enbreathed into the blest,
Stilly Voice and secret — Voice
Making men of peace rejoice,
Voice of sweetness, Voice of bliss,
Voice of voices, ours be this
Sounding through our inmost heart:

Light that bidst all lies depart,
Light that falsehood's router art,

Light that drawest unto Thee
Faith and Truth and Verity;
Light, vouchsafe to us, to all,
Life and health and wealth, that we,
Lit with Light perennial,
Live in sunshine that shall be
Brightening everlastingly.

SIMPLEX IN ESSENTIA.

ADAM OF ST. VICTOR. The first half of this hymn (after the opening stanza), says Archbishop TRENCH, is "in the true spirit of St. Paul and St. Augustine, and hardly to be fully understood without reference to the writings of the latter, above all to his Anti-pelagian tracts; wherein he continually contrasts, as Adam does here, the killing letter of the Old, and the quickening spirit of the New Covenant. A few chapters of his treatise *De Spiritu et Litera*, c. 13-17, would furnish the best commentary on these lines."

This important poem has never, to my knowledge, been presented in an English dress before. I have the pleasure of offering two versions, both made for this Collection. The first is by Dr. EDWARD A. WASHBURN, Rector of Calvary Church, New York. The fifth verse is here omitted, and some liberty taken with the last: these two in the original are of unequal length and inferior merit. With these exceptions, says the translator, "it is as literally done, as I could while keeping the double-endings."

THOU, who One in Essence livest,
   Sevenfold in the Grace Thou givest,
  Holy Spirit, on us shine!
All the shadows o'er us brooding,
All the snares our flesh deluding,
  Lighten by Thy beam divine.

Clad in fear, in darkness clouded,
Came the Law in figure shrouded:

Now behold the Gospel ray,
Now the Spirit's wisdom better,
Hidden by the leafy letter,
   Open into perfect day.

'Neath the mount the people trembled:
In the upper room assembled,
   Heard a few the word of Grace:
Nobler law than Sinai telling,
Newer precepts, gifts excelling,
   Learn we in that holy place.

Trumpet clang and fiery wonder,
Midnight and the muttering thunder,
   Bickering lamps and sounds of dread,
Shook the Hebrew, conscience-stricken;
But the love it could not quicken,
   By the Oil of gladness shed.

See the fathers, fore-appointed,
God's ambassadors anointed,
   Break the chains of human ill:
Raining truth, and judgment pealing,
With new tongues and doctrines healing,
   Heavenly signs attend them still.

See, the sick they kindly cherish:
Man's lost nature, nigh to perish,
   Love divine will seek, will find:
But the guilty, past repentance,
Scourge they with pursuing sentence;
   Theirs to loose, and theirs to bind.

This the time to by-gone ages,
If you search the mystic pages,
  In the Jubilee foreshowed;
Lo! the long-descried fulfilling,
When three thousand converts willing
  Bloomed within the Church of God.

Jubilee! the glorious token,
When the captive's bonds were broken,
  Rose anew Redemption's morn;
So from sin's dark, hapless prison,
By the law of love newrisen,
  Sons of God are we freeborn.

ANOTHER VERSION.

By the Rev. SAMUEL W. DUFFIELD, of Bergen, N.J. Contributed.

SINGLE in essential place,
  But of sevenfold power and grace,
May the Spirit shine on us;
May the light divinely shown
For all gloom of heart atone
  And temptations perilous.

Law in symbols went before us,
Dark with threats of judgment o'er us,
  Ere we saw the Gospel rays:
May the Spirit of the sages,
Hidden in their lettered pages,
  Venture forth in open ways.

Law men heard from mountain-peaks:
Unto few the New Grace speaks
  Softly in a room above:
Thus the spot itself is teaching
Which are best within our reaching,
  Works of Law, or words of Love.

Flame and trumpet sounding loud,
Thunder through the smoky shroud,
  Sudden-flashing lightnings, — those
Strike a terror to the soul;
Nourishing no sweet control
  Which the Spirit's gift bestows.

Thus the sundered Sinai thundered,
  Fixing Law on guilty man:
Law most fearful and uncheerful,
  Crushing sin by rigid plan.

But the fathers long selected
And by power divine directed,
  How they loose the bonds of sin!
Words refreshing, threats astounding,
Through new tongues in concord sounding;
  Thus their miracles begin.

Showing care for them that languish,
Sparing man, they spare not anguish:
  In pursuit of evil things
Smiting sinners and reminding:
Only loosing, only binding,
  By the power which freedom brings.

Type of Jubilee returning
In that day — if thou art learning
　　Mysteries of holy time —
On the which three thousand hearing
Came in faith, no longer fearing,
　　And the Church sprang up sublime.

Jubilee, for so they knew it
Who were changed and succored through it,
Since it freely called unto it
　　Debts and doubts, and set them right.
May the lovingkindness spoken
Unto us, distrest and broken,
Give release and, as a token,
　　Make us worthy of the light.

PART OF A HYMN OF ADAM OF ST. VICTOR.

Translated in EDWARD CASWALL's *Poems*, 1858.

O INEXHAUSTIVE Fount of Light!
　　How does Thy radiance put to flight
The darkness of the mind!
The pure are only pure through Thee;
Thou only dost the guilty free,
　　And cheer with light the blind.

Thou to the lowly dost display
The beautiful and perfect way
　　Of justice and of peace:

Shunning the proud and stubborn heart,
Thou to the simple dost impart
   True wisdom's rich increase.

Thou teaching, naught remains obscure:
Thou present, every thought impure
   Is banished from the breast;
And full of cheerfulness serene
The conscience, sanctified and clean,
   Enjoys a perfect rest.

Dear Soother of the troubled heart!
At Thine approach all cares depart,
   And melancholy grief:
More balmy than the summer breeze,
Thy presence lulls all agonies,
   And lends a sweet relief.

Thy Grace eternal Truth instils,
The ignorant with knowledge fills,
   Awakens those who sleep;
Inspires the tongue, informs the eye,
Expands the heart with charity,
   And comforts all who weep.

O Thou the weary pilgrim's Rest!
Solace of all that are opprest,
   Befriender of the poor:
O Thou in whom the wretched find
A sweet Consoler ever kind,
   A Refuge ever sure!

Teach us to aim at Heaven's high prize,
And for its glory to despise
　The world and all below:
Cleanse us from sin; direct us right;
Illuminate us with Thy Light;
　Thy peace on us bestow.

And as Thou didst in days of old
On the first Shepherds of the Fold
　In tongues of flame descend,
Now also on its pastors shine,
And flood with fire of Grace divine
　The world from end to end!

Lord of all sanctity and might,
Immense, immortal, infinite,
　The Life of Earth and Heaven!
Be, through eternal length of days,
All honor, glory, blessing, praise,
　And adoration given.

SPIRITUS SANCTE, PIE PARACLITE.

HILDEBERT, bishop of Mans (1097), and Archbishop of Tours (1125): died 1133. This fine hymn, which seems to have hitherto escaped the attention of translators, is of very irregular and complicated structure, full of alliteration and interlaced rhymes. Our version was made for this work by Dr. E. A. WASHBURN of New York, and is in his judgment the most satisfactory of several experiments by him in different measures.

O PIOUS Paraclete! O Holy Spirit!
　Love of the Father and the blessed Son!
Goodness of each, the Heart of their twin-Being,
　Kindness Thou art, Sweetness and Joy in one.

O Chain, the highest God with man allying,
    Strength, man uplifting to the Power divine,
Meek, lowly, pure, the vain world purifying;
    All worship due, all honor true be Thine!

Voice, sweetly singing to the exiles lonely,
    Music, still ringing 'mid the city's mirth;
For those in fell despair their Solace only,
    For these a prayer for joys beyond the earth.

Inspirer of the good, Consoler, Healer
    Of all who mourn, Enlightener of the blind,
Purger of every lie, and the Revealer
    Of mysteries that try the groping mind.

Thou holdest up the weak; all those who perish
    Dost kindly seek, dost gather all that stray;
The fainting and the fallen ever cherish,
    And tread before us in our toilsome way.

Ripening our early love, the soul perfected
    Thou drawest above from slimy pools of sin,
Into the happy road of peace directed,
    Fair Wisdom's hall through cloud it enters in.

Pillar of sanctity, and Bread of chasteness!
    Gem of all gentleness, in want our Balm,
Increase of generous wealth, the upright's Fastness,
    The wretched's Port of health, the captive's Arm.

Spirit of Truth, all brother-hearts embracing!
　　Judge of the world, as once Thou didst create,
With honors glad the worthy alway gracing;
　　Shaming the bad with his self-chosen fate.

Thou blowest where Thou listest; out of error
　　Dost lead the doubting, and with knowledge fill:
Thy might our weakness stays in sudden terror;
　　Thou rulest in sure ways of wisdom still.

Order that beauty to each creature giveth,
　　Beauty that ordereth each with grace from Thee,
In word, in deed, in thought, in all things liveth,
　　Words sooth, deeds truth, thoughts of Thy purity.

Good Gift and perfect Good! Thine every motion
　　Of intellect, of heart! on each endeavor
Thy Spirit waits; shapes, guides our true devotion,
　　And at Heaven's gates crowneth the blest forever.

(FROM THE ITALIAN.)

DISCENDI, AMOR SANTO.

BIANCO DA SIENA (died 1434) was of a good family, and entered in 1367 the Order of JESUATES, founded that year, and composed of laymen who followed the rule of S Augustine, and engaged in benevolent labors. He is said to have lived long at Venice. His *Spiritual Songs*, 92 in number, were printed at Lucca in 1851. Three of them (this being one) were translated by Dr. RICHARD FREDERICK LITTLEDALE, in *The People's Hymnal*, 1867.

COME down, O Love divine!
    Seek Thou this soul of mine,
And visit it with Thine own ardor glowing.
    O Comforter, draw near,
    Within my heart appear,
And kindle it, Thy holy flame bestowing.

    O let it freely burn,
    Till earthly passions turn
To dust and ashes in its heat consuming:
    And let Thy glorious Light
    Shine ever on my sight,
And clothe me round, the while my path illuming.

    Let holy Charity
    Mine outward vesture be,
And lowliness become mine inner clothing,
    True lowliness of heart,
    Which takes the humbler part,
And o'er its own shortcomings weeps with loathing.

And so the yearning strong
With which the soul will long
Shall far outpass the power of human telling,
For none can guess its grace
Till he become the place
Wherein the Holy Spirit makes His dwelling.

GERMAN HYMNS.

The hymnic provision of Germany is supposed to be the largest and finest in the world. It is dangerous to pronounce on so wide a subject without an exhaustive knowledge of it, in all languages; but the German hymns, however much or little more numerous than our own, are certainly sounder, purer, wholesomer. Devotion in them is more spontaneous; she moves less awkwardly and seems to feel at home. We however are doing better now, since we lately began to study other hymns than those native to our own soil and tongue.

The German stock may well be larger than ours, for they got two centuries the start of us. "The trade of hymn-making," which our ancestors did not seriously take up till Dr. Watts' time, on the continent began with the Reformation, and was pushed vigorously forward from that on. The Germans have perhaps no one hymnist of the preëminence (in their different ways) of Wesley and Watts; but they have a chain, extending through the last 350 years, of writers far above the average of ours. Sufficient information on this subject is given in Miss WINKWORTH's *Sacred Poets of Germany*, 1869, and the Rev. THEODORE KÜBLER's *Historical Notes to the Lyra Germanica*, London, 1865. For students of the originals, an invaluable Thesaurus is KNAPP's *Liederschatz*, 1837, 1850, containing over 3000 hymns; and another, WACKERNAGEL's *Kirchenlieder*. For important smaller books, the Chevalier BUNSEN's Collection, 1833, was chiefly used by Miss Winkworth; and in America Dr. SCHAFF's *Deutsches Gesangbuch*, Philadelphia, 1860, is made with great judgment and taste.

Of translators into English, J. C. JACOBI, 1722, seems to have been the first who did much. JOHN WESLEY, 1739-40, rendered or paraphrased some 40 German hymns, and often grandly; his work indeed is a unique phenomenon, which no successors have equalled or are likely to equal. HABERKORN (1760) and the Moravian versifiers are of very inferior quality. But most of our stores in this department, like those of Latin origin, are recent contributions: and one benefactor outweighs all others in claims to our gratitude. Miss CATHERINE WINKWORTH, by the amount and quality at once of her translations, reigns unquestioned in this field. She has been preceded or followed, at a distance, but with more or less eminent ability, by Miss COX, RUSSELL, MASSIE, Miss BORTHWICK (*Hymns from the Land of Luther*, 1854-62), and others, who, except the last-mentioned, are represented in our pages.

O Holy Ghost, Thou precious Gift,
   Thou Comforter unfailing,
O'er Satan's snares our souls uplift,
   And let Thy power availing
Avert our woes and calm our dread :
For us the Saviour's Blood was shed ;
   We trust in Thee to save us.
Nicholas Von Hofe, 1529.

O Holy Ghost, Thou Fire of Love !
   Enkindle with Thy flame my will ;
Come with Thy strength, Lord. from above,
   Help me Thy bidding to fulfil :
Forgive that I so oft have done
What I as sinful ought to shun :
Let me with pure and quenchless fire
Thy favor and Thyself desire.
Angelus Silesius, 1657.

O Spirit of the Lord, all Life is Thine !
Now fill Thy Church with life and power divine,
That many children may be born to Thee,
And spread Thy knowledge like the boundless sea.
A. G. Spangenberg, 1747.

O Comforter of priceless worth,
Send peace and unity on earth ;
Support us in our final strife,
And lead us out of death to Life.
Luther, 1542.

O Holy Spirit, at the end,
Sweet Comforter, be Thou my Friend !
When Death and Hell assail me sore,
Leave me, O leave me, nevermore,
But bear me safely through the strife,
As Thou hast promised, into Life !
Nicholas Selnecker, 1587.

O LOVING SPIRIT, the Cleanser of our sins, and Restorer of all innocence, and especial Restorer of sanctification, fill me with the Spirit of wisdom and understanding, the Spirit of counsel and ghostly strength, the Spirit of knowledge and true godliness, and the Spirit of Thy fear and love Clear off all the rust of my sins, that I may be confounded for the errors of my past frailty : but lead me into all true knowledge, and guard me from all wickedness, depravity, and worldly-mindedness, from the attacks and assaults of all my enemies, visible and invisible, and lead me to the grace and glory of Thy kingdom, Who livest and reignest with the FATHER and the SON, one GOD blessed forever. Amen.

O GENTLE Spirit, Fountain, Source, and Consummation of all goodness, mercifully wipe away the pollutions of my mind, and make me fruitful by watering me within with the dew of Thy blessing. Open Thy unfailing treasures of piety and knowledge. Give a teachable disposition and an active intellect, a courteous tongue flowing with pleasing converse : grant me to hold fast the line of rectitude and equity : to discern true from false, right from wrong, and to prefer and reverence Thee above all things, who art the true Arbiter and Disposer of life. Amen.

GERMAN HYMNS.

MARTIN LUTHER, 1483-1546.

The great Reformer wrote 36 or more hymns (the number is variously estimated), which formed no inconsiderable part of the machinery of the German Reformation. Says the Rev THEODORE KÜBLER (*Historical Notes to the Lyra Germanica*: London, 1865), "These simple, childlike, yet strong, fervent, and joyful hymns were printed at first on single sheets with the tunes; they spread like wildfire, and greatly promoted the work of the Reformation. 'Luther,' said the Romanists, 'has done us more harm by his songs than by his sermons.' In the years 1524 and 1525, when Luther composed most of his hymns, four printers in Erfurt alone were fully engaged in publishing them."

LUTHER's *Spiritual Songs*, as he preferred to call them, have in the mass found at least three translators: the Rev. JOHN ANDERSON, Edinburgh, 1846; JOHN HUNT, London, 1853; and Mr. RICHARD MASSIE, London, 1854. The two former versions are of small poetic value. Three of LUTHER's hymns are for Whitsuntide; we give several renderings of each. Their historic importance, and the great influence they have exerted, rather than any special intrinsic beauty, demand for them a prominent and large place in this collection.

KOMM HEILIGER GEIST, HERRE GOTT.

This hymn has an abundant history of its own. Says Mr. KÜBLER: "This is Luther's amplification of an old German version of the Latin Antiphona de Spiritu Sancto (*Veni Sancte Spiritus*). Luther added two verses to the one which he already found in use, and his hymn, with its old tune, was first published in 1524. It spread rapidly among the common people, in proof of which the fact may be adduced, that in the Peasants' War it was sung by the fanatical peasants at the bloody battle of Frankenhausen, in the year 1526. For when the Landgrave Philip of Hesse gave the signal for the attack against them, the peasants remained unmoved, neither retreating nor defending themselves, but waiting for the miraculous help of God, which their leader Thomas Münzer had predicted; they began to sing this Pentecostal hymn, and continued singing, until 50,000 of them were slain and the rest dispersed.

"When Leonhard Kayser, on account of his Evangelical preaching, was burned alive in Passau on the 16th August, 1527, he asked the people to sing this hymn while he was tied to the stake. This they did, and when the flames rose high, he was heard several times to call, 'Jesu, I am Thine, save me!'" And so he died. It has since often been used by ministers of the Gospel, not only in their preaching, but also on their dying beds. In many churches it was the standing hymn at the opening of divine service. A family in Silesia sang it during a fearful storm in 1535, when the roof of their house was blown away, but they themselves escaped without any injuries. The wife of the celebrated Frederic Perthes in Hamburg, the daughter of Matthias Claudius, wrote to her son, who was studying at the University, on his birthday: "My most earnest birthday wish and prayer for you is —

> 'Thou strong Defence, Thou Holy Light,
> Teach him to know our God aright,
> And call Him Father from the heart:
> The Word of Life and Truth impart,
> That he may love not doctrines strange,
> Nor e'er to other teachers range,
> But Jesus for his Master own,
> And put his trust in Him alone.'

"My beloved child, may God fulfil this prayer to you!'

The original of v. 1 is given by WACKERNAGEL, and after him by KÜBLER: its identity with the great hymn of Robert of France extends no further than the first line.

> Veni, Sancte Spiritus:
> Reple tuorum corda fidelium,
> Et tui amoris in eis ignem accende ;
> Qui per diversitatem linguarum cunctarum
> Gentes in unitate fidei congregasti.
> Alleluia, Alleluia.

German translations of this Antiphon had been made at a very early date: the oldest known is found in one of the first books printed in the 15th century.

LUTHER's hymn first appeared in the Erfurt *Enchiridion* of 1524, where it has this title: "Here follows the hymn, *Veni Sancte Spiritus*, sung of the Holy Spirit, very useful and good." It was admitted into the Roman Catholic Collection of M. VEHE, 1537.

FIRST VERSION.

Undoubtedly the first translations from German into English, as almost or quite the first hymnic provision in our language, were made by MYLES COVERDALE (1488?-1569), Bishop of Exeter in 1551, one of the earliest translators of the Bible, and a prominent Reformer. His *Goostly Psalmes and Spirituall Songes*, forty in number, appeared before 1539: a copy is preserved in the library of Queen's College, Oxford, and they are reprinted in his "Remains," published by the Parker Society in 1846. The first three are addressed "To the Holy Goost," and two of them are from Luther. They are here given accurately, even to the rude antique spelling, as memorials of a time when "the rules of religion," though "strict," were matters of fierce debate, but "orthography was optional."

COME, Holy Spirite, most blessed Lorde,
    Fulfyl our hartes nowe with Thy Grace;
And make our myndes of one accorde,
Kyndle them with love in every place.

O Lorde, Thou forgevest our trespace,
And callest the folke of every countre
To the ryght fayth and truste of Thy Grace,
That they may geve thankes and synge to Thee.
                    Alleluya, Alleluya.

O holy Lyght, moste principall,
The Worde of Lyfe shewe unto us;
And cause us to knowe God over all
For our owne Father moste gracious.
Lorde, kepe us from lernyng venymous,
That we folowe no masters but Christe.
He is the Verite, His Worde sayth thus;
Cause us to set in Hym our truste.
                    Alleluya, Alleluya.

O holy Fyre, and conforth moste swete,
Fyll our hertes with fayth and boldnesse,
To abyde by The in colde and hete,
Contente to suffre for ryghteousnesse:
O Lord, geve strength to our weaknesse,
And send us helpe every houre;
That we may overcome all wyckednesse,
And brynge this olde Adam under Thy power.
                    Alleluya, Alleluya.

SECOND VERSION.

From that rare and important volume, *Psalmodia Germanica, or, The German Psalmody. Translated from the High German* by JOHN CHRISTIAN JACOBI 1722. A Supplement was added in 1725: the second edition, with Supplement, 1732: reprinted by JOHN HABERKORN, with a Supplement of his own, 1760: the second edition of this, 1765. There is also a very rare reprint by Hugh Gaine, New York, 1756, "with which," says good Dr. Kunze, Lutheran pastor there in 1795, "many serious English persons have been greatly delighted." JACOBI was indeed, except JOHN WESLEY, the only respectable translator from the German prior to our time; though far from a great poet, he is several steps above his Moravian successors. He rendered 94 hymns, and HABERKORN, who is inferior to him, 33. JACOBI seems to have been Lutheran or Reformed rather than Moravian: but nothing is known about him.

COME, Holy Ghost! come, Lord our God!
Spread faith and love divine abroad;
And fill Thy longing people's minds
With precious gifts of sundry kinds.
O Lord, who by Thy heavenly Light
Hast called Thy Church from sinful night,
Out of all nations, tribes, and tongues,
Thy praise shall make our choicest songs.
       Hallelujah! Hallelujah!

Thou Light of glory, gracious Lord!
Revive us by Thy holy Word,
And teach Thy flock in truth to call
On Thee, the Father of us all.
Delusive errors far remove,
And guide us always by that love,
Which, keeping close to Jesu's path,
Rejects all other guides of faith.
       Hallelujah.

Thou great Dispenser of that Love
Which sent Redemption from above,
O grant us faith and constancy
To conquer sin, and yield to Thee.
O Lord, by Thine almighty Grace
Prepare us so to run our race
That we, from bonds of sin kept free,
May gain a blest eternity.
       Hallelujah.

THIRD VERSION.

By ARTHUR TOZER RUSSELL, then Vicar of Caxton: from a Collection of Psalms and Hymns published by him in 1851: an important book, made up largely of originals and translations from the German.

BLEST Comforter, come, Lord our God!
    And pour Thy gifts of Grace abroad;
Thy faithful people fill with blessing,
    Love's fire their hearts possessing.
O Lord, Thou by Thy heavenly Light
Dost gather and in faith unite
Through all the world a holy nation,
To sing to Thee with exultation,
        Hallelujah! hallelujah!

O Holiest Light! Rock adored!
Give us Thy light, Thy living word,
To God Himself our spirits leading,
    With Him as children pleading.
From error, Lord, our souls defend,
That they on Christ alone attend,
In Him with faith unfeigned abiding,
In Him with all their might confiding.
        Hallelujah! hallelujah!

O Holiest Fire! Source of rest!
Grant that with joy and hope possest,
And in Thy service kept forever,
    Naught us from Thee may sever.

Lord, may Thy power prepare each heart;
To our weak nature strength impart,
That we may, firmly here contending,
To Thee be daily hence ascending.
      Hallelujah! hallelujah!

FOURTH VERSION.

Miss CATHERINE WINKWORTH, 1855. The most gifted translator of any foreign sacred lyrics into our tongue, after Dr. NEALE and JOHN WESLEY: and in practical services rendered, taking quality with quantity, the first of those who have labored upon German hymns. Our knowledge of them is due to her more largely than to any or all other translators: and by her two series of *Lyra Germanica*, her *Choral Book*, and her *Christian Singers of Germany*, she has laid all English-speaking Christians under lasting obligation.

COME, Holy Spirit, God and Lord!
    Be all Thy graces now outpoured
On the believer's mind and soul,
And touch our hearts with living coal.
Thy Light this day shone forth so clear,
All tongues and nations gathered near,
To learn that faith, for which we bring
Glad praise to Thee, and loudly sing,
      Hallelujah, Hallelujah!

Thou strong Defence, Thou holy Light,
Teach us to know our God aright,
And call Him Father from the heart:
The Word of life and truth impart:
That we may love not doctrines strange,
Nor e'er to other teachers range,

But Jesus for our Master own,
And put our trust in Him alone.
    Hallelujah!

Thou sacred Ardor, Comfort sweet,
Help us to wait with ready feet
And willing heart at Thy command,
Nor trial fright us from Thy band.
Lord, make us ready with Thy powers;
Strengthen the flesh in weaker hours,
That as good warriors we may force
Through life and death to Thee our course!
    Hallelujah!

NUN BITTEN WIR DEN HEILIGEN GEIST.

This was first printed in Joh. Walther's Hymn Book, 1524. The first verse is very old. A Franciscan monk, BERTHOLD OF RATISBON, about A.D. 1250, in one of his sermons gives the text of it, and exhorts his hearers to sing it often and heartily. That verse is attributed, says Miss WINKWORTH (*Christian Singers of Germany*, 1869) to SPERVOGEL, a priest and favorite sacred poet of the twelfth century. Other verses, having some resemblance to Luther's, appeared in Romanist books a few years after the publication of his hymn, but there is no evidence that they are old. Luther's hymn was translated into Latin by Reinhart Lorich in 1550, and into Tamil by Ziegenbulg in 1723.

The hymn was once used under very peculiar circumstances, whereof the tale is told by Pastor Heiberg in his account of *Peter Palladius, the First Evangelical Bishop of Seeland*: see KARL HEINRICH's *Erzählungen uber Evan. Kirchenlieder*.

In the earlier part of the 16th century, on the day preceding the festival of the Annunciation of the Virgin, about eighty fishermen were on the ice between Copenhagen and the island of Saltholm, catching eels, when the ice gave way and broke up. They were carried along by the current, parted from each other, and in the end nearly thirty of them drowned. While they were still near together, one of them, Hans Vensen, who had been a pupil of Bishop Palladius, called out to the rest: "Dear brethren, let us not fall into despair because we shall lose our lives: but let us prove by our conduct that we have been bearers of God's Word." Whereupon they sang together *Nun bitten wir den Heil'gen Geist*, and after it the hymn of the dying, *Mit*

NUN BITTEN WIR.

Fried und Freud ich fahr dahin, Luther's metrical version of *Nunc Dimittis*. When they had done singing, they fell on their knees, the water reaching their breasts, and prayed that God would grant them a happy death.

Our first version is by MYLES COVERDALE, 153–. It is said to have been used at the deathbed of Queen Elizabeth.

THOU holy Spirite, we pray to The,
    Strengthe oure faythe and increase it alwaye;
Comforthe oure hertes in adversite
With trewe beleve bothe nyght and daye.
                      Kirieleyson.

Thou worthy Lyght, that art so cleare,
Teache us Christe Jesu to knowe alone;
    That we have never cause to feare
In Hym to have redempcyon.
                      Kirieleyson.

Thou swete Love, graunt us altogether
To be unfayned in charite;
    That we may all love one another,
And of one mynde alwaye to be.
                      Kirieleyson.

Be Thou our Confortoure in all nede;
Make us to feare nether deth nor shame;
    But in the treuth to be stablyshed,
That Sathan put us not to blame.
                      Kirieleyson.

GERMAN HYMNS.

SECOND VERSION.

By A. T. RUSSELL, 1851.

NOW pray we all God the Comforter
Into every heart true faith to pour,
And that He defend us,
Yea, till Death tend us,
When for Heaven we leave this world of sorrow.
Have mercy, Lord.

Shine into us, O most holy Light,
That we Jesus Christ may know aright,
Stayed on Him forever,
Our only Saviour,
Who to our true home again hath brought us.
Have mercy, Lord.

Spirit of Love! now our spirits bless;
Them with Thy own heavenly fire possess;
That in heart uniting,
In peace delighting,
We may henceforth all be one in spirit.
Have mercy, Lord.

Our highest Comfort in all distress!
O let naught with fear our hearts oppress:
Give us strength nnfailing,
O'er fear prevailing,
When the accusing foe would overwhelm us.
Have mercy, Lord.

NUN BITTEN WIR.

THIRD VERSION.

By RICHARD MASSIE, Esq., of Eccleston: from *Martin Luther's Spiritual Songs*, 1854.

NOW crave we of the Holy Ghost,
What of all things we need the most,
True faith in Christ, when life is ending,
And from this grief we home be wending.
    Kyrie eleison.

Shine in our hearts, Thou worthy Light,
And teach us Christ to know aright;
Abiding in Thee, whose faithful hand
Hath brought us safe to our Fatherland.
    Kyrie eleison.

Grant us Thy favor, heavenly Dove,
And let us feel the glow of love,
That we may live with one another
As brother ought to live with brother.
    Kyrie eleison.

O Thou who hast so sweet a name,
Keep us from fear of death and shame,
Nor comfort in the hour refuse us
When Sin and Satan shall accuse us.
    Kyrie eleison.

KOMM GOTT, SCHÖPFER, HEILIGER GEIST.

This first appeared, with the last, in the Erfurt Enchiridion of 1524: a tolerably close rendering of Veni Creator Spiritus. It was admitted into the Romanist collection of Joh. Leisentritt, 1567. This version is by R. MASSIE, 1854.

CREATOR Spirit, Holy Dove,
　Visit Thy people from above;
Fill them with graces, and restore
Thy creatures as they were before.

For Comforter is Thy sweet name,
A Gift which from the Highest came;
A ghostly Ointment from above,
A living Fount, a Fire of Love.

Our minds enlighten, and inspire
Our souls with love's celestial fire;
And since Thou know'st how frail we be,
Confirm and make us strong in Thee.

Thou, with Thy Grace's sevenfold band,
The Finger art on God's right hand:
Thou dost the Father's promise send
With tongues to earth's remotest end.

Drive far away our wily foe,
And by Thy Grace sweet peace bestow;
That in Thy footsteps we may run,
And soul-destroying mischief shun

Let us by Thee the Father know,
His Son Christ Jesus also show,
That, full of faith, we may know Thee
Derived from Both eternally.

To God the Father, and the Son
Who rose again, be honor done,
With Him who came at Pentecost,
The Comforter, the Holy Ghost.

ANOTHER VERSION.

Or rather a loose paraphrase of the first three verses: from the Hymn Book of the *Methodist New Connexion*, London, 1865. It is there anonymous, but has the date 1852.

O HOLY Spirit, now
    With all Thy graces come,
And make the temple of our hearts
    Thine own abiding home.

Visit each waiting mind,
    For Thou alone canst bless:
Stamped with Thy signet, we shall shine
    Complete in righteousness.

The Comforter art Thou,
    Thrice blessed is the name;
The dearest, choicest Gift of Love
    That human hearts may claim.

O kindle in each breast
  The hallowed flame of love,
The fire of zeal, the light of joy,
  Our dark cold hearts to move.

Thus in our weakness we
  Thy holy aid shall prove:
Thy perfect work none can destroy,
  Nor quench Thy deathless Love.

O DU ALLERSÜSZSTE FREUDE.

PAUL GERHARDT, 1606-1676: the greatest of German hymnists, though he left but 123 hymns Of these 75 have been translated (very badly) by John Kelly, 1867. A man of many trials; says Mr. KÜBLER: "His portrait, in the church of Lübben, bears the inscription, 'Theologus in cribro Satanæ versatus'; i.e. A divine sifted in Satan's sleeve." Of this lovely poem, first printed in Chr. Runge's Collection, 1653, we give three versions. The first, which renders the whole hymn, is from JACOBI'S *Psalmodia Germanica*, second edition, 1725; his best effort. Half a century later, part of it was rewritten by Toplady: see below.

O THOU sweetest Source of gladness,
    Faith and Hope and heavenly Light,
Who in joy, as in our sadness,
    Dost convince us of Thy might!
  Holy Spirit, God of peace,
  Great Distributer of Grace,
Life and Joy of the creation,
Hear, O hear my supplication.

O Thou best of all donations
    God can give, or we implore!
Having Thy sweet consolations,
    We need wish for nothing more.

O DU ALLERSÜSZSTE FREUDE.

Come, Thou Lord of love and power,
On my heart Thy graces shower:
Work in me a new creation,
Make my heart Thy habitation.

From that Height that knows no measure
As a shower Thou dost descend,
And bring'st down the richest treasure
Man can wish or God can send.
O Thou Glory, shining down
From the Father and the Son,
Grant me Thy communication,
Which makes all a new creation.

Wise Thou art, know'st all recesses
Of the earth and spreading skies;
Every sand the shore possesses
Thy omniscient Mind descries.
Lord, Thou knowest that I am
Quite corrupted, blind and lame.
Give me such a wise behavior
As may please my God and Saviour.

Holy Lord! who lov'st to visit
Souls of pure and chaste desire,
But abhorrest an heart that's busied
With what flesh and blood admire:
Wash my soul, O Spring of Grace,
Clean from all unrighteousness;
Make me fly what Thou refusest,
And delight in what Thou choosest.

Like a lamb Thou art in nature,
　　Of a meek and tender mind,
Doing good to every creature,
　　Though they 're still to sin inclined.
　　O forgive, and grant I may
　　Follow Thy forgiving way,
Love my foes as my own lineage,
And hate none that bear Thy image.

Dearest Lord, I live contented
　　In the assurance of Thy Love,
Which, if not by sin prevented,
　　Does my highest comfort prove.
　　Make my soul Thy property;
　　All I have shall be to Thee
And Thy glory dedicated,
Here, and when I am translated.

I renounce what's prejudicial
　　To the glory of Thy Name,
Counting only beneficial
　　What's from Thee and from the Lamb.
　　At what Satan can contrive
　　I will never once connive,
But with earnest opposition
Cross that author of perdition.

O support my weak endeavor;
　　Second me on every side;
Thine assistance, great Reliever!
　　Grant me still, and be my Guide.

O DU ALLERSÜSZSTE FREUDE.

Mortify my selfishness,
Turn the old will from sinful ways,
And conform it to Thy Nature,
That my God may love His creature.

Be my Guard on each occasion;
  When I'm sinking, be my staff;
When I die, be my Salvation;
  When I'm buried, be my Grave:
  And when from the grave I rise,
  Take me up above the skies;
Seat me with Thy saints in glory,
There forever to adore Thee.

THE SAME REWRITTEN.

By Augustus Montague Toplady, 1776. A comparison with the above will show that this is merely a partial revision of Jacobi's, though a manifest improvement. Again altered and abridged, in one form or another, this has long been a popular English hymn.

HOLY Ghost, dispel our sadness,
  Pierce the clouds of sinful night:
Come, Thou Source of sweetest gladness,
  Breathe Thy Life, and spread Thy Light!
Loving Spirit. God of peace,
  Great Distributer of Grace,
Rest upon this congregation!
Hear, O hear our supplication.

From that height which knows no measure
  As a gracious shower descend;

Bringing down the richest treasure
  Man can wish, and God can send.
  O Thou Glory, shining down
  From the Father and the Son,
Grant us Thy illumination!
Rest upon this congregation.

Come, Thou best of all donations
  God can give, or we implore:
Having Thy sweet consolations,
  We need wish for nothing more.
  Come with unction and with power;
  On our souls Thy graces shower;
Author of the new creation,
Make our hearts Thy habitation.

Known to Thee are all recesses
  Of the earth and spreading skies;
Every sand the shore possesses
  Thy omniscient Mind descries.
  Holy Fountain, wash us clean,
  Both from error and from sin:
Make us fly what Thou refusest,
And delight in what Thou choosest.

Manifest Thy Love forever;
  Fence us in on every side;
In distress be our Reliever;
  Guard and teach, support and guide.
  Let Thy kind, effectual Grace
  Turn our feet from evil ways:
Show Thyself our New Creator,
And conform us to Thy Nature.

Be our Friend on each occasion,
  God, omnipotent to save!
When we die, be our salvation;
  When we 're buried, be our Grave:
And when from the grave we rise,
  Take us up above the skies;
Seat us with Thy saints in glory,
There forever to adore Thee.

A MODERN VERSION OF THE SAME.

From Miss WINKWORTH's *Chorale Book for England*, 1862.

SWEETEST Fount of holy gladness,
  Fairest Light was ever shed,
Who alike in joy and sadness
  Leavest none unvisited;
Spirit of the highest God,
Lord, from Whom is life bestowed,
Who upholdest every thing,
Hear me, hear me, while I sing.

Thou art shed like gentlest showers
  From the Father and the Son,
Bringing to us quickened powers,
  Purest blessing from their throne;
Suffer then, O noble Guest,
That rich gift by Thee possest,
That Thou givest at Thy will,
All my being now to fill.

Thou art ever true and holy,
  Sin and falsehood Thou dost hate,
But Thou comest where the lowly
  And the pure Thy presence wait:
Wash me then, O Well of Grace,
Every stain and spot efface;
Let me flee what Thou dost flee,
Grant me what Thou lov'st to see.

Well content am I if only
  Thou wilt deign to dwell with me:
With Thee I am never lonely,
  Never comfortless with Thee.
Thine forever make me now,
And to Thee, my Lord, I vow
Here and yonder to employ
Every power for Thee with joy.

When I cry for help, O hear me;
  When I sink, O haste to save;
When I die, be inly near me,
  Be my Hope even in the grave.
Bring me when I rise again
To the Land that knows no pain,
Where Thy followers from Thy stream
Drink forever joys supreme.

ZEUCH EIN ZU DEINEN THOREN.

PAUL GERHARDT. Written "during the Thirty Years' War," and in some sense a hymn for Church and State: first printed in Joh. Crüger's *Praxis Pietatis Melica*, 1656. The original has 16 verses, of which one is omitted in this version by Miss WINKWORTH, 1855. There are two versions of most of it, in the *Psalmodia Germanica*, by Jacobi and Haberkorn, of 13 and 12 verses severally: and a more modern one, also in 13 verses, by F. E. Cox, 1864. Dr. Schaff, in his *Deutsches Gesangbuch* (Philadelphia, 1860), omits vv 8-12, which have special reference to the thirty years' war, and are less adapted to general use.

COME to Thy temple here on earth,
    Be Thou my spirit's Guest,
Who givest us of mortal birth
    A second birth more blest;
Spirit beloved, Thou mighty Lord,
    Who with the Father and the Son
    Reignest upon an equal throne,
Art equally adored!

O enter, let me feel and know
    Thy mighty power within,
That can alone our help bestow
    And rescue us from sin.
O cleanse my soul and make it white,
    That I with heart unstained and true
    May daily render service due
And honor Thee aright.

I was a wild unfruitful vine
    Which Thou shouldst prune and train;
Death pierced through all this life of mine,
    But Thou my foe hast slain.

Thy holy Baptism is his grave,
   He perishes beneath the flood
   Of His most precious Death and Blood
Who died our life to save.

Thou art the Spirit who dost teach
   To pray aright, for all
Our prayers are heard if Thou beseech,
   Thy songs have sweetest fall.
They soar on tireless wings to heaven,
   They fail not from before God's throne,
   Till all His goodness we have known
By whom all help is given.

Thou art the Spirit of all joy,
   Sadness Thou lovest not;
Thy comfort beaming from on high
   Lights up the darkest lot.
Ah yes, how many a time of old
   Thy voice hath rapt my soul away
   To yon bright halls of endless day,
And oped the gates of gold!

Thou art the Spirit of all love,
   The Friend of kindly life;
Thou wouldst not that our hearts should prove
   The pangs of wrath and strife.
Thou hatest hatred's withering reign;
   In souls that discord maketh dark
   Dost Thou rekindle Love's bright spark,
And make them one again.

On Thee is all this world upstaid
  And in Thy hands doth rest;
And Thou canst wayward hearts persuade
  To turn as seems Thee best.
O therefore give Thy love and peace,
  That they may join in strongest bands
  Long parted foes, and through our lands
These sad divisions cease.

Thou art the true, the only Source
  Whence concord comes to men:
O that Thy power might have free course
  And bring us peace again!
O hear, and stem this mighty flood
  That o'er us death and sorrow spreads;
  Alas! each day afresh it sheds
Like water human blood.

And let our nation learn to know
  What, and how deep, our sin;
Nay, let God's judgments come, if so
  A fire be lit within
The hearts that loved themselves to please:
  In bitter shame now let them burn,
  And loving Thee, repentant spurn
Their selfish worldly ease.

Grace for the contrite heart abounds,
  Joy to the sad is given;
To serve God's Truth will heal our wounds
  And bring us help from Heaven.

Lord, for Thine honor's sake, make known
    Thy power: convert the wicked now,
    And teach the hard to weep, for Thou
Canst soften steel and stone!

Arise, and make an end of all
    Our heartache and our pain:
Thy wandering flock at last recall
    And grant them joy again:
To peace and wealth the lands restore,
    Wasted with fire or plague or sword;
    Come to Thy ruined churches, Lord,
And bid them bloom once more!

The rulers of our land defend,
    Our sovereign's throne uphold;
That he and we may prosper, send
    True wisdom to the old:
With piety the young men bless,
    And through the nation shed abroad
    True virtue and the fear of God,
A nation's happiness.

Fill every heart with holy zeal
    To keep the Faith unstained;
Let house and land Thy blessing feel,
    Whence all true wealth is gained.
Him who resists Thy inward powers,
    The evil spirit, make Thou flee;
    What'er delights Thy heart, would he
Fain root from out of ours.

ZEUCH EIN ZU DEINEN THOREN.

Give strong and cheerful hearts to stand
  Undaunted in the wars
That Satan's fierce and mighty band
  Is waging with Thy cause.
Help us to fight as warriors brave,
  That we may conquer in the field,
  And not one Christian man may yield
His soul to sin a slave.

Order according to Thy mind
  Our life from day to day;
And when this life must be resigned,
  And Death has seized his prey,
When all our days have fleeted by,
  Help us to die with fearless spirit,
  And let us after death inherit
Eternal life on high.

ANOTHER VERSION.

A more vigorous and graceful version of part of the same poem, in the original measure, from *The Chorale Book for England*, 1862.

O ENTER, Lord, Thy temple,
  Be Thou my spirit's Guest,
Who at my birth didst give me
  A second birth more blest.
  Thou in the Godhead, Lord,
Though here to dwell Thou deignest,
Forever equal reignest,
  Art equally adored.

O enter, let me know Thee
   And feel Thy power within,
The power that breaks our fetters
   And rescues us from sin.
   So wash and cleanse Thou me
That I may serve Thee truly,
And render honor duly
   With perfect heart to Thee.

'Tis Thou, O Spirit, teachest
   The soul to pray aright;
Thy songs have sweetest music,
   Thy prayers have wondrous might.
   Unheard they cannot fall,
They pierce the highest Heaven,
Till He His help hath given
   Who surely helpeth all.

Joy is Thy gift, O Spirit!
   Thou wouldst not have us pine;
In darkest hours Thy comfort
   Doth aye most brightly shine.
   Ah then how oft Thy voice
Hath shed its sweetness o'er me,
And opened Heaven before me,
   And bid my heart rejoice!

All love is Thine, O Spirit!
   Thou hatest enmity;
Thou lovest peace and friendship,
   All strife wouldst have us flee.

When wrath and discord reign
Thy whisper inly pleadeth,
And to the heart that heedeth
  Brings love and light again.

The whole wide world, O Spirit!
  Upon Thy hands doth rest:
Our wayward hearts Thou turnest
  As it may seem Thee best.
  Once more Thy power make known!
As Thou hast done so often,
Convert the wicked, soften
  To tears the heart of stone.

With holy zeal then fill us,
  To keep the Faith still pure;
And bless our lands and houses
  With wealth that may endure.
  And make that foe to flee
Who in us with Thee striveth;
From out our heart he driveth
  Whate'er delighteth Thee.

Order our path in all things
  According to Thy mind;
And when this life is over
  And must be all resigned,
  O grant us then to die
With calm and fearless spirit,
And after death inherit
  Eternal life on high.

O HEIL'GER GEIST, KEHR' BEI UNS EIN.

MICHAEL SCHIRMER, 1606–1673: headmaster of the Grayfriars' Grammar School at Berlin. The date of this is 1650: it has seven verses, and is one of the most popular Spirit-hymns among the Germans both in Europe and America. Translated by Miss WINKWORTH, *Chorale Book*, 1862.

O HOLY Spirit, enter in,
    Among these hearts Thy work begin,
  Thy temple deign to make us;
Sun of the soul, Thou Light divine,
Around and in us brightly shine,
  To strength and gladness wake us.
Where Thou shinest Life from Heaven
    There is given:
    We before Thee
For that precious gift implore Thee.

Left to ourselves we shall but stray;
O lead us on the narrow way,
  With wisest counsel guide us,
And give us steadfastness, that we
May henceforth truly follow Thee,
  Whatever woes betide us.
Heal Thou gently hearts now broken,
    Give some token
    Thou art near us,
Whom we trust to light and cheer us.

O mighty Rock, O Source of Life,
Let Thy dear Word, 'mid doubt and strife,
  Be so within us burning

That we be faithful unto death
In Thy pure Love and holy Faith,
　　From Thee true wisdom learning.
Lord, Thy graces on us shower;
　　　By Thy power
　　　Christ confessing,
Let us win His Grace and blessing.

O gentle Dew, from Heaven now fall
With power upon the hearts of all,
　　Thy tenderness instilling;
That heart to heart, more closely bound,
Fruitful in kindly deeds be found,
　　The law of love fulfilling.
No wrath, no strife here shall grieve Thee;
　　　We receive Thee.
　　　Where Thou livest
Peace and love and joy Thou givest.

Grant that our days, while life shall last,
In purest holiness be past;
　　Our minds so rule and strengthen
That they may rise o'er things of earth,
The hopes and joys that here have birth:
　　And if our course Thou lengthen,
Keep Thou pure, Lord, from offences,
　　　Heart and senses:
　　　Blessed Spirit,
Bid us thus true Life inherit.

GERMAN HYMNS.

BRUNQUELL ALLER GÜTER.

JOHN FRANK, 1618–1677: a Lutheran lawyer and burgomaster at Guben in Saxony. He wrote 110 hymns: the date of this is 1660. Translated by RICHARD MASSIE, 1854. Some of the expressions in vv. 3 and 4 are rather untastefully erotic. These have been corrected in MERCER's *Church Psalter and Hymn Book*, 1854–6, and in KENNEDY's *Hymnologia Christiana*, 1863: the emendations are given below.

SOURCE of good, whose power controls
    Every movement of our souls;
Wind that quickens where it blows;
Comforter of human woes;
Lamp of God, whose ray serene
In the darkest night is seen;
Come, inspire my feeble strain,
That I may not sing in vain.

God's own Finger, skilled to teach
Tongues of every land and speech,
Balsam of the wounded soul,
Binding up and making whole;
Flame of pure and holy love;
Strength of all that live and move:
Come, Thy gifts and fire impart,
Make me love Thee from the heart.

Bridegroom of believing souls!
Let me in the sheltering holes [1]
Of the Rock of Ages find
Refuge from the stormy wind;

---

[1] Succor of the soul bereft,
    Let me in some sheltering cleft. — *Mercer's Collection.*

Like a bird unto its nest
Flee away and be at rest.
Shine, Thou Sun of grace and bliss,[1]
Breathe upon me with Thy kiss.

Precious Gift, by God bestowed,
Come, and make me Thine abode.
See, I languish; see, I faint;
Listen to my sad complaint.
Come, O come to me, my Love,[2]
Come with unction from above,
That my heart may smile anew
At Thy soul-entrancing view.[3]

As the hart with longing looks
For refreshing water-brooks,
Heated in the burning chase,
So my soul desires Thy Grace;
So my heavy-laden breast,
By the cares of life opprest,
Longs Thy cooling streams to taste
In this dry and barren waste.

Mighty Spirit, by whose aid
Man a living soul was made,
Everlasting God, whose fire
Kindles chaste and pure desire!

---

[1] Shine, thou Sun of Grace and Joy,
And inspire me from on high. — *Kennedy*.

[2] Come, O fill me with Thy Love. — *Mercer*.

[3] Make me strong and pure and bright
With thy soul-reviving light. — *Kennedy*.

Grant in every grief and loss
I may calmly bear the cross,
And surrender all to Thee,
Comforting and strengthening me.

Lord, to Thy safe keeping take,
When I sleep and when I wake,
Every feature, limb, and bone,
Every thing I call my own;
That each word, and work, and way,
And even this my humble lay,
May, O heavenly Father, be
Good and pleasing unto Thee.

Let not Hell with frowns or smiles,
Open force or cunning wiles,
Snap[1] the thread of my brief days;
And when gently life decays,
Take to Heaven Thy servant dear,
Who hath loved and served Thee here;
There eternal hymns to raise,
Mighty Spirit, to Thy praise.

KOMM, O KOMM, DU GEIST DES LEBENS.

JOACHIM NEANDER, 1640-1680. A German Reformed minister at Bremen, and the greatest hymnist of that communion, though the author of but 71 hymns. Version by Miss WINKWORTH, 1858. The Rev. Theodore Kübler, in his Historical Notes to the *Lyra Germanica*, tells a curious story about the sixth verse of this hymn, given below. It "was once used under very peculiar circumstances. In a town of Northern Germany a very poor woman, who with her two children had had nothing to eat for four days, was driven to despair, and in the night she resolved to murder her chil-

---

[1] Break. — *Mercer.*

dren. She was just taking up the youngest, with a knife in her hand, when the night watchman, who at that moment passed under her low window, and saw through a hole of the shutter what she was intending, suddenly knocked, and entered the room. He inquired about her misery, and gave her fourpence, promising to procure her more help. The good man then went out to sing a verse according to his custom when calling out the hours, and he sang in all the streets of the town this one: —

> 'And whene'er a yearning strong
> Presses out the bitter cry,' &c."

HOLY Spirit, once again
   Come, Thou true Eternal God!
Nor Thy power descend in vain,
   Make us ever Thine abode;
So shall Spirit, joy, and light
Dwell in us where all was night.

Pour into our heart and mind
   Wisdom, counsel, truth and love;
That we be to naught inclined
   Save what Thou mayst well approve;
Let Thy knowledge spread and grow,
Working error's overthrow.

Guide us, Lord, from day to day,
   Keep us in the paths of Grace,
Clear all hindrances away
   That might foil us in the race;
When we stumble hear our call,
Work repentance for our fall.

Witness in our hearts that God
   Counts us children through His Son,
That our Father's gentle rod
   Smites us for our good alone;
So when tried, perplexed, distrest,
In His Love we still may rest.

Quicken us to seek His face
  Freely, with a trusting heart;
In our prayers O breathe Thy Grace;
  Go with us when we depart;
So shall our requests be heard,
And our faith to joy be stirred.

And whene'er a yearning strong
  Presses out the bitter cry,
Ah my God, how long, how long?
  Then O let me find Thee nigh,
And Thy words of healing balm
Bring me courage, patience, calm.

Spirit Thou of strength and power,
  Thou new Spirit God hath given,
Aid us in temptation's hour,
  Train and perfect us for Heaven;
Arm us in the battle field,
Leave us never there to yield.

Lord, preserve us in the faith,
  Suffer naught to drive us thence,
Neither Satan, scorn, nor death;
  Be our God and our Defence;
Though the flesh resist Thy will,
Let Thy Word be stronger still.

And at last when we must die,
  O assure the sinking heart
Of the glorious realm on high
  Where Thou healest every smart,
Of the joys unspeakable
Where our God would have us dwell.

KOMM, DU GEIST DES LEBENS.

SECOND VERSION.

Partial translation by Dr. CHARLES W. SCHAEFFER, Lutheran pastor in Germantown, Pennsylvania; made 1866. From the *Church Book* of the Lutheran General Council, 1868.

COME, O come, thou quickening Spirit!
    Thou forever art divine:
Let Thy power never fail me,
    Always fill this heart of mine:
Thus shall Grace and Truth and Light
Dissipate the gloom of night.

Grant my mind and my affections
    Wisdom, counsel, purity;
That I may be ever seeking
    Naught but that which pleases Thee.
Let Thy knowledge spread and grow,
Working error's overthrow.

Lead me to green pastures, lead me
    By the true and living Way;
Shield me from each strong temptation
    That might draw my heart astray:
And if e'er my feet should turn,
For each error let me mourn.

Holy Spirit, strong and mighty,
    Thou who makest all things new,
Make Thy work within me perfect;
    Help me by Thy Word so true;
Arm me with that sword of Thine,
And the victory shall be mine.

In the faith O make me steadfast:
  Let not Satan, death, or shame
Of my confidence deprive me:
  Lord, my refuge is Thy Name.
When the flesh inclines to ill,
Let Thy Word prove stronger still.

And when my last hour approaches,
  Let my hopes grow yet more bright,
(Since I am an heir of heaven,)
  In Thy glorious courts of light,
Fairer far than voice can tell,
There, redeemed by Christ, to dwell.

SCHMÜCKT DAS FEST MIT MAIEN.

BENJAMIN SCHMOLKE, 1672-1737: Lutheran pastor in Schweidnitz. He wrote 1188 hymns, some of them of great beauty. The date of this is 1715; translated by Miss WINKWORTH, 1855.

COME, deck our feast to-day
  With flowers and wreaths of May,
And bring an offering pure and sweet;
  The Spirit of all Grace
  Makes earth His dwelling-place;
Prepare your hearts your Lord to meet.
  Receive Him, and He shall outpour
  Such light, all hearts with joy run o'er,
And sound of tears is heard no more.

Thou Harbinger of peace,
Who makest sorrows cease,
Wisdom in word and deed is Thine;
Strong Hand of God, Thy seal
The loved of Jesus feel;
Pure Light, o'er all our pathway shine!
  Give vigorous life and healthy powers;
  O let Thy sevenfold gifts be ours,
  Refresh us with Thy gracious showers!

O touch our tongues with flame,
When speaking Jesu's name!
And lead us up the heavenward road.
Give us the power to pray,
Teach us what words to say,
Whene'er we come before our God.
  O Highest Good, our spirits cheer;
  When raging foes are strong and near,
  Give us brave hearts undimmed by fear.

O golden Rain from heaven!
Thy precious dews be given
To bless the churches' barren field!
And let Thy waters flow
Where'er the sowers sow
The seed of Truth, that it may yield
  A hundred-fold its living fruit,
  O'er all the land may take deep root,
  And mighty branches heavenward shoot.

Thou fiery Glow of Love!
Let us Thy ardors prove,

Consume our hearts with quenchless fire!
　Come, O Thou trackless Wind!
　Breathe gently o'er our mind!
Nor let the flesh to rule aspire;
　Help us our free-born right to take,
　The heavy yoke of sin to break,
　And all her tempting paths forsake.

　Be it Thine to stir our will;
　Our good intents fulfil;
Be with us when we go and come;
　Deep in our spirits dwell,
　And make their inmost cell
Thy temple pure, Thy holy home!
　Teach us to know our Lord, that we
　May call His Father ours through Thee,
　Thou Pledge of glories yet to be!

　O make our crosses sweet,
　And let Thy sunshine greet
Our longing eyes in clouded hours!
　Wing Thou our upward flight
　Toward yonder mountain bright,
Girded about with Zion's golden towers!
　Forsake us not when our last foe
　Puts forth his strength to lay us low,
　Then joyful victory bestow!

　Let us, while here we dwell,
　This one thought ponder well,

That in God's likeness we are made.
As o'er a fruitful land
Rich harvests waving stand,
We, serving Him, bear fruits that never fade,
Till Thou in whom all comfort lies
Lift us to fields above the skies,
And bid us bloom in Paradise!

HOCHGELOBTER GEIST UND HERR.

From *Liturgic Hymns of the United Brethren. Translated from the German,* 1793. The only hymn of distinctly Moravian origin that I have found fit for use here. The English hymns of that body are generally very rude, and owe their reputation largely to the fact that John Wesley's and Jacobi's translations, being found in the Moravian books, have been commonly supposed to be themselves Moravian. This is freely translated from a hymn by CHRISTIAN GREGOR (1723-1801; Moravian Bishop), and JOHN M. LAUTERBACH.

HOLY Ghost, Thou God and Lord
   Of Thy congregation,
We to Thee with one accord
   Pay our adoration.

For Thy teachings, heavenly Guide,
   O accept our praises;
Have we Thee, we're well supplied
   With good gifts and graces.

Thou explainest unto us
   Jesu's Incarnation,
And how He upon the Cross
   Purchased our salvation.

Thou fillest with the Gospel light
   Every land and nation,
Aid'st Thy witnesses with might
   Under tribulation.

Us to Jesus Thou hast brought,
   And wilt keep us ever
In the faith, which Thou hast wrought
   Through Thy Grace and favor.

With maternal faithfulness
   Lead His ransomed people,
And, to please Him, give them Grace;
   Bear them up when feeble.

Daily Jesu's flock thanks Thee
   For Thy kind tuition:
O may we obedient be
   Through Thy benediction.

Grant that we may never lose
   Till our dying moment
The rich comfort, which to us
   Flows from Christ's Atonement.

For our heavenly Father's Love,
   Jesu's great compassion,
And Thy patience, ever prove
   Our strong consolation.

Amen, Lord God, Holy Ghost!
   Endless thanks and praises
Gives to Thee the ransomed host
   In the name of Jesus.

O GOTT, O GEIST, O LICHT DES LEBENS.

GERHARD TERSTEEGEN, 1697-1769. A very eminent Pietist: wrote 111 hymns, some of which, including this one, appeared 1731. Translated by Miss WINKWORTH, 1855.

O GOD, O Spirit, Light of all that live,
   Who dost on us that sit in darkness shine,
Our darkness ever with Thy Light doth strive;
   In vain Thou lur'st us with Thy beams divine;
Yet none, O Spirit, from Thine eye can hide;
Gladly will I Thy searching glance abide.

Search all my hidden parts, whate'er impure
   Thy Light discovers there, do Thou destroy;
The bitterest pain I willingly endure,
   Such pain is followed by eternal joy:
Thou 'lt cleanse me from my stains of darkest hue,
And in Christ's image form my soul anew.

I cannot stay the venomed power of sin,
   'Tis Thy anointing only can avail:
O make my spirit new and right within;
   Without Thee all my utmost efforts fail.
Life to my cold dead soul I cannot give:
Be Thou my Life; so only shall I live.

O Breath from out the Eternal Silence, blow
   All softly o'er my spirit's barren ground;
The precious fulness of my God bestow,
   That where erst sin and shame alone were found,
Faith, love, and holy reverence may upspring,
In spirit and in truth to worship God our King.

O let my thoughts, my actions and my will
    Obedient solely to Thy impulse move;
My heart and senses keep Thou blameless still,
    Fixed and absorbed in God's unuttered Love.
Thy praying, teaching, striving, in my heart,
Let me not quench, nor make Thee to depart.

O Fount, O Spirit, who dost take and show
    Things of the Son to us, who crystal clear
From God's throne and the Lamb's dost ceaseless
        flow
    Into the quiet hearts that seek Thee here;
I open wide my mouth, and thirsting sink
Beside Thy stream, its living waves to drink.

I give myself to Thee, to Thee alone:
    From all else sundered, Thou art ever near.
The creature and myself I all disown,
    Trusting with inmost faith that God is here.
O God, O Spirit, Light of Life, we see
None ever wait in vain, who wait for Thee.

ANOTHER VERSION.

From Dr. KENNEDY's *Hymnologia Christiana*, 1863.

SPIRIT of Grace, Thou Light of Life
    Amidst the darkness of the dead,
Bright Star, whereby through worldly strife
    The people of the Lord are led,
Thou Dayspring in the deepest gloom,
Wildered and dark, to Thee I come.

Burn up in me, Thou Fire of heaven,
    The evil seen by Thee alone;
Nor spare, though heart and flesh be riven;
    For joy shall dawn when grief is gone,
And in my soul shall be restored
The glorious image of my Lord.

I languish in the plague of sin;
    O heal Thou me, and I shall live;
Renew my fainting heart within,
    And give the balm I cannot give.
Live Thou in me, O Life Divine!
The new creation's work is Thine.

O Breath from deep Eternity,
    Breathe o'er my soul's unfertile land;
So shall the pine and myrtle-tree
    Spring up amidst the desert sand,
And where Thy living water flows,
The wild shall blossom as the rose.

Let me in will and deed and word
    Obey Thee as a little child,
And in Thy love abide, O Lord,
    For ever pure and undefiled:
Teach me to work, and strive and pray,
And keep me in Thy heavenward way.

THOU WHO LOVEST US AS A FATHER.

DAVID BRUHN, 1727-1782, was a pupil of the devout Jacob Baumgarten, and was afterwards preacher in Berlin, and author of eleven hymns of no particular repute. He is not mentioned by KÜBLER. The original of this is inaccessible, and the translation is anonymous and cut from a newspaper.

THOU who lovest us as a Father,
 Faithful God! and who hast said
Thou wilt give Thy Holy Spirit
 To all those who seek His aid,
Humbly I beseech of Thee,
Father, send Him now to me,
That He may renew my heart
And set it for Thy shrine apart.

Without Him fails all my knowledge,
 Fruitfulness, and strength and life,
And my heart forgets Thy presence,
 Drowned in earthly toil and strife,
If He do not, through His might,
Set both heart and will aright,
That I to Thee may wholly give
Myself, and to Thy honor live.

Fount divine of holy blessings,
 Glorious Spirit of the Lord,
Thou by whom the human spirit
 Is to peace and truth restored;
After Thee I thirst and pine,
I to Thee myself resign;
Make me holy to God's praise,
Wise to walk in heavenly ways.

Mould me wholly in Thine image,
  Blessed Source of love and peace;
Let me love and meekness cherish,
  Let me count my gains increase,
Whene'er I with faithful hand
Can cement a peaceful band,
Or can lighten, soothe, or share
Any human load of care.

Teach me, Lord, with true self-knowledge,
  All my secret faults to see,
Humbly to my God to tell them,
  And to Him for pardon flee.
Daily make my earnest striving
To forsake them in me new:
To the work of growing holy
Ever Thou my strength renew.

To Thy work of Grace I owe it
  If there's any good in me;
This desire Thyself hast kindled,
  That I thirst and long for Thee;
Oh, to prosper through Thy word
This Thy gracious working, Lord,
That in the happy end it be
All gloriously complete in me.

O GEIST DES HERRN, NUR DEINE KRAFT.

JOHN CASPAR LAVATER, 1741-1801. The physiognomist: pastor at Zürich: remarkable for eccentricity, enthusiasm, benevolence, purity, and piety. In proof of all these qualities, see his very curious and able *Aphorisms*. This translation is by FRANCES ELIZABETH COX, whose *Hymns from the German*, 1841 (2d ed. enlarged, 1864), is a book of interest and value. I give the older text: it was afterwards revised.

O HOLY Ghost! Thy heavenly dew
   The hearts of sinners can renew;
Thou dost within our breasts abide,
And still to holy actions guide.

Thou makest the soul with joy to sing
When sorrow's clouds are deepening;
With Jesus Christ Thou makest us one,
Earnest of Heaven, from God's high throne.

Best Gift of God, and man's true Friend,
Into my inmost soul descend;
The mind of Jesus Christ impart,
And consecrate to Thee my heart.

Teach me to do my Father's will,
Beneath His guidance to lie still;
Lighten my mind, and O, incline
My heart to make His pleasure mine.

From spot and blemish make me pure,
My heavenly happiness secure;
When lost in darkness, give me light,
And cheer me through death's dreary night.

GEIST DES GLAUBENS, GEIST DER STÄRKE.

"The Spirit of the Fathers." CHARLES JOHN PHILIP SPITTA, D.D., 1801-1859: Lutheran pastor and superintendent. His hymns, 106 in number, were published in 1833 and 1843, under the title *Psaltery and Harp*. They went through a number of editions at home, and have all been translated by RICHARD MASSIE, Esq., in the First and Second Series of *Lyra Domestica*, 1860 and 1863. This and the next belong to the earlier dates.

SPIRIT, by whose operation
   Faith and holiness proceed,
Source of heavenly conversation,
   Strength in weakness, Help in need!
Spirit, by whose inspiration
   Prophets and Apostles spake,
Martyrs bled, and tribulation
   Saints endured for Jesus' sake!

Lord, endue us with Thy blessing,
   That, though babes we be in Grace,
Faith, and love, and zeal possessing
   For Thy house and holy place,
We may stake our dearest treasures,
   All the good things of this life,
Honor, wealth and darling pleasures,
   In the great and holy strife.

Give us Abram's faith unshaken
   That the promise must be true,
And what God hath undertaken
   He assuredly will do;
Which not only could unmovèd
   Trust the Covenant of Grace,
But the thing which he most lovèd
   At the Lord's disposal place.

Give us Joseph's chaste behaviour,
 When the world with crafty wiles
Seeks to draw us from the Saviour
 To herself, with frowns or smiles.
Give us grace and strength, for shunning
 This ensnaring Potiphar;
Wisdom to elude her cunning,
 Strength her open hate to bear.

Give us Moses' intercession,
 When he pleaded, wept and prayed,
That the people's sore transgression
 Might not to their charge be laid.
Let us not with selfish coldness
 See the sinner go astray,
But with Moses' holy boldness
 Plead and wrestle, weep and pray.

Give us David's bold defiance
 Of the Lord's and Israel's foes,
And, in trouble, the reliance
 Which on God, his Rock, he shows;
His right princely disposition,
 Friendship, constancy, and truth,
But still more, his deep contrition
 For the errors of his youth.

Arm us with the stern decision
 Of Elijah, in these days,
When men led by superstition
 To false gods new altars raise.

Let us shun the mere profession
  Common in our days and land,
Witnessing a good confession,
  Even if alone we stand.

Give us the Apostles' daring,
  And their bold, undaunted mood,
Threats, and fierce reproaches bearing,
  To proclaim a Saviour's Blood.
Let us to the truth bear witness,
  Which alone can make us free,
Nor leave off, until its sweetness
  All shall taste and know through Thee.

Give us Stephen's look collected,
  And his calm and cheerful mind,
When we meet with unexpected
  Trials of the sharpest kind.
In the midst of shouts and crying
  Let us with composure stand,
Open Heaven to us in dying,
  Show us Christ at God's right hand.

Spirit, by whose operation
  Faith and love and might are given,
Source of holy conversation,
  Bearing seed and fruit for heaven;
Spirit, by whose inspiration
  Prophets and Apostles spake,
Visit us with Thy salvation,
  Dwell with us for Jesus' sake!

O KOMM, DU GEIST DER WAHRHEIT.

SPITTA, 1833: translated by R. MASSIE, 1860.

DRAW, Holy Spirit, nearer,
    And in our hearts abide;
O make our judgment clearer,
    Our minds inform and guide.
O come, Thou great Renewer,
    Touch heart and lip with fire;
Make every bosom truer,
    Our aims and objects higher.

O come, Thou true Consoler,
    Thou Fire, that warms the cold;
The haughty breast's Controller,
    O come and make us bold.
On all sides danger threatens;
    Lord, to our succour come,
And arm us with the weapons
    Of early Christendom.

Hard unbelief and folly
    The Truth of God deny;
O arm us, Lord most holy,
    With weapons from on high,
With faith that never falters,
    Unmoved by fear or praise,
And love that never alters,
    And hope in darkest days.

We need a free confession
    In this our lukewarm age;
A frank and full profession
    In spite of scorn and rage;
To friend alike and foeman,
    On this, or heathen ground,
To every man and woman,
    The Gospel-trump to sound.

Where'er Thy Word is sounded,
    In far and savage lands,
The Heathen are confounded,
    And cast off Satan's bands.
On every side they waken
    To hear Thy blessed Word:
Shall it from us be taken,
    By us remain unheard?

On us, O Thou most holy,
    Thy wrath doth justly fall,
Who hear, yet through our folly
    Have not obeyed the call:
Let us with deep prostration,
    Implore God's Grace, that thus
The Word of His salvation
    Be not withdrawn from us.

Give power to those who witness
    And preach Thy holy Word,
That all may taste its sweetness,
    And rally round the Lord.

Be this our preparation,
   A heart and tongue of fire!
That this our proclamation
   May speed as we desire.

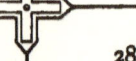

From the Danish.

THOU HOLY SPIRIT, COMFORTER SUBLIME.

The hymns of Denmark are little known here: but Mr. GILBERT TAIT has recently (London, 1868) translated a hundred of them. This one is by CHRISTENSEN.

THOU Holy Spirit, Comforter sublime;
   Thou purest Fountain of eternal Truth;
Thou who, enthroned above all space and time,
   Cleavest the darkness with Thy rays of ruth;
     Come, Thou exalted, mystic Guest,
      Through Thee may Pentecost be blest!
       O Thou, high Heaven's Dove,
        In glory, life, and love,
   Fly down, and be our rapture and our rest!

Into our bosom may Thy message steal,
   A word recalling the eternal Word:
A holy joy, a holy strength reveal;
   Enrich, inspire with things unseen, unheard.
     O cleanse our soul from leprous sin;
      Lead potent Grace in triumph in.
       Renew us in Christ's peace,
        And through the grand release
May we our deathless, priceless heirdom win!

Bound by the bonds of sacred peace we dwell
  In sweetest, in the Spirit's unity.
Through faith ecstatic may our anthems swell,
  Tones in the mighty concert of the sky!
    Let seeds from heaven scattered grow
      As heaven, fruitful here below;
    Let earth, so barren, cold,
      Bring forth a hundredfold
The trees of life, that heal all human woe.

Thou, Spirit, hast the strong foundations laid
  Which never, never can be overthrown;
Stablished thereon, in noblest grace arrayed,
  May Thy true Church increasing converts own!
    Us in our combats strengthen, cheer;
    In our temptations be Thou near;
    Us with faith's valors shield;
    Ne'er may we craven yield,
But seek immortal homes in holy fear.

RETURNED IS SACRED PENTECOST.

<small>The three which follow are taken from *Hymns for the use of the Lutheran Congregations in the Danish West India Islands. Copenhagen,* 1850. *Authorized by the Danish Government.* Of 150 hymns therein, the majority appear to be original translations, made by a person not thoroughly familiar with English. In naïve rudeness and "sweet simplicity," they resemble the early Moravian versions from the German, one of which we have ventured to insert in this book.</small>

RETURNED is sacred Pentecost:
  Be Thou our Guest, O Holy Ghost!
With God the Father and the Son
Thou from eternity art One.

O Lord, support me, proofs to give
That Jesus Christ in me doth live,
And that in none I hope and trust
But Him who came to save the lost.

I pray Thee, Holy Ghost, abide
With me, and be to Truth my Guide,
That I may never from the way
Of faith in Christ one moment stray.

Should carelessly asleep I fall,
Rouse me by Thy almighty call,
And keep me, that with greater care
I may avoid sin's hidden snare.

Without Thee I should vainly seek
The way to God and Jesus meek:
Grant therefore that Thy heavenly light
Shine always to me clear and bright.

In grief and fear and poverty
And in temptation, stay with me;
Thou art my Comforter; supply
Me with Thy comfort till I die.

Then gladly I shall bear my cross
And count as gain my worldly loss,
If thus I gain the treasure which
In Jesus Christ doth make me rich.

O Holy Ghost, I trust in Thee:
I pray that Thou wilt strengthen me,
And fill my heart with hope and faith,
And make me cheerful in my death.

BE OUR SUPPORT, O HOLY GHOST!

From the same source.

BE our support, O Holy Ghost!
　　Our lot is naught but weakness.
To dangers we are here exposed,
　　To wants, to grief and sickness.
　　　　Our flesh and blood
　　　　Are foes, O God,
　　That threaten to enslave us:
　　　　We should be lost
　　　　If, Holy Ghost,
　　Thou wert not sent to save us.

We often should be led astray
　　And lose the path forever,
If Thou didst not enlight our way,
　　And wert a Guide that never
　　　　Wilt us forsake;
　　　　If we but wake
　　When Thou dost kindly call us,
　　　　If we obey,
　　　　O Spirit, Thee,
　　No evil can befall us.

O Holy Ghost, send us Thy light,
　　Thy strength and consolation;
Watch over us by day and night,
　　Complete Thou our salvation:

Until we see
What here must be
To mortal eyes concealed,
Until at length
In light and strength
Our happiness is sealed.

GOD HOLY GHOST, TEACH US IN FAITH.

Apparently founded, to some extent, on Luther's Nun bitten wir den Heilgen Geist.

GOD Holy Ghost, teach us in faith
   To love our Saviour truly,
With all our heart, in life and death,
   And thus to serve Him duly:
That we may get from death release,
In Jesus' wounds obtain the peace
   Which is alone His merit.

Help always, that Thy doctrine sound
   May be our heart's best treasure,
And that Thy blessed Word be found
   A source of life and pleasure!
Yea, render us dead unto sin,
Born new to Heaven's peace again,
   With fruits of faith abounding!

When life and breath shall pass away,
   When death will make us shiver,
Let us Thy comfort feel, we pray,
   From sadness us deliver:

That we may then our soul commend
With confidence in Jesus' hand,
  To rest in peace and safety.

From the French.

SPIRIT OF CHARITY.

JEANNE DE LA MOTHE GUION (1647-1717), the celebrated Quietest. Her poems were written during a ten-years' imprisonment. Some of them were translated in 1782 by WILLIAM COWPER (1731-1800), and given to his friend the Rev. William Bull, who published them in 1801. Two brief extracts are here given.

SPIRIT of Charity, dispense
  Thy Grace to every heart;
Expel all other spirits thence,
  Drive self from every part.
Charity Divine, draw nigh,
Break the chains in which we lie!

All selfish souls, whate'er they feign,
  Have still a slavish lot;
They boast of liberty in vain;
  Of love, and feel it not.
He whose bosom glows with Thee,
He, and he alone, is free.

O blessedness, all bliss above,
  When Thy pure fires prevail!
Love only teaches what is love;
  All other lessons fail.
We learn its name, but not its powers;
Experience only makes it ours.

O MESSENGER of dear delight,
    Whose voice dispels the deepest night,
Sweet peace-proclaiming Dove!
With Thee at hand to soothe our pains,
No wish unsatisfied remains,
    No task, but that of love.

"HE SHALL TESTIFY OF ME."

JOHN xv. 26.

The celebrated Dr. CÉSAR MALAN, of Geneva, wrote some 83 hymns, which have been translated by JANE E. ARNOLD, and printed in London, 1866, under the title *Lyra Evangelica*. From that volume are taken the two which follow.

O HOLY Spirit, blessed Comforter,
    Who hast revealed the Saviour to my heart,
Lead me again to Him whom I adore,
    And the assurance of His Love impart.

Once in blind ignorance I loved to stray,
    And only lived the world's vain smile to share,
And thus while wandering in error's way,
    My onward path was darkness and despair.

Eternal Spirit! Thine almighty power
    Illumined this dark scene with heavenly light,
And graciously revealed in that blest hour
    Jesus, the anointed Saviour, to my sight.

But, Lord, I could not realize Thy Love,
  Nor dared to trust Thy Word and venture near,
Until, through faith in Jesus' precious Blood,
  "Peace in believing" banished all my fear.

O Holy Comforter! I bless Thy Name,
  Who hast my soul to Life eternal sealed:
By Thee my precious Saviour's Love I claim,
  And to His Will would glad obedience yield.

Lord! ever speak of Jesus to my heart;
  Help me to love Him, serve Him, and adore;
And thus prepare my spirit, here on earth,
  To dwell with Him in Heaven forever more.

"HE SHALL GUIDE YOU INTO ALL TRUTH."

JOHN xvi. 13.

SPIRIT of Truth! Thy gracious beams
  Of heavenly light impart;
Revealing all the Father's Love
  To every waiting heart.

Cause us to taste and feed upon
  The sweetness of Thy Word;
There may our precious Saviour's voice
  Celestial peace afford.

From pride and error guard our steps,
   Their latent evils show;
And lead us to the sacred founts
   Whence living waters flow.

Show us the glory of our Lord,
   And consecrate our powers
To Him through whose victorious Love
   Eternal Life is ours.

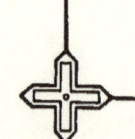

OLD ENGLISH HYMNS.

1530–1700.

O BLESSED Spirit, Who guidest and governest the Church of Christ in all truth, illuminating its doctors, strengthening its martyrs and perfecting its saints: Thou Bond of the mystical union between Christ our Head and us His members, and between the Church above and the Church below, have mercy upon us, and keep us in the unity of the faith. Amen.

OLD ENGLISH HYMNS.

1530-1700.

BISHOP MYLES COVERDALE, 1488-1569.

<small>One of the leading Reformers; translator of the Scriptures (1535), and Bishop of Exeter (1551-53). His forty *Goostly Psalmes and Spirituall Songes* appeared before 1539. Two of them, translated from Luther, are given at pp. 231, 237, of this volume. This one, which stands first of the forty in his *Remains*, is perhaps in part founded on Luther's *Komm Gott, Schöpfer*.</small>

O HOLY Spirite our Comfortoure,
    For grace and help, Lorde, now we call;
Teach us to know Christ our Savioure,
And His Father's mercy over all.
From His swete Worde let us not fall;
But lyft up our hertes alway to The,
That we may receave it thankfully.

Nowe seynge we are come together
To heare the wordes of verite;
In understandynge be Thou Guyder,
That we may folowe the voyce of The.
From straunge lernynge, Lorde, kepe us fre,
That we thorowe them be not begyled:
Kepe our understandynge undefyled.

We praye The also, blessed Lorde,
Enflame our hertes so with Thy Grace,

That in our lives we folowe Thy Worde,
And one forgeve another's trespace.
To amende our lyves, Lord, geve us space;
With Thy godly frutes endewe us all,
That from Thy Worde we never fall.

Let us not have Thy Worde only
In our mouthe and in our talkynge;
But both in dede and verite
Let us shewe it in our lyvynge.
Make us frutefull in every thynge,
And in good workes so to encrease
That whyle we lyve, we may The please.

O Lorde, lende us Thy strength and power,
To mortifie all carnall luste:
In all our trouble send us succour,
That we faynt not in The to truste.
And make us stronge to suffer with Christe,
Beynge pacient in adversite,
And in all thynges thankfull to The.

ANONYMOUS.

From the *Old Version* of the Psalms, by STERNHOLD, HOPKINS, and others, completed in 1562: or rather one of the hymns added thereto, and partly by the same writers. I know no way of ascertaining the precise date and authorship of this.

COME, Holy Spirit, God of might,
 The Comforter of all;
Teach us to know Thy Word aright,
 That we may never fall.

BEFORE SERMON.

O Holy Ghost, visit our land,
   Defend us with Thy shield;
Against all sin and wickedness,
   Lord, help us win the field.

O Lord, preserve our King, and bless
   His council, that they may
Be steadfast in the Gospel of
   Our Saviour Christ alway.

O Lord, that giv'st Thy holy Word,
   Send preachers plenteously,
That in the same we may accord,
   And therein live and die.

O Holy Spirit, guide aright
   The preachers of Thy Word,
That Thou by them may'st cut down sin
   As it were with a sword.

Depart not from Thy pastors pure,
   But aid them at their need,
Who break to us the Bread of Life
   Whereon our souls do feed.

Blessèd Spirit of Truth, keep us
   In peace and unity;
Keep us from sects and errors all
   And from all heresy.

Convert all those that are our foes
  And bring them to Thy light,
That they and we may all agree,
  And praise Thee day and night.

True faith in us, O Lord, increase,
  And let love so abound
That man and wife may live in peace
  And all about us round.

In our time give Thy peace, O Lord,
  To nations far and nigh,
And teach them all Thy Word, that they
  May sing to Thee most high.

FRANCIS KINWELMERSH.

"A member of Gray's Inn," friend of Gascoigne, and a "noted poet in the age of Elizabeth." From *The Paradise of Daintie Devises*, 1576. Reprinted in Edward Farr's *Select Poetry of the Reign of Queen Elizabeth*, 1845.

COME, Holy Ghost, eternall God,
    And ease the wofull greefe,
That through the heapes of heavy sinne
  Can noewhere find releefe:
  Do Thou, O God, redresse
    The great distresse
  Of sinfull heavinesse.

Come, comfort the afflicted thoughts
  Of my consumèd heart:

O rid the pearcing pricking paines
  Of my tormenting smart.
O Holy Ghost, graunt me
  That I by Thee
From sinne may purgèd be.

Thou art my God; to Thee alone
  I will commend my cause:
Nor glittering golde, nor precious stone,
  Shall make me leave Thy lawes.
  O teach me then the way
    Whereby I may
Make Thee my onely stay.

My lippes, my tung, my heart, and all
  Shall spread Thy mightie Name;
My voice shall never cease to sound
  The praises of the same.
  Yea, everie living thing
    Shall sweetly sing
To Thee, O heavenlie King.

RICHARD VENNARD.

"A gentleman of Lincoln's Inn," who wrote three books. This is from *The Right Way to Heaven*, 1601, through Farr's *Select Poetry*.

O HEAVENLY Spirit of especiall power,
  That in Thy hand Thy praise of praises holdest,
And from the top of Truthe's triumphant tower
The hidden fence of fairest thoughts unfoldest,

Inspire this hart and humble soule of mine
With some sweet sparkle of Thy power divine.

Teach me to think but on that onely thought,
Wherein doth live the grace of vertue's glory;
　And learn no more than what Thy Truth hath taught
To those best wits that write Thy worthie story;
Wherein is seene in heaven and earth's preserving
The highest point of praises, praise deserving.

Let not compare come neere unto none such:
　Heaven bee my thought, and let the world go by:
And say with all that, say I ne'er so much,
　All are but trifles to Thy treasurie:
For all no more than what Thy mercy giveth,
Who can behold wherein Thy glory liveth?

No, I can see the shining of the sunne,
　But cannot sound the essence of the light:
Then of Thy face, in whom that faire begunne,
　How can my soule presume to have a sight?
No, my deere God, Thy glory hath a beeing,
Where eye, nor heart, nor soule, may have a seeing.

And therefore, Lord, since such Thy glory is
As cannot be but of Thyselfe conceivèd;
　And heaven nor earthe containes that sparke of blisse
But from Thy hand of mercy is receivèd;
　What spirit can her sweetest passion raise
Neare to the due of Thy deservèd praise?

Yet since all glory doth belong to Thee,
   Thy Name in all things must bee magnified;
And by Thy mercy Thou hast made me see
   How in my soule Thou may'st be glorified:
In that sweet mercy make my soule to know
How best I may that blessed glory show.

ANONYMOUS.

<small>From a MS. of about 1600, first printed by the Religious Tract Society, 1846, under the title, *Ancient Devotional Poetry*.</small>

O HOLY Spirit, assist me with Thy Grace,
   And ope my eyes that I may see my shame;
How lewdlie I have lived before Thy face,
   And how I still persever in the same.
O Holy Comforter of all distrest,
   Behold my wretched state and pittie mee:
Lend help at length, inspire within my brest
   Thy wholesome counsells to recomfort mee:
O daigne to inhabite in my house of clay,
   And purifie it with Thy clensing power;
My ouglie sins let them be chased away.
   Regenerate me, Lord; O let this hour
Be the last instant of my fowle offending
And blest beginning of my life's amending.

EDMUND SPENSER, 1553-1598.

The seventh verse of An Hymne of Heavenly Love, and the second and third of An Hymne of Heavenlie Beautie; 1596.

YET, O most blessed Spirit! pure Lampe of Light,
    Eternal Spring of Grace and Wisdom trew,
Vouchsafe to shed into my barren spright
    Some little drop of Thy celestiall dew,
    That may my rymes with sweet infuse embrew,
And give me words equall unto my thought,
To tell the marveiles by Thy mercy wrought.

VOUCHSAFE then, O Thou most almightie
    Spright!
    From whom all gifts of wit and knowledge flow,
To shed into my breast some sparkling light
    Of Thine eternall Truth, that I may show
    Some little beames to mortall eyes below
Of that immortall Beautie there with Thee,
Which in my weake distraughted mind I see:

That with the glorie of so goodly sight
    The hearts of men, which fondly here admire
Faire seeming shewes, and feed on vaine delight,
    Transported with celestiall desire
    Of those faire formes, may lift themselves up
      hyer,
And learn to love, with zealous humble dewty,
The eternall Fountaine of that heavenly beauty.

GEORGE HERBERT, 1593–1632.

<small>Prebend of Layton Ecclesia (1626) and Rector of Bemerton (1630): the leading sacred poet of an age rich in meditative and devotional verse.</small>

WHIT-SUNDAY.

LISTEN, sweet Dove, unto my song,
    And spread Thy golden wings in me;
Hatching my tender heart so long,
Till it get wing, and fly away with Thee.

    Where is that fire which once descended
    On Thy Apostles? Thou didst then
    Keep open house, richly attended,
Feasting all comers by twelve chosen men.

    Such glorious gifts Thou didst bestow,
    That the earth did like a heaven appear;
    The stars were coming down to know
If they might mend their wages, and serve here.

    The sun, which once did shine alone,
    Hung down his head, and wished for night,
    When he beheld twelve suns for one
Going about the world, and giving light.

    But since those pipes of gold, which brought
    That cordial water to our ground,
    Were cut and martyred by the fault
Of those who did themselves through their side
        wound;

Thou shutt'st the door, and keep'st within;
Scarce a good joy creeps through the chink;
And if the braves of conquering sin
Did not excite Thee, we should wholly sink.

Lord, though we change, Thou art the same,
The same sweet God of love and light:
Restore this day, for Thy great Name,
Unto his ancient and miraculous right.

PROVIDENCE.

Some verses (the seventh to the eleventh, and the last three) of his long poem with this title. Whether they strictly belong here may be open to question.

WHEREFORE, most sacred Spirit, I here present
For me and all my fellows, praise to Thee:
And just it is that I should pay the rent,
Because the benefit accrues to me.

We all acknowledge both Thy power and love
To be exact, transcendent, and divine;
Who dost so strongly and so sweetly move,
While all things have their will, yet none but Thine.

For either Thy command, or Thy permission,
Lay hands on all: they are Thy right and left:
The first puts on with speed an expedition;
The other curbs sin's stealing pace and theft.

Nothing escapes them both; all must appear,
And be disposed, and dressed, and tuned by Thee,
Who sweetly temper'st all. If we could hear
Thy skill and art, what music would it be!

Thou art in small things great, not small in any;
Thy even praise can neither rise, nor fall.
Thou art in all things one, in each thing many:
For Thou art infinite in one and all.
. . . . . .
But who hath praise enough? nay, who hath any?
None can express Thy works, but he that knows
   them;
And none can know Thy works, which are so
   many,
And so complete, but only he that owes them.

All things that are, though they have several ways,
Yet in their being join with one advice
To honor Thee: and so I give Thee praise
In all my other hymns, but in this twice.

Each thing that is, although in use and name
It go for one, hath many ways in store
To honor Thee: and so each hymn Thy fame
Extolleth many ways, yet this one more.

GRIEVE NOT THE HOLY SPIRIT.

Ephesians iv. 30.

AND art Thou grievèd, sweet and sacred Dove,
    When I am sour,
      And cross Thy Love?
Grievèd for me? the God of strength and power
    Grieved for a worm, which when I tread,
    I pass away and leave it dead?

Then weep, mine eyes, the God of Love doth grieve.
    Weep, foolish heart,
      And weeping live;
For earth is dry as dust. Yet if ye part,
    End as the night, whose sable hue
    Your sins express: melt into dew.

When saucy mirth shall knock or call at door,
    Cry out, Get hence,
      Or cry no more.
Almighty God doth grieve, He puts on sense:
    I sin not to my grief alone,
    But to my God's too: He doth groan.

O take thy lute, and tune it to a strain
    Which may with Thee
      All day complain:
There can no discord but in ceasing be.
    Marbles can weep; and surely strings
    More bowels have than such hard things.

Lord, I adjudge myself to tears and grief;
  Even endless tears
  Without relief.
If a clear spring for me no time forbears,
  But runs, although I be not dry;
  I am no crystal, what shall I?

Yet if I wail not still, since still to wail
  Nature denies,
  And flesh would fail
If my deserts were masters of mine eyes;
  Lord, pardon, for Thy Son makes good
  My want of tears with store of blood.

THE SAME REWRITTEN.

By JOHN WESLEY, 1739. In his *Hymns and Sacred Poems* of that date he printed some 42 hymns modernized and popularized "from Herbert." Only one of them has come into use, the noble "Teach me, my God and King": and only one other has any special merit: they have usually been passed by without notice. And yet John Wesley had it in him to be nearly or quite as great a poet as his brother Charles. Some of his versions from the German (chiefly published in the same book of 1739) are among the grandest of all our English hymns. None of them, unfortunately for us, come within the range of this volume.

AND art Thou grieved, O Sacred Dove,
  When I despise or cross Thy Love?
Grieved for a worm; when every tread
Crushes, and leaves the reptile dead?

Then mirth be ever banished hence,
Since Thou art pained by my offence:
I sin not to my grief alone,
The Comforter within doth groan.

Then weep, my eyes, for God doth grieve!
Weep, foolish heart, and weeping live:
Tears for the living mourner plead,
But ne'er avail the hopeless dead.

Lord, I adjudge myself to grief,
To endless tears without relief:
Yet O! to exact Thy due forbear,
And spare a feeble creature, spare!

Still if I wail not, (still to wail
Nature denies, and flesh would fail)
Lord, pardon — for Thy Son makes good
My want of tears, with store of blood.

JOSEPH BEAUMONT, D.D., 1615-1699.

King's Professor of Divinity at Cambridge; a man of great repute in his day, and author of *Psyche*, the longest poem in the language, now utterly forgotten. A selection from his shorter poems was published in quarto half a century after his death, and seems to have been overlooked by the critics and collectors, though some of them are extremely fine. The verses which follow are probably from his *Cathemerina*, or morning devotions, written in the summer of 1652.

WHIT-SUNDAY.

I.

FOUNTAIN of sweets! Eternal Dove!
  Which leav'st Thy glorious perch above,
And hovering down, vouchsafest thus
To make Thy nest below with us:

Soft as Thy softest feathers, may
We find Thy Love to us to-day;
And in the shelter of Thy wing
Obtain Thy leave and grace to sing.

II.

TUNE we our heart-strings high,
  And to the Heavenly Dove,
As we are able, fly
  On vocal wings of love :
To Him our thanks and praises pay
In all the tongues He gave to-day.

ROBERT HERRICK. Born 1591.

From his *Noble Numbers*, 1647. Two very curious verses, the fourth and fifth, are here, as in most editions of the poem, omitted.

LITANIE TO THE HOLY SPIRIT.

IN the houre of my distress,
  When temptations me oppresse,
And when I my sins confesse,
  Sweet Spirit, comfort me.

When I lie within my bed,
Sick in heart and sick in head,
And with doubts discomforted,
  Sweet Spirit, comfort me.

When the house doth sigh and weepe,
And the world is drowned in sleepe,
Yet mine eyes the watch doe keepe,
    Sweet Spirit, comfort me.

When the passing bell doth tole,
And the furies, in a shole,
Come to fright a parting soule,
    Sweet Spirit, comfort me.

When the tapers now burn blue,
And the comforters are few,
And that number more than true,
    Sweet Spirit, comfort me.

When the priest his last hath praid,
And I nod to what is said,
'Cause my speech is now decaid,
    Sweet Spirit, comfort me.

When God knowes I'm tost about,
Either with despaire or doubt,
Yet, before the glasse be out,
    Sweet Spirit, comfort me.

When the tempter me pursu'th
With the sins of all my youth,
And half damns me with untruth,
    Sweet Spirit, comfort me.

When the flames and hellish cries
Fright mine ears and fright mine eyes,
And all terrors me surprise,
    Sweet Spirit, comfort me.

When the judgment is revealed,
And that opened which was sealed,
When to THEE I have appealed,
　　Sweet Spirit, comfort me.

HENRY MORE, 1614-1687.

Fellow and Tutor of Christ's College, Cambridge. From his *Psychozoia, or the Song of the Soul, containing a Christiano-Platonic Display of Life*, 1640.

O THOU eternal Spright! cleave ope the skie,
　　And take Thy flight into my feeble breast;
Enlarge my thoughts, enlight my dimmer eye,
That wisely, of that burthen (closely prest
In my strait mind) I may be dispossest.
My muse must sing of things of mickle weight;
The soule's eternitie is my great guest.
Do Thou me guide: Thou art the soule's sure Light;
Grant that I never err, but ever wend aright.

JOHN AUSTIN. Died 1669.

A Romanist, and author or compiler of *Devotions in the Ancient Way of Offices*, 1668. This was "reformed" by THEOPHILUS DORRINGTON, 1686, and by Mrs. SUSANNA HOPTON a little later: her version, edited by Dean (or Bishop) Hickes, has been several times reprinted.

I.

COME, Holy Spirit, come and breathe
　　Thy spicy odors on the face
Of our dull regions here beneath,
　　And fill our souls with Thy sweet Grace.

Come and root out the poisonous weeds
  Which overrun and choke our lives;
And in our hearts plant Thine own seeds,
  Whose quickening power our spirit revives.

First plant the humble violet there,
  Which dwells secure by dwelling low;
Then let the lily next appear,
  And make us chaste, yet fruitful too.

But O, plant all the virtues, Lord,
  And let the metaphors alone:
Repeat once more that mighty word;
  Thou need'st but say, Let it be done.

We can, alas, nor be, nor grow,
  Unless Thy powerful mercy please;
Thy Hand must plant and water too,
  Thy Hand alone must give the increase.

Do then what Thou alone canst do,
  Do what to Thee so easy is:
Conduct us through this world of woe,
  And place us safe in Thine own bliss.

All glory to the sacred Three,
  One ever-living sovereign Lord;
As at the first, still may He be
  Beloved and praised, feared and adored.

A modern abridgment of the above is found in JOHN BICKERSTETH's *Psalms and Hymns*, 4th edition, 1832.

COME, Holy Spirit, come and breathe
  Fresh fragrance on a weary soil;
By Thee, dispelled the shades of death,
  The barren wilderness shall smile.

All noxious weeds root out, destroy;
  Plant trees of righteousness around;
Thy quickening gracious power employ,
  And plenteous may the fruit be found.

Let holy graces live and grow,
  Faith, hope, and love, and joy and peace:
Thou art their Source, from Thee they flow;
  O grant the wished for rich increase.

II.

This fine hymn has been introduced into a few collections, and lately rewritten by the Rev. W. J. BLEW.

COME, mild and holy Dove,
  Descend into our breast;
Do Thou in us, make us in Thee
  Forever dwell and rest.

Come, and spread o'er our heads
  Thy soft all-cherishing wing,
That in its shade we safe may sit,
  And to Thee praises sing:

To Thee who giv'st us Life,
  Our better Life of Grace;
Who giv'st us breath, and strength, and speed
  To run and win our race.

If by the way we faint,
    Thou reachest forth Thy hand;
If our own weakness makes us fall,
    Thou mak'st our weakness stand.

When we are sliding back,
    Thou dost our danger stop;
When we again, alas, are fallen,
    Again Thou tak'st us up.

Else there we still must lie,
    And still sink lower down;
Our hope to rise is all from Thee,
    Our ruin's all our own.

O my ingrateful soul!
    What shall our dulness do
For Him that does all this for us,
    Only our love to woo?

We'll love Thee then, dear Lord,
    But Thou must give that love;
We'll humbly beg it of Thy Grace,
    But Thou our prayers must move.[1]

---

[1] This is Mr. BLKW's revision of vv. 8 and 9:—

    Be Thou our Strength, O Lord,
      Our Life by which we live;
    Our Love, our Joy, our Hope; but Thou
      That Life of love must give.

    Speak Thou within our souls;
      Our prayers within us pray:
    And hear Thyself within us speak,
      For Thine own prayers are they.

O hear Thine own Self speak,
    For Thou in us dost pray;
Thou canst as quickly grant as ask,
    Thy Grace knows no delay.

Glory to Thee, O Lord,
    One coeternal Three;
To Father, Son, and Holy Ghost,
    One equal glory be.

JOHN RAWLET.

Author of *Poetick Miscellanies*, 1687. I take this and the next through the great Moravian Collection of 1754, and cannot answer for the text.

O SACRED Spirit, within my soul repeat
    Those blessings, which once made this day so great;
Breathe Thou upon me with that heavenly Wind
Which may refresh and purify my mind.

Kindle within me and preserve that Fire
Which may with holy love my breast inspire,
And with an active zeal my mind inflame
To do Thy will, to glorify Thy Name.

Furnish me richly both with gifts and Grace
To fit me for the duties of my place:
So open Thou my lips, my heart so raise,
That both my heart and mouth may give Thee
    praise.

As in Thy temple, keep Thou residence
Within my soul, and never part from thence,
Till I am framed and fitted by Thy Hand
A pillar in God's House above to stand.

LANCELOT ADDISON, D.D., 1632–1703.

Dean of Lichfield, and father of Joseph Addison. He published some theological treatises, and a small volume, now rare, of *Devotional Poems*, 1699.

COME, blessed Spirit, descend and light on me;
    Give me one beam of Thy Divinity;
One, 'bove whatever yet Thou didst impart,
Since first Thou didst inflame my teeming heart.

Thou didst descend in cloven tongues and fire;
O touch my tongue, and my cold heart inspire,
That the one may praise Thee, and the other love
Thee, and those mansions (whence Thou cam'st)
    above.

Thou say'st Thou 'rt grieved, when we refuse Thy
    Grace,
And Thy blest intimations find no place:
And art Thou grieved for me, blest Spirit of Love?
Oh, though Thou grieve, do not from me remove!

For me hast Thou been grieved, been grieved by
    me:
O let me grieve, that e'er I grievèd Thee;
And by Thy conduct, aid, and sacred fires,
Yet may I see the Land of my desires.

ENGLISH HYMNS

OF THE

EIGHTEENTH CENTURY.

O GOOD Paraclete, O eternal Virtue, O true Charity, and loving Eternity, gentle SPIRIT, abundantly replenish my heart with the sweetness of faith, hope, and charity; ever inflame it with the love of Thee and of my neighbor, that, ever cleaving to Thy service, I may obtain remission of my sins from Thee, the Fountain of mercies. Amen.

O HOLY SPIRIT, drive from me the cruel enemy; bestow on me true affection, and the plentiful gifts of charity; and grant that my conscience, serving Thee, may advance from day to day, and may submit itself to Thy unfailing Grace. Amen.

ENGLISH HYMNS OF THE EIGHTEENTH CENTURY.

ISAAC WATTS, D.D., 1674-1748.

The father of English hymnody, and perhaps still, by suffrage of the majority, the most popular of English hymnists; though hardly to be accounted the best. Of his 800 hymns and more (including his paraphrases of the Psalms) all that celebrate the Holy Ghost, except a few scattered verses, are here given. He has another beginning, "Descend from Heaven, immortal Dove," but the bulk of it is about a different subject. The first and third of these appeared in 1707, the second in 1709.

THE WITNESSING AND SEALING SPIRIT.

Rom. viii. 14, 16. Eph. i. 13, 14.

WHY should the children of a King
    Go mourning all their days?
Great Comforter! descend and bring
    Some tokens of Thy Grace.

Dost Thou not dwell in all the saints,
    And seal them [1] heirs of heaven?
When wilt Thou banish my complaints,
    And show my sins forgiven?

Assure my conscience of her part
    In the Redeemer's Blood;
And bear Thy witness with my heart
    That I am born of God.

---

[1] In many editions it is *the* heirs.

Thou art the Earnest of His Love,
The Pledge of joys to come;
And Thy soft wings, celestial Dove,
Will safe convey me home.

THE OPERATIONS OF THE HOLY SPIRIT.

ETERNAL Spirit, we confess
And sing the wonders of Thy Grace:
Thy power conveys our blessings down
From God the Father and the Son.

Enlightened by Thine heavenly ray,
Our shades and darkness turn to day;
Thine inward teachings make us know
Our danger, and our refuge too.

Thy power and glory work[1] within,
And break the chains of reigning sin;
Do our imperious lusts subdue,
And form our wretched hearts anew.

The troubled conscience knows Thy voice;
Thy cheering words awake our joys;
Thy words allay the stormy wind,
And calm the surges of the mind.

---

[1] In some early editions the verb throughout this verse is singular, — *works* within, *breaks, doth, forms.*

BREATHING AFTER THE HOLY SPIRIT: OR FERVENCY OF DEVOTION DESIRED.

COME, Holy Spirit, heavenly Dove,
    With all Thy quickening powers;
Kindle a flame of sacred love
    In these cold hearts of ours.

Look, how we grovel here below,
    Fond of these trifling toys:
Our souls can neither fly nor go
    To reach eternal joys.

In vain we tune our formal songs,
    In vain we strive to rise;
Hosannas languish on our tongues,
    And our devotion dies.

Dear Lord! and shall we ever lie[1]
    At this poor dying rate?
Our love so faint, so cold to Thee,
    And Thine to us so great?

Come, Holy Spirit, heavenly Dove,
    With all Thy quickening powers,
Come, shed abroad a Saviour's Love,
    And that shall kindle ours.

---

[1] In some modern editions, *live*.

SIMON BROWNE, 1680-1732.

Pastor at Portsmouth, and at the Old Jewry, London. In 1723 he met with some misfortunes, which preyed upon his mind, and produced that singular case of monomania, recorded in the text-books of Mental Philosophy: he thought that God had "annihilated in him the thinking substance, and utterly divested him of consciousness." Notwithstanding, says Toplady, "instead of having no soul, he wrote, reasoned, and prayed as if he had two." His works amount to 23, some of them still in repute. His *Hymns and Spiritual Songs, in Three Books, designed as a Supplement to Dr. Watts*, appeared in 1720, and again in 1741 and 1760. They number 166, of which this is far the best.

THE SOUL GIVING ITSELF UP TO THE CONDUCT AND INFLUENCE OF THE HOLY SPIRIT.

COME, Holy Spirit, heavenly Dove,
    My sinful maladies remove:
Be Thou my Light, be Thou my Guide;
O'er every thought and step preside.

The light of Truth to me display,
That I may know and choose my way;
Plant holy fear within mine heart,
That I from God may ne'er depart.

Conduct me safe, conduct me far
From every sin and hurtful snare;
Lead me to God, my final Rest,
In His enjoyment to be blest.

Lead me to Christ, the living Way,
Nor let me from His pastures stray.
Lead me to Heaven, the seat of bliss,
Where pleasure in perfection is.

Lead me to holiness, the road
That I must take, to dwell with God;
Lead to Thy Word, that rules must give,
And sure directions how to live.

Lead me to Means of Grace, where I
May own my wants, and seek supply;
Lead to Thyself, the Spring from whence
To fetch all quickening influence.

Thus I, conducted still by Thee,
Of God a child beloved shall be;
Here to His family pertain,
Hereafter with Him ever reign.

ANONYMOUS, 1733.

<small>From a very curious "Specimen" of ten hymns, with music, appended to a sermon by Arthur Bedford, *The Excellency of Divine Music*, 1733. This is probably older, but I have not traced it further back. Six verses of it, altered, are in John Arnold's *Compleat Psalmodist*, third edition, 1753; and four (vv. 1, 4, 5, and 6) in the American Prayer-Book Collection.</small>

HE'S come! let every knee be bent,
    All hearts new joys resume;
Let nations sing with one consent,
    The Comforter is come!

No troubled thoughts molest our peace,
    This day all grief retire;
Let every fear forever cease,
    And every doubt expire.

There is no end of the content
    And joy the Spirit brings;
Happy the man to whom 'tis lent!
    That man sees wondrous things.

What greater gift, what greater love
    Can God on man bestow?
'Tis half the angels' heaven above,
    And all our heaven below.

Hail, blessed Spirit! not a soul
    But doth Thy goodness feel;
Thou dost our darling sins control,
    And fix our wavering zeal.

Thou to the conscience dost convey
    The checks that all must know;
Thy motions first do show the way,
    Then give us strength to go.

As pilots by the compass steer,
    Till they their harbor find,
So do Thy sacred breathings here
    Guide every wandering mind.

The flesh may strive our course t' impeach,
    The world's rough billows roar,
But by Thy help we're sure to reach
    The safe eternal shore.

THOMAS CONEY, D.D.

Prebendary of Wells, and Rector of Chedzoy in Somersetshire: author of several volumes of Sermons, and of *The Devout Soul: consisting of Meditations, Poems, Hymns, and Prayers*, 1722. It is in two parts, the first being "An Entertainment for a Penitent," and the other "An Entertainment for the Thankful." The second of these affords us the following "Poem."

O THOU propitious Paraclete!
    Thou Holy Spirit, Eternal Lord!
Who man's redemption didst complete,
    And still to man dost aid afford!

Whilst I to Thee address my song,
    And venture on Thy boundless praise,
Be pleased to guide my faltering tongue,
    And elevate my humble lays.

When the almighty God declared
    This spacious fabric of a world
From barren Nothing should be reared,
    And round its infant axis hurled;

Thy brooding and prolific wings
    On medly Chaos sat at first,
To hatch the seeds of future things
    And fix the vital stamp on dust.

'Twas Thou the holy Prophets' breast
    With sacred ecstasy didst fill,
And mad'st unerring tongues confess
    The latent counsels of Thy Will.

Great David's soul Thou didst inspire,
   When the melodious harp he strung;
Thou didst supply the poet's fire
   And fit the numbers of his song.

And when no thoughts Thou wilt impart,
   Ye wretched rhymers, 'tis in vain
For you, the meaner sons of art,
   To torture your unteeming brain.

Great Guardian of my Saviour's Spouse,
   Who dost her faithful sons secure;
Who dost maintain the servant's cause,
   And the declining Master's power!

Thou art of learning's stores possest,
   And dost Thy various gifts impart
To inspire the sacred pastor's breast,
   And the dull stupid flock convert.

Into the pious martyr's mind
   What rapturous joy dost Thou inspire,
When, to the burning stake confined,
   He triumphs in the midst of fire!

Thou mak'st the timorous virgins dare
   Boldly resign their holy breath;
Virgins, whose softer natures fear
   The rude alarms of ghastly death.

Even these (the foremost in the list of fame),
   When Thou Heaven's glories dost display,
Have clasped and hugged the friendly flame
   Which bore their struggling life away.

O blessed Spirit! whether I
   By lingering pains must end my days,
Or by some sudden stroke must die,
   Assist me as my strength decays.

Through all the frightful paths of death,
   Aid me with Thy reviving Grace;
And when I quit this mortal earth,
   Transport me to a better place.

THOMAS HARRISON.

Poems on Divine Subjects, Second Edition, 1721. I take this from the Moravian Collection of 1754.

COME, Holy Ghost, celestial Dove,
   Fill me with light, with joy and love;
By Thee inspired, to Thee I 'll raise
A tribute of unfeignèd praise.

My soul, by sin's strong chains confined,
Thou in a moment canst unbind:
All solid pleasures flow from Thee,
Whose office 'tis to comfort me.

JAMES CRAIG, 1682-1744.

"A native of East Lothian; one of the most popular preachers in Edinburgh." He published three volumes of Sermons, and *Spiritual Life: Poems on Several Divine Subjects*, 1727: Second Edition, 1751. I give the last of eleven verses, composing a very long piece on the various offices of the Spirit.

A HYMN TO THE HOLY SPIRIT.

DEAR Comforter of pious souls!
    How sweet the heavenly torrent rolls,
When from on high Thou dost impart
Thy consolations to the humble heart!
How oft have I by sweet experience found,
    When sore dejected and opprest
    With troubles like to rend my breast,
Thy joys control my grief, and heal my bleeding wound!
    O God of Grace, what thanks I owe
To Thee, from whom my daily succors flow!
    How kind, how potent Thy supplies,
    Which balance my infirmities;
    Which strengthen me, a feeble worm,
    To bear the burden, stand the storm
    Of trials and hard-pressing woes!
    By Thee I triumph o'er my foes,
    The world, my lusts, the powers of hell;
    By Thee I am instructed well
    In dear religion's pleasant ways.
    By Thee I vent my heart in praise:
    By Thee with humble zealous care
    My task I ply: with me in prayer

  Thou interced'st with mighty moans,
  With secret sympathizing groans,
Which though I can't express, attentive Heaven
    does hear.
  Yea, by sure signs in me revealed,
  Methinks I dare be bold to say
  That by Thy Grace divine I'm sealed
  To the complete redemption-day.
  Meanwhile, my Guide, to Thee resigned,
  With humble and obsequious mind,
  Whate'er Thou bid'st I'll willing do,
  Where'er Thou lead'st I cheerful go;
Till at the end of Life's laborious path
  I smiling meet approaching Death:
  And then, my God, in transports lost,
'Midst a detachment of the heavenly host
With speed my soul her flight to Heaven shall wing,
  Where Father, Son, and Holy Ghost
She ever shall behold, and ever, ever sing.

JOHN WRIGHT.

Author of *The Best Mirth; or the Melody of Zion.* 1727. The abrupt and awkward ending of this piece is given unchanged, from a reprint (1800) of "the Second Edition corrected," 1745.

ON THE NORTH AND SOUTH WIND.

CANTICLES iv. 16.

A WAKE, awake, Thou Spirit sweet,
  Give me a taste of Thee,
And deal with me as Thou seest meet;
  Let me Thy power see.

But since Thou know'st my frame is weak,
    Deal tenderly with me;
My soul is sore; wound me no more,
    But make me trust in Thee.

My soul is blasted with the cold
    Of winter, and I fade.
Forsake me not when I am old:
    Of dust Thou hast me made.

What is my garden, Lord, to Thee,
    That Thou should'st dwell therein?
What have I done, that Thy dear Son
    Should save me from my sin?

My ground is dry, but, Lord, draw nigh,
    And water me this day:
My spices shall bring forth withal,
    If Thou Thy Love display.

Come, eat Thy pleasant fruit, my Joy,
    My Love, my Lord, my Life;
And let no evil me destroy,
    But free my soul from strife.

Indeed there is no grace in me
    To make Thy soul rejoice:
The stock of Grace is laid in Thee;
    O let me hear Thy voice.

The voice of others change so oft
    There is no certainty;
When they have set my hopes aloft,
    They leave me with a lie.

SAMUEL WESLEY, Jr., 1690–1739.

Elder brother of John and Charles, and no mean poet. He was usher at Westminster School till 1732, and then head-master of the Free School at Tiverton. His Poems appeared 1736, and were reprinted 1743 and 1862. This is one of a series of four hymns to the Trinity.

AN HYMN TO GOD THE HOLY GHOST.

HAIL, Holy Ghost, Jehovah, Third
    In order of the Three,
Sprung from the Father and the Word
    From all eternity!

Thy Godhead brooding o'er the abyss
    Of formless waters lay,
Spoke into order all that is,
    And darkness into day.

In lowest hell, or heaven's height,
    Thy presence who can fly?
Known is the Father to Thy sight,
    The depths of Deity.

Thy power through Jesu's life displayed,
    Quite from the Virgin's womb,
Dying, His soul an offering made,
    And raised Him from the tomb.

God's image, which our sins destroy,
    Thy Grace restores below,
And truth and holiness and joy
    From Thee their Fountain flow.

Hail, Holy Ghost, Jehovah, Third
  In order of the Three,
Throned with the Father and the Word
  Through all eternity.

CHARLES WESLEY, 1708-1788.

"Author of a great number of the best hymns in the English, or any other language." So says JAMES MONTGOMERY in his *Christian Poet*, 1827. Yet from reasons apparent to the thoughtful reader, the immense mass of Wesley's poetry can be more freely used in books intended merely for private reading, than in such as aim to assist "the service of song in the house of the Lord." We have here drawn without stint from the liberal store. His verses, when taken at random, are in style far above the average of other reputable writers, and in matter generally of historical if not of intrinsic interest. Our extracts are given chronologically, in the order of their appearance.

HEAR, HOLY SPIRIT, HEAR.

From his first volume, *Hymns and Sacred Poems*, 1739.

HEAR, Holy Spirit, hear,
  My inward Comforter!
Loosed by Thee, my stammering tongue
  First essays to praise Thee now:
This the new, the joyful song:
  Hear it in Thy temple Thou!

Long o'er my formless soul
  The dreary waves did roll:
Void I lay and sunk in night:
  Thou, the overshadowing Dove,
Call'dst the chaos into light,
  Bad'st me be, and live, and love.

Thee I exult to feel,
   Thou in my heart dost dwell:
There Thou bear'st Thy witness true,
   Shed'st the Love of God abroad;
I in Christ a creature new,
   I, even I, am born of God!

Ere yet the time was come
   To fix in me Thy home,
With me oft Thou didst reside:
   Now, my God, Thou in me art!
Here Thou ever shalt abide;
   One we are, no more to part.

Fruit of the Saviour's prayer,
   My promised Comforter!
Thee the world cannot receive,
   Thee they neither know nor see;
Dead is all the life they live,
   Dark their light, while void of Thee.

Yet I partake Thy Grace
   Through Christ my Righteousness:
Mine the gifts Thou dost impart,
   Mine the unction from above,
Pardon written on my heart,
   Light, and life, and joy, and love.

Thy gifts, blest Paraclete,
   I glory to repeat:

Sweetly sure of Grace I am,
　　Pardon to my soul applied,
Interest in the spotless Lamb;
　　Dead for all, for me He died.

　　Thou art Thyself the Seal:
　　　　I more than pardon feel,
　　Peace, unutterable peace,
　　　　Joy that ages ne'er can move,
　　Faith's assurance, hope's increase,
　　　　All the confidence of love.

　　Pledge of Thy promise given,
　　　　My antepast of Heaven;
　　Earnest Thou of joys divine,
　　　　Joys divine on me bestowed;
　　Heaven, and Christ, and all is mine,
　　　　All the plenitude of God.

　　Thou art my inward Guide,
　　　　I ask no help beside:
　　Arm of God, to Thee I call,
　　　　Weak as helpless infancy:
　　Weak I am — yet cannot fall,
　　　　Stayed by faith, and led by Thee.

　　Hear, Holy Spirit, hear,
　　　　My inward Comforter!
　　Loosed by Thee, my stammering tongue
　　　　First essays to praise Thee now:
　　This the new, the joyful song:
　　　　Hear it in Thy temple Thou!

COME, HOLY GHOST, ALL QUICKENING FIRE.

1739.

COME, Holy Ghost, all-quickening Fire,
    Come, and in me delight to rest;
Drawn by the lure of strong desire,
    O come and consecrate my breast:
The temple of my soul prepare,
And fix Thy sacred presence there!

If now Thy influence I feel,
    If now in Thee begin to live,
Still to my heart Thyself reveal;
    Give me Thyself, for ever give.
A point my good, a drop my store:
Eager I ask, and pant for more.

Eager for Thee I ask and pant,
    So strong the principle divine
Carries me out with sweet constraint,
    Till all my hallowed soul be Thine;
Plung'd in the Godhead's deepest sea,
And lost in Thy Immensity.

My Peace, my Life, my Comfort now,
    My Treasure, and my All Thou art!
True Witness of my sonship Thou,
    Engraving pardon on my heart;
Seal of my sins in Christ forgiven,
Earnest of Love, and pledge of Heaven.

Come then, my God, mark out Thy heir,
  Of Heaven a larger earnest give;
With clearer light Thy witness bear;
  More sensibly within me live;
Let all my powers Thy entrance feel,
And deeper stamp Thyself the Seal.

Come, Holy Ghost, all-quickening Fire,
  Come, and in me delight to rest;
Drawn by the lure of strong desire,
  O come and consecrate my breast:
The temple of my soul prepare,
And fix Thy sacred presence there!

HYMN TO GOD THE SANCTIFIER.

From Hymns and Sacred Poems, 1740.

COME, Holy Ghost, all-quickening Fire,
  Come, and my hallowed heart inspire,
    Sprinkled with the atoning Blood:
Now to my soul Thyself reveal;
Thy mighty working let me feel,
    And know that I am born of God.

Thy witness with my spirit bear
That God, my God, inhabits there:
    Thou, with the Father and the Son,
Eternal Light's coeval Beam:
Be Christ in me, and I in Him.
    Till perfect we are made in one.

HYMN TO GOD THE SANCTIFIER.

When wilt Thou my whole heart subdue?
Come, Lord, and form my soul anew,
　Emptied of pride, self-will, and hell;
Less than the least of all Thy store
Of mercies, I myself abhor;
　All, all my vileness may I feel.

Humble, and teachable, and mild,
O may I, as a little child,
　My lowly Master's steps pursue!
Be anger to my soul unknown;
Hate, envy, jealousy, be gone:
　In love create thou all things new.

Let earth no more my heart divide;
With Christ may I be crucified,
　To Thee with my whole soul aspire;
Dead to the world and all its toys,
Its idle pomp and fading joys,
　Be Thou alone my one desire.

Be Thou my joy, be Thou my dread;
In battle cover Thou my head.
　Nor earth nor hell so shall I fear;
So shall I turn my steady face,
Want, pain defy, enjoy disgrace,
　Glory in dissolution near.

My will be swallowed up in Thee;
Light in Thy light still may I see,

Beholding Thee with open face:
  Called the full power of faith to prove,
  Let all my hallowed heart be love,
    And all my spotless life be praise.

Come, Holy Ghost, all-quickening Fire,
My consecrated heart inspire,
  Sprinkled with the atoning Blood:
Still to my soul Thyself reveal;
Thy mighty working may I feel,
  And know that I am one with God!

BEFORE READING THE SCRIPTURES.

1740.

COME, Holy Ghost, our hearts inspire;
  Let us Thy influence prove;
Source of the old prophetic fire,
  Fountain of life and love.

Come, Holy Ghost, (for moved by Thee
  Thy prophets wrote and spoke,)
Unlock the Truth, Thyself the Key,
  Unseal the sacred Book.

Expand Thy wings, prolific Dove;
  Brood o'er our nature's night;
On our disordered spirits move,
  And let there now be light.

God through Himself we then shall know,
  If Thou within us shine;
And sound, with all Thy saints below,
  The depths of Love divine.

HYMNS ON THE LORD'S SUPPER.

1745.

I.

COME, Thou everlasting Spirit,
  Bring to every thankful mind
All the Saviour's dying merit,
  All His sufferings for mankind:
True Recorder of His Passion,
  Now the living faith impart;
Now reveal His great Salvation,
  Preach His Gospel to our heart.

Come, thou Witness of His dying;
  Come, Remembrancer divine;
Let us feel Thy power applying
  Christ to every soul, and mine;
Let us groan Thine inward groaning,
  Look on Him we pierced, and grieve;
All receive the Grace atoning,
  All the sprinkled Blood receive.

II.

COME, Holy Ghost, Thine influence shed,
    And realize the sign,
Thy life infuse into the bread,
    Thy power into the wine.

Effectual let the tokens prove,
    And made by heavenly art
Fit channels to convey Thy Love
    To every faithful heart.

III.

COME, Thou Spirit of contrition,
    Fill our souls with tender fears;
Conscious of our lost condition,
    Melt us into gracious tears.
Just and holy detestation
    Of our bosom sins impart,
Sins that caused our Saviour's Passion,
    Sins that stabbed Him to the heart.

Fill our flesh with killing anguish,
    All our members crucify;
Let the offending nature languish
    Till on Jesu's Cross it die.
All our sins to death deliver,
    Let not one, not one survive:
Then we live to God forever,
    Then in heaven on earth we live.

SPIRIT OF FAITH, COME DOWN.

From Hymns of Petition and Thanksgiving for the Promise of the Father, *otherwise called* Hymns for Whit-Sunday, 1746.

SPIRIT of Faith, come down,
    Reveal the things of God,
And make to us the Godhead known,
    And witness with the Blood:
'Tis Thine the Blood to apply,
    And give us eyes to see
Who did for every sinner die
    Hath surely died for me.

No man can truly say
    That Jesus is the Lord,
Unless Thou take the veil away,
    And breathe the living Word;
Then, only then we feel
    Our interest in His Blood;
And cry with joy unspeakable,
    "Thou art my Lord, my God!"

I know my Saviour lives,
    He lives, who died for me;
My inmost soul His voice receives
    Who hangs on yonder Tree:
Set forth before my eyes
    Even now I see Him bleed,
And hear His mortal groans and cries,
    While suffering in my stead.

O that the world might know
　　The great atoning Lamb!
Spirit of Faith, descend, and show
　　The virtue of His Name:
The Grace which all may find,
　　The saving power impart;
And testify to all mankind,
　　And speak in every heart!

Inspire the living faith,
　　(Which whosoe'er receives
The witness in himself he hath,
　　And consciously believes;)
The faith that conquers all,
　　And doth the mountain move,
And saves whoe'er on Jesus call,
　　And perfects them in love.

COME, HOLY, CELESTIAL DOVE.
1746.

COME, holy, celestial Dove,
　　To visit a sorrowful breast,
My burden of guilt to remove,
　　And bring me assurance and rest.
Thou only hast power to relieve
　　A sinner o'erwhelmed with his load;
The sense of acceptance to give,
　　And sprinkle his heart with the Blood.

With me if of old Thou hast strove,
   And strangely withheld from my sin,
And tried, by the lure of Thy Love,
   My worthless affections to win:
The work of Thy mercy revive;
   Thine uttermost mercy exert;
And kindly continue to strive,
   And hold, till I yield Thee, my heart.

Thy call if I ever have known,
   And sighed from myself to get free,
And groaned the unspeakable groan,
   And longed to be happy in Thee;
Fulfil the imperfect desire!
   Thy peace to my conscience reveal,
The sense of Thy favor inspire,
   And give me my pardon to feel.

If when I had put Thee to grief,
   And madly to folly returned,
Thy pity hath been my relief,
   And lifted me up as I mourned;
Most pitiful Spirit of Grace,
   Relieve me again, and restore;
My spirit in holiness raise,
   To fall and to suffer no more.

If now I lament after God,
   And gasp for a drop of Thy Love,
If Jesus hath bought Thee with Blood,
   For me to receive from above;

Come, heavenly Comforter, come,
True Witness of mercy divine;
And make me Thy permanent home,
And seal me eternally Thine!

AUTHOR OF EVERY WORK DIVINE.

In the *Hymns for Whit-Sunday*, 1746, this is numbered as four successive hymns: but it is evidently a unit, and is best given as four parts of the same poem. The first part, with its breadth and beauty of thought, recalls some of the finer mediæval hymns.

I.

AUTHOR of every work divine,
Who dost through both Creations shine,
The God of Nature and of Grace!
Thy glorious steps in all we see,
And wisdom attribute to Thee,
And power, and majesty, and praise.

Thou didst Thy mighty wings outspread,
And brooding o'er the chaos, shed
Thy Life into the impregned abyss,
The vital principle infuse,
And out of Nothing's womb produce
The earth and heaven, and all that is.

That all informing Breath Thou art
Who dost continued life impart,
And bidd'st the world persist to be:

Garnished by Thee, yon azure sky,
And all those beauteous orbs on high,
  Depend in golden chains from Thee.

Thou dost create the earth anew,
(Its Maker and Preserver too,)
  By Thine almighty arm sustain:
Nature perceives Thy secret force,
And still holds on her even course,
  And owns Thy providential reign.

Thou art the Universal Soul,
The plastic Power that fills the whole,
  And governs earth, air, sea, and sky:
The creatures all Thy breath receive,
And who by Thy inspiring live,
  Without Thy inspiration die.

Spirit immense, eternal Mind,
Thou on the souls of lost mankind
  Dost with benignest influence move,
Pleased to restore the ruined race,
And new create a world of Grace
  In all the image of Thy Love.

II.

Spirit of Grace, we bless Thy name,
Thy works and offices proclaim,
  Thy fruits, and properties, and powers:

Thou dost with kind intendering care
The godless heart of man prepare,
   That God may yet again be ours.

Thou didst Thy fallen creature see,
Fallen from happiness and Thee,
   And swiftly to our rescue come:
Well-pleased amongst the sons of men
To fix Thy residence again,
   And make them Thy eternal home.

Thou dost the first good thought inspire;
The first faint spark of pure desire
   Is kindled by Thy gracious breath;
By Thee made conscious of his fall,
The sinner hears Thy sudden call,
   And starts out of the sleep of death.

Convinced of sin and unbelief
He sinks o'erwhelmed with sacred grief,
   And pines disconsolate for God,
Till Thou the healing balm apply,
The sinner freely justify,
   In Jesu's name and Jesu's Blood.

III.

Spirit of Power, 'tis Thine alone
To finish what Thyself begun,
   And crown Thy work with full success;
To them that groan beneath their sin
Thou bring'st the sweet refreshment in,
   The everlasting righteousness.

Thou dost by Thine almighty Grace
Again the abject sinner raise,
   Again our fleshly souls refine;
Spirit of Spirit born, we love,
And only seek, the things above,
   And live on earth the Life divine.

Thou dost the vital seed infuse,
Thou dost the creature new produce,
   In all its glorious parts complete;
The subjects of the kingdom here
Thou makest, ere the Judge appear,
   For all Thy Heavenly Kingdom meet.

Thou that revealing Spirit art
Who dost the hearing ear impart,
   The clear illuminated sight;
Spirit of Wisdom from on high,
Of Knowledge that shall never die,
   Of holy, true, eternal Light.

Thou art the end of doubtful care;
The antidote of sad despair
   We feel in that sweet power of Thine:
Through Thee, who lift'st the fallen up,
We rise, rejoice, abound in hope,
   And bless Thine energy divine.

Author of never-failing peace!
Whene'er we languish in distress,
   O'erwhelmed with sin and misery,

Thy presence brings us sure relief,
To gladness turns our every grief,
  And joy in God is joy in Thee.

Spirit of meek and godly fear,
The children, taught of Thee, revere
  And do their heavenly Father's will;
Pierced with an humble filial awe,
They love to keep His blessed Law,
  And all His kind commands fulfil.

Spirit of pure and holy Love,
We feel Thee streaming from above
  In calm unutterable peace;
The love by Thee diffused abroad
Unites our happy hearts to God,
  And seals our everlasting bliss.

IV.

Spirit of Holiness and Root,
Thy gracious God-delighting fruit
  Is joy, fidelity, and peace;
Meekness which no affront can move,
Truth, temperance, long-suffering, love,
  And universal righteousness.

Restorer of the sin-sick mind,
Our souls a perfect soundness find
  Through all their powers in Thee renewed:

Spirit of Life and Might divine,
By Thee we in the image shine,
  In all the strength and life of God.

Thou dost the living power exert
To invigorate and confirm the heart
  Of those who feel Thy work begun,
To exercise our every grace,
Quicken us in the glorious race,
  Till all the glorious race is run.

Through Thee the flesh we mortify,
A daily death rejoice to die,
  To live from sin forever free:
An holy sinless life to lead
Is only in Thy track to tread,
  To walk in love, in God, in Thee.

Through Thee we render God His due,
The worship spiritual and true
  With loving hearts rejoice to pay;
Him, while we find Thy present power,
In truth and spirit we adore,
  And pray — whene'er in Thee we pray.

Thou pleadest in the living stones
With speechless eloquence of groans,
  Which pierce our pitying Father's ear:
The answer of Thy prayer we feel,
The glorious joy unspeakable,
  And triumph in the Comforter.

True Witness of our sonship, Thee
We feel, from fear and sorrow free,
 And Father, Abba Father, cry:
Seal of our endless bliss Thou art,
Foretaste and Earnest in our heart
 Of pleasures that shall never die.

First fruits of yonder Land above,
Celestial joy, seraphic love
 To us, to us in Thee is given;
And all that to the Spirit sow
Shall of the Spirit reap, and know
 The ripest happiness of Heaven.

SPIRIT OF TRUTH, DESCEND.

1746.

JOHN xvi. 13-15.

SPIRIT of Truth, descend,
 And with Thy Church abide,
Our Guardian to the end,
 Our sure unerring Guide:
Us into the whole counsel lead
 Of God revealed below,
And teach us all the truth we need
 To Life Eternal know.

Whate'er Thou hear'st above
 To us with power impart,
And shed abroad the love
 Of Jesus in our heart:

One with the Father and the Son,
  Thy record is the same ;
O make to us the Godhead known
  Through faith in Jesu's Name.

To all our souls apply
  The doctrine of our Lord,
Our conscience certify,
  And witness with the Word.
Thy realizing light display,
  And show us things to come,
The after state, the final Day,
  And man's eternal doom.

The Judge of quick and dead,
  The God of Truth and Love,
Who doth for sinners plead,
  Our Advocate above,
Exalted by His Father there
  Thou dost exalt below,
And all His Grace on earth declare,
  And all His glory show.

Sent in His Name Thou art,
  His work to carry on,
His Godhead to assert,
  And make His mercy known.
Thou searchest the deep things of God,
  Thou know'st the Saviour's mind,
And tak'st of His atoning Blood
  To sprinkle all mankind.

Now then of His receive,
    And show to us the Grace,
And all His fulness give
    To all the ransomed race:
Whate'er He did for sinners buy
    With His expiring groan,
By faith in us reveal, apply,
    And make it all our own.

Descending from above,
    Into our souls convey
His comfort, joy, and love,
    Which none can take away;
His merit and His righteousness
    Which makes an end of sin;
Apply to every heart His peace,
    And bring His kingdom in.

The plenitude of God
    That doth in Jesus dwell,
On us through Him bestowed,
    To us secure and seal:
Now let us taste our Master's bliss,
    The glorious heavenly powers:
For all the Father hath is His,
    And all He hath is ours.

ETERNAL SPIRIT, COME.

1746.

ETERNAL Spirit, come
    Into Thy meanest home:
From Thine high and holy place
    Where Thou dost in glory reign,
Stoop in condescending Grace,
    Stoop to the poor heart of man.

    For Thee our hearts we lift,
    And wait the heavenly Gift.
Giver, Lord, of Life divine,
    To our dying souls appear;
Grant the Grace for which we pine,
    Give Thyself the Comforter.

    No gift or comfort we
    Would have distinct from Thee:
Spirit, Principle of Grace,
    Sum of our desires Thou art;
Fill us with Thy holiness,
    Breathe Thyself into our heart.

    Our ruined souls repair,
    And fix Thy mansion there:
Claim us for Thy constant shrine;
    All Thy glorious Self reveal;
Life, and Power, and Love divine,
    God in us forever dwell.

FOR CHRISTIAN FRIENDS.

<small>The eighteenth of a series of fifty-six hymns with the above title, in the second volume of *Hymns and Sacred Poems*, 1747. They were mostly or all written as letters to Sarah Gwynne, before or after her marriage with Wesley; the correspondence of the lovers being conducted chiefly "in verse, and remarkable for its piety."</small>

HOLY sanctifying Dove,
   God of Truth, and God of Love,
On my feeble soul descend,
On my dearest earthly friend.
Come, and all our wants supply;
Now the pardoned sanctify,
Now our little faith increase,
Fill us now with perfect peace.

Lead us, Thou, our constant Guide!
Witness, in our hearts abide;
Earnest of the joys to come,
Make our souls Thy glorious home.
Every precious promise seal;
All the depths of God reveal;
Keep us to that happy Day,
Bear us on Thy wings away.

If Thou didst the grace impart,
Mad'st us of one mind and heart,
Still our friendly souls unite
Partners in the realms of light.
Let us there together soar,
Quickly meet to part no more;
There our ravished spirits join,
Mingled, lost in Love divine.

PENITENTIAL.

The last of nine "Penitential Hymns," in the first volume of 1749.

STAY, Thou insulted Spirit, stay,
   Though I have done Thee such despite;
Nor cast the sinner quite away,
   Nor take Thine everlasting flight.

Though I have steeled my stubborn heart,
   And still shook off my guilty fears;
And vexed, and urged Thee to depart,
   For forty long rebellious years:

Though I have most unfaithful been
   Of all who e'er Thy Grace received;
Ten thousand times Thy goodness seen,
   Ten thousand times Thy goodness grieved:

Yet O, the chief of sinners spare,
   In honor of my great High Priest;
Nor in Thy righteous anger swear
   To exclude me from Thy people's rest.

This only woe I deprecate,
   This only plague, I pray, remove,
Nor leave me in my lost estate,
   Nor curse me with this want of love.

If yet Thou canst my sins forgive,
   From now, O Lord, relieve my woes;
Into the rest of love receive,
   And bless me with the calm repose.

From now, my weary soul release;
  Upraise me with Thy gracious hand,
And guide into Thy perfect peace,
  And bring me to the promised land.

AFTER A RECOVERY.

I.e., from Backsliding. 1749, volume first. A curious example of Wesley's softer style, and of the lengths to which his emotional views and habits sometimes led him.

O THOU meek and injured Dove,
  Wherefore dost Thou strive with me?
Me, who still abuse Thy Love,
  Me who grieve and fly from Thee?
Thee why should I longer grieve?
Leave me, Lord, Thy rebel leave.

Well Thou know'st, if now my heart
  Melts to feel Thy softening Grace,
Ready am I to depart,
  Thine to quit for sin's embrace:
Take Thy mercy back again:
Wherefore shouldst Thou strive in vain?

O that I might never feel
  One desire or drawing more!
Rather than provoke Thee still,
  Now let all the strife be o'er:
Drive me from Thy blissful face,
Let me go to my own place.

Or if Thy unwearied Love
Will not yet the rebel leave,
Stronger let Thine influence prove;
Let me double grace receive:
Give me more, or give me less;
Fix my doom, or seal my peace.

IN NATIONAL DANGER.

The third part of a hymn on Ezekiel ix., from Hymns for the Year 1756, *particularly for the Fast Day, February 6, when a French invasion was expected.*

STAY, Thou departing Spirit, stay,
Nor take Thy presence quite away!
Though now our languid hearts bemoan
Thy glory to the threshold gone,
Yet do not, Lord, withdraw Thy light,
Or leave us to eternal night.

Arise into Thy resting-place,
As in those wondrous ancient days
When God appeared, to dwell with men,
Betwixt the mystic cherubs seen,
Worshipt by all the angel-choir,
And symbolized by living fire.

Now to Thy drooping Church return,
Thou Comforter of all that mourn;
Thy suppliants in Thy temple meet
And bless us from Thy mercy-seat,
And still in our assemblies shine,
The dazzling Shéchinah divine.

The tokens of Thy presence show
And guard us from the invading foe:
Thy glory be our sure defence,
Our buckler Thy Omnipotence;
Nor ever from Thine house remove,
When filled with all the life of Love.

SCRIPTURE HYMNS.

From *Short Hymns on Select Passages of the Holy Scriptures*, two volumes, 1762.

GENESIS i. 2, 3.

EXPAND Thy wings, celestial Dove,
    And brooding o'er my nature's night,
Call forth the ray of heavenly Love,
    Let there in my dark soul be light;
And fill the illustrated abyss
With glorious beams of endless bliss.

Let there be Light (again command),
    And light there in our hearts shall be;
We then through faith shall understand
    Thy great mysterious Majesty,
And by the shining of Thy Grace,
Behold in Christ Thy glorious face.

John xv. 26.

SPIRIT of Truth, the Comforter,
  Proceeding from the Father's throne,
Come, and Thine inward witness bear
  Of Jesus, His eternal Son:
Him, the great uncreated Word,
  Give me the God supreme to call,
Essence, I AM, Jehovah, Lord,
  My God, who made and died for all.

John xvi. 15.

HOLY Ghost, by Him bestowed
  Who suffered on the Tree,
Take of my Redeemer's Blood
  And show it unto me.
Witness with the Blood Thou art:
  Apply it to this soul of mine:
Now assure my sprinkled heart
  It is the Blood divine.

Romans viii. 25.

SPIRIT of interceding Grace,
  I know not how, or what to pray:
Assist my utter helplessness,
  The power into my heart convey;
That God, acknowledging Thy groan,
May answer in my prayers His own.

Romans xv. 13.

HOLY Ghost, the power inspire,
  The taste of things above;
Set my panting soul on fire
  With hope of perfect love.
Hope's full confidence infuse,
Till it bursts the earthen shrine,
Till my hope, myself, I lose
  Within the Arms divine.

1 Corinthians vi. 19.

HOLY Ghost, we know Thou art
  Still in every faithful heart.
Yes, we tremble, Lord, to know
God resides in man below!
O might all our bodies be
Sensibly replete with Thee!
O might all Thy temples shine
Bright with holiness divine!

2 Corinthians iii. 17.

COME then, and dwell in me,
  Spirit of power within,
And bring the glorious liberty
  From sorrow, fear, and sin:
The seed of sin's disease,
  Spirit of health, remove,
Spirit of finished holiness,
  Spirit of perfect love.

2 COR. v. 5.

COME, Thou beatific Spirit,
   Earnest of the joys above,
Taste of what the saints inherit,
   Author of seraphic love!
When Thou unto me art given,
   Full of immortality,
Sure I am to dwell in heaven,
   Sure that heaven dwells in me.

GALATIANS ii. 20.

HOLY Ghost, remove the grief
   And burthen of my sins;
Me, convinced of unbelief,
   Of righteousness convince.
Comforter, on Thee I call:
Apply the Blood that sets me free;
   Tell my heart, Who died for all
     Hath loved and died for me.

Faith's appropriating power
   With Thee I long to feel:
Come in this accepted hour,
   My Saviour-Lord reveal;
By Thine energy constrain
My soul to cry with joy unknown,
   Very God was very Man,
     And Christ is all my own.

GALATIANS v. 17.

HOLY Ghost, with grace inspire
My heart against my sin;
When I feel the base desire,
Exert Thy power within:
Keep me till the conflict 's o'er,
That nature's will I may not do,
Till the Kingdom Thou restore
And all my heart renew.

THE FRUIT OF THE SPIRIT.

GALATIANS v. 22, 23.

This is altered, and, strange to say, much improved, in the Leeds Independent Selection of 1822, a book to which James Montgomery was a contributor. As a good and unknown hymn, I give the revision.[1]

HOLY Spirit, dwell in me:
Then the fruit shall show the Tree;
Every grace its Author prove,
Rising from the root of love.

---

[1] Here is WESLEY's original, 1762:—

> JESUS, plant Thy Spirit in me:
> Then the fruit shall show the Tree,
> Every grace its Author prove,
> Rising from the root of love.

Joy shall then my heart o'erflow,
Peace which only Christians know :
Peace, the seal of cancelled sin,
Joy, the pledge of Heaven within.

Gentle then to all, and kind,
Transcript of the Saviour's mind,
Full of sympathy and care
In another's woe to share ;

Prompt and tender to relieve,
Faithful never to deceive ;
All Thy virtues, Lord, be mine,
Brighter Thy resemblance shine !

THE SPIRIT AND THE WORD.

2 TIMOTHY iii. 16, 17.

(This should have been in our first *Introductory* part, rather than here.)

INSPIRER of the ancient Seers,
  Who wrote from Thee the sacred page,
The same through all succeeding years ;
  To us, in our degenerate age,

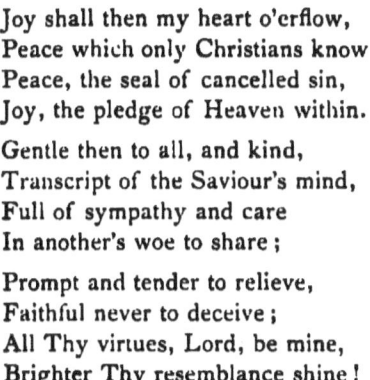

Joy shall then my heart o'erflow,
Peace which only saints can know,
Peace, the seal of cancelled sin,
Joy, the taste of heaven within.

Gentle then to all, and kind
To the wicked and the blind,
Full of tenderness and care,
I shall every burthen bear ;

Glad the general servant be,
Serve with strict fidelity,
Life itself for them deny,
Meekly in their service die.

The Spirit of Thy Word impart,
And breathe the life into our heart.

The Word if Thou vouchsafe to give,
  We find its efficacious power,
The saving benefit receive,
  And taught aright our God to adore,
The living sentiment we feel,
Conformed to all Thy righteous will.

While now Thine Oracles we read
  With earnest prayer and strong desire,
O let Thy Spirit from Thee proceed,
  Our souls to waken and inspire;
Our weakness help, our darkness chase,
And guide us by the Light of Grace.

Whene'er in error's paths we rove,
  The living God through sin forsake,
Our conscience by Thy Word reprove,
  Convince, and bring the wanderers back,
Deep wounded by Thy Spirit's sword,
And then by Gilead's Balm restored.

The secret lessons of Thy Grace,
  Transmitted through the Word, repeat,
To train us up in all Thy ways,
  To make us in Thy Will complete;
Fulfil Thy Love's redeeming plan,
And bring us to a perfect man.

Furnished out of Thy treasury,
  O may we always ready stand
To help the souls redeemed by Thee
  In what their various states demand;
To teach, convince, correct, reprove,
And build them up in holiest love.

ANOTHER.

2 TIMOTHY iii. 16.   2 PETER i. 21.

This and the five following are from *Hymns on the Trinity*, 1767

SPIRIT of truth, essential God,
  Who didst Thine ancient saints inspire,
Shed in their hearts Thy Love abroad,
  And touch their hallowed lips with fire;
. Our God from all eternity,
World without end we worship Thee!

Still we believe, almighty Lord,
  Whose presence fills both earth and heaven,
The meaning of the written Word
  Is still by inspiration given;
Thou only dost Thyself explain
The secret mind of God to man.

Come then, divine Interpreter,
  The Scriptures to our hearts apply;
And, taught by Thee, we God revere,
  Him in Three Persons magnify;
In each the Triune God adore,
Who was, and is for evermore.

2 THESSALONIANS iii. 5.

COME, Holy Ghost, Thou Lord most high,
   The veil of unbelief remove,
And in us Abba Father cry,
   And lead our hearts into His Love;
Our hearts into His patience lead
   Whose Blood hath washed our sins away,
And, perfected like Christ our Head,
   Seal and preserve us to that Day.

MATTHEW ix. 38. ACTS xiii. 4.

HOLY Ghost, regard our prayers,
   Third of the glorious Three,
Send forth faithful laborers
   To gather souls for Thee:
Sovereign, everlasting Lord,
The harvest is entirely Thine,
   Thine the preachers of the Word,
     The messengers divine.

  Move their hearts, and more stir up
     Salvation to proclaim,
  Bold on every mountain-top
     To shout in Jesus' name,
Tidings of great joy to tell
Of peace obtained and sin forgiven;
   Then, Thy Word of Grace to seal,
     O God, come down from Heaven.

LUKE ii. 16, 28.

HOLY Ghost, apply Thy word
  And promise to my heart;
Tell me I shall see the Lord
  Before I hence depart.
When my faith the Christ hath seen,
Creator of that inward eye,
  Thee I shall acknowledge then,
    The Lord and God most high.

Spirit of faith, reveal in me
  The sure approaching grace;
Then I shall the Deity
  Of my Inspirer praise,
Bless my God forever blest,
Glory in salvation given,
  Late obtain the promised rest,
    And go in peace to Heaven.

2 CORINTHIANS i. 3.

GOD of all consolation,
  The Holy Ghost Thou art;
Thy secret inspiration
  Hath told it to my heart.
The blessing I inherit,
  Through Jesus' prayer bestowed,
The Comforter, the Spirit,
  The true eternal God.

With God the Son and Saviour,
    With God the Father One,
The tokens of His favor
    Thou mak'st to sinners known;
An antepast of heaven
    Thou dost in me reveal,
Attest my sins forgiven,
    And my salvation seal.

The indubitable witness
    Of Thy own Deity,
Thou giv'st my soul its fitness
    Thy glorious face to see:
Thy comforts, gifts, and graces
    My largest thoughts transcend,
And challenge all my praises,
    When faith in sight shall end.

A PRAYER TO THE HOLY GHOST.
1767.

KINDLER of seraphic fire
    Glowing in Thy hosts above,
Giver of the pure desire,
    Spirit of celestial Love,
Heavenly love to us impart,
Comfort every drooping heart.

If Thou hast a token given,
    If our want of love we feel,
Bless us with that taste of heaven,
    Pardon on our conscience seal;

Then with cordial charity,
  Gracious God, we cleave to Thee.

Then, because Thou first hast loved,
  We shall love our God again,
Happy, till from earth removed,
  Joy consummate we obtain,
Dazzled with the glorious sight,
Lost in an abyss of light.

COME, THOU ALL-INSPIRING SPIRIT.

This and the two following are from *Hymns for the Use of Families*, 1767.

COME, thou all-inspiring Spirit,
  Into every longing heart!
Bought for us by Jesu's merit,
  Now Thy blissful Self impart.
Sign our uncontested pardon,
  Wash us in the atoning Blood;
Make our souls a watered garden,
Fill our sinless[1] souls with God.

If Thou gav'st the enlarged desire,
  Which for Thee we ever feel,
Now our panting hearts inspire,
  Now our cancelled sin reveal:
Claim us for Thine habitation;
  Dwell within our hallowed breast;
Seal us heirs of full salvation,
  Fitted for our heavenly rest.

---

[1] In the reprint, *spotless*.

Give us quietly to tarry,
    Till for all Thy glory meet;
Waiting like attentive Mary,
    Happy at our Saviour's feet:
Keep us from the world unspotted,
    From all earthly passions free,
Wholly to Thyself devoted,
    Fixt to live and die for Thee.

Wrestling on in mighty prayer,
    Lord, we will not let Thee go,
Till Thou all Thy mind declare,
    All Thy Grace on us bestow:
Peace, the seal of sin forgiven,
    Joy and perfect love impart,
Present, everlasting heaven;
    All Thou hast, and all Thou art!

SPIRIT OF SUPPLICATION.

SPIRIT of supplication,
    Through Jesus Christ bestowed,
Visit this habitation,
    And make us Thine abode:
To pour a mournful prayer
    Help our infirmity,
And all our souls prepare,
    Great God, to compass Thee.

Spirit of faith, discover
    To us the Crucified,
The sinner's Friend and Lover,
    Who for His haters died.
Set forth the Lamb atoning,
    As slaughtered in our stead,
And let us hear Him groaning,
    And see Him bow His head.

Help us to look upon Him
    By us transfixt and torn,
The Lord of all to own Him,
    And o'er our Saviour mourn;
With tears of true contrition
    Bewail a tortured God,
And find Him a Physician
    Who heals us by His Blood.

O might we now relenting
    Confess the Deicide,
And while we lie lamenting
    Perceive His Blood applied!
No longer let us grieve Him
    Who joy to us imparts,
But lovingly receive Him
    Into our broken hearts!

SPIRIT OF LOVE, RETURN.

SPIRIT of Love, return
    To every troubled breast,
And comfort us who mourn
    For permanence of rest:
Thou dost Thy mourners' steps attend,
    Our undiscovered Guide;
But come, our grief and sin to end,
    And in our hearts abide.

With us residing here
    We know Thee now in part,
The Author of our fear
    And all our hope Thou art.
Thou often visitest Thine own:
    But in an hour or day
Our transitory Guest is gone,
    Our joy is fled away.

How short, alas, our taste
    Of those celestial powers,
When, a few moments blest,
    We know that Christ is ours,
That Christ hath quenched the wrath of God,
    His Father's Grace revealed,
And bought our pardon with His Blood,
    And on our conscience sealed.

FOR LOVE.

O might we always know
  The Father reconciled!
Set up Thy throne below
  In each adopted child:
Restore the Kingdom of Thy Grace,
  And fill us from above
With purest joy, and perfect peace,
  And everlasting love.

FOR LOVE.

One of 34 *Hymns for Love*, apparently among WESLEY's latest writings: no date is given to them.

SPIRIT of revelation,
  Jehovah, Thee we own:
Make by Thy inspiration
  To us the Father known:
Of Jesus testifying,
  His Deity assert,
His Blood divine applying
  To every longing heart.

With Love beyond expression
  Bless each expecting soul,
And take entire possession
  And consecrate the whole:
By Thy own signet seal us
  Thy permanent abode;
With all the graces fill us,
  With all the Life of God.

The Earnest and the Witness,
  Vouchsafe in us to dwell,
And give the blissful meetness
  For bliss ineffable:
With heavenly joy transported
  We then our course shall run,
By angel-hosts escorted
  To the eternal throne.

JOHN CENNICK, 1717-1755.

Teacher of John Wesley's school at Kingswood, afterwards associated with Whitefield, and finally a Moravian. He published six volumes, now very scarce, of *Sacred Hymns for the Children of God in the Days of their Pilgrimage*, and *for the Use of Religious Societies*. A few of his hymns are familiar, and many of the others are not without attractions. He imitated Charles Wesley largely, and had some talent of his own, though but little taste or culture.

TO THE HOLY GHOST.

1742.

AWAKE and blow, Thou purest Wind,
  Awake and blow on me:
Let me Thy quickening influence find,
  And be baptized in Thee.

Unveil Thy power, Thy Grace unveil,
  And all Thy virtues show;
With living streams my spirit fill,
  In me let rivers flow.

AFTER A DISPUTE.

I wait Thy light; O let it be
    A lantern to my feet;
And lead me home to reign with Thee
    On Heaven's eternal seat.

HOLY GHOST, ANOINTING DOVE!

The seventh and eighth of ten verses of "A Hymn to the Trinity," 1741.

HOLY Ghost, anointing Dove,
    Well of Life, and God of Love!
Breath of the almighty Sire!
Our uplifted hearts inspire.

Shed in us Thy Love abroad,
Seal, O seal us sons of God;
Bring the Father's blessing down;
Thou the heirs of glory crown!

AFTER A DISPUTE.

1741.

COME, Holy Spirit, heavenly Guest,
    Reveal the faith divine!
Come from Emmanuel's peaceful breast,
    In one Thy servants join!

Forbid disputes, dispel our doubts,
  Our wide dissension heal;
To every servant of the Lord
  Thy sacred truths reveal.

One God, the Father, lives and reigns:
  One Jesus Christ we know:
One mind above the Church enjoys,
  So let the flocks below.

Then concord, peace, and holy love
  Shall bless our golden days;
Then all the fold in one glad voice
  Shall sing our Maker's praise!

AT ADULT BAPTISM.

1742.

DESCEND, celestial Dove,
  In every bosom dwell;
Upon the present water move,
  While we the influence feel.

Anoint with holy fire,
  Baptize with purging flames,
This soul, and with Thy Grace inspire
  In ceaseless living streams.

AT THE OPENING OF WORSHIP.

Thy heavenly unction give,
    Thy promise, Lord, fulfil,
Give power Thy Spirit to receive,
    And strength to do Thy Will.

Thy ordinance we obey;
    O meet us in the same!
And with this water now convey
    The virtues of Thy Name.

Witness to this Thy sign
    And grant the inward grace;
Let this Thy servant, sealed for Thine,
    From hence depart in peace.

ROBERT SEAGRAVE. Born 1693.

A Cambridge man, and clergyman of the English Church, from which he withdrew about 1739 and connected himself with Whitefield. His *Hymns for Christian Worship* appeared 1742: among them is "Rise, my soul, and stretch thy wings."

AT THE OPENING OF WORSHIP.

NOW may the Spirit's holy Fire,
    Descending from above,
His waiting family inspire
    With joy, and peace, and love!

Thee we the Comforter confess:
    Shouldst Thou be absent here,
Our songs of praise are vain address,
    We utter heartless prayer.

Drop as the dew on tender grass,
  Or like a shower abound,
Vouchsafed by Heaven's indulgent Grace
  To glad the weary ground.

With unction consecrate our frame
  To search the depths of God:
Teach us to know His Love, who came
  By water and by Blood.

Wake, heavenly Wind, arise and come,
  Blow on the drooping field:
The plants and flowers shall breathe perfume,
  By Thee their incense yield.

In rushing or in gentle gale
  Pour forth Thy gifts divine:
O'er darkness, weakness, sin prevail,
  Till all we are is Thine.

Touch with a living coal the lip
  That shall proclaim Thy Word,
And bid each awful hearer keep
  Attention to the Lord.

Converts add Thou, delivered far
  From falsehood's specious guise:
Let Truth and Righteousness appear,
  The latter glory rise.

Hasten the Restitution-day
  Which now corruption shrouds;
New heavens and new earth display,
  With Jesus in the clouds.

FOR AN AWAKENING.

COME, Holy Spirit, heavenly Power,
    Kindly Thy quickening work begin;
Visit a formal, dead mankind,
    And lift them from their graves of sin.

Amongst the tombs Thy circuit take,
    Bring Sinai's wakening thunders there,
Followed by Grace's softer voice:
    But give the slumberers ears to hear.

The dead can ne'er Thy praise advance,
    The living shall Thy worth proclaim:
Bid many rise, and they shall bless
    With us the great Redeemer's Name.

Rebellious flinty hearts subdue,
    Chase stubborn unbelief away;
Pour on the blind, that think they see,
    The sevenfold light of Gospel day.

The deaf, the dumb, restored by Thee,
    Shall soon the wondrous change confess;
Nor aught their future song employ
    Save the sweet riches of free Grace!

Even Thy own saints await Thy power,
    Our trembling lamps ask fresh supplies:
Do Thou each virtuous light sustain,
    And teach our feeble flame to rise.

Faith, hope, and charity we ask,
  And purity still more to feel:
Deep in our hearts Thy work engrave,
  And still more deep the heavenly seal.

Inspire our love, inspire it high,
  To Jesus our affections raise:
We more would thank, we more would bless,
We more would live our Jesu's praise.

WILLIAM HAMMOND. Died 1783.

A graduate of St. John's College, Cambridge, and a man of some learning; he was associated with John Cennick, and spent the best part of his life among the Calvinistic Methodists. His *Psalms, Hymns, and Spiritual Songs* appeared 1745. Some of them are founded on the Latin, and this one is headed

VENI CREATOR.

HOLY Spirit, gently come,
    Raise us from our fallen state;
Fix Thy everlasting home
    In the hearts Thou didst create:
  Gift of God most high,
    Visit every troubled breast;
Light and life and love supply,
    Give our spirits perfect rest.

Heavenly unction from above,
  Comforter of weary saints,
Fountain, Life, and Fire of Love,
  Hear and answer our complaints.

Thee we humbly pray,
  Finger of the living God,
Now Thy sevenfold Grace display,
  Shed our Saviour's Love abroad.

Now Thy quickening influence bring,
  On our spirits sweetly move;
Open every mouth to sing
  Jesu's everlasting Love.
    Lighten every heart,
    Drive our enemies away,
Joy and peace to us impart,
  Lead us in the heavenly way.

Take the things of Christ, and show
  What our Lord for us hath done;
May we God the Father know
  Only in and through the Son.
    Nothing will we fear,
    Though to wilds and deserts driven,
While we feel Thy presence near,
  Witnessing our sins forgiven.

Glory be to God alone,
  God whose Hand created all;
Glory be to God the Son,
  Who redeemed us from our fall:
    To the Holy Ghost
    Equal praise and glory be,
When the course of time is lost,
  Lost in wide eternity.

PHILIP DODDRIDGE, D.D., 1702–1751.

Pastor and teacher at Northampton. His hymns, to the number of 374, were first published in 1755 by Job Orton. A larger and professedly more accurate edition was issued in 1838 by his grandson, John Doddridge Humphreys.

THE LOVE OF GOD SHED ABROAD IN THE HEART BY THE SPIRIT.

ROMANS v. 5.

DESCEND, immortal Dove,
    Spread Thy kind wings abroad,
And, wrapt in flames of holy love,
    Bear all my soul to God.

Jesus my Lord reveal
    In charms of Grace divine,
And be Thyself the sacred Seal
    That Pearl of Price is mine.

Behold, my heart expands
    To catch the heavenly fire;
It longs to feel the gentle bands,
    And groans with strong desire.

Thy Love, my God, appears,
    And brings salvation down,
My cordial through this vale of tears,
    In paradise my crown.

THE HEART PURIFIED TO LOVE UNFEIGNED BY THE SPIRIT.

1 Peter i. 22.

GREAT Spirit of Immortal Love,
　Vouchsafe our frozen hearts to move;
With ardor strong these breasts inflame
To all that own a Saviour's name.

Still let the heavenly fire endure
Fervent and vigorous, true and pure;
Let every heart and every hand
Join in the dear fraternal band.

Celestial Dove, descend and bring
The smiling blessings on Thy wing;
And make us taste those sweets below
Which in the blissful mansions grow.

SEEKING TO GOD FOR THE COMMUNICATION OF HIS SPIRIT.

Ezekiel xxxvi. 37.

HEAR, gracious Sovereign, from Thy throne,
　And send Thy various blessings down:
While by Thine Israel Thou art sought,
Attend the prayer Thy word hath taught.

Come, Sacred Spirit, from above,
And fill the coldest heart with love:
Soften to flesh the rugged stone,
And let Thy godlike power be known.

Speak Thou, and from the haughtiest eyes
Shall floods of pious sorrow rise;
While all their glowing souls are borne
To seek that Grace, which now they scorn.

O let a holy flock await
Numerous around Thy temple-gate,
Each pressing on with zeal to be
A living sacrifice to Thee.

In answer to our fervent cries,
Give us to see Thy Church arise;
Or if that blessing seem too great,
Give us to mourn its low estate.

THOMAS RAWSON.

COMMUNION WITH JESUS.

Mr. Sedgwick gives the date of this as 1757. I take the text from an early edition of Whitefield's *Collection*, where it has the above title. It is found in several other old books, and seems to have been popular among the early Calvinistic Methodists. In the Inghamite Collection, 1756-61, it has a fourth verse, and several variations in the text.

COME, descend, O heavenly Spirit!
Fan each spark into a flame;

Blessings let us now inherit,
  Blessings that we cannot name.
Whilst hosannas we are singing,
  May our hearts in rapture move,
Feel new grace in them still springing,
  Breathe the air of purest love.

Let us sail in Grace's ocean,
  Float on that unbounded sea,
Guided into pure devotion,
  Kept from paths of error free;
On Thy heavenly manna feeding,
  Screened from every envious foe,
Love, O Love for sinners bleeding,
  All for Thee we would forego.

Keep us, Lord, still in communion,
  Daily nearer drawn to Thee;
Sinking in the sweetest union
  Of that heartfelt mystery.
Keep us safe from each delusion,
  Well protected from all harms;
Free from sin and all confusion,
  Circle us within Thine arms.

JOSEPH HART, 1712–1768.

Minister of Jewin Street Independent Chapel. In 1759 he published 119 hymns, including those here given: 96 were added in subsequent editions. Dr. Johnson has a curious passage, quoted by Belcher (Historical Sketches of Hymns, Philadelphia, 1859): "I went to church; and seeing a poor girl at the Sacrament in a bedgown, I gave her privately half-a-crown, though I saw Hart's hymns in her hand."

COME, Holy Spirit, come,
   Let Thy bright beams arise;
Dispel the darkness from our minds,
   And open all our eyes.

Cheer our desponding hearts,
   Thou heavenly Paraclete;
Give us to lie, with humble hope,
   At our Redeemer's feet.

Revive our drooping faith,
   Our doubts and fears remove;
And kindle in our breasts the flames
   Of never-dying love.

Convince us of our sin,
   Then lead to Jesus' Blood;
And to our wondering view reveal
   The secret Love of God.

Show us that loving Man
   That rules the courts of bliss,
The Lord of hosts, the mighty God,
   The eternal Prince of Peace.

'Tis Thine to cleanse the heart,
　　To sanctify the soul,
To pour fresh life on every part,
　　And new create the whole.

If Thou, celestial Dove,
　　Thine influence withdraw,
What easy victims soon we fall
　　To conscience, wrath, and law!

No longer burns our love;
　　Our faith and patience fail;
Our sin revives, and death and hell
　　Our feeble souls assail.

Dwell, therefore, in our hearts;
　　Our minds from bondage free;
Then shall we know, and praise, and love
　　The Father, Son, and Thee.

WHIT-SUNDAY.

The three opening verses are omitted.

BLEST God, that once in fiery tongues
　　Cam'st down in open view,
Come, visit every heart that longs
　　To entertain Thee too.

And though not like a mighty wind,
　　Nor with a rushing noise,
May we Thy calmer comforts find,
　　And hear Thy still small voice.

Not for the gift of tongues we pray,
    Nor power the sick to heal;
Give wisdom to direct our way,
    And strength to do Thy Will.

We pray to be renewed within,
    And reconciled to God;
To have our conscience washed from sin
    In the Redeemer's Blood.

We pray to have our faith increased;
    And O, celestial Dove,
We pray to be completely blest
    With that rich blessing, love.

BLEST SPIRIT OF TRUTH.

BLEST Spirit of Truth, eternal God,
    Thou meek and lowly Dove,
Who fill'st the soul, through Jesus' Blood,
    With faith and hope and love:

Who comfortest the heavy heart
    By sin and sorrow prest;
Who to the dead canst life impart,
    And to the weary rest:

Thy sweet communion charms the soul,
    And gives true peace and joy,
While Satan's power cannot control,
    Nor all his wiles destroy.

Come from the blissful realms above;
  Our longing breasts inspire
With Thy soft flames of heavenly Love,
  And fan the sacred fire.

Let no false comfort lift us up
  To confidence that's vain;
Nor let their faith and courage droop
  For whom the Lamb was slain.

Breathe comfort where distress abounds;
  Make the whole conscience clean;
And heal with balm from Jesus' wounds
  The festering sores of sin.

Vanquish our lusts; our pride remove;
  Take out the heart of stone;
Show us the Father's boundless Love,
  And merits of the Son.

The Father sent the Son to die;
  The willing Son obeyed;
The Witness Thou, to ratify
  The purchase Christ has made.

DESCEND FROM HEAVEN.

DESCEND from Heaven, celestial Dove;
  With flames of pure seraphic love
Our ravished breasts inspire:

Fountain of joy, blest Paraclete!
Warm our cold hearts with heavenly heat,
   And set our souls on fire.

Breathe on these bones, so dry and dead;
Thy sweetest, softest influence shed
   In all our hearts abroad;
Point out the place where Grace abounds;
Direct us to the bleeding wounds
   Of our incarnate God.

Conduct, blest Guide, Thy sinner-train
To Calvary, where the Lamb was slain,
   And with us there abide;
Let us our loved Redeemer meet,
Weep o'er His piercèd hands and feet,
   And view His wounded side.

From which pure Fountain if Thou draw
Water to quench the fiery Law,
   And Blood to purge our sin,
We'll tell the Father in that Day
(And Thou shalt witness what we say),
   "We're clean, just God, we're clean."

Teach us for what to pray and how:
And since, kind God, 'tis only Thou
   The Throne of Grace canst move,
Pray Thou for us; that we through faith
May feel the effects of Jesus' death,
   Through faith that works by love.

A PRAYER FOR GRACE.

Thou, with the Father and the Son,
Art that mysterious Three in One,
  God blest for evermore;
Whom though we cannot comprehend,
Feeling Thou art the sinner's Friend,
  We love Thee and adore.

WILLIAM WILLIAMS, 1717-1791.

A celebrated Welsh itinerant, of the Calvinistic Methodist body. From his *Hosannah to the Son of David*, 1759. This, and his *Gloria in Excelsis*, 1772, were reprinted by Mr. SEDGWICK, 1859.

A PRAYER FOR GRACE.

COME, Holy Spirit, now descend,
  And shower from above
Upon my dry and withered soul
  Thy everlasting Love.

Reveal Thy glories and Thy Grace,
  The beauties of Thy Name;
Remove my sin, that heavy load
  Of painful guilt and shame.

Allure my soul above the world,
  Where vanities abound;
And lulled secure upon Thy breast
  May I be ever found;

Taught to be wise above the wiles
    Of the malicious foe,
And trample on his secret snares
    Wherever I may go.

Thou, God, alone canst make me strong,
    Thy Word can faith convey;
When with Thy strength I am endued
    I 'll never more dismay.

AUGUSTUS MONTAGUE TOPLADY, 1740–1778.

Vicar of Broad Hembury, Devon, and author of "Rock of Ages," the greatest of English Hymns. His Poems on Sacred Subjects *appeared 1759. The only complete and reliable edition of his hymns is that of Mr.* SEDGWICK, *1860.*

THE SPIRIT'S WITNESS.

ROMANS viii. 16.

EARNEST of future bliss,
    Thee, Holy Ghost, we hail:
Fountain of holiness
    Whose comforts never fail;
The cleansing Gift on saints bestowed,
The Witness of their peace with God.

With our perverseness here
    How often hast Thou strove,
And spared us year by year
    With never-ceasing Love!
O set from sin our spirits free,
And make us more and more like Thée.

What wondrous Grace is this,
　For God to dwell with men!
Through Jesus' Righteousness
　His favor we regain,
And feeble worms, by nature lost,
Are temples of the Holy Ghost.

Though Belial's sons would prove
　That Thou no Witness art,
Thanks to redeeming Love,
　We feel Thee in our heart.
O mayst Thou still persist to bear
Thine inward testimony there.

By Thee on earth we know
　Ourselves in Christ renewed,
Brought by Thy Grace into
　The family of God:
Of His adopting Love the Seal,
And faithful Teacher of His Will.

Great Comforter, descend
　In gentle breathings down:
Preserve us to the end,
　That no man take our crown:
Our Guardian still vouchsafe to be,
Nor suffer us to go from Thee.

THE BELIEVER'S WISH.

The last three verses of a poem of ten, which appeared in the Gospel Magazine, *April, 1771.*

FAIN would I mount, fain would I glow,
    And loose my cable from below:
But I can only spread my sail;
Thou, Thou must breathe the auspicious gale!

At anchor laid, remote from home,
Toiling I cry, Sweet Spirit, come!
Celestial Breeze, no longer stay,
But swell my sails, and speed my way.

Open my heart; the key is Thine:
My will effectually incline:
Possess a soul, that fain would be,
Lord, only intimate with Thee.

SAMUEL DAVIES, 1724–1761.

A native of Newcastle, Delaware, and from 1759 President of Princeton College; he held a high place in early American literature. His sermons were published in London by Dr. Thomas Gibbons, who also inserted Davies' 16 hymns in his own volume of 1769. This is the best of them.

THE HOLY SPIRIT INVOKED, AND HIS PURIFYING AND QUICKENING INFLUENCES IMPLORED.

ETERNAL Spirit, Source of light,
    Enlivening, consecrating Fire,

THE HOLY SPIRIT INVOKED.

Descend, and with celestial heat
    Our dull, our frozen hearts inspire;
Our souls refine, our dross consume:
    Come, condescending Spirit, come!

In our cold breasts O strike a spark
    Of the pure flame which seraphs feel;
Nor let us wander in the dark,
    Or lie benumbed and stupid still.
Come, vivifying Spirit, come,
And make our hearts Thy constant home.

Whatever guilt and madness dare,
    We would not quench the heavenly Fire:
Our hearts as fuel we prepare,
    Though in the flame we should expire.
Our breasts expand to make Thee room;
Come, purifying Spirit, come!

Let pure devotion's fervors rise;
    Let every pious passion glow;
O let the raptures of the skies
    Kindle in our cold hearts below.
Come, condescending Spirit, come,
And make our souls Thy constant home.

ELIZABETH SCOTT.

Little is known of this lady: Josiah Miller supposes that she was a sister of Thomas Scott, of Norwich (the hymn-writer, not the commentator). Twenty-one hymns by her appeared in Ash and Evans' *Collection*, 1769, and fourteen others in Dobell's *New Selection*, 1806. This is among the latter.

THE BIBLE INDITED AND PRESERVED BY THE SPIRIT.

ISAIAH xl. 8.

ETERNAL Spirit! 'twas Thy Breath
    The Oracles of Truth inspired,
And kings and holy seers of old
    With strong prophetic impulse fired.

Filled with Thy great almighty power,
    Their lips with heavenly science flowed;
Their hands a thousand wonders wrought
    Which bore the signature of God.

With gladsome hearts they spread the news
    Of pardon through a Saviour's Blood,
And to a numerous seeking crowd
    Marked out the path to His abode.

The powers of earth and hell in vain
    Against the sacred Word combine;
Thy Providence through every age
    Securely guards the work divine.

Thee, its great Author, Source of Light,
    Thee, its Preserver, we adore;
And humbly ask a ray from Thee,
    Its hidden wonders to explore.

JOHN WILLISON.

"Minister of the Gospel in Dundee," and author of *One Hundred Gospel-Hymns*, 1767. The three opening verses of the following piece are omitted.

COME, Holy Ghost, Thou heavenly Dove
    Descending from above;
Renew our souls, and fill our hearts
    With precious faith and love.

We are Thy workmanship; but sin
    Hath every thing misplaced;
Come o'er Thy handiwork again:
    Thy image is defaced.

Create in us all things anew,
    Cause old things pass away;
Our córrupt habits quite subdue,
    Sin weaken every day.

Let David's house in us grow strong,
    But weak the house of Saul;
Let Satan's holds and all our lusts
    Before God's Spirit fall.

O kindly guide poor travellers
    Into the paths of peace,
And bring us to our Father's house
    Where sins and sorrows cease.

JAMES NEALE, M.A.

"Of Pembroke Hall, Cambridge: late Head Master of the Royal Grammar School, Henly upon Thames, and Curate of Bix in the County of Oxford." His *Select Hymns*, 1763, seem never to have been known or used. He was connected with the early Methodists.

BREATHE, DESCENDING HOLY SPIRIT.

BREATHE, descending Holy Spirit,
   Let our bliss
   E'er be this,
Thee to still inherit.

Give divine and blest communion,
   Knit in bands
   Hearts and hands
With increasing union.

Arm us to the battle glorious;
   Let us wield
   In the field
Thy bright sword victorious.

Let us through Thy mighty power
   Glad fulfil
   All Thy Will,
Thou our Rock and Tower.

Then beyond all tribulation,
   Happy we
   Soon shall see
Zion's great salvation.

ADMIRAL RICHARD KEMPENFELT, 1718–1782.

The brave and blameless officer who went down in "The Royal George" was author of a tract of twelve pages, *Original Hymns and Poems, by Philotheorus*, Exeter, 1767: it has been reprinted by Mr. Sedgwick. The two pieces which we extract from it — and more especially the second — perhaps do not strictly belong here; but their intrinsic merit, added to the interest derived from the tragic fate of their author, has turned the balance in their favor.

THE SOUL LONGING FOR HOLINESS.

GENTLE Spirit, waft me over
   Jordan's intervening flood;
Lead me to the bleeding Lover,
   Bear me to the rest of God!
Glad I eye the rich possession,
   Land of peace and perfect love;
Joy, without an intermission,
   Ever streaming from above.

Raise me, Lord, to solemn action;
   Breathe the energetic breath;
Crown me with the true perfection,
   Previous to the stroke of death.
Now commence the holy union;
   Let a living seeker prove
All the riches of communion,
   All the tenderness of love.

O, my agonizing spirit!
   Thou shalt surely enter in,
Pluck the fruit of Jesu's merit,
   And expel the poison Sin.

Far must all thy foes be driven,
   Hell's invaders forced to flee,
While the potent arm of Heaven.
   Brings thee into liberty.

Yes, through Jesu's intercession,
   I shall reach the fruitful shore;
There receive a saint's impression,
   And be happy evermore.
By the force of love attracted,
   Fluttering spirit, fly away;
Jesu calls; by Him directed,
   Gain the path of perfect day.

THE RAPTURE:

IN IMITATION OF THE MANNER OF HERBERT.

(One of the finest rhapsodies in our language. Part of it, beginning with the third verse, may be found in the *Plymouth Collection* (No. 1258) and some other hymn-books.)

HASTEN, hasten, sweetest Dove,
   Sacred Sanctifier!
Breathe the soul-abasing love;
   Form the true desire;
Clear the gloomy mists away;
Tune the heart to harmony;
Then we'll sing, and then we'll pray,
   With celestial energy.

Bear me on Thy rapid wing,
   Everlasting Spirit!
Where the young-eyed cherubs sing,
   And the saints inherit
(Fluttering round the flaming throne)
Joys eternally their own:
This the cry of every one,
Glory to the incarnate Son!

Burst, ye emerald gates, and bring
   To my raptured vision
All the ecstatic joys that spring
   Round the bright Elysian:
Lo! we lift our longing eyes;
Break, ye intervening skies!
SON OF RIGHTEOUSNESS, arise!
Ope the gates of Paradise.

See! the exalted SON of GOD
   Pours the intercession!
Mark the sin-atoning Blood,
   Bend in adoration!
Endless glory is secured;
True perfection is restored;
Sinner, see! and be assured
All thy wants in JESUS stored.

Floods of everlasting light
   Freely flash before Him;
Myriads, with supreme delight,
   Instantly adore Him:

Angels' trumps resound His fame;
Lutes of lucid gold proclaim
All the music of His Name,
Heaven echoing the theme.

Hark! the thrilling symphonies
   Seem, methinks, to seize us;
Join we too the holy lays;
   JESUS! JESUS! JESUS!
Sweetest sound in seraph's song,
Sweetest note on mortal's tongue,
Sweetest carol ever rung,
JESUS! JESUS! flow along.

Four and twenty elders rise
   From their princely station;
Shout His glorious victories;
   Sing the great salvation:
Cast their crowns before His throne,
Cry in reverential tone,
Holy! Holy! holy One!
T' whom be endless praise alone.

Martyrs in a grand array
   Circle the REDEEMER;
Now their crimson banners play
   Near the imperial streamer;
And before His piercèd feet
Down they cast the coronet,
Ruby wreath superbly set
With the dazzling saphiret.

High ascend the mingling throngs,
  Filled with heavenly fire;
Raise, believers! raise your songs;
  Join the sacred choir.
Soon in yonder faith-viewed plain,
Ye shall shout in rapturous strain,
Free from sin, and free from pain,
While eternal ages reign.

JOHN FELLOWS.

A Baptist shoemaker of Birmingham, author of various books in verse and prose. These are from his *Hymns on Believers' Baptism*, 1773. The extravagant statements in vv. 3 and 4 are of course made from a sectarian standpoint.

MATTHEW iii. 16, 17.

DESCEND, celestial Dove,
  And make Thy presence known;
Reveal our Saviour's Love,
  And seal us for Thine own.
    Our works are vain,
    Unblest by Thee,
    Nor e'er can we
    Acceptance gain.

When Heaven's incarnate God,
  The sovereign Prince of Light,
In Jordan's swelling flood
  Received the holy rite;

Thy form came down
In open view,
And dove-like flew
The King to crown.

The day was never known
Since Time began his race,
In which such glory shone,
Or which obtained such grace,
As that which shed
In Jordan's stream
Thy heavenly beam
On Jesus' head.

There never was a deed
Thus honored from above:
Father and Son agreed
With the celestial Dove,
To crown the rite
With equal rays
In boundless blaze
And floods of light.

Continue still to shine
And fill us with Thy fire:
This ordinance is Thine,
And Thou our souls inspire.
Thou wilt attend
On all Thy sons
(Thy promise runs)
Till time shall end.

INVOCATION.

Baptizèd into Christ,
Lord, we our tribute bring
To Thee, our Prophet, Priest,
And our exalted King:
On Thee we call:
O deign to bless!
Thee we confess,
Our All in all.

THE INVOCATION.

ROMANS viii 9.

BLEST Harbinger of future joys,
Immortal Herald of the skies,
Great Partner of the eternal throne,
Descend, and make Thy presence known.

Shine on our souls, eternal God,
And take amongst us Thine abode:
Why shouldst Thou at a distance stand,
Or be a stranger in our land?

Whatever to our Lord belongs
Is always worthy of our songs;
And all Thy works, and all Thy ways
Demand our wonder and our praise.

But are we not without Thy Grace
Cold as the stream through which we pass?
Our hearts attempt Thy praise in vain,
Nor can our works acceptance gain.

If Thou refuse to aid our songs,
Thy praises falter on our tongues;
The chariot of our love stands still,
Or heavily drives up the hill.

But when Thy cheering beams inspire
These lifeless souls with heavenly fire,
Our rapid wheels outstrip the wind,
And leave earth's empty toys behind.

O touch our lips, eternal King,
While of Thy sovereign Will we sing!
We languish, if Thou cease to shine;
For all our songs and joys are Thine.

———oOo———

ANONYMOUS.

From the "Foundling Hospital Collection," 1775. Long overlooked, this hymn, more or less altered, is now in nearly general use. Compare the revised text in *Hymns Ancient and Modern.*

WHIT-SUNDAY.

SPIRIT of mercy, truth, and love,
    Shed Thy blest influence from above,
And still from age to age convey
The wonders of this sacred day.

In every clime, in every tongue,
Be God's eternal praises sung:
Through all the listening earth be taught
The acts our great Redeemer wrought.

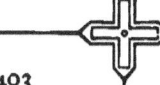

Unfailing Comfort, Heavenly Guide,
Over Thy favored Church preside;
Still may mankind Thy blessings prove,
Spirit of mercy, truth, and love.

JOHN STOCKER.

He was of Honiton, Devon, and nothing more is known of him. His nine hymns were reprinted by Mr. Sedgwick in 1861: they originally appeared in the *Gospel Magazine*, this one in July, 1777.

GRACIOUS Spirit, Dove divine!
   Let Thy light within me shine:
All my guilty fears remove,
Fill me full of heaven and love.

Speak Thy pardoning Grace to me,
Set the burdened sinner free:
Lead me to the Lamb of God,
Wash me in His precious Blood.

Life and peace to me impart;
Seal salvation on my heart;
Breathe Thyself into my breast,
Earnest of immortal rest.

Let me never from Thee stray,
Keep me in the narrow way:
Fill my soul with joy divine,
Keep me, Lord, for ever Thine.

Guard me round on every side;
Save me from self-righteous pride:
Me with Jesu's mind inspire;
Melt me with celestial fire.

Thou my dross and tin consume;
Let Thy inward kingdom come:
All my prayer and praise suggest;
Dwell and reign within my breast.

JONATHAN EVANS, 1749–1809.

Independent minister at Foleshill, near Coventry. From George Burder's *Supplement to Watts, 1784.*

COME, Thou soul-transforming Spirit!
　　Bless the sower and the seed;
Let each heart Thy Grace inherit;
　　Raise the weak, the hungry feed:
　　　From the Gospel
Now supply Thy people's need.

O may all enjoy the blessing
　　Which Thy Word's designed to give!
Let us all, Thy Love possessing,
　　Joyfully the Truth receive;
　　　And for ever
To Thy praise and glory live.

JOHN RYLAND, D.D., 1753–1825.

An eminent Baptist minister at Bristol. His hymns have been collected by Mr. Sedgwick, 1862. This one was written in 1786.

THOU Source of all vigor divine,
    Sweet Spirit of life and of love,
How long shall I languish and pine,
    And when Thy full influence prove?

So far Thou hast quickened my heart,
    It now its own hardness can feel:
When wilt Thou more softness impart,
    And turn it like wax to Thy seal?

I trust I oft feel in my breast
    Some spark of celestial fire:
Without Thee my soul cannot rest;
    No creature can fill my desire.

My deadness and coldness I hate:
    I long to be all on a flame
With love that shall never abate,
    But rise to the skies whence it came.

Lord, cause my cold bosom to glow,
    From odious lukewarmness set free;
Invincible ardor bestow,
    And make me all active for Thee.

SAMUEL MEDLEY, 1738-1799.

Baptist minister at Liverpool, and author of 232 hymns, 77 of which, including this, appeared as a "Second Edition, Enlarged," in 1785. The confusion of thought here apparent is often found among writers of the last century, when they touch the unfamiliar doctrine of the Holy Ghost.

THE SPIRIT AND GRACE OF PRAYER.

ETERNAL Spirit, mighty Lord!
    Jehovah is Thy name:
Thy glories here will we record
    And sing Thy wondrous fame.

'Twas Thy almighty Power and Love
    Which called our souls from death:
O raise our hearts to Thee above
    In praise, while we have breath.

Of heavenly Love Thou art the Pledge,
    The Witness, and the Seal;
O that in prayer when we engage
    We may their influence feel.

Help our infirmities, we pray,
    Our ignorance remove:
O smile our darkness into day,
    And fill us with Thy Love.

Our faint attempts, Lord, kindly own,
    And for us intercede:
Hear every sigh and every groan
    Which from our hearts proceed.

View every painèd, throbbing heart
  That would, but cannot pray;
Thy gracious liberty impart
  To teach them what to say.

Great Searcher of the heart! to Thee
  Let every groan ascend;
Thou know'st the Spirit's mind, and we
  Upon His help depend.

He intercedes for every saint
  According to Thy Will;
True praying souls shall never faint,
  For He is with them still.

THOMAS HAWEIS, LL.B., M.D., 1732–1820.

Rector of All Saints, Aldwinkle, Northamptonshire, and Chaplain to the Countess of Huntingdon: author of several prose works, and of *Carmina Christo, or Hymns to the Saviour*, 1792.

DAY OF PENTECOST.

GREAT Spirit, by whose mighty power
  All creatures live and move,
On us Thy benediction shower,
  Inspire our souls with love.

Hail, Source of light! arise and shine,
  Darkness and doubt dispel;
Give peace and joy, for we are Thine;
  In us for ever dwell.

From death to life our spirits raise,
    Complete redemption bring:
New tongues impart, to speak the praise
    Of Christ our God and King.

Thine inward witness bear, unknown
    To all the world beside:
Exulting then we feel and own
    Our Jesus glorified.

---

2 THESSALONIANS iii. 5.

SPIRIT of God and glory, send
    Thine influence from above;
Reveal in us the sinner's Friend,
    And shed abroad His Love.

Direct our hearts with power divine
    To know the Father's Grace,
And open all His great design
    To save our wretched race.

Of things unseen the evidence give,
    Rejoicing in Thy light;
May we in hope's assurance live
    By faith, and not by sight.

To suffer or to serve our Lord
    With patience persevere,
Till we, according to His word,
    With Him in Heaven appear.

EPHESIANS iv. 15.

SPIRIT of power, descend,
    And dwell in every breast;
Reveal in us the sinner's Friend,
    And bring the promised rest.

His blest new name impart,
    Which the world cannot know,
And stamp His image on our heart,
    That like Him we may grow.

His tender Love inspire,
    His lowliness of mind;
His patience, truth, and holy fire
    Of zeal, with meekness joined.

Thus still from grace to grace
    Advancing as we go,
Bring us to see the Saviour's face,
    And share His glory too.

MARIA FRANCES COWPER, 1727-1797.

Daughter of Colonel Madan of the Guards, sister of Martin Madan, wife of Major Cowper, and cousin of the poet : author of Original Poems, on various Occasions. *by a Lady. Revised by William Cowper, Esq.* 1792. This little book, which was reprinted in Philadelphia 1793. and once or twice in England, is now nearly unknown, though it possesses considerable merit in the way both of poetry and of devotion.

THE WORK OF THE SPIRIT.

THOU Spirit of eternal Truth,
    Thou to whose only power
My soul can look for faith and hope
    In every trying hour;

O work in me to will and do
    The thing that pleaseth Thee:
For in myself no good I know,
    But sore depravity.

Thou Spirit of consummate Grace,
    Fountain of Love divine,
Author of heavenly blessedness,
    Come, fill this heart of mine.
Jesus, Thou everlasting Strength!
    My only Refuge, God!
Behold Thy willing servant bow
    Beneath Thy chastening rod.

Weak and unstable as I am,
    Thy willing servant made,
Boldly Thy promises I claim,
    Through covenant Love conveyed.
Almighty Power! defend my heart,
    Its inmost thoughts control;
Let not the faithless world have part,
    Do Thou possess the whole.

Abate my pride, restrain my will,
    My unbelief subdue:
Cleanse me from every secret ill,
    And all my powers renew.
According to Thy richest Grace,
    My life from sin secure,
And lead me in Thy steadfastness
    To joys for ever pure.

THE RETROSPECT.

COME, Holy Spirit, Love divine,
    Thy cleansing power impart;
Each erring thought and wish refine,
    That wanders near my heart.
There let Thy quickening breezes blow,
    Thine influences be
Such as revive Thy hidden ones,
    And lift their souls to Thee.

Through darkening rains and threatening storms
    My little bark doth ride:
O save me from the fatal wreck
    Of sin's devouring tide.
By past corrections humbled still,
    Let no vain passion start
Within the consecrated veil
    Of a believer's heart.

Oft hast Thou cast me to the ground,
    O'erwhelmed with grief and pain;
Yet hath Thy pitying hand restored
    And led me forth again;
Forth from the shade of sullen woe,
    From darkness and dismay,
And o'er my anguish poured the sweet
    Consolatory ray.

O Lord, how mingled was Thy Love
    In all my deep distress!
Thou gav'st the knowledge of Thy Word,
    That gift of sovereign Grace.

And shall my peevish heart regret
  The momentary pain
That follows on departed joys
  In life's contracted span?

Time's little inch, that steals away
  With every fleeting breath,
And points to an eternity
  Beyond the reach of Death.
Enough, my soul, enough of Time,
  And Time's uncertain things;
Farewell that busy hive, the world,
  And all its thousand stings.

As feathers on the passing stream
  Our earthly pleasures move,
And transient as the evening beam
  That gilds the verdant grove.
To other climes, to other skies,
  My lifted soul aspires;
Thither my wandering thoughts ascend,
  And all my best desires.

Awhile I strive, awhile I mourn,
  Midst thorns and briers here;
But God vouchsafes with Love divine
  My drooping heart to cheer.
Though meaner than the meanest saint,
  My heavenly Guide I see;
I hear a voice behind me say
  That Jesus died for me.

BENJAMIN BEDDOME, 1717-1795.

Baptist minister at Bourton, Gloucestershire, for over half a century. His hymns, to the number of 830, were published in 1818, with a recommendation from Robert Hall: they have been praised by James Montgomery.

INVOCATION.

COME, Holy Spirit, come,
    With energy divine,
And on this poor benighted soul
    With beams of mercy shine.

From the celestial hills
    Light, life, and joy dispense;
And may I daily, hourly feel
    Thy quickening influence.

O melt this frozen heart,
    This stubborn will subdue;
Each evil passion overcome,
    And form me all anew.

The profit will be mine,
    But Thine shall be the praise;
Cheerful to Thee will I devote
    The remnant of my days.

TEACHINGS OF THE SPIRIT.

<small>Dr. Rogers, in his *Lyra Britannica*, gives what purports to be the original text — a very inferior one — of this, and says it was revised by another hand.</small>

COME, blessed Spirit, Source of light,
    Whose Power and Grace are unconfined;
Dispel the gloomy shades of night,
    The thicker darkness of the mind.

To mine illumined eyes display
    The glorious truths Thy Word reveals;
Cause me to run the heavenly way;
    The Book unfold, and loose the seals.

Thine inward teachings make me know
    The mysteries of Redeeming Love,
The emptiness of things below,
    And excellence of things above.

While through this dubious maze I stray,
    Spread, like the sun, Thy beams abroad,
To show the dangers of the way,
    And guide my feeble steps to God.

RENEWING INFLUENCE.

ETERNAL Spirit, Source of good,
    Too little known or understood,
Thy saving gifts to us dispense,
And bless us with Thine influence.

Form every faculty anew,
Our lusts restrain, our hearts subdue;
Our fears suppress, our guilt remove,
Inspire with zeal, enflame with love.

Let all our powers to Thee submit,
And bow adoring at Thy feet;
Thy holy light may we receive,
And mourn whene'er Thyself we grieve.

Thus will we bless Thy name, O Lord,
And Thine efficient Grace record;
Thou with the Father and the Son
Art One in Three and Three in One.

GRIEVE NOT THE SPIRIT.

MY faith is weak, my foes are strong,
  My wandering heart with anguish pained:
Celestial Dove, where art Thou fled,
  Since I Thine influence restrained?
O come again and ease my heart;
There dwell, and never thence depart.

Teach me Thy sovereign will to know,
  From paths of folly to return;
O let me never grieve Thee more,
  Nor ever hence Thine absence mourn.
Come then, celestial Dove, impart
Thy sacred peace to soothe my heart.

Vouchsafe, in answer to my prayer,
    To form my inward powers anew;
Confirm my faith, my fears dispel,
    And guide me all my journey through.
Come then, celestial Spirit, come,
And lead a lonely pilgrim home.

SAMUEL PATTISON.

Author of *Original Poems, chiefly on Sublime Subjects;* published 1801, but apparently prepared for the press in 1792: a curious volume, with a singularly humorous preface. Our extracts are taken from a poem in 33 Odes (covering 57 pages) on the *Te Deum:* they are the 8th and 17th.

TO GOD THE HOLY GHOST.

ERE Nature, lovely child, arose,
    With all her ample spheres,
Thou didst with Deity repose,
    And know coequal years.

Thine agency the GODHEAD sought,
    When Wisdom formed the plan
To rear creation out of naught,
    Or rescue prisoned man.

And from the everlasting throne
    Thy dove-formed radiance flew,
Making its power omnific known
    To all the ethereal view.

Primeval horrors felt Thy glade
    Enter their central gloom;
And downs, with all their charms arrayed,
    Immerged from the hideous womb.

We celebrate Thee, Light of Light!
　By whom the prophets told
Of Israel's freedom from the weight
　Of Babel's yoke of old.

Both Jew and Gentile, seer and sage,
　Drank in their moral day,
Of every clime and every age,
　From Thy inspiring ray.

But O, the effulgence Zion boasts!
　With matchless glow she flames;
Brightened with glory are her coasts
　Of rich immortal beams:

While every member honored is
　With Thy renewing power,
And Thee their Pledge of deathless bliss
　Their grateful souls adore.

Hail, Thou irradiating Fire
　From the eternal Sun!
Through every host and heavenly choir
　Thy boundless praises run.

ALSO THE HOLY GHOST, THE COMFORTER.

HOLY Ghost, the Comforter,
　Thee the sons of light revere;
Own the Paraclete alone,
Hail Thee welcome to Thy throne.

Every humble patient breast,
Of sweet charity possest,
Is the throne of Deity,
Is a temple, Lord, for Thee.

Poor your state, ye splendid domes,
If in you He never homes:
Solemn piles are reared in vain,
If His Grace no glories gain.

Softening as Spring's genial showers
Are the dews He sweetly pours:
Grateful for the drops benign,
Meekened spirits drink them in.

Culture sacred they receive,
By His emanations live;
Down in holy tempers shoot,
Upwards bear celestial fruit.

While His fragrant breezes blow,
Fan the cedars as they grow,
Till they gain their perfect rise,
Gladsome both to earth and skies.

Holy Ghost, the Comforter,
Thee the sons of Heaven revere;
As One of the eternal Three,
Praise, adore, and worship Thee.

RICHARD BURNHAM, 1749–1810.

A London Baptist minister. From his *Hymns*, 1796.

HOLY Spirit, now descend!
   Now reveal the dying Friend:
Give the Christ-endearing light,
Peace, and joy, and vast delight.

Come, Thou sweetest, purest Dove!
Blow up all the fire of love:
Love victorious may we feel,
Love that conquers party zeal:

Love that frees from vile restraint,
Kindly smiles on every saint,
Runs through all the shining road,
Grasps a world, and flies to God.

ANONYMOUS.

From the *Gospel Magazine*; reprinted in Thomas Humphreys' *Collection*, Bristol, 1798.

COME, Holy Ghost, and warm my heart;
   Thy animating power impart,
 Sweet dawn of life divine:
'Tis Jesu's Love alone can give
The power to rise, the power to live;
 Eternal Life is Thine.

If in my heart Thy heavenly day
Has e'er diffused its vital ray,
  I bless the smiling dawn;
But O, when gloomy clouds arise
And veil Thy glory from mine eyes,
  I mourn my joys withdrawn.

Then faith and hope and love decay;
Without Thy life-inspiring ray
  Each cheerful grace declines:
Yet I must live on Thee, my Lord,
For still in Thy unchanging Word
  A beam of comfort shines.

The vital principle within,
Though oft deprest with fear and sin,
  Can never cease to be;
Though doubt prevails, and grief complains,
Thy Hand omnipotent sustains
  The life derived from Thee.

O come, Thou Life of every grace,
Reveal, reveal Thy lovely face;
  These gloomy clouds remove,
And bid my fainting hope arise
To Thy fair mansions in the skies
  On wings of faith and love.

There Life divine no languor knows,
But with immortal vigor glows,
  By joys immortal fed:
No cloud can spread a moment's night,
For there Thy smiles immense delight
  And boundless glory shed.

SIMON BROWNE, 1720.

This piece was overlooked in its proper place, which should be after BROWNE's other hymn on pp. 318-19. It is a fine sample of the theological thought of that day.

HAIL, Holy Spirit, bright immortal Dove!
　　Great Spring of light, of purity and love;
Proceeding from the Father and the Son,
Distinct from Both, and yet with Both but One.

By Thy prolific influence empty space
Grew fruitful, and old Chaos changed its face·
Upon the wasteful deep Thou didst but move,
And Life and Light straight through the fluid strove.

When 'twas foreseen that man would soon rebel,
And yet decreed to save the wretch from hell,
Thou didst in the eternal consult join,
And freely bear a part in that design.

How dim and faded did the apostate look,
How changed his nature, when he God forsook!
How did his glory wane, his life decay,
And all his native beauty fade away!

Before, he shone with heavenly lustre bright,
Bore God's own image, and was His delight:
Basked in His smiles, and on His Love did feast,
And settled in Him as his central Rest.

But ah, what waste the invader Sin has made!
His lustre's lost, his mind involved in shade:
His God is gone, the very man is dead,
And in his room the brute erects his head.

Dusky and callous all his mind is grown,
Dark as the grave, and hard as any stone;
Insensible to things divine become,
Stained all with guilt and thick impervious gloom.

But, Lord, from Thee one kind and quickening ray
Will pierce the gloom, and re-enkindle day;
'Twill waken all the primogenial fire,
Revive the man, and Life divine inspire.

Thy secret energy diffused within
Will purify the soul, and purge out sin;
'Twill warm the frozen heart with love divine,
And with its Maker's image make it shine.

O shed Thine influence, and Thy power exert,
Clear my dark mind, and thaw my icy heart;
Pour on my drowsy soul celestial day,
And heavenly Life to all its powers convey.

Say but the powerful word, and 'twill be done:
Soon shall I put my Maker's image on,
And shine again with His resemblance bright,
Enjoy His favor and be His delight.

The brute in me shall die, and in its stead
The man revive, and lift again his head:
God reconciled shall to my breast return,
And all my soul with strong devotion burn.

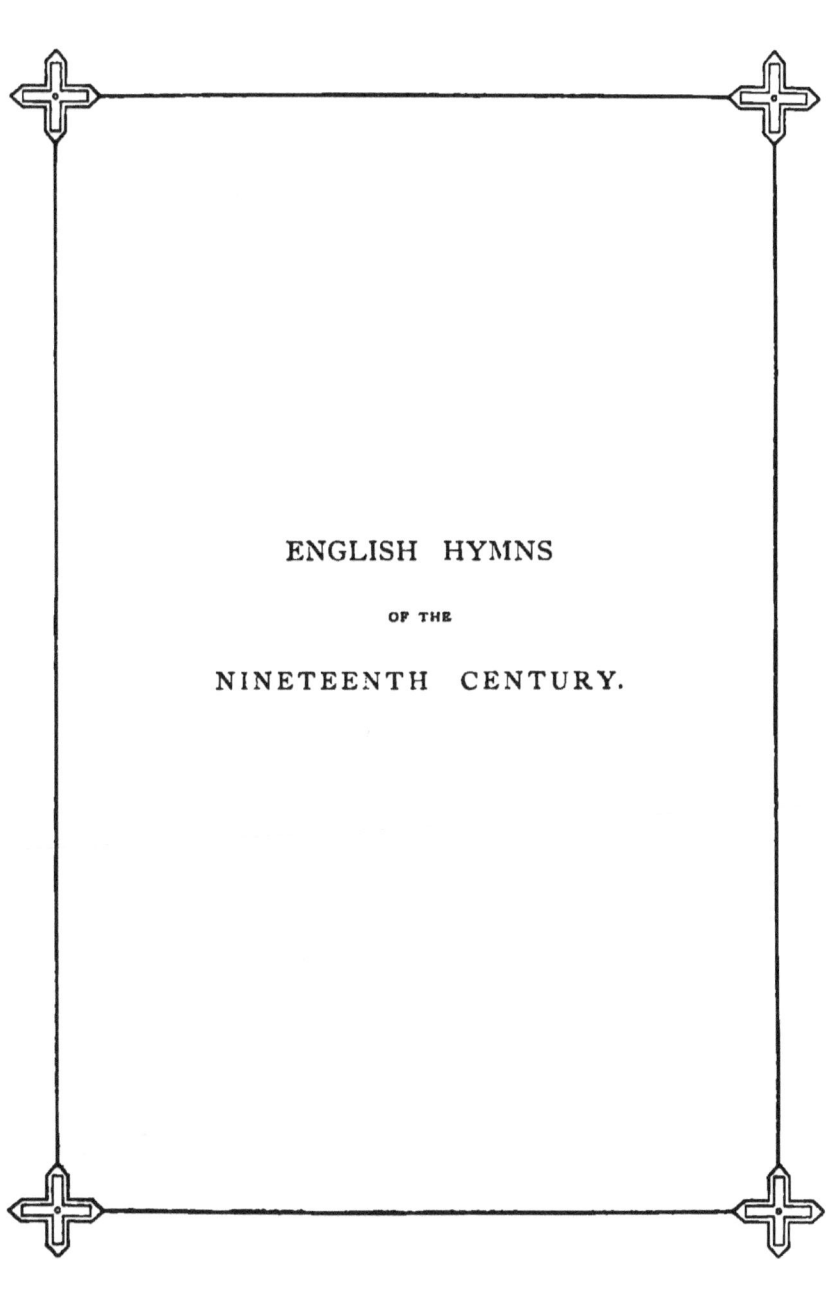

ENGLISH HYMNS

OF THE

NINETEENTH CENTURY.

O HOLY SPIRIT of Grace, be Thou my Wisdom, to teach me my faith; my Understanding, to teach me my duty; my Counsel, in all my doubts; my Strength, against all temptations; my Knowledge, in what belongs to the state of life to which I am called; my Godliness, in all my actions; my Fear, all the day long: that Thou mayst be my Comfort at the last, and my Bliss for ever. Amen.

ENGLISH HYMNS OF THE NINE-TEENTH CENTURY.

BASIL WOODD, 1760–1831.

Morning preacher at Bentinck Chapel, Marylebone, and rector of Drayton-Beauchamp, Buckinghamshire. His *New Metrical Version of the Psalms, with an Appendix of Hymns*, appeared in or about 1800: second edition, 1821. Of this piece he says in his Preface that it "was a favorite hymn of the late lamented Princess Charlotte. She frequently played and sang it to the tune of Haydn's celebrated German hymn: and had marked in her copy the passages which particularly interested her." Joseph Hart (1759) has a hymn beginning with the same words, but after the opening lines entirely different.

HOLY Ghost, inspire our praises;
   Shed abroad a Saviour's Love:
While we chant the name of Jesus,
   Deign on every heart to move.
Source of sweetest consolation!
   Breathe Thy peace on all below;
Bless, O bless this congregation;
   Bid our hearts with influence glow.

Come with heavenly inspiration,
   Jesus in our souls reveal;
Manifest this great salvation;
   As Thy own our spirits seal.
Light divine, on darkness shining,
   Deign the light of Truth to give;
Every grace and joy combining,
   May we to Thy glory live.

Hail, ye spirits bright and glorious,
  High exalted round the throne!
Now with you we join in chorus,
  And your Lord we call our own.
God to us His Son hath given:
  Saints, your noblest anthems raise:
All in earth and all in Heaven
  Shout the great Jehovah's praise.

DANIEL HERBERT, 1751–1833.

Independent minister at Sudbury, Suffolk; a voluminous but feeble versifier. His *Hymns and Poems, Doctrinal and Experimental*, fill three volumes, of which the first, containing this, appeared 1801.

LONGING AFTER GOD.

COME, Thou almighty Comforter,
  And bring upon Thy wing
Sweet consolations to each soul,
  That we may praise and sing.

We want to feel, we want to see,
  We want to know Thee more;
We want sweet foretastes of Thy Love,
  As we have had before.

And shall we come in vain to God?
  Dear Lord, that cannot be;
Thy promise stands engaged to come
  And bless even two or three.

Come, Lord, and grant each soul to feel
    Its interest in Thy Grace,
And give us faith and hope and love,
    And strength to run the race.

For if Thou draw'st us, we can run;
    Upheld by Thee, we stand:
Lord, work in us to will and do,
    And lead us by the hand.

If Thou should'st leave us, we must fall,
    Without Thee cannot rise;
For when our Jesus hides His face
    Our hope and comfort dies.

Lord, give more faith, more solid faith,
    More confidence in Thee;
Break off our legal chains, O God,
    And let our souls go free.

JOHN STEWART, 1803.

This hymn has been wrongly ascribed to George Burder: Mr. Sedgwick gives it as above. I know nothing of the author, and cannot answer for the text.

COME, Holy Spirit! calm my mind,
    And fit me to approach my God;
Remove each vain, each worldly thought,
    And lead me to Thy blest abode.

Hast Thou imparted to my soul
   A living spark of holy fire?
O kindle now the sacred flame;
   Make me to burn with pure desire.

Impress upon my wandering heart
   The Love that Christ to sinners bore;
That I may mourn the wounds I caused,
   And my redeeming God adore.

A brighter faith and hope impart,
   And let me now my Saviour see;
O soothe and cheer my burdened heart,
   And bid my spirit rest in Thee.

JOHN KEMPTHORNE, 1810.

From *Select Portions of Psalms*, &c. So says Mr. Sedgwick. I find it in a *Selection of Psalms and Anthems* by W. MORGAN of Bradford: 1815-1822.

SPIRIT OF GOD, ON THEE WE CALL.

SPIRIT of God, on Thee we call;
   O hear us, and Thy gifts impart.
Lamenting, penitent, we fall:
   Descend into our inmost heart.

Our strongest efforts all are vain;
   Spirit of Mercy! set us free:
Captive to sin we shall remain
   Till we are sanctified by Thee.

In time of wealth, Protecting Power!
From pride and worldly snares defend;
And in affliction's keenest hour,
Be Thou our Comforter and Friend.

Vouchsafe to lend a gracious ear,
And quickly come, Thou heavenly Guest!
Come and abide for ever here;
Thy temple is the Christian's breast.

THOMAS COTTERILL, 1779–1823.

Perpetual Curate of St. Paul's, Sheffield. His *Selection*, in which James Montgomery helped him, appeared 1810, and reached an eighth edition, enlarged, 1819. The date of this is 1811: it is founded on a hymn of HART's: see pp. 384-5.

FOR A WELL-GROUNDED HOPE OF SALVATION.

ETERNAL Spirit! Source of Truth!
Our contrite hearts inspire;
Kindle a flame of heavenly love,
And feed the pure desire.

'Tis Thine to soothe the sorrowing soul,
With Satan's yoke oppressed;
'Tis Thine to bid the dying live,
And give the weary rest.

Let no false joy deceive our minds;
Lest, while we boast Thy light,
We fall from all our towering hopes
Down to eternal night.

Subdue the power of every sin,
  Whate'er that sin may be;
That we, in singleness of heart,
  May worship only Thee.

Then with our spirits witness bear,
  That we're the sons of God,
Redeemed from sin, and death, and hell,
  Through Christ's atoning Blood.

SPIRIT OF TRUTH, THY GRACE IMPART.

The above has been rehashed as follows. This compilation, found in many books, owes its second verse to C. Wesley, and its third and fourth to Hart and Cotterill; while v. 1 alone boasts a semblance of originality.

SPIRIT of truth, Thy grace impart,
  To guide our doubtful way;
Thy beams shall scatter every cloud,
  And make a glorious day.

Light in Thy light O may we see,
  Thy Grace and mercy prove,
Revived and cheered and blessed by Thee,
  Spirit of peace and love!

'Tis Thine to soothe the sorrowing mind,
  With guilt and fear opprest;
'Tis Thine to bid the dying live,
  And give the weary rest.

Subdue the power of every sin,
  Whate'er that sin may be,
That we, in singleness of heart,
  May worship only Thee.

ANONYMOUS, 1815.

From a Cornish Selection, 1815, and others.

HOLY Ghost, whose fire celestial
    Light and Life divine imparts;
Come and dwell in breasts terrestrial;
    Heaven reveal in earthly hearts.
Come and pour in blest effusion
    Heavenly unction from above,
Scattering wide, in rich diffusion,
    "Comfort, light, and fire of love."

Keep Thy Church in holy union;
    Foes remove, give peace at home:
Source of peace and sweet communion,
    Where Thou dwellest, no ill can come.
Teach us humbly to adore Thee,
    While on earth we pass our days:
Thence transport our souls to glory,
    Lost in wonder, love, and praise.

SPIRIT OF TRUTH, O HOLY GHOST.

From a Collection prepared by the Revs. E. Maltby, R. Tillard, and J. S. Banks, and sanctioned by the Bishop of Lincoln, 1815.

SPIRIT of Truth, O Holy Ghost,
    Fruit of our Saviour's Love!
Come, as on Day of Pentecost,
    Descending from above.

Like the first saints, with one accord
 Behold us met to hail
Our risen and ascended Lord:
 His promise will not fail.

And though no mighty rushing sound,
 Or cloven tongues of fire,
Or gifts of speech attend Thee down,
 With comfort us inspire.

Teach us to feel His heavenly peace,
 To walk the paths He trod;
Confirm our faith, our hope increase,
 And fix our love on God.

WILLIAM GADSBY, 1773-1844.

Author of The Nazarene's Songs, 1814. This piece is here abridged.

HOLY Ghost, we look to Thee!
 Raise the dead, the captive free;
From the mighty take the prey,
Teach the weak to watch and pray.

Blessed Spirit, holy God,
'Tis Thy work to shed abroad
Love divine in Zion's heart,
And true holiness impart.

HOLY SPIRIT, HEAVENLY DOVE.

Thine it is the Church to bless,
And to comfort in distress;
Trembling, helpless souls to guide
Safe to Jesu's wounded side.

Carry on Thy work with power,
Lead us safely to Thy tower;
Jesu's matchless fulness show,
Suited to our every woe.

Out of self to Jesus lead;
For and in us intercede:
Guide us down to death, and there
Banish all our guilt and fear.

There, and then, support the mind;
May we be to death resigned;
And with an immortal song
Haste to join the heavenly throng.

JOSEPH IRONS, 1785-1852.

Independent minister in London, and father of Dr. W. J. Irons, who has made the best version of *Dies Iræ*. Author of *Zion's Hymns*, 1816.

HOLY Spirit, heavenly Dove,
Breathe upon us from above,
And with sweet celestial fire
Zeal inflame, and love inspire.

On this congregation pour
Heavenly blessings like a shower;
Streams of Grace upon us shed;
Teach the living, raise the dead.

Bid each groundless doubt depart;
Bind up every broken heart.
Warm the frozen, cheer the faint;
Feed and comfort every saint.

Every soul do Thou engage;
Every Christian's grief assuage;
Be our Counsellor and Guide;
Lead to Jesus crucified.

THE WITNESS.

Romans viii. 16.

HOLY Spirit, heavenly Witness,
    Whose almighty unction darts
Life to souls once dead, and fitness
    For the heavenly state imparts;
      Bear Thy witness
    To Thy work in all our hearts.

Witness to our souls of Jesus,
    Let us now His Grace record:
Thou and Thou alone canst ease us;
    Shed the Saviour's Love abroad,
      And bear witness
    That we are the sons of God.

Witness every frame and feeling,
  Every want and every woe;
And the Blood of Christ for healing
  On our helpless souls bestow:
    Holy Witness,
  Let us covenant blessings know.

Witness in us, for us, by us,
  With Thine agency divine;
Nor in that great Day deny us,
  When the saints in glory shine.
    Then bear witness
  Of our souls, that they are Thine.

INVOCATION.

ETERNAL Spirit, let me know
  The Love of Christ to me;
Its conquering, quickening power bestow,
  To set my spirit free.

I long to know its depth and height,
  To scan its breadth and length,
Drink in its ocean of delight,
  And triumph in its strength.

It is Thine office to reveal
  The Saviour's wondrous Love;
O set upon my heart Thy seal,
  And bless me from above.

Thy quickening power to me impart,
   And be my constant Guide;
Remove my sorrows, warm my heart,
   And be Thou glorified.

THOMAS ROW.

An obscure but voluminous rhymer. His two volumes of Spiritual Poems, or Evangelical Hymns, appeared 1817 and 1822. I take this and the next from DAVID DENHAM'S Selection, 1837.

ALMIGHTY Spirit, we
   Thy Godhead now adore;
We bring our praise to Thee,
   And thanks for evermore.
For once we slept in darkness deep,
But Thou hast raised us from the sleep.

Through all Thy work within
   Thy greatness we admire:
It breaks the reign of sin,
   And lights the sacred fire,
To make us burn with love to God,
Through the atoning Saviour's Blood.

Thy Power and Grace divine
   Have raised us from the dead,
And taught our souls to twine
   Around our living Head:
And none but God could bless us so,
Or raise us from such depths of woe.

     To Jesus Thou dost lead
     Our souls for life and rest,
     And on His Cross to feed
     Till we are truly blest.
We now to Thee our praises bring,
And thus Thy glorious Godhead sing.

ROBERT HAWKER, D.D., 1753–1827.

<small>Vicar of Charles-the-Martyr, Plymouth. His *Collection of Psalms and Hymns* reached a 15th edition in 1834. Text from Denham's *Selection*.</small>

SPIRIT Jehovah! glorious Lord!
   Vouchsafe Thy presence with Thy Word
  To all Thy Church around:
Lord, grant to each of Thine now here
The seeing eye, the hearing ear,
  To know the joyful sound.

Without renewings of Thy Grace
To see God's glory in Christ's face
  And manifest the Lord,
Our ordinance will barren prove,
Not one will taste of Jesus' Love
  Or savor in Thy Word.

Blest Spirit! on Christ's garden blow,
And cause the spices all to flow,
  As grace for grace each suits;
For then will our Beloved come
Into this garden of His own
  And eat His pleasant fruits.

Almighty Lord! let all around
In sweet communion now abound
  With God and God's dear Son.
If Thou wilt open to our view
The Love of Each, and draw us too,
  Then will our hearts be won.

'Tis Thine, O Lord, in blessing thus
To take of Christ's and show to us,
  Of Him and His to impart:
And Thine no less the same to prove,
And shed abroad the Father's Love
  In each renewèd heart.

'Tis Thine in prayer to help complaints,
To quicken sinners, comfort saints,
  And weary souls refresh;
The heart of stone to take away;
Lord, there are many here this day!
  O give them hearts of flesh.

Sweet Comforter! do Thou behold
The little ones of Jesus' fold
  With special grace this day;
That all Thy children, taught of Thee,
May have their portion full and free,
  And none go lean away.

Then will loud praises through our host
To Father, Son, and Holy Ghost,

By every tongue be given;
And each will say in godly fear,
"This is God's House; the Lord is here;
And this the Gate of Heaven."

And daily, till our Lord shall come
To take His whole redeemèd home
    With Him for ever then,
The Lord send blessings from above!
The Father's, Son's, and Spirit's Love
    Be with us all. Amen.

ANDREW REED, D.D., 1787-1862.

Independent minister in London, and an eminent philanthropist. He published *A Supplement to Dr. Watts*, 1817, enlarged edition 1825; and *The Hymn Book*, 1842. The latter contains nineteen lyrics of his own: two of which are among the most familiar modern Spirit-hymns. The first appeared 1817.

HOLY Ghost, with light divine,
    Shine upon this heart of mine!
Chase the shades of night away,
Turn the darkness into day.
Let me see my Saviour's face,
Let me all His beauties trace;
Show those glorious truths to me
Which are only known by Thee.

Holy Ghost, with power divine,
Cleanse this guilty heart of mine:

Long has sin, without control,
Held dominion o'er my soul:
Oft I of its power complain,
Yet I live beneath its reign;
In Thy mercy pity me,
From this bondage set me free.

Holy Ghost, with joy divine,
Cheer this saddened heart of mine;
Bid my many woes depart,
Heal my wounded, bleeding heart.
Yield a sacred, settled peace,
Bid it grow and still increase;
Till each anxious thought expires,
Till my joy to Heaven aspires.

Holy Spirit, all divine,
Dwell within this heart of mine;
Cast down every idol throne,
Reign supreme, and reign alone.
See, to Thee I yield my heart;
Shed Thy life through every part.
A pure temple I would be,
Wholly dedicate to Thee.

SPIRIT DIVINE! ATTEND OUR PRAYERS.
1842.

SPIRIT Divine! attend our prayers,
   And make this house Thy home;
Descend with all Thy gracious powers;
   O come, great Spirit, come!

Come as the light: to us reveal
    Our emptiness and woe;
And lead us in those paths of life
    Where all the righteous go.

Come as the fire, and purge our hearts,
    Like sacrificial flame:
Let our whole soul an offering be
    To our Redeemer's Name.

Come as the dew, and sweetly bless
    This consecrated hour;
May barrenness rejoice to own
    Thy fertilizing power.

Come as the dove, and spread Thy wings,
    The wings of peaceful Love;
And let Thy Church on earth become
    Blest as the Church above.

Come as the wind, with rushing sound
    And Pentecostal Grace;
That all of woman born may see
    The glory of Thy face.

Spirit divine, attend our prayers,
    Make a lost world Thy home;
Descend with all Thy gracious powers;
    O come, great Spirit, come!

JAMES MONTGOMERY, 1771–1854.

His hymns appeared at various times: some 46 in Thomas Cotterill's *Selection*, 1819; 100 in his own *Christian Psalmist*, 1825; and many were printed for the first time in his *Original Hymns*, 1853.

THE DESCENT OF THE SPIRIT.

Acts ii. 1-4.

1819. Text slightly revised in 1825.

LORD God, the Holy Ghost!
    In this accepted hour,
As on the day of Pentecost,[1]
    Descend in all Thy power.
We meet with one accord
    In our appointed place,
And wait the promise of our Lord,
    The Spirit of all Grace.

Like mighty rushing wind
    Upon the waves beneath,
Move with one impulse every mind,
    One soul, one feeling breathe:
The young, the old inspire
    With wisdom from above;
And give us hearts and tongues of fire,
    To pray, and praise, and love.

Spirit of Light, explore
    And chase our gloom away;
With lustre shining more and more
    Unto the perfect day.

---

[1] *On this* the day of Pentecost. — 1819.

Spirit of Truth, be Thou
    In life and death our Guide;
O Spirit of adoption, now
    May we be sanctified!

THE SPIRIT CREATING ALL THINGS NEW.
1825.

SPIRIT of power and might, behold
    A world by sin destroyed:
Creator-Spirit, as of old,
    Move on the formless void.

Give Thou the word; — that healing sound
    Shall quell the deadly strife;
And earth again, like Eden crowned,
    Produce the Tree of Life.

If sang the morning-stars for joy,
    When Nature rose to view,
What strains will angel-harps employ
    When Thou shalt all renew!

And if the sons of God rejoice
    To hear a Saviour's name,
How will the ransomed raise their voice,
    To whom that Saviour came!

So every kindred, tongue and tribe,
    Assembling round the throne,
Thy new creation shall ascribe
    To sovereign Love alone.

THE SPIRIT ACCOMPANYING THE WORD OF GOD.

1825.

O SPIRIT of the living God!
   In all Thy plenitude of Grace,
Where'er the foot of man hath trod,
   Descend on our apostate race.

Give tongues of fire and hearts of love,
   To preach the reconciling Word;
Give power and unction from above,
   Whene'er the joyful sound is heard.

Be darkness, at Thy coming, light;
   Confusion order in Thy path;
Souls without strength inspire with might;
   Bid mercy triumph over wrath.

O Spirit of the Lord! prepare
   All the round earth her God to meet;
Breathe Thou abroad like morning air,
   Till hearts of stone begin to beat.

Baptize the nations; far and nigh
   The triumphs of the Cross record;
The Name of Jesus glorify,
   Till every kindred call Him Lord.

God from eternity hath willed
All flesh shall His salvation see;
So be the Father's Love fulfilled,
   The Saviour's sufferings crowned through
     Thee.

HENRY LOWE.

<small>Author of a volume of *Psalms and Hymns* for the Church Year, 1820.</small>

THEE will we praise, celestial Power,
   Thee, wondrous, mighty Spirit, sing:
Thou who in young Creation's hour
   Wast present with Thy fostering wing.

From Thee its life and beauty came,
   All that delights and cheers the eye;
The Spirit earth, sea, sky proclaim,
   And tell of blessings from on high.

To man, the fairest work of Heaven,
   O'er all the rest to bear control,
To him Thine energy was given,
   Endowed by Thee, a living soul.

Yet hast Thou blessings dearer far;
   To make our souls Thine own abode;
To form them by Thy holy care
   For endless bliss, the sons of God.

Thanks, blessing, honor, might, and praise
  Be unto Thee, all holy Lord!
To Thee may earth one chorus raise,
  And God the Spirit be adored.

S. B. HASLAM.

From the title-page of his *Divine Aspirations*. 1824–1833.

INSPIRED by Thee, divine triumphant Breath!
  I sing Thy conquests over sin and death:
Or in Thy rich salutes such bliss I prove,
My spirit breathes enraptured strains of love.
But should my muse a mournful theme assume,
Of souls deep buried in a fleshly tomb;
Or songs or sighs, as touching Grace and sin,
Alike are echoes of Thy voice within.

BISHOP REGINALD HEBER, 1783–1826.

WHIT-SUNDAY.

(Compare with Hart's hymn on pp. 383-4.)

SPIRIT of Truth! on this Thy day
  To Thee for help we cry,
To guide us through the dreary way
  Of dark mortality.

We ask not, Lord, Thy cloven flame,
  Or tongues of various tone;
But long Thy praises to proclaim
  With fervor in our own.

We mourn not that prophetic skill
  Is found on earth no more;
Enough for us to trace Thy will
  In Scripture's sacred lore.

We neither have nor seek the power
  Ill demons to control;
But Thou, in dark temptation's hour,
  Shalt chase them from the soul.

No heavenly harpings soothe our ear,
  No mystic dreams we share;
Yet hope to feel Thy comfort near,
  And bless Thee in our prayer.

When tongues shall cease, and power decay,
  And knowledge empty prove,
Do Thou Thy trembling servants stay
  With faith, with hope, with love.

JOHN KEBLE, 1792–1866.

<small>Vicar of Hursley. The two following extracts are from *The Christian Year*, 1827.</small>

CONFIRMATION.

<small>The five opening verses are omitted.</small>

SPIRIT of might and sweetness too!
  Now leading on the wars of God,
Now to green isles of shade and dew
  Turning the waste Thy people trod;

Draw, Holy Ghost, Thy sevenfold veil
  Between us and the fires of youth:
Breathe, Holy Ghost, Thy freshening gale,
  Our fevered brow in age to soothe.

And oft as sin and sorrow tire,
  The hallowed hour do Thou renew,
When, beckoned up the awful choir
  By pastoral hands, toward Thee we drew;

When trembling at the sacred rail
  We hid our eyes and held our breath,
Felt Thee how strong, our hearts how frail,
  And longed to own Thee to the death.

For ever on our souls be traced
  That blessing dear, that dove-like hand,
A sheltering rock in memory's waste,
  O'ershadowing all the weary land.

ORDINATION.

The four opening verses are omitted.

AND where shall Mother's bosom find,
  With all its deep love-learnèd skill,
A prayer so sweetly to her mind
  As, in this sacred hour and still,

Is wafted from the white-robed choir,
  Ere yet the pure high-breathèd lay,
"Come, Holy Ghost, our souls inspire,"
  Rise floating on its dovelike way.

And when it comes, so deep and clear
　　The strain, so soft the melting fall,
It seems not to the entrancèd ear
　　Less than Thine own heart-cheering call,

Spirit of Christ — Thine earnest given
　　That these our prayers are heard, and they
Who grasp this hour the sword of Heaven
　　Shall feel Thee on their weary way.

Oft as at morn or soothing eve
　　Over the holy Fount they lean,
Their fading garland freshly weave,
　　Or fan them with Thine airs serene,

Spirit of Light and Truth! to Thee
　　We trust them in that musing hour,
Till they, with open heart and free,
　　Teach all Thy Word in all its power.

When foemen watch their tents by night,
　　And mists hang wide o'er moor and fell,
Spirit of Counsel and of Might,
　　Their pastoral warfare guide Thou well.

And O, when worn and tired they sigh
　　With that more fearful war within,
When passion's storms are loud and high,
　　And brooding o'er remembered sin

The heart dies down — O mightiest then,
　　Come ever true, come ever near,
And wake their slumbering love again,
　　Spirit of God's most holy Fear!

GRIEVE NOT THE HOLY SPIRIT.

From Henry Allon's *Supplemental Hymns*, 1868. It is there ascribed to Keble, but I cannot find it in his books.

How dare we pray Thee dwell within
  These hearts defiled by wilful sin?
Yet, Holy Ghost, do not depart,
Leave not to earth our earthly heart.
And if Thou seest us erring still,
O bend to Thine our stubborn will,
And bring us to the fold again,
If need, by chastisement and pain.

Bring us, by all the powers of sense,
By all the course of Providence,
By inmost Conscience, not yet dumb,
By all the past, by all to come,
By God's best Gifts, His Son to die,
And then our hearts to sanctify;
Bring us, before our sun go down,
To bear the cross, to win the crown.

ANONYMOUS, 1828.

FOR HELP IN THE FIGHT.

From *A Collection of Prayers, with a Few Hymns*, Oxford, 1828.

Spirit of God, mysterious Power, descend!
  To Thine own victory rule our combat now;
Leave us not to ourselves, but still defend
  Each breast unharnessed, each unhelmèd brow.

Our battle is not against flesh alone,
    The banded world and many a treacherous guide;
But against vigilant fiends, to whom are known
    Our hopes of Heaven, our weakness, and our pride.

Though reft of helm and corselet, we shall war
    To victory, so Thou our cause befriend,
By Him, the Crucified, the Conqueror:
    Spirit of God, mysterious Power, descend!

TURN US.

O TURN, most Holy Spirit! turn
    Our hearts to wisdom, and release
Our souls from Satan: make us learn
    In Christ the lesson of our peace.
For His dear sake, in Whom alone
    Began, continues, and must end
The work of Grace, to us make known
    His Cross: on us Thy power descend!

The sinners Thou dost call to Thee,
    The sinners whom He died to save.
Redeem us from ourselves, and free
    Our souls from bondage and the grave:
Make our ears hear, our eyes discern
    Thy Truth; all our reluctance cease:
O turn, almighty Spirit, turn
    Our hearts to wisdom and to peace.

R. DUNDERDALE.

Poems on Religious and Moral Subjects: Kirkby Lonsdale, 1829.

HAIL, blessed Source of holy Light and Life,
   Our Guide to Heaven and Comfort here below!
Thou kind Defence 'gainst anger, wrath, and strife,
   On my sad heart Thy influence bestow.

Teach me to spurn that idle pomp and state
   From which much ire and discord oft arise:
For purer scenes teach my proud heart to wait,
   And fix my view on worlds beyond the skies.

Inspire my soul with deepest love of Christ;
   His blessed steps incline me to pursue:
Cleanse from my earthly eyes the darkening mist,
   And with Thy Grace my carnal mind renew.

And then whatever here may be my lot,
   Whether proud wealth or poverty betide,
Like the poor hermit's in the lonely grot,
   My heart will be secure from deadly pride.

Then I shall run my mortal course in peace,
   As much as is allowed to Adam's race:
Then, when the throbbing tide of life shall cease,
   Where seraphs reign, I'll reach the happy place.

WILLIAM HILEY BATHURST. Born 1796.

Rector of Barwick-in-Elmet, 1820–1852. His *Psalms and Hymns* appeared 1831

ETERNAL Spirit, by whose power
   Are burst the bands of death,
On our cold hearts Thy blessings shower,
   And stir them with Thy breath.

'Tis Thine to point the heavenly way,
   Each rising fear control,
And with a warm enlivening ray
   To melt the icy soul.

'Tis Thine to cheer us when distrest,
   To raise us when we fall,
To calm the doubting, troubled breast,
   And aid when sinners call.

'Tis Thine to bring God's sacred Word
   And write it on our heart,
There its reviving truths record,
   And there its peace impart.

Almighty Spirit, visit thus
   Our hearts, and guide our ways;
Pour down Thy quickening Grace on us,
   And tune our lips to praise.

SPIRITUAL STRENGTH AND WISDOM DESIRED.

John xvi. 13, 14.

SPIRIT of Life, Thy influence shed,
To wake the careless and the dead,
Light, strength, and comfort to bestow
On many a child of sin and woe.

Behold our frail and feeble state;
Our foes are strong, our danger great:
The force of hostile rage withstand,
And guard us with Thy mighty Hand.

Give us an understanding mind,
The chains of ignorance unbind;
Instruct, enlighten, and prepare
Our hearts the joy of Heaven to share.

Christ's precious truths to us proclaim,
Expound His Word, exalt His Name;
Make known His power, His Love reveal,
And with His Blood our conscience heal.

Lord, in our hearts vouchsafe to dwell,
There every sinful motion quell;
Complete Thy blessed work of Grace,
And fit us for a happier place.

FOR HEALING AND STRENGTHENING GRACE.

SPIRIT of holiness, look down,
    Our fainting hearts to cheer;
And when we tremble at Thy frown,
    O bring Thy comforts near.

The fears which Thy convictions wrought,
    O let Thy Grace remove;
And may the souls which Thou hast taught
    To weep, now learn to love.

Now let Thy saving mercy heal
    The wounds it made before;
Now on our hearts impress Thy seal,
    That we may doubt no more.

Complete the work Thou hast begun,
    And make our darkness light,
That we a glorious race may run,
    Till faith be lost in sight.

Then as our wondering eyes discern
    The Lord's unclouded face,
In fitter language we shall learn
    To sing triumphant Grace.

THE SPIRIT'S DIRECTION IMPLORED.

HOLY Spirit, from on high
  Bend on us a pitying eye;
Animate the drooping heart,
Bid the power of sin depart.

Light up every dark recess
Of our hearts' ungodliness;
Show us every devious way
Where our steps have gone astray.

Teach us with repentant grief
Humbly to implore relief;
Then the Saviour's Blood reveal,
All our deep disease to heal.

Other groundwork should we lay,
Sweep those empty hopes away;
Make us feel that Christ alone
Can for human guilt atone.

May we daily grow in grace,
And pursue the heavenly race,
Trained in wisdom, led by Love,
Till we reach our Rest above.

BAPTIST WRIOTHESLEY NOEL. Born 1799.

This is from his Selection, 1832, second edition, 1838; and is supposed to be from his pen.

HOLIEST Source of consolation,
  Light and life Thy Grace imparts;
Visit us in Thy compassion;
  Guide our minds, and fill our hearts.

Heavenly blessings without measure
  Thou canst bring us from above;
Lord, we ask that heavenly treasure,
  Wisdom, holiness, and love.

Dwell within us, blessed Spirit;
  Where Thou dwell'st no ill can come.
Bless us now, through Jesus' merit;
  Reign in every heart and home.

Saviour, lead us to adore Thee,
  While Thou dost prolong our days;
Then, with angel hosts before Thee,
  May we worship, love, and praise.

ANONYMOUS, 1832.

From a Collection for St. George's church, Hulme; Manchester, 1832. Verses 2 and 3 are from later hymnals.

SPIRIT of God, whose sacred fire
  Wisdom and power and love conveys,
Thy Grace impart, our souls inspire
  With holy hope and fervent praise.

Thee we adore, Spirit divine,
    Proceeding from the eternal Throne,
Whose gifts mysterious all combine
    To glorify our Lord alone.

O Thou who hast Thine unction poured
    In rich abundance o'er the head
Of each ordained to speak Thy Word,
    On us that quickening influence shed.

With beams of heavenly light sent down,
    Dispel the darkness of our mind:
Give us that peace which they alone,
    Who love the Saviour, surely find.

Thy living temples may we be,
    Cleansed by Thy hallowing presence, Lord:
Abide in us, and we in Thee,
    Supremely loved, obeyed, adored:

Our sins effaced by Jesus' Blood,
    Our spirits sanctified by Grace:
Then raise us up to meet our God,
    And see the Saviour face to face.

WHIT-SUNDAY.

From a Collection by R. Frost of Salford, 1832-1842.

ONCE more the Christian Pentecost we hail:
    May love divine in every soul prevail,
And youth and age their hearts and voices raise,
To sing redeeming Love in hymns of praise.

Come, Holy Comforter! our tongues unloose,
And grateful incense from our hearts produce;
Still, still may holiness with years increase,
And our last days be crowned with joy and peace.

From sin and endless woe may all be freed,
Eternal Spirit! in this hour of need.
Descend, and bring to every longing breast
The pledge and earnest of eternal Rest.

By every nation, people, kindred, tongue,
May Jesus' glorious fame be ceaseless sung;
And righteousness and peace salute and reign,
Till man's chief foes, both sin and death, are slain.

O Saviour! may we always feel Thee near,
To fill our hearts with love and holy fear;
May naught from Thee our faithful souls divide,
Nor life, nor death, nor aught on earth beside.

THOMAS JAMES JUDKIN.

"Minister of Somers' Town Chapel, St. Pancras": author of *Church and Home Psalmody*, 1831: a work dedicated to the Bishop of Salisbury.

2 CORINTHIANS iii. 17.

HOLY Spirit, Fount of blessing,
    Ever watchful, ever kind;
Thy celestial aid possessing,
    Prisoned souls deliverance find.

Seal of Truth and Bond of Union,
   Source of Light and Flame of Love,
Symbol of divine communion
   In the olive-bearing dove!

Heavenly Guide from paths of error,
   Comforter to minds distrest,
When the billows fill with terror
   Pointing to an Ark of rest:
Promised Pledge, eternal Spirit,
   Greater than all gifts below;
May our hearts Thy Grace inherit,
   May our lips Thy glories show.

LORD'S DAY MORNING.

Rev. i. 10.

O HOLY Spirit, who didst shed
   Thy heavenly beams on Jesu's head,
When stooping low, He meekly stood
To be baptized in Jordan's flood!

O'er us Thy dove-like wings extend,
To us Thy promised succor lend,
That so this Sabbath-morn may prove
A time for knowledge, peace, and love.

Without Thy light no power have we
The glories of Thy Word to see;
Without Thy proffered strength, in vain
We strive to break our bondage-chain.

Thriceblessed Spirit! hither come
And make our willing hearts Thy home:
Thy wisdom, Grace, and might be given,
To bless on earth, and lead to Heaven.

WILLIAM WINSTANLEY HULL.

He edited, in 1833, *A Churchman's Hymns*, many of them being originals, and presumably his own.

SPIRIT of Mercy, dwell
   With us Thy servants here,
And let each bosom deeply swell
   With love and holy fear.

Ours be the fear that heeds
   A Saviour's warning tone:
Ours be the love that ever speeds
   A Father's will to own.

Bear witness with each heart,
   Spirit of Holiness,
That we would be Thine own: impart
   To us pardon and peace.

MRS. ELIZA JONES FALLOW.

Author of *Poetical Remains*, 1833. This and eight others by her were reprinted in Dr. Leifchild's *Original Hymns*, 1842.

ETERNAL Spirit, Lord of Light,
   Throned in the Heaven of Heavens above,
Descend in Thy renewing might,
   Come in the glory of Thy Love.

Here in this dark disordered heart
   Be Thy creative power displayed;
Thy own undying Life impart
   To Nature's energies decayed.

For Thou canst bid the dead arise;
   And strong in all Thy strength divine,
Armed with celestial energies,
   O what a glorious life were mine!

How would high thoughts in boldest flight
   From their inglorious bondage break,
The soul's deep music of delight
   At Thy harmonious touch awake!

Spirit of Life, in Love descend!
   My dying spirit asks for Thee:
Breathe Thou the Life that cannot end;
   Begin my immortality.

MRS. TONNA, 1790–1846.

Known as "CHARLOTTE ELIZABETH": daughter of the Rev. Michael Browne of Norwich. This piece was written in 1834, and appeared in her *Posthumous and other Poems*, 1847.

PRAYER FOR A MINISTER.

SPIRIT of Grace, of Truth and Power,
   Be near in this auspicious hour;
Thy Pentecostal unction shed,
Almighty! on Thy servant's head.

For him Thy boundless gifts I claim,
The heart of zeal, the tongue of flame:
To him the wisdom give and love
That blend the serpent with the dove:
O bring Thy rich endowments near,
Of counsel, might, and holy fear.
Spirit of Fire, pervade, enfold,
Consume the dross, refine the gold;
Spirit of Healing, sweetly rest
On every wound that scars his breast.
Spirit of Life and Light, display
Salvation's full and finished day,
That his own gladdened soul may share
The gospel-wealth his lips declare.
Beyond my prayer, beyond my thought,
O be the abundant blessing wrought!
In him, a chosen vessel, place
The treasure of Thy boundless Grace;
Yea, with Thyself his spirit fill;
There reign, and work Thy sovereign will.

S. C. E. NEVILLE.

Author of *Sunday Evening Recreation*, 1836. I take these from W. C. Wilson's *Book of General Psalmody*, 1838.

G RACIOUS Spirit, Source of bliss!
Mercy is my only plea;
All I want is simply this,
More of fellowship with Thee.

Lord, illuminate my soul,
   Shed the Light of Life within:
Exercise a sweet control,
   Free me from the power of sin.

Rid me from the grasp of sense,
   Fruitful source of all my grief:
Let Thy sacred influence
   Triumph over unbelief.

Open Christ's eternal Love
   In its depth and breadth and height;
Raise this grovelling soul above,
   Wing it to the world of light.

Consecrate me for Thine own;
   In this body deign to dwell;
On my heart erect Thy throne,
   Crush the thought that would rebel.

AT PUBLIC WORSHIP.

HOLY Ghost, Thy power impart
   To the souls assembled here:
Give the understanding heart;
   Lord, bestow the hearing ear.

Be a Tongue to him who speaks,
   Speaks for Jesus Christ alone:
Be a Guide to him who seeks
   Grace and mercy at the Throne.

Deepen, Lord, the sense of sin,
  Fill us with a holy zeal:
Crush each deadly foe within;
  On our hearts the promise seal.

Lord of Life, we look to Thee,
  Great in wisdom, might, and love:
Let Thy presence set us free;
  Grant Thy teaching, Holy Dove.

JOSIAH CONDER, 1789–1855.

A voluminous author both in prose and verse, and an excellent man. In 1836 he edited the first official *Congregational Hymn-Book*, inserting in it 56 hymns of his own, among them this.

MATTHEW iii. 11.

O BREATHE upon this languid frame,
    Spirit of heavenly might!
Baptize me with the vital flame
    Of purity and light.

Descend like Heaven's self-kindled fire
  On my heart's sacrifice,
Till self in flames of love expire,
  In clouds of incense rise.

Spring up within this flinty heart,
  Well-spring of Life divine!
Health to my feeble pulse impart;
  Light out of darkness shine.

O Light and Power! O Life and Love!
    Of every good the Source!
Send me sweet succor from above,
    To speed me on my course.

Instruct me, rule me, guide my feet,
    My every thought control.
My Teacher, Patron, Paraclete!
    Possess and guard my soul.

Spirit of Christ, sent forth from Him,
    Yet uncreate, divine!
Thine are the songs of seraphim;
    All human praise be Thine.

CHARLOTTE ELLIOTT.

Formerly of Torquay, now of Brighton. Our first and second selections are pleasantly characteristic of this author and her chief occupations.

INVOCATION.

From Hours of Sorrow, 1836.

BLESSED Spirit! Thou who deignest
  In each bosom where Thou reignest
Heavenly thoughts to inspire:
Now, Thy gracious influence lending,
With my strain its virtue blending,
  Wake my simple lyre!

Let it breathe some hallowed numbers,
Ere in death the minstrel slumbers
　　Who implores Thy skill :
Let it soothe some ear that listens,
Let it dry some tear that glistens,
　　Ere my heart be still !

There are bosoms wrung with anguish,
Mourners who in silence languish,
　　Hidden wounds that bleed.
Heavenly Comforter of sorrow !
Balm for these if I might borrow,
　　I were blest indeed.

FOR THE SICK.

The closing piece of the last edition (1854) of The Invalid's Hymn-Book, which Miss Elliott edited It is there headed, " To the Holy Spirit."

GOD of peace and consolation !
　　Human sufferings claim Thy care :
Now, in Thy divine compassion,
　　Grant Thy feeble suppliant's prayer :
Through these simple strains impart
Light and peace to many a heart.

In those hours of sickness lonely,
　　When the body finds no rest,
And the soul by Thee, Thee only,
　　Can be healed, renewed, and blest,
Fill these lines with heavenly power !
Cheer by them each suffering hour.

Let each page, Thy Truth containing,
  Shine illumined with Thy light:
With free Grace and Love constraining
  Make the darkened spirit bright;
And as earth's fair visions fade,
Let Heaven's glories be displayed.

THE REMEMBRANCER.

JOHN xiv. 18.

From *The Invalid's Hymn-Book*, Second Edition, 1841.

HOLY Comforter! Who guidest
  Those who seek Thine aid divine,
Who in contrite hearts abidest,
  Now amidst my darkness shine!
Though around me waves are swelling
  And the storms of life increase,
If my heart be made Thy dwelling,
  I shall still be kept in peace.

'Tis Thine office, blessed Spirit,
  Christ's Remembrancer to be:
Though such Grace I cannot merit,
  Now recall His words to me.
Though with grief my heart seems broken,
  Though the waves go o'er my soul,
Every word by Jesus spoken
  Makes the wounded spirit whole.

God of peace and consolation!
  Pour this balm upon my mind;
In my Saviour's Cross and Passion
  Strength and healing let me find.
Is the outward man decaying?
  Be the inward man renewed:
Now, Thy power and Love displaying,
  Cheer my mournful solitude.

Take the things to Christ belonging,
  Manifest His Love to me;
Check these thoughts of anguish, thronging
  This poor heart, resigned to Thee.
Show me life nor death can sever
  From my soul that heavenly Friend;
Tell me He is mine for ever
  And will love me to the end.

BISHOP RICHARD MANT, 1776–1848.

<small>Bishop of Killaloe, 1820; of Down and Connor, 1823; and of Dromore, 1842: a voluminous writer in prose and verse. Of his volume of *Ancient Hymns*, 1837, despite the title, nearly one half consists of *Original Hymns, principally of Commemoration and Thanksgiving for Christ's Holy Ordinances*: in interest and importance they are far above his translations. His learning, devoutness, and scrupulous accuracy of mind leave nothing to be desired in his hymns but lyrical fire; and the few in which this is found in sufficient degree are of great value.</small>

HYMN TO THE COMFORTER FOR FAITH, HOPE, AND CHARITY.

"COME, Holy Ghost, my soul inspire!"
  Spirit of the Almighty Sire,
Spirit of the Son Divine,
Comforter, Thy gifts be mine!

Holy Spirit, in my breast
Grant that lively FAITH may rest,
And subdue each rebel thought
To believe what Thou hast taught.

When around my sinking soul
Gathering waves of sorrow roll,
Spirit blest, the tempest still,
And with HOPE my bosom fill.

Holy Spirit, from my mind
Thought, and wish, and will unkind,
Deed and word unkind remove,
And my bosom fill with LOVE.

Faith, and Hope, and Charity,
Comforter, descend from Thee.
"Thou the anointing Spirit art;"
These Thy gifts to us impart:

Till our Faith be lost in sight,
Hope be swallowed in delight,
And Love return to dwell with Thee
In the Threefold Deity.

JAMES EDMESTON, 1791–1867.

An architect, and churchwarden of St. Barnabas, Homerton: author of several volumes of sacred verse. These two are taken from Collections, and I cannot answer for the text.

SUNDAY MORNING.

HEAVENLY Spirit! may each heart
 Through these sacred hours be Thine:
May we from the world depart,
 Breathing after things divine.

Lead us forth with joy and peace
  To Thy temple, in Thy ways;
And when this sweet day shall cease,
  May its sun go down with praise.

May Thy ministers declare
  All Thy Word of Truth with power,
Till the sinner bend in prayer,
  Conquered in that mighty hour.

So may we who worship here
  Profit by Thy Word to-day;
And more love and peace and fear
  Carry from Thy house away.

A NEW SPIRIT.

From the Leeds *Sunday School Hymn-Book*, 1862.

HOLY Spirit, come renew me,
  Make me holy, make me just:
I am evil; O subdue me
  To His yoke, in Whom I trust!

I would have new thought and feeling,
  New desire and new delight:
Grant, O grant me the revealing
  Made by Thine own heavenly light!

Make me love my God; and serving
  Him supremely day by day,
Without wandering, without swerving,
  May I tread the heavenly way!

ANONYMOUS, 1837-8.

From *The Comprehensive Hymn-Book*, 1837, by JOHN CAMPBELL. D.D., editor of the *British Banner*. In this, says Mr. Sedgwick, "he gave many for the first time from Matthew Wilks' MSS."

SPIRIT of Life, go forth!
   Let Thy great Word proceed,
Dispensed by whom Thou wilt, to wake
   The spiritually dead.
Send forth to prophesy
   Thy chosen messenger;
And Thou the Word of Life apply,
   Constrain the world to hear!

Lord, while at Thy command
   Thy servants prophesy,
O let it spread through every land
   That Thou in Christ art nigh!
The dead professors shake,
   And with Thy quickening Breath
Make Thou their lifeless souls to wake
   Out of the sleep of death!

O HOLY SPIRIT, COME!

From the same. Supposed to be by WILLIAM ALLEN, 1835.

O HOLY Spirit, come
   With energy divine!
On Nature's deep and cheerless gloom
   In Truth's bright splendor shine!

THE SPIRIT'S WITNESS.

Come, Holy Spirit, now,
   Sent from Messiah's throne!
Let penitential thoughts outflow
   From smitten hearts of stone.

O Holy Spirit, come,
   And speak with mercy's voice:
O come and make each heart Thy home;
   Let every soul rejoice.

THE SPIRIT'S WITNESS.

ROMANS viii. 16.

This and the next two are from WILLIAM CARNS WILSON's Book of General Psalmody, 1838: containing 1031 hymns, and probably the largest hymnal prepared for use in the English Church up to that time.

SPIRIT of Truth and Holiness,
   Whose comforts never fail,
Earnest of everlasting bliss,
   Thee, Holy Ghost, we hail!
The Comforter on saints bestowed,
The Witness of our peace with God.

Children of light and holiness
   We "Abba Father" cry,
In Jesu's Blood and Righteousness
   To God by Thee brought nigh:
Of His adopting Love the Seal,
And faithful Teacher of His Will.

The living fruits of holiness
   And love by Thee we show;
Thus heirs of everlasting bliss
   Ourselves we prove below.
This witness in our hearts we join,
O blessed Comforter, with Thine.

Spirit of Grace and Holiness,
   Still give us light and joy;
Fill us with love, keep us in peace,
   Safe for the world on high:
Of Jesu's faithful Love the Seal,
And Teacher of His holy Will.

THE SPIRIT'S HELP.

Romans viii. 26.

SPIRIT of Power! to Thee I cry:
   Look on my soul's infirmity;
And teach me even my utmost need,
That I may seek Thy help indeed.

Spirit of Love! I ask Thine aid,
That all my sins, before me laid,
May but through Thee to Jesus guide,
To shelter in His piercèd side.

Spirit of Truth! O teach my mind
To turn from subtleties refined;
And seize the faith that makes us free
In all its meek simplicity.

Spirit of Holiness! consecrate
My will, my heart anew create,
Till all its prime affections tend
To Thee, their Author and their End.

Spirit of Faith! O give me wings
To soar above terrestrial things,
And zeal, to fix my ardent eyes
Upon the bright eternal prize.

Spirit of Joy! O lead me on
Through life, and even to Thy throne,
Where I for ever may abide,
In Jesus' likeness satisfied!

FOR AN OUTPOURING.

Isaiah xxxii. 15.

BREATHE, Holy Spirit, from above,
   Until our hearts with fervor glow :
O kindle there a Saviour's love,
   True sympathy with human woe.

Bid our conflicting passions cease,
   And terror from each conscience flee ;
O speak to every bosom peace,
   Unknown to all who know not Thee.

Give us to taste of heavenly joy,
   While here we celebrate Thy praise ;
Guide us to wealth without alloy ;
   Our hopes to cloudless glory raise.

, Extend Thy power to every place
  Where Christ is named, but not adored;
And teach each church, through sovereign
    Grace,
  Once more to seek and serve the Lord.

Pour forth Thy light on heathen lands
  Which under Satan's thraldom groan:
Turn them from idols made with hands
  To bow before Immanuel's throne.

DIANA A. THRUPP, 1840.

From E. H. Bickersteth's *Psalms and Hymns*, 1858.

FOR A CHILD.

COME, Holy Spirit, come;
  O hear an infant's prayer!
Stoop down and make my heart Thy home,
  And shed Thy blessing there.

Thy Light, Thy Love impart,
  And let it ever be
A holy, humble, happy heart,
  A dwelling-place for Thee.

Let Thy rich Grace increase
  Through all my early days
The fruits of righteousness and peace
  To Thine eternal praise.

HENRY O'NEILE.

From *The Church of England Magazine*, 1840.

FOR EMBER WEEK.

SPIRIT divine! from Whom
All heavenly gifts do come,
Thy suppliant Church now lowly turns to Thee.
Her chosen servants bless,
Fountain of holiness!
With wisdom, light, and inward purity.

Give them discerning grace
To fill Thy sacred place
With priests and pastors for the Saviour meet,
Who scorn each selfish end,
Willing themselves to spend,
And seek His scattered flock with patient feet.

Spirit of fire! impart
Zeal to the waiting heart,
And clothe the glowing tongue with words divine;
Like to gold, fine and tried,
Moulded and purified,
Do Thou from earthly dross their thoughts refine.

Spirit of Love! control
The motions of each soul,
And on this hour Thy dove-like influence shed:
So may their fervor be
Tempered by charity,
And with the Truth, peace and good-will be spread.

Spirit of comfort! pour
Thy healing unction o'er
The troubled Church, and all her discord still;
For one harmonious end
Her varied powers blend,
And with Thyself her peaceful precincts fill!

ANONYMOUS. "J. C. H."

<small>From *The Church of England Magazine*, October, 1842.</small>

GRACIOUS, free, and sovereign Spirit,
    With Thy presence visit me;
All my plea and all my merit
    Is in Him who promised Thee.

Reign within, and then those sorrows
    Which oppress this sinking heart —
Then these clouds, now big with horrors, —
    At Thy beaming shall depart.

When to dust my soul is cleaving,
    Quicken me, Thou Lord of Life;
When this breast 'gainst sin is heaving,
    Aid me in the mortal strife.

All Thy graces, gentle Teacher,
    Patience, hope, humility,
Love, peace, joy, — Thy every feature,
    Mighty Spirit, stamp on me!

These Thy fruits, and not my merit,
Shall approve me in that Day
When Thou bidst Thy saints inherit
Through "the Life, the Truth, the Way."

WILLIAM PRESCOT SPARKS.

From *The Church of England Magazine*, November, 1842.

FOUNTAIN of Life, most pure, most bright!
Sun of the soul, the spirit's Light!
Great Source of joy, and End of rest,
For ever blessing, ever blest!

As the young dayspring's glorious birth
Calls into life rejoicing earth,
And with new beauty, love, and power,
Robes field and stream and tree and flower:

As the high noon's unbroken blaze,
Deep-searching with resistless rays,
From frost-bound caves and darksome springs
Wakes rainbow hues and radiant things:

As cooling dews, like gentle sleep
On hearts that bleed and eyes that weep
In the sweet hour of evening's calm,
On feverish earth shed heavenly balm:

Shine on our souls, in mercy shine,
Thou living Beam, Thou Fire divine!
Bid sin's distracting turmoil cease,
Thou Comforter, Thou God of peace!

Lamp of the Church, the polar Star
That o'er the dark world gleams afar,
Gilding the Truth's immortal page
Held by her hand from age to age:

In days of old how wondrously
Men drew from Thee the rich supply
Of grace and strength, that led them on
Through flood and flame to victory won!

Travelling on time's dark borders, we
Our light alone derive from Thee:
The same as in the days gone by
Thou art, unseen, yet ever nigh.

The suffering Church is still Thy care;
Thou art her Guide, her hope, her prayer.
Arm of the Lord! put forth Thy might
To shield her in the heathen's sight.

A sevenfold strength she needs, to stand,
Obedient to her Lord's command,
The Truth's firm champion, undismayed,
Against a world in arms arrayed.

Her lot is cast in evil days
Of blasphemy, and crooked ways,
Where open force meets latent guile,
The scorner's threat, the traitor's smile.

A waveless faith, a judgment clear,
A tempered zeal, a holy fear,
She asks: O God of Grace, do Thou
Grant to her prayer Thy fulness now!

Armed with Thy quick and two-edged sword —
The undefiled, heart-piercing Word, —
Along the path her fathers trod
Lead her to glory and to God:

That path, where flowers of beauty spring
From blood of martyrs' suffering,
Opened by Him who died to save,
And rose victorious from the grave.

Spirit of Life! we pray, we pray,
As on Thine old, Thy glorious day,
When Thou wert found the saints among,
With rushing wind and fiery tongue,

Descend, Almighty, from above
On beams of light, on wings of Love;
Abide, the Church's hallowed Guest,
Her weal Thy care, her ark Thy rest;

Till o'er the earth, from pole to pole,
The Truth's full ocean broadly roll,
And every soul a temple be,
Meet, holy Lord, for Heaven and Thee!

JOSEPH JONES.

Of Bower Hill, Repton: author of some "theological publications," 1840-53, and of *Sacred Rhymes*, 1842.

H OLY Spirit, mystic Dove,
    Giver Thou of light and love!
Come in mercy and in might,
Scatter far the shades of night.

We are feeble, slumbering, dead;
But reviving influence shed;
Grace, the blest celestial dew,
Might, creating all things new.

Melt and purify the heart;
Health and strength and peace impart.
Fill our souls with faith and love,
With blest hope of joys above.
Every lofty thought expel;
Dwell within us, ever dwell:
Be Thy temple every breast,
Cleansed, and made Thy place of rest.

While this misty vale we tread,
By Thy power may we be led:
Daily give us victory here
Over foes and over fear.
Daily guide us, rule and bless;
Daily cheer us in distress:
Give us life and give us peace,
Holy joys that shall not cease.

Holy Spirit, mystic Dove,
Fill our souls with fervent love:
Teacher, Purifier, Friend!
On Thy goodness we depend.
Pour upon us brighter light,
More of life and more of might;
All we need till life is o'er,
Till with angels we adore.

ANOTHER.

SPIRIT of Truth! my mind illume;
　　Dispel the clouds of mental gloom,
And bid the beams of Light divine
On my glad soul with splendor shine.

Spirit of Grace! my heart renew;
Its hardness and its pride subdue:
Be Thou to me refiner's Fire,
And fill my soul with blest desire.

Spirit of Might! all power is Thine;
The weakness of a reed is mine:
But in Thy strength may I prevail,
Nor in the days of trial fail.

Spirit of Comfort! in distress
My soul with peace and patience bless:
In days of gloom and hours of pain
My fluttering, trembling heart sustain.

Spirit of Goodness, mystic Dove!
Fill me with faith and hope and love:
Christ to my inmost soul reveal,
And fix upon my heart Thy seal.

As pass the hours of life away,
Thy gifts, Thyself to me convey;
That I may now Thy temple be,
Emptied of self, and full of Thee.

HENRY ALFORD, D.D., 1810–1871.

Vicar of Wymeswold, 1835-1853; in 1857 Dean of Canterbury. From his Collection of *Psalms and Hymns*, 1844.

SAVIOUR, Thy Father's Promise send:
  Spirit of holiness, descend:
Lo, we are waiting for Thee, Lord,
All in one place with one accord.

Come and convince us all of sin,
Lighting Thy lamp our hearts within:
Thy temples, but alas, how slow
Thy presence and Thy voice to know.

Convince us all of Righteousness:
By that great Work Thy people bless,
Which our High Priest hath wrought alone,
And carried to His Father's throne.

Of judgment, Lord, convince us too:
Teach us in Christ all things to view:
O make us pure, with lightened eyes,
Harmless as doves, as serpents wise.

NATHANIEL MEERES.

Curate of Cradley, Worcestershire, and author of *Original Psalms and Hymns*, 1845.

SPIRIT of Life and Light, descend,
  While we bow before Thy face:
On Thee alone we can depend;
  Grant us, Lord, Thy quickening Grace:

Waft our praises
To Thy blessed throne on high.

Disperse the clouds of nature's night:
Shine upon our dark abode:
Reveal Thy blest celestial light
As we journey on the road:
Make us watchful
For the coming of our Lord.

When we descend the vale of death,
Lift our hopes beyond the skies;
Thus, when we yield our dying breath,
May our souls to glory rise,
And with angels
Tune our harps to sound Thy praise.

JOHN LEIFCHILD, D.D.

From his *Original Hymns by Various Authors*, 1842.

FOR A BLESSING ON PREACHING.

ETERNAL, Holy Spirit, bend
To us in mercy down;
O hear Thy suppliants, and descend
Our humble work to crown.

No more we wait the rushing wind
That marked Thy viewless wing;
Breathe softly o'er each willing mind
As earliest breath of spring.

The seed by us in winter sown —
  The winter of the heart —
Shall soon by holy fruits be known,
  If Thou Thine aid impart.

No more we ask the cloven flame
  To shed a glory round;
Be but the savor of Thy Name
  On us like unction found.

What though in plain unvarying speech
  The wanderers home we call?
'Tis ours with childlike art to teach,
  But Thine to perfect all.

Yea, uninstructed lips may wake
  The guilty slumbering soul,
If Thou from Héaven's high altar take
  For them the living coal.

What though no more our potent word
  The demon may expel:
Even now, where'er in faith 'tis heard,
  No rebel sin can dwell.

Do Thou, with fructifying shower,
  Complete what we begin;
We plant, then pray Thine heavenly power
  To ripen all within.

WILLIAM MACLARDIE BUNTING, 1805–1866.

An eminent Wesleyan minister. Thirty-five of his hymns appeared in Dr. Leifchild's Collection, 1842.

BLEST Spirit, from the Eternal Sire
   And Son proceeding, promised, sent!
'Tis Thine the first good thought to inspire;
   By Thee the obdurate repent,
The penitent by Thee believe,
The saints Thy holiness receive.

Thy Deity the saints adore,
   Thy offices of mercy bless,
Thy help in utmost need implore,
   Thy all-sufficiency confess;
Without Thee, wretched, poor, and blind,
Wealth, wisdom, joy, in Thee they find.

If e'er to forms of truth I gave
   The homage due, great Lord, to Thee,
E'er deemed the Cross could, spell-like, save,
   While yet Thou dwelledst not in me;
Reprove my folly, but forgive,
And make me understand and live.

Thou gavest the Word, and must apply;
   Thou knowest the Son, and must make known;
In vain He died and rose on high,
   And stoops beseeching from His throne,
Till Thou this alien heart prepare,
And gain for Christ an entrance there.

O could I always know Thee near,
  Midst means and ministries of Grace,
Thy footstep in my closet hear,
  Thy finger on my Bible trace!
My God, here find, here grant Thy rest,
Pleased Inmate of my peaceful breast!

Nor me alone instruct, rejoice:
  All souls are Thine; teach, comfort all!
Let each soon recognize Thy voice
  In every evangelic call;
Each feel Thy halcyon-rest within,
Calming the storms of dread and sin.

Thus searching the deep things of God,
  And witnessing His mind to us,
Where'er Peace dwells or Truth hath trod,
  Reveal Thy own true Person thus!
And with all Majesty divine,
All praise, blest Spirit, shall be Thine.

ISAAC WILLIAMS, B.D., 1802–1865.

Rector of Bisley from 1842 to 1845: a voluminous author both in verse and prose. Several of his translations from the Latin have appeared in preceding pages. The three following pieces are from his *Hymns on the Catechism*, 1843.

I BELIEVE IN THE HOLY GHOST.

O HOLY Ghost, Who didst descend
  At hallowed Whitsuntide,
With us, until the world shall end,
  And with Thy Church abide!

Thou camest like the wind, with rushing mighty
    sound,
And fiery tongues were seen to burn on all around.

    Even like the wind Thou camest down,
      With footsteps all unseen;
    For only by the fruit 'tis known
      Where'er Thy Grace hath been:
Thy power to cheer and cleanse is seen in awful
    flame;
The tongues set forth Thy will the Gospel to pro-
    claim.

    O Holy Ghost, great God from Heaven!
      I tremble at Thy name;
    For he shall never be forgiven
      Who sins against the same.
And when Thou camest down, and they Thy power
    belied,
Then Ananias false and false Sapphira died.

    Thou dwellest with Thy Church below,
      An unseen present God;
    And in all Christian souls, we know,
      Thy holy feet have trod.
O Giver of all light, O Giver of all love!
Fit us to dwell with Thee in Thine own House
    above.

THE COMMUNION OF SAINTS.

O HOLY Ghost, Thou God of peace,
   Pity Thy Church now rent in twain;
Let these dissents and schisms cease,
   And let us all be one again:

One with our brethren here in love,
   And one with saints that are at rest,
And one with angel-hosts above,
   And one with God for ever blest.

O make on earth all churches one,
   All one with churches gone before;
All knit in sweet communion,
   To love Thee, worship, and adore.

For love is life, and life is love,
   And Thou Thyself art Love and Life;
And we in Thee shall live and move,
   If Thou wilt keep us free from strife.

THE BAPTISM OF THE HOLY GHOST

GLORY, Holy Ghost, to Thee,
   Who the saints from sin dost free,
And hast washed and hallowed me.

Thou didst come down like a Dove,
Opening erst the heavens above
On the Son of God's dear Love:

So Thou, at our Baptism given,
Callest us to homes in Heaven;
Children, and of God forgiven.

O keep us, blessed Trinity,
In substance One, in Person Three;
For we are all baptized in Thee.

JOHN MASON NEALE, D.D., 1818–1866

Warden of Sackville College, East Grinstead, and one of the most remarkable men of our time; eminent alike for ability, learning, energy, integrity, and devotion. "His life was divided between excessive literary toil and exhausting labors of piety and benevolence." His services to hymnody were invaluable, and, in our century at least, unsurpassed. The following is from his chief untranslated work, *Hymns for Children*, 1844.

WHIT-SUNDAY.

THOU Who camest from above,
    Bringing light and shedding love,
Teaching of Thy perfect way,
Giving gifts to men to-day:

Thou Who once didst change our state,
Making us regenerate,
Help us evermore to be
Faithful subjects unto Thee.

Where Thou art not, none can do
What is holy, just, and true;
Those whose hearts Thy wisdom leads
Think good thoughts and do good deeds.

We have often grieved Thee sore;
Never let us grieve Thee more.
Thou the feeble canst protect,
Thou the wandering canst direct.

We are dark — be Thou our Light.
We are blind — be Thou our Sight.
Be our Comfort in distress;
Guide us through the wilderness.

To the blessed Three in One,
To the Father and the Son
And the Holy Ghost, arise
Praise from all below the skies.

ANONYMOUS, 1844.

From the Comprehensive Edition of Rippon's Selection, 1844.

BLEST Comforter, Balm of the mind,
   Long have I Thy absence deplored;
Nor peace nor contentment can find,
   Till Thou to my soul art restored.

With comfort I once passed the day,
   With comfort I laid me to rest;
But now Thou art fled far away,
   And sorrow oppresseth my breast.

Return and revive me once more
   With joys that are pure and divine:
Thy presence is what I implore;
   O grant it, and comfort is mine.

But if Thou delay to impart
  The earnest and foretaste of Heaven;
In duty I'll give Thee my heart,
  And wait till the blessing is given.

And should it yet tarry awhile,
  Yea, till I'm resigning my breath,
O step in and give me a smile,
  And let me find comfort in death.

BISHOP JOHN HARDING, D.D.

<small>Bishop of Bombay, 1851. This is from *Hymns for Church Sunday Schools*, 1847.</small>

O SPIRIT of Love, Who dwellest on high,
  Descend from above, and answer our cry.
Thou ne'er hast denied us the blessings we crave;
Unerring to guide us, and mighty to save.

All fallen and weak, polluted and blind,
Thy comfort we seek, Thy light in the mind,
Thy strength against evil, Thy succor within,
To combat the devil and overcome sin.

Though laden with guilt and covered with shame,
Revive us Thou wilt with the Blood of the Lamb.
Receiving His merit for peace to the soul,
The broken in spirit are perfectly whole.

Thou Comforter true to the children of Grace,
Their love is Thy due, their worship and praise.
To Thee with the Father, to Thee with the Son,
Our homage we offer: The Godhead is One.

JULIA C. GRIMANI.

From her Sacred Lyrics, 1849.

1 CORINTHIANS iii. 16.

SPIRIT, that dwellest where the stream
  Of life is ever flowing,
Where round the Throne the rainbow's beam
  Its emerald light is throwing,
Where bright and holy seraphim
  Are bending to adore Thee,
And even their radiant forms seem dim
  To Thine eternal glory :
Where all is fitted for Thy rest,
  And worthy even Thee,
So beautiful it is, so blest,
  So calm in purity !

Yet not in Heaven's light alone
  Is fixed Thy glorious dwelling,
As in Thy holy Book Thine own
  Celestial voice is telling.
For Thou, O Spirit, deignest to seek
  A temple for Thy Name,
An earthly temple, in the weak
  And sinful human frame :
Not to consume upon that shrine
  The trembling light of earth,
But to impart the Breath divine
  Which gave that light its birth.

If every voice that e'er has breathed
    Thy glory were confessing,
If every dying sigh bequeathed
    To Thee an endless blessing;
If on each wave of Time's swift stream
    The light of love could glow,
If the dark waters 'neath its beam
    Could praise Thee as they flow,
Then, blending in the eternal Sea
    That laves the heavenly Shore,
Bear with those sparkling waves to Thee
    Glory for evermore:
That love, that glory, all would seem,
    If balanced with Thy Grace,
A passing shade, a vanished dream,
    A cloud in boundless space.

O take the faint, weak breath of praise
    Which Thou Thyself hast taught,
And let me through eternal days
    Adore Thee as I ought.
Yes, for that dear Redeemer's sake
    By Whom Thine aid is given,
Abide with me through life, and make
    My soul Thine own in Heaven.

MISS J. E. BROWNE.

From *The Dove on the Cross, and other Thoughts in Verse*, 1849.

O HOLY Ghost, the Comforter,
    How is Thy Love despised,
While the heart longs for sympathy,
    And friends are idolized.

O Spirit of the living God,
    Brooding with dove-like wings
Over the helpless and the weak
    Among created things:

Where should our feebleness find strength,
    Our helplessness a stay,
Didst Thou not bring us strength and help
    And comfort day by day?

O Spirit of the living God,
    In Whom our spirits live,
Who from the cradle to the grave
    Dost never cease to give

Such sustenance and daily bread,
    Showered down in bounteous meed,
Such streams of living water,
    As our fainting spirits need:

Great are Thy consolations, Lord,
    And mighty is Thy power,
In sickness and in solitude,
    In sorrow's darkest hour.

O if the souls that now despise
    And grieve Thee, heavenly Dove,
Would seek Thee and would welcome Thee,
    How would they prize Thy Love!

ROBERT MONTGOMERY.

Author of *Luther*, *Satan*, and other epics, and of two less ambitious but perhaps more attractive volumes, *The Christian Life*, 1848, and *Lyra Christiana*, 1851. From the latter, which is a volume of extracts from his other poems, these selections are taken.

ETERNAL Former of the holy mind,
　　Vicar of Christ! Who art to men redeemed
Soul of their souls, and Light of light within,
Vast in Thy sway, and viewless in Thy strength,
How full, how free, unfathomed, undefined,
Yet felt, art Thou, in purity and power!
Thou o'er the chaos of the earth newborn
Didst move, and print it with Thy plastic seal
And inspiration. Beauty hence began;
Order, and shape, and symmetry arose;
For Thou of all the Consummator art,
In the green earth or garnished heaven displayed;
And Nature still is but Thine organ, moved
Responsive to the impulse of Thy sway terrene.
Her laws, and lineaments, and loveliness,
Are but expressions of Thy shaping will,
The outward index to Thine inward hand
Creative: beauty is Thy vital power;
Grandeur and Grace Thine intimations are,
And Second Causes form but stepping-stones
O'er which Thou marchest to Thy works and ways.

SINGLE VERSES

Extracted from his Poems.

COME, Holy Spirit, mystic Dove,
    Thine innocence from Heaven impart:
Our hate transform to heavenly love,
    And build Thy temple in our heart.

SPIRIT of Wisdom! pure and perfect Light!
    Come from Thy region of celestial Grace;
Through the bad gloom of unbelieving night
    Dart the mild beams of Thy majestic face.
By loving Thee, saints learn to grow divine,
And as they live, resemble Thee and Thine.

DEEP Spirit of divinest calm,
    Descend, and soothe unquiet hearts:
Breathe o'er each ruffled mind the balm
    Thy perfect nobleness imparts:
And then, O Lord, Thy saints will be
Secure in heaven, and safe in Thee.

ANNE BRONTË, 1820–1849.

The youngest of the three famous sisters, whose touching history is well known. Her few hymns were given by Charlotte Brontë in the biographical sketch of Ellis *and* Acton Bell, *published in 1850.*

SPIRIT of Truth, be Thou my Guide!
    O clasp my hand in Thine,
And let me never quit Thy side;
    Thy comforts are divine.

Pride scorns Thee for Thy lowly mien,
   But who like Thee can rise
Above this toilsome sordid scene,
   Beyond the holy skies?

Weak is Thine eye and soft Thy voice
   But wondrous is Thy might
To make the wretched soul rejoice,
   To give the simple light.

And still to all that seek Thy way
   This magic power is given;
Even while their footsteps press the clay
   Their souls ascend to Heaven.

BENJAMIN SAMUEL HOLLIS.

Formerly minister of Islington Chapel. In 1849 he published *The One Book of Psalms and Hymns*.

GREAT Spirit, like a rushing wind,
   Diffuse abroad Thy Grace:
Now let the careless sinner find
   That God is in this place.

Assist the preacher to proclaim
   With living power Thy Word,
The glories of His Saviour's Name,
   The mercies of his God.

Sit on our heads like cloven tongues,
    Our grovelling spirits raise;
Devout and cheerful be the songs
    That speak Thy lofty praise.

Lord, we are dark; be Thou our Light!
    And cold; be Thou our Fire.
Lord, we are weak; be Thou our Might!
    And dead; Thy Life inspire!

Hear how our pleading voices cry,
    "Come, Holy Spirit, come!
Our drooping spirits vivify,
    And make our hearts Thy home."

THE SPIRIT'S POWER AND LOVE.

This and the three following are from Mr. HOLLIS' Collection, and are supposed to be his. The chorus is meant to follow each verse here.

O HOLY Ghost, we praise Thy Name,
    With God the Father and the Word:
All Thy perfections are the same,
    Co-equal, co-eternal Lord!
We sing, with all the heavenly host,
The Godhead of the Holy Ghost.

This wondrous world was wholly wrought
    To order by Thy potent Will,
And all is with Thy goodness fraught,
    And every part proclaims Thy skill.

Through what mysterious events
  Our guilty souls to Christ were led!
Praise to Thy ruling Providence,
  That brought us from among the dead!

'Tis by Thy mighty Grace we stand,
  Nor are we ever safe alone;
And all who gain the Heavenly Land
  Thy love, and power, and keeping, own.
We sing, with all the heavenly host,
The Godhead of the Holy Ghost.

NEW CREATION.

HOLY Ghost, whose potent word
  Earth's primeval chaos heard,
Hurling back the shades of night,
Turning darkness into light;
May a ruined creature's cry
Importune Thy Majesty?

All my restless pride subdue,
All my shattered powers renew;
My disordered will control,
New-create my wretched soul:
By Thy life-inspiring Breath
Scatter all these shades of death.

Shall the earth all vocal be
With the praise of Deity,

And my soul a blank appear,
Dumb and deaf and dead and drear?
Light of Life! to Thee I pray;
Turn my darkness into day.

THE SPIRIT OF ADOPTION.

(In imitation of Charles Wesley.)

ROMANS viii. 15.

SPIRIT of God! I cannot rest
  Till with the glorious hope possest,
The sense of sin forgiven:
O let me not my soul deceive,
Without the inward witness live,
  The antepast of Heaven.

Whate'er prevents assuring Grace,
Whate'er beclouds Thy smiling face,
  Great Comforter! remove:
Now let my soul to God draw nigh,
And freely *Abba, Father* cry,
  And prove redeeming Love.

This hallowed joy my strength shall be,
This confident access to Thee,
  My Father reconciled:
Thy Love shall purify my heart,
Thy smiles fresh energy impart,
  To converse as Thy child.

FREDERIC WILLIAM FABER, D.D., 1815–1863.

He entered the Roman communion in 1846, and in 1849 established the Brotherhood of the Oratory of St. Philip Neri. His *Jesus and Mary*, or *Catholic Hymns*, appeared 1849 (enlarged 1852), and his collected *Hymns*, 8vo, 1862.

THE ETERNAL SPIRIT.

1849 or 1852.

FOUNTAIN of Love! Thyself true God!
   Who through eternal days
From Father and from Son hast flowed
   In uncreated ways!

O Majesty unspeakable!
   O Person all divine!
How in the Threefold Majesty
   Doth Thy Procession shine!

Fixed in the Godhead's awful light
   Thy fiery Breath doth move;
Thou art a wonder by Thyself
   To worship and to love.

Proceeding, yet of equal age
   With Those whose Love Thou art;
Proceeding, yet distinct, from Those
   From whom Thou seem'st to part:

An undivided Nature, shared
   With Father and with Son;
A Person by Thyself; with Them
   Thy simple essence One!

Bond art Thou of the other Twain!
　　Omnipotent and free,
The consummating Love of God,
　　The limit of the Three!

Thou limitest Infinity,
　　Thyself all infinite;
The Godhead lives and loves and rests
　　In Thine eternal light.

I dread Thee, Unbegotten Love!
　　True God! Sole Fount of Grace!
And now before Thy blessed throne
　　My sinful self abase.

Ocean, wide-flowing Ocean Thou
　　Of uncreated Love:
I tremble as within my soul
　　I feel Thy waters move.

Thou art a Sea without a shore;
　　Awful, immense Thou art;
A Sea which can contract itself
　　Within my narrow heart.

And yet Thou art a Haven too
　　Out on the shoreless sea,
A Harbor that can hold full well
　　Shipwrecked humanity.

Thou art an unborn Breath outbreathed
　　On angels and on men,
Subduing all things to Thyself,
　　We know not how or when.

Thou art a God of fire, that doth
  Create while He consumes;
A God of light, whose rays on earth
  Darken where He illumes!

All things, dread Spirit! to Thy praise
  Thy presence doth transmute;
Evil itself Thy glory bears,
  Its one abiding fruit.

O Light, O Love, O very God!
  I dare no longer gaze
Upon Thy wondrous Attributes
  And their mysterious ways.

O Spirit, beautiful and dread!
  My heart is fit to break
With love of Thy humility
  For us poor sinners' sake.

Thy Love of Jesus I adore:
  My comfort this shall be,
That when I serve my dearest Lord
  That service worships Thee!

HOLY GHOST, COME DOWN UPON THY CHILDREN.

<small>1854 or 1862. In the original the first verse is added as a refrain to every stanza.</small>

HOLY Ghost, come down upon Thy children,
  Give us Grace, and make us Thine;
Thy tender fires within us kindle,
  Blessed Spirit! Dove Divine!

For all within us good and holy
　　Is from Thee, Thy precious gift;
In all our joys, in all our sorrows,
　　Wistful hearts to Thee we lift.

For Thou to us art more than father,
　　More than sister in Thy Love,
So gentle, patient, and forbearing,
　　Holy Spirit! heavenly Dove!

O we have grieved Thee, gracious Spirit!
　　Wayward, wanton, cold are we;
And still our sins, new every morning,
　　Never yet have wearied Thee.

Dear, Paraclete! how hast Thou waited
　　While our hearts were slowly turned!
How often hath Thy Love been slighted,
　　While for us it grieved and burned!

Now, if our hearts do not deceive us,
　　We would take Thee for our Lord;
O dearest Spirit! make us faithful
　　To Thy least and lightest word.

Ah, sweet Consoler! though we cannot
　　Love Thee as Thou lovest us,
Yet if Thou deign'st our hearts to kindle,
　　They will not be always thus.

With hearts so vile how dare we venture,
　　Holy Ghost, to love Thee so?
And how canst Thou with such compassion
　　Bear so long with things so low?

Holy Ghost, come down upon Thy children,
Give us Grace, and make us Thine;
Thy tender fires within us kindle,
Blessed Spirit, Dove divine!

MATTHEW BRIDGES.

He entered the Roman Church about 1848. Author of various books, from 1825 to 1864. From his *Hymns of the Heart*, 1848–51.

O FOR those solitary hours
When Grace descends in silent showers;
When all the Visible withdraws
In solemn, fitful, awful pause,
And memory, like a glassy sea,
Looks up in calmness, Lord, to Thee!

Then let Thine image on this heart
Be deeply felt in every part:
Each motion of the will subdue,
Inform, correct, instruct, renew;
The motives guide, the thoughts refine,
Thyself the Type, from line to line.

Come then, Thou Holy Spirit, come,
And worthy make a worthless home;
All folly into wisdom turn,
And let me live, to love and learn;
Pride with its piteous dross consume,
And lay in lowliness its tomb.

Eternal, brooding, glorious Dove!
Breathe sweetly from Thy throne above;
The weight of every wave control,
Be Thou the Conscience of my soul,
Till, self absorbed, I sit and sing
Beneath the shadow of Thy wing.

Through Thee let all the peace of Heaven
In every sacrament be given;
The precious Eucharistic Bread,
That Body of our Priest and Head,
O let it prove my ransom price,
A daily paschal sacrifice!

So, dead to sin, when Thou art near,
Preserve me from corruption clear;
Feed me with rich celestial food,
Whilst trials rage, yet work for good;
Till final perseverance crown
The conflict Thou hast made Thine own!

EDWARD CASWALL. Born 1814.

<small>He became a Romanist in 1847: Priest of the Oratory, Birmingham: author of *Lyra Catholica*. From his *Poems*, 1858.</small>

GRACE Increate!
From Whose vivific fire
All acts that to immortal glory tend
Their force acquire!

Hail, Life of life!
Hail, Paraclete divine!
All justice, sanctity, obedience, love,
And truth, are Thine.

Thou in the Blood
Of Him who died for men,
By sacramental element applied,
Dost wash us clean.

Thou to the deeds
Of every passing hour
In Thee performed, impartest merit new
And heavenly power.

From grace to grace
O grant me to proceed;
And with assisting hand my faltering steps
To Sion lead!

So may I mount
In peace the holy hill;
And safe at last by Life's eternal Fount,
There drink my fill!

ARTHUR TOZER RUSSELL, B.C.L. Born 1806.

Of St. John's College, Cambridge; 1830-1852 Vicar of Caxton: since then he has held several preferments, and is now incumbent of Wellington, Salop. Author of several prose works, and of *Psalms and Hymns, partly Original, partly Selected*, Cambridge, 1851. This very interesting little volume, which is now scarce, consists almost entirely of translations and originals from his own pen, and has given him rank among the half-dozen most important translators from the German. His originals, however, are equal or superior to his translations.

> HOLY Spirit, given
>   For our Guide to Heaven,
>   Gift of Love divine!
>   Us with peace consoling,
>   Every ill controlling,
>   On our darkness shine!
> Come, faith, hope, and love increasing,
> Fill our hearts with joy unceasing.
>
>   O Lord and Life-giver,
>   Dwell with us for ever;
>   Heavenly life inspire:
>   All within renewing,
>   With Thy Grace enduing
>   Heart, mind, thought, desire:
> Fount of Life for ever flowing,
> Grace and peace on us bestowing.
>
>   Fill our meditation
>   With Thine inspiration:

Graft in us Thy Word:
O may we, possessing
Thine all-fruitful blessing,
Glorify our Lord,
Following Him with faith unfeignèd,
Till we have His Rest attainèd.

Only through His merit
We Thine aid inherit:
By His Name we plead:
Never let us grieve Thee,
But with thanks receive Thee,
Fulness of our need!
Both in joy and in affliction,
Crown us with Thy benediction.

O THOU, WHO BY THE LORD WAST GIVEN.

From the Dalston *Hymns*, 1848 (see p. 515): also found in his book, 1851.

O THOU Who by the Lord wast given,
   In tongues of fire to spread His praise!
Now on our souls, with fire from Heaven,
   Descend, and bless these latter days;
Till all the earth His praise proclaim,
And every tongue confess His Name.

Blest Comforter and Guide, defend us,
   Whose Saviour dwells unseen on high;
But if Thy light and power attend us,
   We still shall feel His presence nigh.
O be our strength, our shield, our might,
And bring us to the land of light.

WHIT-SUNDAY.

NOW is the Church's joyous feast,
    Day of her coronation!
O be thy joy this day increased,
    Christ's consecrated nation!
O Holy Ghost, of Life the Lord,
    Descend with gifts of blessing,
Thou by our prayers again implored,
    Our tongues Thy might confessing.

Touch Thou our lips with fire of love,
    From Love's true Home descending:
Almighty Spirit, from above
    Come, Satan's kingdom rending.
Thy herald-host send forth again,
    Their minds with Truth inspiring:
O may Thy zeal within them reign,
    Pure, peaceable, untiring.

O come, the idol-train destroy,
    All tongues in one uniting;
Christ's Church cleanse Thou from all alloy,
    On all His fold alighting.
O Holy Ghost! His promised sway
    Haste Thou, all hearts preparing;
In holiness the earth array,
    Again Thy presence sharing.

BLEST COMFORTER, WHO DIDST INSPIRE.

BLEST Comforter, Who didst inspire
　　The Apostles' glorious company,
O kindle through the earth that fire,
　　That light which beams from God on high.

O speak with Thine own power the Word
　　Of Jesus; speak His Name divine:
His Name by every land be heard;
　　O may o'er all His glory shine.

Let long-lost Israel again
　　Return, and her Deliverer own:
O may her Lord o'er Sion reign,
　　The Lord, Whose is the eternal throne.

Prepare in every heart His way;
　　Renew His fold in truth and love,
Till earth and Heaven alike obey,
　　And all is praise, on earth, above.

HOLY GHOST, WHO US INSTRUCTEST.

HOLY Ghost, Who us instructest,
　　And unto Heaven our feet conductest,
　　Now pour on us Thy gifts divine.
Let Thy gracious consolation
Uphold us in all tribulation,

Who all our soul to Thee resign.
Be Thou our constant stay
Along this mortal way:
Lord, have mercy!
O let Thy light still cheer our sight,
Till o'er us shines eternal Day.

COME, O PROMISED COMFORTER.

"Ancient": apparently based on parts of *Veni Sancte Spiritus* and *Adsis Superne Spiritus.*

1848. Rewritten 1851.

COME, O promised Comforter;
Light upon our darkness pour.
Father of the poor Thou art:
Then to us Thy gifts impart.
Light of everlasting Day!
Lord, direct us on our way.

Consolation all divine,
Blessed Comforter, is Thine.
Be our strength in weariness:
Thou the weeping heart dost bless.
Sweet repose in every toil,
Thou dost all our griefs beguile.

Lord, Thy perfect gifts bestow
On the fold of Christ below:

Crown our days with heavenly Grace,
Help us when we close our race:
Help us when we look to Thee:
Grant us endless joy to see.

COME, HOLY GHOST, ON US DESCEND.

1 Cor. xii. 13.

Mr. Sedgwick ascribes this to RUSSELL, though it is not in his volume. It appeared without name in Mr. Ernest Bunsen's *Hymns for the Benefit of the London German Hospital, Dalston*, 1848; a Collection to which Mr. Russell contributed largely.

COME, Holy Ghost, on us descend,
　　Our hearts renewing;
With life and peace that know no end,
　　All enduring.
　Fit us for Thy blest abode:
　Thou man to God unitest.
We in Thy holy temple join,
　　Thy gifts imploring;
Own us, O Holy Ghost, for Thine,
　　Thee adoring.
Here inspire our minds with light,
Here, Lord, the blind enlighten.
Here by Thy presence cleanse each heart
　　With Truth celestial;
So from our spirits shall depart
　　Cares terrestrial.
　Bear us on Thy wings above
　To Him who us redeemed.

THE ABOVE REWRITTEN.

In Dr. B. H. Kennedy's *Hymnologia Christiana*, 1863.

COME, Holy Ghost, on us descend,
   Our waiting souls renew :
With peace and hope that know no end,
   Our fears subdue.
Come, fit us for Thy blest abode,
   Our souls to God unite :
Guide us upon the heavenward road,
   And give us light.

Sole Strength of all our weariness,
   Our sorrowing spirits' Stay ;
Thou Who the weeping heart dost bless
   Through all the way !
Come, Holy Ghost, the flock to cheer,
   For whom the Saviour died ;
And ever to His Church be near,
   Her heavenly Guide !

GEORGE RAWSON.

"A Leeds layman." He contributed fourteen hymns, some of them of striking merit, to the Leeds Congregational Collection, 1853.

JOHN xiv. 16.

COME to our poor nature's night
   With Thy blessed inward light,
Holy Ghost the Infinite,
   Comforter Divine.

We are sinful: cleanse us, Lord;
Sick and faint: Thy strength afford;
Lost, — until by Thee restored,
   Comforter Divine!

Orphans are our souls, and poor.
Give us from Thy heavenly store
Faith, love, joy, for evermore,
   Comforter Divine!

Like the dew, Thy peace distil;
Guide, subdue our wayward will,
Things of Christ unfolding still,
   Comforter Divine!

Gentle, awful, holy Guest,
Make Thy temple in each breast,
Shrine of purity confessed,
   Comforter Divine!

In us, for us, intercede,
And with voiceless groanings plead
Our unutterable need,
   Comforter Divine!

Dwell in us, as in the Son,
With His Father ever One
In adoring union;
   Comforter Divine!

In us "Abba, Father," cry:
Earnest of our bliss on high,
Seal of immortality,
   Comforter Divine!

Search for us the depths of God;
Bear us up the starry road
To the height of Thine abode,
 Comforter Divine!

"HE DWELLETH WITH YOU."

JOHN xiv. 17.

From the Leeds *Sunday School Hymn-Book*, 1852.

AND will the mighty God,
 Whom Heaven cannot contain,
Make me His temple and abode,
 And in me live and reign?

Come, Spirit of the Lord,
 Teacher and Heavenly Guide!
Be it according to Thy Word,
 And in my heart reside.

O Holy, Holy Ghost!
 Pervade this soul of mine:
In me renew Thy Pentecost,
 Reveal Thy power divine!

Make it my highest bliss
 Thy blessed fruits to know;
Thy joy, and peace, and gentleness,
 Goodness and faith to show.

Be it my greatest fear
Thy holiness to grieve;
Walk in the Spirit even here,
And in the Spirit live.

Now let me live in Thee,
My inner life of love:
So only shall I meetened be
For spirit-life above.

JOHN FLESHER.

Editor of *The Primitive Methodist Hymn-Book*, 1853.

O HOLY Spirit, send
Thy power to all mankind:
Their hearts subdue, their follies end,
And let them mercy find.

The only Saviour show,
The virtue of His Blood;
By faith this Saviour let them know,
And feel they're born of God.

Increase Thy Church below,
Her members multiply;
Let faith and love among them grow,
Their God to glorify.

Be Thou their inward Fire,
  Their Guide to things above:
Their hearts with purity inspire
  And fill them with Thy Love.

Thus make them one in Thee
  For fellowship and fight;
May Satan own their victory,
  And yield to Thee Thy right.

One God in Persons Three!
  Thy Spirit breathe on all,
Till Jew and Gentile, bond and free,
  Before Thee prostrate fall.

ANONYMOUS.

From *The Evangelical Hymn-Book*, by John H. Rutherford, 1853.

O SPIRIT of the living God,
  Whose heart yearns o'er a dying world!
Against sin's raging, swelling flood
  Thy glorious banner be unfurled!

Roll back the fierce outbursting tide
  Of unbelief and crime and woe:
The wanderer to Jesus guide;
  Christ's Love to every sinner show.

Lift up the Cross, till every soul
  Bends to its pure and gentle sway;
Till over earth, from pole to pole,
  Hell's night gives place to Heaven's glad day.

MRS. MARGARET MACKAY.

Daughter of one Scotch officer, and wife of another; author of the popular lyric, "Asleep in Jesus, blessed sleep," and of several volumes, poetic and other. This hymn is taken through Rogers' *Lyra Britannica*, 1867, from her *Thoughts Redeemed, or Lays of Leisure Hours*, 1854.

GRACIOUS Spirit, from on high,
Sent to show a Saviour nigh!
In the darkest hours of night
Cheer me with Thy quenchless light.

By Thine holy office led,
Testify of Him who bled;
Testify how Jesus slain
Rose, revived, and reigns again.

Turn the sinner from his sin,
Teach him how the crown to win;
Bring him to Immanuel's feet,
Lead him to the mercy-seat.

Thou canst make the soul to feed
On the ever-living Bread;
Thou canst calm his newborn fears,
Dry his penitential tears.

Bid him hear the Shepherd's voice,
Think of Jesus and rejoice:
Daily, though earth's woes increase,
Thou canst sweetly whisper peace.

While in just avenging ire
God is "a consuming Fire,"
Yet, Thou new life-giving Dove,
Thou canst show how God is Love.

GEORGE CROLY, LL.D., 1780–1860.

1781–1860: a poet of some eminence, and from 1835 Rector of Walbrook. In 1854 he issued a Collection of Psalms and Hymns, containing ten of each by himself. This is taken through Rogers' Lyra Britannica.

SPIRIT of God! descend upon my heart;
   Wean it from earth; through all its pulses move;
Stoop to my weakness, mighty as Thou art,
   And make me love Thee as I ought to love.

I ask no dream, no prophet-ecstasies,
   No sudden rending of the veil of clay,
No angel-visitant, no opening skies;
   But take the dimness of my soul away.

Hast Thou not bid us love Thee, God and King?
   All, all Thine own, — soul, heart, and strength, and mind:
I see Thy Cross — there teach my heart to cling:
   O let me seek Thee, and O let me find!

Teach me to feel that Thou art always nigh;
   Teach me the struggles of the soul to bear;
To check the rising doubt, the rebel sigh:
   Teach me the patience of unanswered prayer.

Teach me to love Thee as Thine angels love,
   One holy passion filling all my frame,
The baptism of the heaven-descended Dove;
   My heart an altar, and Thy Love the flame.

HENRY GEORGE TOMKINS.

Now Vicar of Branscombe, Sidmouth. He published in 1855, before his ordination, A Remembrance of Drachenfels, and other Poems

WHEN across the inward thought
    Comes the emptiness of life,
And it seems that earth has naught
    But a vain and weary strife:

All to do, and nothing done,
    Useless days fast fleeting by,
Wanderings many, progress none,
    Faltering steps by fountains dry:

Shall we, in that hapless mood,
    Fainting fall beside the way?
Help us, Giver of all good!
    Teach Thy wretched ones to pray!

Thou that with the Father art
    One in power, in glory One,
Yet within the trusting heart
    Bearest witness with the Son:

O forgive our faithless mind,
    Raise us from our low estate;
Breathe in us the will to find
    Higher life in small and great!

Give us watchful eyes and clear,
    Purgèd from the scales of sense,
Seeing still the Master near,
    And the City far from hence.

Higher lead our love and faith,
   Lower our humility;
Let the words that Jesus saith
   Be illumined all by Thee!

And in them let us discern,
   Çalming all our sinful strife,
While our hearts within us burn,
   Him, the Word, the Truth, the Life!

THOMAS TOKE LYNCH, 1819–1871.

Independent minister at Mornington Chapel, Hampstead Road, London, and a man of singular ability; author of several prose works, and of *The Rivulet, a Contribution to Sacred Song*, 1855; third edition, enlarged, 1868. This is a book far out of the common way, full of fresh thought, and deserving of much more notice than it has received in America. It was attacked with great vehemence on its first appearance, and thence arose "The Rivulet Controversy," which for a time shook the British dissenting world. The early editions contain 100 lyrics, the third has 67 more. Our selections, except the last, bear date 1855.

SUPPLICATION.

GRACIOUS Spirit, dwell with me;
   I myself would gracious be,
And with words that help and heal
Would Thy life in mine reveal,
And with actions bold and meek
Would for Christ my Saviour speak.

Truthful Spirit, dwell with me;
   I myself would truthful be,

And with wisdom kind and clear
Let Thy Life in mine appear,
And with actions brotherly
Speak my Lord's sincerity.

Tender Spirit, dwell with me;
I myself would tender be,
Shut my heart up like a flower
At temptation's darksome hour,
Open it when shines the sun,
And His Love by fragrance own.

Silent Spirit, dwell with me;
I myself would quiet be,
Quiet as the growing blade
Which through earth its way has made,
Silently, like morning light,
Putting mists and chills to flight.

Mighty Spirit, dwell with me;
I myself would mighty be,
Mighty so as to prevail
Where unaided man must fail;
Ever by a mighty hope
Pressing on and bearing up.

Holy Spirit, dwell with me;
I myself would holy be;
Separate from sin, I would
Choose and cherish all things good,
And whatever I can be
Give to Him Who gave me Thee!

LIFE.

SPIRIT! Whose various energies
    By dew and flame denoted are,
By rain from the world-covering skies,
    By rushing and by whispering air:

Be Thou to us, O gentlest One,
    The brimful River of sweet peace,
Sunshine of the celestial Sun,
    Restoring Air of sacred ease.

Life of our life, since Life of Him
    By Whom we live eternally.
Our heart is faint, our eye is dim,
    Till Thou our spirit purify.

The purest airs are strongest too,
    Strong to enliven and to heal:
O Spirit purer than the dew,
    Thine holiness in strength reveal.

Felt art Thou, and the heavy heart
    Grows cheerful and makes bright the eyes;
Up from the dust the enfeebled start,
    Armed and re-nerved for victories.

Felt art Thou, and relieving tears
    Fall, nourishing our young resolves:
Felt art Thou, and our icy fears
    The sunny smile of Love dissolves.

O Spirit, when Thy mighty wind
   The entombing rocks of sin hath rent,
Lead shuddering forth the awakened mind,
   In still voice whispering Thine intent.

As to the sacred light of day
   The stranger soul shall trembling come,
Say, "These thy friends," and "This thy way,"
   And "Yonder thy celestial home."

HAPPINESS.

SPIRIT of sacred happiness,
   Who makest energy delight,
   And love to be in weakness might;
Now with enlivening impulse bless,
Now reconfirm our steadfastness,
   And make us vigorous and bright.

Blessed be Thou, O Heart supreme,
   Sweet Charity's unfailing Well,
   Whose bounty all the countries tell;
Drinking of Thee, with sunny gleam
Forth-leaping into action's stream,
   Our hearts' replenished fountains swell.

Both work and sport Thou hallowest,
   Canst blissful make the busiest days,
   And woes that else benumb and craze
By Thee to finer joys are blest,
And hearts, of deeper power possest,
   With grateful tears Thy wisdom praise.

Spirit of bliss and sanctity,
  Who art invincible in good,
  Who hate and mockery hast withstood
In every age; how coward we,
How selfish, restless, till by Thee
  Inspired to do the thing we would!

By unremorseful joys, O woo
  Our hearts to holy effort still:
  Now with young life volition fill;
For child-like, we are God-like too,
Likest our Father when we do
  With filial love and haste His Will.

BEAUTY.

SPIRIT of Beauty! Thy presence confessing,
  God can we see in a sparkle of ore;
Flowers and shells to our heart are expressing
  Love like its own, but transcendently more.

Spirit of Beauty! each bough in its bending,
  Skies in their curve, and the sea in its swell,
Streams as they wind, hills and plains in their blending,
  All, in our own, of God's happiness tell.

Spirit of Beauty! Thou Soul of our Maker,
  Suddenly shown in a gleam or a tint;
O be each heart of Thy joy a partaker;
  Love, and its store, are alike without stint.

Spirit of Beauty! Thou teachest us sweetly;
Prophets and psalmists yield holy delight:
Show us our Lord, and we then shall completely
Know Thee as gentle, omnipotent Might.

Spirit of Beauty! our offering we render;
Thee in Thy skyey dominion we praise;
Lark-like we rise to the shadowless splendor,
Pouring out song as the sun pours his rays.

HOLY COMMUNION.

The third of ten equal stanzas of a very lovely hymn with this title, 1868.

O SPIRIT of Remembrance, tell
   The tale of Love and Sin;
Their mighty strife, and how He fell
   Whose was the right to win.
Then, kind Interpreter, explain
   How, rising from His fall,
He bore aloft our broken chain,
   And shone the Life of all.

ELIZA HUMPHREYS.

From her Metrical Collects, 1856.

GOD the Spirit, we aspire
   To receive those tongues of fire:
Sanctify the high desire:
   Descend, O Lord!

Magnify Thy gifts of Grace
In all those who seek Thy face
In their due appointed place:
    Descend, O Lord!

God the Spirit, we beseech,
Sanctify the gift of speech
To those called Thy Word to preach:
    Descend, O Lord!

Give to us the hearing ear,
Give to us the heart to fear,
Give the penitential tear:
    Descend, O Lord!

Cause the rightful seed be sown;
When the blade be newly grown,
Deign Thy gracious work to own:
    Descend, O Lord!

Let the plant deep-rooted be,
Watered, nurtured aye by Thee
Till the fruits of faith we see:
    Descend, O Lord!

Come forth, Thou soft-rushing Wind;
With Thy sacred effluence bind
The cold hearts of all mankind:
    Descend, O Lord!

Suffer our glad eyes to see
Restorèd grace of unity,
In the called Thine own to be:
    Descend, O Lord!

CONFIRMATION.

God the Spirit, we inquire
For Thy baptism of fire,
Our dross to burn, our hearts to inspire:
    Descend, O Lord!

Christ's own Church has daily prayed:
Inspirer, hear her cry: O aid!
Now let Satan's wiles be stayed:
    Descend, O Lord!

Come, O come! descend, and bring
Christ the glorious Lord and King
In His perfect triumphing:
    Descend, O Lord!

JOSEPH HENRY BUTTERWORTH.

Vicar of Stapleton near Bristol. He contributed this hymn in 1857 to his curate, the Rev. R. R. Chope, who inserted it in his *Hymnal*, 1858. It is for Confirmation

SPIRIT of Wisdom! guide Thine own,
    Who make Thee now their choice;
That they may never walk alone,
    But hear Thy heavenly voice.

Spirit of Understanding! Light
    Shed that the world ne'er saw;
Open their eyes, to see aright
    The wonders of Thy Law.

Spirit of Counsel! 'neath the cloud
    Of sorrow and dismay,
Cheer Thou their souls with anguish bowed,
    And chase all doubt away.

Spirit of Strength! infuse Thy might,
    Nerve Thy young soldiers' arms;
Temptation let them put to flight,
    And banish hell's alarms.

Spirit of Knowledge! Whose deep things
    Are now but darkly shown;
Lead them, on Resurrection-wings,
    To know as they are known.

Spirit of Godliness! unfold
    The joys of heavenly Grace;
Give peace on earth, the bliss untold
    Of saints who see God's face.

Spirit of holy Fear! inspire
    Dread reverence of Thy Name;
That we, with the celestial choir,
    May praise Thee without blame.

CHRISTINA FORSYTH, 1825–1859.

Hymns by C. F., Second Edition, 1861.

O HOLY Spirit, now descend on me
    As showers of rain upon a thirsty ground;
Cause me to flourish as a spreading tree;
    May all Thy precious fruits in me be found.

Be Thou my Teacher: to my soul reveal
  The length, breadth, depth, and height of Jesu's Love;
And on my soul Thy blest instructions seal,
  Raising my thoughts and heart to things above.

Be Thou my Comforter: when I'm distrest
  O gently soothe my sorrows, calm my grief,
Help me to find upon my Saviour's breast
  In every hour of trial sure relief.

Be Thou my Guide into all Truth divine:
  Give me increasing knowledge of my God:
Show me the glories that in Jesus shine,
  And make my heart the place of His abode.

Be Thou my Intercessor: teach me how
  To pray according to God's holy will;
Cause me with deep and strong desire to glow,
  And my whole soul with heavenly longings fill.

Be Thou my Earnest of eternal Rest,
  And witness with me I am God's own child,
With His unchanging Love and favor blest,
  By Jesus' merits fully reconciled.

Be Thou my Sanctifier: dwell within,
  And purify and cleanse my every thought;
Subdue the power of each besetting sin,
  And be my will to sweet submission brought.

Be Thou my Quickener: in me revive
  Each drooping grace, so prone to fade and die;
Help me on Jesus day by day to live,
  And loosen more and more each earthly tie.

Blest Spirit! I would yield myself to Thee;
  Do for me more than I can ask or think:
Let me Thy holy habitation be,
  And daily deeper from Thy fulness drink.

ANOTHER.

O HOLY Spirit! Comforter Divine!
    On me descend;
Into my soul with heavenly radiance shine,
    And condescend
To make this heart of mine a fit abode
For the indwelling presence of my God.
    O quicken me to run
With holy patience my appointed race,
Until at last through Thine almighty Grace
    My crown of glory's won.
Fill Thou my soul with light and life and love,
And gently draw my every thought above:
Make me to grow in knowledge of Thy Word
And daily closer likeness to the Lord.

CHRISTOPHER NEWMAN HALL, LL.B.
Born 1816.

<small>Minister of Surrey Chapel, London, and well known and honored here, as in England. His hymns appeared 1857. I take this through the English Presbyterian Collection, 1867.</small>

HOLY Spirit, Source of Light!
　　Beam upon our nature's night:
Make my doubts and darkness flee,
Clearly let me Jesus see.
Holy Spirit, Fount of Love!
Breathe upon me from above;
Warm this cold ungrateful heart,
Bid its selfishness depart.

Holy Spirit, Lord of Life!
Make me victor in the strife
Over Satan, death, and hell:
Fit me thus in Heaven to dwell.
Praises then I'll ever sing
Unto Christ my Saviour-King;
To the Father and to Thee
Praise I'll sing eternally.

CHARLES B. TAYLER.

<small>Rector of Otley in Suffolk: author of *Earnestness, Thankfulness*, &c. From one of his tales, called *Truth, or Persis Clareton*: I suppose the verses are his own.</small>

WIND of the North! awake and bring
　　Thy spirit-searching breath:
For feeble, faint, and withering,
　　We languish unto death.

Thy living energies bestow,
  Thy bracing strength impart,
And cause a vigorous health to flow
  Into each failing heart.

And thou, sweet South! with gentlest powers
  Our drooping graces raise;
Like freshened beds of fragrant flowers
  Expanding to Thy praise.

Then livelier tints shall greet Thine eyes,
  And spicy odors be
Drawn forth as incense, Lord, to rise
  In gratitude to Thee.

Spirit of gentleness and love,
  Combined with strength divine!
Come like the eagle and the dove,
  To make our spirits Thine.

Bear us aloft on eagles' wings,
  To soar with heavenward flight
Above the clouds of earthly things
  And drink the orient light.

And while our fervent prayers ascend
  In Jesus' name to Heaven,
O let the Dove of peace descend,
  The Comforter be given.

HORATIUS BONAR, D.D., 1808-1869.

Minister of the Free Church of Scotland at Kelso; a voluminous and well-known author. His *Hymns of Faith and Hope*, in three volumes, appeared severally in 1857, 1861, and 1866.

TILL THE DAY DAWN.
1857.

The third of four verses, under the title, "Hope of Day."

TILL the day dawn,
    And the Day-Star arise,
Spirit of gentle Love,
Thou tempest-calming Dove,
Come, and within me dwell,
Come, and all gloom dispel.
Most blessed Comforter,
My weary footsteps cheer.
O Light and Lamp divine,
Upon my midnight shine,
Better than star or moon,
Brighter than day's bright noon:
O let Thy joyous ray
Turn all my night to day.
When Thou art absent, even my joy is sad;
When Thou art with me, even my grief is glad:
Let not Thy silence now sorrow to sorrow add.

LIFE FROM THE DEAD.
1857.

SPIRIT of everlasting Grace,
    Infinite Source of Life, come down!
These tombs unlock, these dead upraise,
    Thy glorious power and Love make known.

Breathe o'er this valley of the dead;
  Send forth Thy quickening might abroad,
Till, rising from their tombs, they spread,
  In full array, — the host of God!

Thy heritage lies desolate,
  And all Thy pleasant places mourn.
O look upon our low estate,
  In loving-kindness, Lord, return!

Now let Thy glory be revealed,
  Now let Thy presence with us rest:
O heal us, and we shall be healed!
  O bless us, and we shall be blest!

COME, MIGHTY SPIRIT.
1861.

COME, mighty Spirit, penetrate
  This heart and soul of mine,
And my whole being with Thy Grace
  Pervade, O Life divine!

As this clear air surrounds the earth,
  Thy Grace around me roll;
As the fresh light pervades the air,
  So pierce and fill my soul.

As from these clouds drops down in love
  The precious summer rain,
So from Thyself pour down the flood
  That freshens all again.

As these fair flowers exhale their scent
    In gladness at our feet,
So from Thyself let fragrance breathe,
    More heavenly and more sweet.

Thus Life within our lifeless hearts
    Shall make its glad abode,
And we shall shine in beauteous light,
    Filled with the light of God.

TO THE COMFORTER.
1861.

MIGHTY Comforter, to Thee
    In our feebleness we flee;
O unveil Thy gracious face,
Spread out all Thy wondrous Grace.

Strengthener of the poor and weak,
To Thy power for strength we seek;
Heavenly Fulness from above,
O descend in blessed Love.

Patient Teacher of the blind,
Opener of the sin-sealed mind,
Fix in us Thy sure abode,
And reveal the Christ of God.

Guider of the erring feet
In the waste or busy street,
Lead us through life's Babel-crowds,
Through its pathless solitudes.

True Enricher of the poor,
Enter Thou our lowly door;
Let Thy liberal Hand impart
Heavenly riches to our heart.

Looser of the bonds of sin,
O make haste and enter in;
Break each link, till there remains
Not one fragment of our chains.

Loving Spirit, come, O come!
Find in us Thy endless home;
Find in this our world below
A dwelling for Thy glory now.

Holy Light, upon us shine
With Thy energy divine;
Heavenly Brightness, break Thou forth
Over this benighted earth.

With the eternal Father One,
One with the eternal Son,
Eternal Spirit, Thee we praise,
Now and through eternal days.

PRAYER TO THE SPIRIT.

1866.

ALMIGHTY Comforter and Friend,
    Eternal Spirit, now descend,
Fill us from Thy heavenly store!

Thou art the Church's holy Guest,
Earnest of her eternal rest,
   Let us grieve Thee never more.

Great Promise of the Father, come,
The Church's fading lamps relume;
   Come, rekindle joy and love!
Wisdom, and Truth, and Love are Thine,
Life, light, and holiness divine;
   Shed Thy gifts down from above!

Witness of Him Who died and rose,
Who as the Conqueror of our foes
   Took His seat upon the throne!
Great Gift of Jesus glorified,
Revealer of the Crucified,
   Unto us reveal the Son!

THE COMFORT OF THE HOLY GHOST.
1866.

Compare Herrick's " Litany to the Holy Spirit," pp. 305-7.

WHEN the leaves of life are falling,
   When the shadows flit appalling,
When the twilight voice is calling;
   Mighty Spirit, comfort!

When youth's verdure all is fading,
When I pass into the shading,
Life's long load at last unlading;
   Mighty Spirit, comfort!

When the frost of time has found me,
When the chains of age have bound me,
When the evening mists surround me;
    Mighty Spirit, comfort!

When the worn-out flesh is sinking,
When from burdens it is shrinking,
And from earthly ties unlinking:
    Mighty Spirit, comfort!

When the gates of life are closing,
All its lattice-bolts unloosing,
And the spirit seeks reposing;
    Mighty Spirit, comfort!

When these skies look wan and dreary,
When the inner man is weary,
Worn out by the adversary;
    Mighty Spirit, comfort!

When the once keen eye is failing,
When the steadfast heart is quailing,
Flesh, and fiend, and world assailing;
    Mighty Spirit, comfort!

When past sins are flocking round me,
When the fiery arrows wound me,
As if hell would then confound me;
    Mighty Spirit, comfort!

When I think on manhood wasted,
Cups of pleasure vilely tasted,
Holy longings madly blasted;
    Mighty Spirit, comfort!

When my farewells I am taking,
And these lower rooms forsaking,
To my upper home betaking ;
　　Mighty Spirit, comfort !

Holy Spirit, Strength in weakness,
Holy Spirit, Health in sickness,
Give me comfort, patience, meekness !
　　Mighty Spirit, comfort !

Ah, Thou wilt not then forsake me ;
Strong in weakness Thou wilt make me,
To Thy bosom Thou wilt take me :
　　Mighty Spirit, comfort !

ROBERT WILSON EVANS, B.D.

Vicar of Heversham, and Archdeacon of Westmoreland: author of *The Rectory of Valehead, Bishopric of Souls*, and several other prose works: and of *Daily Hymns*, 1860. This very remarkable book of elaborate, cultivated, and uncommonplace verse is written throughout in a single difficult measure, recommended to the author by being "entirely unassociated with any utterance of secular poetry."

INVOCATION.

HOLY Ghost, Thou satest brooding,
　　Under Thy warm wing including
Heaven and earth, Thou Dove of ages,
Rudimental atoms quickening,
Points to primal masses thickening,
　　Through Thy plastic nurture's stages.

So disposed for form and figure
Stood they in attempered vigor,
   Reined in for impetuous sally
Into sun and all life's fountains,
Into earth and sea and mountains,
   When the Word life's ranks should rally.

Thou all this creative earnest
Into bright fulfilment turnest,
   O'er our hearts with warmth dost flutter;
All preparing, upper, nether,
Into form to run together,
   When the Word "Be Light" shall utter.

Blessed Spirit, mighty Maker,
Bid my spirit be partaker
   In Thy Pentecostal newness;
All my heart's close chamber rending
With Thy fiery storm descending
   In its sempiternal trueness.

'Mid its waste of night and deadness
There unto life-giving redness
   Wake the fire from smouldering embers;
Let the heavenly heat be teeming,
Let the heavenly light be beaming
   Through my brain, my reins, my members.

Soften this hard frame, thus soften,
Visiting it long and often,
   Turn to flesh its stone obdurate;
Melt each passage hard contorted,
Through which hell hath long resorted
   To my breast in bands conjurate.

Temper thus a mould for casting
Christ's own image everlasting
  On my soul in perfect beauty;
From His Word's outpouring treasure
Filling up with daily measure
  Every empty nook of duty.

For affection and for reason
Ever make that Word's blest season
  Homeward bring its ministration,
That with its deep tide of fulness
It may whelm all clog of dulness,
  Soak with quickening penetration.

THE BODY'S TEMPLE.

O INVINCIBLE Compeller
  In the breast where Thou art Dweller,
Holy Spirit, Lord enlightening:
Fill this body with pure essence,
Temple of Thy glorious presence,
  Daily growing, daily brightening.

Temper Thou this spirit, cooling
Passion, ere it strive for ruling,
  While from nature's caldron seething:
Sweeten every gale that sallies
Through thought's labyrinthine alleys,
  With Thy perfumed incense breathing.

Fast against the day's offences
Shut the portal of my senses,
   Setting watch at every station.
Help my weakness when I falter,
Offering on heart's high altar
   Struggling will's long-due oblation.

Thus let all within bear witness
To Thy habitation's fitness,
   To Thy temple's pure condition.
Be the font of sins remitted
Unto souls by Jesus pitied
   Imaged in my deep contrition.

Be the pulpit of Thy teaching
To my spirit daily preaching,
   Seeds of Life immortal sowing;
While my heart's secreted table
Set by faith, adorned and stable,
   Christ in flesh and blood is showing.

Thence in order long bid issue,
Bound in action's varied tissue,
   Outward token of the inner,
Services to each dear brother,
Hailing still in him another
   Fellow-saint and fellow-sinner.

Bless this increase, which augmenteth
Day by day, as heart relenteth
   From its shapeless stony nature
Into heavenly plan and moulding,
Storied height and wings unfolding
   Duly in harmonious stature.

There let Faith her portal furnish,
Joy her front of golden burnish,
   Hope her spire of bright adventure,
Knowledge her wide windows, fretting
From the sun that knows no setting,
   Love his harmonizing centre.

As the Spirit's springs awaken,
Hands in fond salute are shaken,
   Heads are pressed in fervent blessing:
Alms are dealt with secret pressure,
Heart is opening hidden treasure,
   Hungry feeding, naked dressing.

Lord, may thus my part immortal,
Set at inner life's last portal,
   Empty on this world external,
Poured from all its well-stored niches,
All its treasures, all its riches,
   Lasting cheer to gloom diurnal.

Holy Spirit! now heart's station
Opens to Thy inspiration;
   Words come prompt, my lips I sever.
Glory from all spirits living,
Glory, blessing, and thanksgiving,
   Glory be to Thee for ever.

MEEKNESS OF SPIRIT.

Blessed Spirit, that preparest
　From Thy unction's vial rarest
　For the kingdom ever-during,
Nature with new beauty gracing,
Guilt's imprinted soil effacing,
　Sin's heart-eating cancer curing:

With Thy quickening sunbeams reach me,
With Thy holy lessons teach me,
　Change me, Thou almighty Changer.
Like the flame from altar's embers,
Pierce my heart, my reins, my members,
　Never more to be a stranger.

Where Thy virtue Thou suppliest,
There the lowest is the highest,
　There the servant is the master,
And Thy new-born child is wiser
Than the world's gray-haired adviser,
　Sees scenes brighter, regions vaster.

Royalty in shame Thou shroudest;
Reed of scorn is sceptre proudest,
　Robe of mockery is glorious;
Thorns are crowns of jewelled whiteness,
And the Cross a throne of brightness,
　Grave's deep cry a shout victorious.

So uphold my fixed endeavor,
Let me live Thy child for ever,
  Child to sin, but man to duty;
Down to dust all proud looks veiling,
Up to Heaven with clear eye scaling,
  Wondering at Thy heavenly beauty.

Led by Thee, O Spirit Holy,
It is pleasant to be lowly,
  Calm to lie in that green valley,
Where, unseen from world's proud mountains,
Sweet with Love of Christ, full fountains
  From His rock of freshness sally.

Lord, there is a winsome sweetness,
Lord, there is a gladsome meetness,
  When the[1] soul hath found her station,
And no further fall can try her,
But each flutter lifts her higher
  On Thy pinions of salvation.

Thus renewed to nature's centre,
That blest kingdom may I enter,
  There where service shall be lording,
There where cities ruled in meekness
Shall not blame the ruler's weakness,
  Love with faithfulness according.

---

[1] Original, "when *thus* soul": probably a misprint.

THOMAS HORNBLOWER GILL. Born 1819.

Author of *The Papal Drama*, 1866, *The Anniversaries*, 1858, and *The Golden Chain of Praise*, 1869. The latter contains 165 hymns, which are remarkable for freshness and delicacy of thought, warmth of feeling, and frequent melody of rhythm: in the judgment of Dr. Freeman Clarke, who reprinted some of his earlier lyrics, this author is a more intellectual Charles Wesley. He lives at Lewisham in Kent, and is chiefly occupied with historical and theologic studies. Some account of him may be found in *Hours at Home* for February, 1868.

A BREATHING AFTER THE HOLY SPIRIT.
1863.

O HOLY Ghost who down dost come
    To make each contrite heart Thy home,
On me descend! within me dwell,
My soul renew, my sin expel!

Spirit of Truth, who makest bright
All souls that long for heavenly light,
Appear and on my darkness shine!
Descend and be my Guide divine!

Spirit of Power, whose might doth dwell
Full in the souls Thou lovest well,
Unto this fainting heart draw near,
And be my daily Quickener!

Spirit of Joy, who makest glad
Each broken heart by sin made sad,
Pour on this mourning soul Thy cheer;
Give me to bless my Comforter!

O tender Spirit, who dost mourn
Whene'er from Thee Thy people turn,
Give me each day to grieve Thee less:
Enjoy my fuller faithfulness!

Come mightier down! Thyself impart
More largely to this longing heart;
My Comforter more dearly be;
More sweetly guide and hallow me:

Till Thou shalt make me meet to bear
The sweetness of Heaven's holy air,
The light wherein no darkness is,
The eternal, overflowing bliss!

THE FELLOWSHIP OF THE HOLY SPIRIT.

1848.

HOLY Spirit! dwell with me!
    Glorify this humble home!
Meet again mortality,
    To another temple come!

Holy Spirit! forth from me!
    Sweetly forth — ah, not away:
Kept Thou mayst, yet given be;
    Mighty go, yet mighty stay.

Spirit that with me dost dwell,
    Make Thy presence richly known:
Holy deeds send forth to tell
    Of the bright communion!

Peaceful Spirit! hath the soul
   Where Thy voice so sweet doth sound,
Of Thy mighty music full,
   Ears to hear the roar around?

Cheerful Spirit! where but here
   In this happy home of Thine,
Floweth on such gladsome cheer?
   Ever fresh the feast divine.

Holy Spirit! give not o'er;
   Leave not, leave not hallowing me;
Me Thy temple evermore;
   Mine Thine own Eternity!

THE DIVINE RENEWER.

"Thou renewest the face of the earth."
"Be renewed in the spirit of your mind."

1867.

THE glory of the Spring how sweet!
   The new-born life how glad!
What joy the happy earth to greet
   In new, bright raiment clad;

The blessed vernal airs to hail
   In their renewing power,
The new song of each nightingale,
   The new birth of each flower!

THE DIVINE RENEWER.

Divine Renewer! Thee I bless;
   I greet Thy going forth:
I love Thee in the loveliness
   Of Thy renewèd earth.

But O these wonders of Thy Grace,
   These nobler works of Thine,
These marvels sweeter far to trace,
   These new-births more divine!

These sinful souls Thou hallowest,
   These hearts Thou makest new,
These mourning souls by Thee made blest,
   These faithless hearts made true!

This new-born glow of faith so strong,
   This bloom of love so fair;
This new-born ecstasy of song
   And fragrancy of prayer!

Creator Spirit, work in me
   These wonders sweet of Thine!
Divine Renewer, graciously
   Renew this heart of mine!

Grant me the grace of the New Birth,
   The joy of the New Song!
The vernal bloom, the vernal mirth
   In my new heart prolong!

Still let new life and strength upspring,
   Still let new joy be given,
And grant the glad new song to ring
   Through the new earth and Heaven!

THE UNCHANGING RENEWER.

"Immutabilia, mutans omnia." — St. Augustine.

(Written 1869, and now first printed. Contributed to this Collection.)

LORD God, by Whom all change is wrought,
By Whom new things to birth are brought,
   In Whom no change is known;
Whate'er Thou dost, whate'er Thou art,
Thy people still in Thee have part;
   Still, still Thou art our own.

Ancient of Days! we dwell in Thee;
Out of Thine own Eternity
   Our peace and joy are wrought;
We rest in our eternal God,
And make secure and sweet abode
   With Thee Who changest not.

Each steadfast promise we possess;
Thine everlasting Truth we bless,
   Thine everlasting Love;
The Unfailing Helper close we clasp,
The Everlasting Arms we grasp,
   Nor from the Refuge move.

Spirit, Who makest all things new,
Thou leadest onward: we pursue
   The heavenly march sublime.
'Neath Thy renewing fire we glow,
And still from strength to strength we go,
   From height to height we climb.

Darkness and dread we leave behind,
New light, new glory still we find,
   New realms divine possess:
New births of Grace new raptures bring;
Triumphant the new song we sing,
   The great Renewer bless.

To Thee we rise, in Thee we rest;
We stay at home, we go in quest,
   Still Thou art our abode.
The rapture swells, the wonder grows,
As full on us new life still flows
   From our unchanging God.

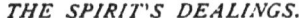

THE SPIRIT'S DEALINGS WITH THE HEART.

1854

WEET Spirit! would Thy Breath Divine
  O'er a void waste all fragrant blow?
Bright Presence! would that fire of Thine
  All lonely in Thy temple glow?

Thou dost not sure an empty heart
  For Thy dear dwelling-place desire;
To glorify Thy holy art
  Thou dost a peopled realm require.

O sternly all the robbers chase,
  But give the dwellers leave to stay;
Unpeople not the yielded place,
  Nor all its treasure cast away.

The taken treasure-house explore
  With Thine all-searching fire divine :
And put upon the dross-blent store
  The glory of Thy gold most fine.

O teach the conquered realm Thy law,
  Each passion 'neath Thy sweet sway bring;
From each dark depth Thy glory draw,
  From each dull chord Thy music ring!

Each mounting thought, each strong desire
  Help on Thy heavenly wings to rise,
And light in hearts with love on fire
  Thine own pure flame that never dies.

O teach our wrath the holy glow
  Wherewith Thine awful anger burns,
And make our grovelling sorrow know
  How gloriously the Spirit mourns!

O lend our hope's dim, dying light
  The steadfast glory of Thy flame,
And grant our joy, divinely bright,
  The witness of Thy smile to claim.

Take all this heart, its wealth, its powers,
  Its yearnings soft, its longings high,
Its bleeding wounds, its golden hours,
  And on them all Thy sweet skill try.

O breathe on them Thy Breath divine!
  O steep them in Thy heavenly glow!
Nor let one smile unhallowed shine,
  Nor let one tear unhallowed flow.

THE FREE SPIRIT.

LORD, when we come at Thy dear call,
    Our scanty store we bring:
Sweet Spirit! Thou dost ask our all
    For Thine own hallowing.

We need not ask of our right hand
    Its cunning to forget:
May not it move at Thy command?
    Hast not Thou tasks to set?

Why need we, Lord, our hearts deny,
    Why bid our love begone?
The Heavenly Dove comes down to try
    His own sweet skill thereon.

Why should our minds repent their pains,
    Unlearn their little lore?
Spirit of Truth! advance their gains;
    Mingle Thine own bright store.

Our tender tears we need not hide,
    Our yearnings deep reprove;
Teach us a glorious grief allied
    To Thine, sin-vexèd Dove!

We need not dread our golden while,
    Nor shun each blissful bower;
Bright Presence! bless it with Thy smile!
    Make it Thine own sweet hour!

For us no height, for us no deep
    Whereon Thou mayst not shine;
O Spirit sweet! Thou wouldst not keep
    From us one gift divine.

TAKE NOT THY HOLY SPIRIT FROM ME.
1868.

O SPIRIT sweet and pure,
    Wilt Thou at last depart?
Canst Thou no more endure
    This faithless, fallen heart?
      These lusts that reign,
        These sins that cleave,
      Will they constrain
        My Lord to leave?

Was not this heart of mine
    Thy dwelling fair and bright?
Didst not Thou, Guest divine,
    In that abode delight?
      With me to dwell
        My Lord did love;
      I pleased Thee well,
        Celestial Dove.

Thou madest all Thy power
    And glory known to me;
Thou broughtest all Thy dower
    Of gifts divine with Thee.
      Thy cheer ran o'er,
        Thy Love o'erflowed;
      Thy precious store
        Was all bestowed.

Those tender tears and sighs,
    Those strivings strong and blest,
Those prayers that rend the skies,
    They came with Thee, sweet Guest.

That joy divine,
   That gladsome strain,
They once were mine,
   Thy glorious train.

And now I grieve Thee sore,
   I scarce resist the foe:
The song ascends no more;
   The stream of prayer runs low.
   Sweet Holy Ghost,
      And art Thou gone?
   Bright Heavenly Host,
      And have ye flown?

Lord, shall I never more
   Thy Spirit entertain?
In vain do I implore
   A visit sweet again?
   Ah, well I mourn;
      Thou well dost chide:
   But yet return!
   But yet abide!

More mightily descend,
   More graciously come in!
Thy fuller presence lend,
   A fairer temple win!
   O go away,
      Sweet Guest, no more,
   But come and stay
      With all Thy store!

CHARLOTTE MARGARET NOEL.

An invalid lady, daughter of the Hon. and Rev. Gerard Thomas Noel. From her little volume, The Name of Jesus and other Verses for the Sick and Lonely, Second Edition, 1862. The earlier verses of this piece are on page 107.

O SPIRIT of our spirit, Life's pure Fount!
   True Friend of the true Bridegroom Whom
      we wait,
Reveal Him clearer to our souls, that mount
With keen expectance towards their promised state.

'Tis not enough that He our place prepares,
With beauty infinite adorns our Home,
And by the power of His unceasing prayers
Prevails, that those He loves shall thither come.

We would be like Him Whom we call our Lord,
We would reflect the Image that we love;
O chasten our whole being to accord
With the deep tides of life that in Him move.

Thou gracious Spirit! Comforter most meek!
As Christ His glory veiled in flesh of man,
So Thou Thy Godhead dost conceal in weak
Blind spirits, who Thy working cannot scan.

But when He comes for Whom we hourly pray,
And we are one with Him in heart and mind,
He will unfold to us the wondrous way
In which Thy Love and His for us combined.

SPIRIT OF BONDAGE UNTO FEAR. 561

Till then we yield ourselves in deepest trust
Into Thy Hands, their impress to receive;
We would adore Thee, humbled to the dust:
O Holy Ghost! we do in Thee believe.

SAMUEL DUNN.

A Wesleyan minister. From his *Hymns for Pastors and People*, 1862.

ACTS xix. 2.

SPIRIT of Bondage unto fear,
    Fill me with sacred grief;
Make all my dangerous state appear,
    Shut up in unbelief.

Spirit of Faith, to me reveal
    Jesus the Crucified;
Let me behold His face, and feel
    His cleansing Blood applied.

Spirit of Liberty, impart
    The sense of sin forgiven;
Engrave the pardon on my heart,
    And seal the heir of heaven.

Spirit of Life, the Grace divine
    In quickening power bestow;
Transform my nature into Thine,
    The new Creation show.

Spirit of Love, diffuse abroad
    Throughout my longing soul
The Love, the perfect Love of God,
    And purify the whole.

May I receive the Holy Ghost,
    Then stand before the throne,
And join the bright celestial host
    To praise the Three in One.

ROMANS viii. 9.

SPIRIT of Christ, descend
    On every waiting heart;
On Thee, Thee only, we depend;
    Thy help to us impart.

Come as the shining Light,
    The things of Christ reveal,
That we may see His glories bright,
    And all His goodness feel.

Come as refining Fire,
    On all our spirits move;
Kindle the pure and strong desire
    To be transformed by Love.

Come as a mighty Wind
    And fill this favored place;
Let every heart Thy presence find
    And taste Thy richest Grace.

ADESTE SUMMA CARITAS.

Come as the gentle Dew
Upon the thirsty field,
And all our barren souls renew
The fruit of Grace to yield.

Come as the peaceful Dove
And dwell in every breast,
Till we from all our toils remove
To Heaven's eternal Rest.

FRANCIS POTT.

Incumbent of Northill in Bedfordshire. His *Hymns fitted to the Order of Common Prayer*, 1861-4, include a number of versions from the Latin, of which this is one. Its origin was not known when the "Latin Hymns" in this volume were set.

ADESTE SUMMA CARITAS.

HEAR, Holy Spirit, Fount of Sweetness,
Binding the Eternal Three in One by Love!
Hear and descend, that in our weakness
We may the fulness of Thy comfort prove.

By Thee the Virgin-Maid conceiving
Brought forth the Second Adam, who hath burst
The death-bonds which the arch-deceiver
Had drawn around the children of the first.

By Thee the Apostles' souls were lighted,
To trace the mysteries of God the Word:
Through Thee the Truth that Israel slighted
The Gentile nations at their preaching heard.

Thy Strength upheld the noble martyrs
In death the rulers of the world to face;
Thy Light illumined holy Fathers
Each subtle error in the Church to trace.

And we too now need all Thy goodness,
The Oil of Thine anointing on the soul:
O pour it out in all its fulness,
Till all Thy fallen creatures are made whole.

Good Spirit! let no abject trembling
Place us at last amid the slaves disowned;
But give us at that great assembling
The loving awe of children round the throne.

And now, O Lord, with this our pleading,
We praise Thee, with the Father and the Son;
We praise Thee, who from Both proceeding,
With Both from all eternity art One.

WHITSUN-EVE.

<small>This is from Mr. POTT's Collection, and may be his.</small>

THE Lord is gone; His people watch and pray,
   Until fulfilled is His consoling word;
In patience for that Promised One they stay,
   The Comforter foretold them by their Lord.

Come, blessed Comforter, Thy light reveal!
   Strengthen our faith in sorrow's gloomy hour!
Teach us to know Thou carest for our weal,
   And wilt preserve us from the tempter's power.

Come, blest Remembrancer, Thy Grace bestow,
  That we remember all that Christ has taught;
Make us His saving truths on earth to know,
  Ourselves to be with Christ's own likeness fraught.

Thrice holy Paraclete! Thy power revealed,
  We shall no more lament that Christ is gone;
For by Thy mercy purified and sealed
  We shall hereafter with our Lord be one.

BISHOP CHRISTOPHER WORDSWORTH. D.D.
Born 1807.

A nephew of William Wordsworth, and since 1868 Bishop of Lincoln. In 1862 he published *The Holy Year; or Hymns for Sundays and Holy Days, and for Other Occasions.*

WHIT-SUNDAY.

WHEN the Lord of Hosts ascended
  To His heavenly citadel;
Soon the Holy Ghost descended,
  Sent by Him with men to dwell;
Sign of Christ's inauguration
  In the kingdom of His power,
Largess of His coronation,
  Royal Bounty, promised Dower.

When the faithful there assembled
  On the Day of Pentecost,
Rushed the wind, the place it trembled;
  Came from Heaven the Holy Ghost;

Golden shower of consecration,
   Tongues of fire were on them shed,
And that holy dedication
   Made an altar of each head.

Now the festive Pentecostal
   Harvest-home of souls they keep;[1]
With his sickle each Apostle
   Whitening fields goes forth to reap:
God with holy flame from Heaven
   Writes on hearts the law of love;[2]
Jubilee[3] of sins forgiven
   Sounds its trumpet from above.

Holy Ghost, divine Creator,
   Who didst on the waters move;
Holy Ghost, Regenerator,
   Author of all life and love;
Holy Ghost, Illuminator,
   Who didst then with fire baptize;
Holy Ghost, great Renovator,
   Come, the world evangelize.

Not in fire from Heaven descending,
   Not in earthquake nor in shower,
Not in wind the mountains rending,
   Now, O Lord, we seek Thy power;

---

[1] The Feast of Pentecost introduced the Wheat Harvest.
[2] The Law of Moses was given on Mount Sinai, fifty days after the Passover.
[3] In the Fiftieth year: so the Pentecost, or Fiftieth, introduces the Christian Jubilee, when the Apostles began to preach remission of sins to all nations.

But in holy aspirations
  Do we seek and find Thee, Lord,
And in quiet meditations
  On Thy everlasting Word.

With the kneeling congregation
  Thou art in the house of prayer;
Laver of Regeneration
  Is o'ershadowed by Thee there;
Thou dost shed at Confirmation
  From Thy wing a gift of Grace;
Eucharistic Celebration
  Has revealings of Thy face.

Guide of erring, go before us;
  Breeze in heat, refresh our soul;
Shed Thy genial lustre o'er us;
  Balm of sickness, make us whole.
In the hour of danger hear us;
  After labor give repose;
In the days of sickness cheer us;
  Guard in danger from our foes.

Strengthen, warm, and purify us;
  From the bands of sin release;
Comfort, counsel, sanctify us;
  Give us love and joy and peace:
Patience, faith, and resignation
  Breathe upon us with Thy Breath;
Give us heavenly consolation
  In the solemn hour of death.

So when earth with fruit aboundeth,
    And shall angel reapers see,
And the great archangel soundeth
    God's eternal Jubilee,
We may join their gratulation;
    To the Father and the Son
And the Spirit, adoration
    Ever be, blest Three in One.

ASCENSION DAY.

(The last half of a hymn of ten verses.)

HOLY Ghost, Illuminator, shed Thy beams upon
    our eyes,
Help us to look up with Stephen, and to see, be-
    yond the skies,
Where the Son of Man in glory standing is at God's
    right hand,
Beckoning on His martyr army, succoring His faith-
    ful band.

See Him, Who is gone before us heavenly mansions
    to prepare,
See Him, Who is ever pleading for us with prevail-
    ing prayer;
See Him, Who with sound of trumpet and with His
    angelic train,
Summoning the world to Judgment, on the clouds
    will come again.

Lift us up from earth to Heaven; give us wings of faith and love,
Gales of holy aspirations wafting us to realms above;
That, with hearts and minds uplifted, we with Christ our Lord may dwell,
Where He sits enthroned in glory in His heavenly Citadel.

So at last, when He appeareth, we from out our graves may spring,
With our youth renewed like eagles, flocking round our Heavenly King,
Caught up on the clouds of heaven, and may meet Him in the air,
Rise to realms where He is reigning, and may reign for ever there.

Glory be to God the Father; glory be to God the Son,
Dying, risen, ascending for us, Who the heavenly realm has won;
Glory to the Holy Spirit; to One God in Persons Three,
Glory both in earth and heaven, glory, endless glory be.

QUINQUAGESIMA.

1 Corinthians xii. 31; xiii.

Gracious Spirit, Holy Ghost,
  Taught by Thee, we covet most
Of Thy gifts at Pentecost
  Holy, heavenly Love.

Faith, that mountains could remove,
Tongues of earth or Heaven above,
Knowledge — all things — empty prove
  Without heavenly Love.

Though I as a martyr bleed,
Give my goods the poor to feed,
All is vain, if Love I need;
  Therefore, give me Love.

Love is kind and suffers long,
Love is meek, and thinks no wrong.
Love than death itself more strong;
  Therefore, give us Love.

Prophecy will fade away,
Melting in the light of day;
Love will ever with us stay;
  Therefore, give us Love.

Faith will vanish into sight;
Hope be emptied in delight;
Love in Heaven will shine more bright;
  Therefore, give us Love.

Faith and Hope and Love we see
Joining hand in hand agree;
But the greatest of the three,
   And the best, is Love.

From the overshadowing
Of Thy gold and silver wing
Shed on us, who to Thee sing,
   Holy, heavenly Love.

CONFIRMATION.

(Three verses, the third and the last two, out of eleven.)

O HOLY Ghost, by Whom we live,
   To Thee we praise and glory give:
Thou blessed Spirit, Holy Dove.
Who dost on hallowed waters move,
By Whom in them we joinèd are
To Christ, and God's own Nature share:
Brood o'er us with the shadowings
For ever of Thy golden wings.

Come, ever-blessed Spirit, come,
And make Thy servants' hearts Thy home;
Thus consecrated, Lord, to Thee,
May each a living temple be.
Enrich that temple's holy shrine
With sevenfold gifts of Grace divine;
With wisdom, light, and knowledge bless,
Strength, counsel, fear, and godliness.

O Trinity in Unity,
One only God and Persons Three,
In Whom, through Whom, by Whom we live,
To Thee we praise and glory give.
O grant us so to use Thy Grace,
That we may see Thy glorious face,
And ever with the heavenly host
Praise Father, Son, and Holy Ghost.

CECIL FRANCES ALEXANDER.

Wife of the present Bishop of Derry: author of Hymns for Little Children, Verses for Holy Seasons, &c., and compiler of The Sunday Book of Poetry. From her Hymns Descriptive and Devotional, 1858.

SPIRIT of God, that moved of old
    Upon the water's darkened face,
Come, when our faithless hearts are cold,
    And stir them with an inward grace.

Thou that art Power and Peace combined,
    All highest Strength, all purest Love,
The rushing of the mighty wind,
    The brooding of the gentle dove;

Unseal the well within our hearts
    Whose fount in Heaven immortal springs;
Bid all our troublous fears depart,
    And soothe us with Thy quiet wings.

Come, give us still Thy powerful aid,
   And urge us on, and make us Thine;
Nor leave the hearts that once were made
   Fit temples for Thy Grace divine.

Nor let us quench Thy sevenfold light;
   But still with softest breathings stir
Our wayward souls; and lead us right,
   O Holy Ghost, the Comforter!

OSWALD ALLEN.

Born 1816; a banker at Kirkby-Lonsdale, Westmoreland. *Hymns of the Christian Life*, 1862. The following was revised for Dr. Rogers' *Lyra Britannica*, 1867.

O HOLY Spirit, come,
   And Jesu's Love declare;
O tell us of our heavenly Home,
   And guide us safely there.

Our unbelief remove
   By Thine almighty breath;
O work the wondrous work of love,
   The mighty work of faith!

Come with resistless power,
   Come with almighty Grace,
Come with the long-expected shower,
   And fall upon this place.

We know Thou hast the power,
    O let that power be shown!
We know that this is mercy's hour,
    O make Thy mercy known!

We now besiege Thy throne,
    We fall before Thy face;
Our only hope, Thy Love alone;
    Our only trust, Thy Grace.

Thy sceptre, Lord, extend;
    Pity our deep distress:
Thou art the contrite sinner's Friend;
    Thy waiting servants bless.

Give us the melting soul,
    Give us the will subdued,
Give us the streams of Grace, to roll
    Over a heart renewed.

We bless Thee for Thy Grace
    And Thine almighty power;
We bless Thee for Thy holy place,
    And this accepted hour.

WILLIAM LINDSAY ALEXANDER, D.D.

Born 1808: Congregationalist pastor and professor in Edinburgh, and "the greatest ornament of Independency in Scotland": author of various works, among them a few hymns. This is taken through *Lyra Britannica*. The date of this is 1849.

SPIRIT of Power and Truth and Love,
    Who sitt'st enthroned in light above,
Descend, and bear us on Thy wings
Far from these low and fleeting things.

'Tis Thine the wounded soul to heal;
'Tis Thine to make the hardened feel;
Thine to give light to blinded eyes,
And bid the grovelling spirit rise.

Compassed by foes on every side,
By sin and sore temptation tried,
Where can we look or whither flee,
If not, great Strengthener, to Thee?

When faith is weak and courage fails,
When grief or doubt the soul assails,
Who can like Thee our spirits cheer?
Great Comforter, be ever near!

Like captives at their prison gate,
We mourn our languishing estate:
Thou only canst our bonds untie;
Great Sanctifier, hear our cry!

Come, Holy Spirit, like the fire,
With burning zeal our souls inspire;
Come like the south wind, breathing balm;
Our joys refresh, our passions calm.

Come like the sun's enlightening beam;
Come like the cooling, cleansing stream;
With all Thy graces present be:
Spirit of God, we wait for Thee.

THOMAS BURBIDGE.

Eleven pieces by this author are included in that very interesting Collection. *Poems of the Inner Life*, London, 1866. Of this hymn Mrs. C. F. Alexander has inserted four verses in her *Sunday Book of Poetry*, 1864.

PRAISE be Thine, most Holy Spirit,
    Honor to Thy Holy Name!
May we love it, may we fear it,
    Set in everlasting fame!
Honor, honor, praise, and glory,
    Comforter, Inspirer, Friend,
Till these troubles transitory
    End in glory without end.

By Thy hand, in secret working,
    Like a midnight of soft rain,
Seeds that lay in silence lurking
    Spring up green, and grow amain.
Roots which in their dusty bosoms
    Hid an age of golden days,
Stirring with a cloud of blossoms,
    Clothe their bareness for Thy praise.

We should sleep but Thou awakest;
    Sometimes like a morning sun
On the dazzled soul Thou breakest,
    Heaven at once on earth begun.
Sometimes like a star appearing,
    Seen and lost as earth-winds blow,
Wishing, hoping, thinking, fearing,
    Thou hast saved us ere we know.

Thou dost set the mute world speaking
  To the sinner in his sin;
Thou to spirits humbly seeking
  Answerest by a voice within.
Happier souls, like fruit-trees leading
  Ordered branches o'er the wall,
Find in Thee the solace needing.
  Shower or sunshine, Thou art All!

When the proud one builds a wonder
  Overshadowing the earth,
Oft its turrets, split asunder,
  Cast the homeless wanderer forth:
Underneath his towers derided
  Conscience lurked, as strong as hell,
But Thine eye the times divided,
  And the spark in season fell.

As an island in a river,
  Vexed with ceaseless rave and roar,
Keeps an inner silence ever
  On its consecrated shore,
Flowered with flowers and green with grasses;
  So the poor through Thee abide,
Every outer care that passes
  Deepening more the peace inside.

Led by Thee, the loving pastor,
  Anxious night and weary day,
In the footsteps of his Master
  Seeks the sheep that run astray;

Glad to warm, and glad to cherish,
  With a faithful tender tongue
Cheers the weak ones near to perish,
  Gently leads the ewes with young.

When our heart is faint Thou warmest,
  Justifiest our delight;
Thou our ignorance informest,
  And our wisdom shapest right;
Thou in peace dost keep, defendest
  In the hour of doubt and strife;
Thou beginnest and Thou endest
  All that Christians count of life.

Gracious Spirit, Spirit Holy,
  Take our spirits unto Thee;
Fain we would be happy, lowly:
  Make us as we fain would be!
'Tis not our own will approves us;
  If we praise or if we sue,
'Tis Thine own kind Spirit moves us,
  For 'tis Thine to will and do.

ANONYMOUS.

From *The Monthly Packet*, a magazine now edited by Miss Yonge, which has long "maintained the reputation of being the best Church Monthly for Young Persons." These sonnets are founded on Collects for certain days.

O COME, Consoler! vivifying Dove!
  And o'er our hearts, with sins and sorrows rife,
Stretch forth Thy hovering wings, as erst above
  The dim abyss of elemental strife,

Fraught with Creation's mission, Thou didst move,
　　Evoking morning from primordial night.
E'en thus o'ershadowing in the might of Love,
　　Create anew our souls to life and light.
Enlightener, come! and with Thy conquering fire
　　Enkindle the sweet flame of charity,
And fervent zeal, that ne'er shall halt or tire,
　　And love that taught the martyrs how to die;
Yea, with Thy seven blest gifts our hearts inspire,
　　Till earth recedes, and Heaven seems drawing nigh.

EIGHTH SUNDAY AFTER TRINITY.

O HOLY Ghost, Whose pitying Providence
　　Doth temper all things, both in heaven and earth,
We pray Thee, Lord, with Thy blest influence,
　　To rule our spirit, by the second birth
Regenerate, and dead to things of sense;
　　That we henceforth, redeemed from sin and wrath,
May labor to fulfil all excellence,
　　All fruit of love in patience bringing forth.
Nor let the leaven of hypocrisy
　　With empty hopes our carnal hearts inflate;
But teach us so on earth to mortify
　　The flesh, with its desires inordinate,
That we, in meekness and all purity,
　　At length may enter by the narrow gate.

TWENTY-THIRD SUNDAY AFTER TRINITY.

O GOD, our Strength, our Refuge in the hour
    Of tears, of trembling, and of tribulation,
Our Light in darkness, and our Fortress-Tower,
    Our Help, our Shield, the Rock of our salvation:

O Holy Spirit, with Thy guiding power,
    Grant us to walk as worthy our vocation;
Yea, o'er our path Thy gifts as dew-drops shower,
    And save us in the day of visitation.

And let us labor, looking for the day
    When Christ our Righteousness, from Heaven
        descending,
    Shall come again in glorious majesty;

When, clothed with immortality, the clay
    Transfigured shall awake to life unending,
    "While death is swallowed up in victory!"

HERBERT KYNASTON, D.D.   Born 1809.

<small>Rector of St. Nicholas Cole Abbey, London, and Prebendary of St. Paul's: from his vigorous *Occasional Hymns, Original and Translated*, 1862.</small>

SILENCE IN HEAVEN.

COME, Holy Ghost; the Lamb has broke
    The hidden Scripture's seals;
Yet from the Throne no thunders woke,
    No golden trumpet peals:

HOLY SPIRIT! LONG EXPECTED.

Mysterious rest of Light represt, —
  As when the day was won,
The sun stood still on Gibeon's hill,
  The moon on Ajalon!

'Tis silence still in all the heaven,
  Above, below, around;
The angels with the trumpets seven,
  Who stand prepared to sound,
The saint before the golden shrine,
  The River by the Tree,
And where the pictured harps recline
  Upon the glassy Sea.

Hold fast the Rock, thou little flock,
  So fainting, and so few;
Lift, lift your hands, — the angel stands
  With incense lit for you:
Those prayers shall be a cloudy sea,
  From myriad censers hurled;
Earth's utmost space your meeting-place,
  Your upper-room the world.

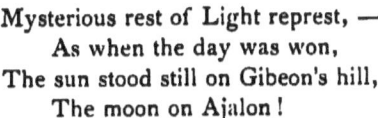

JOHN SAMUEL BEWLEY MONSELL, LL.D.
Born 1811.

Vicar of Egham, Surrey, and Rural Dean: author of *Parish Musings*, *Spiritual Songs*, and several other books. The hymns here given are from his *Hymns of Love and Praise for the Church's Year*, 1863.

CANTICLES ii. 14.

HOLY Spirit! long expected,
  Come, Thou slow-returning Dove,
And the olive-branch rejected
  O bring with Thee from above!

Holy Spirit!
Let the savor
Of Thy favor
Comfort all our hearts with love!

Comforter of those in sorrow,
  Guide to those who go astray!
Teacher, all Whose lessons borrow
  Light from what the Lord did say;
    Holy Spirit!
    Let Thy guiding,
    Grace providing,
Lead us upward into Day!

O Thou Advocate![1] Whose pleading
  Wins back those whose souls have erred,
While, for sinners interceding,
  Christ their Advocate[2] is heard;
    Holy Spirit!
    Let Thy praises
    Help to raise us
Nearer to the Eternal Word!

Praise to God, the glorious Giver!
  Praise to Christ, the Gift bestowed!
Praise to Thee, the Spirit! ever
  Make our hearts Thy blest abode.
    Holy Spirit!
    Dwell within us,
    Gently win us
Back, in Thy good time, to God!

---

[1] John xiv. 16.   [2] 1 John ii. 1.

THE HEART'S GARDEN.

ISAIAH xlv. 8.

GIFT of the Father's living Love,
    Hope of the Saviour's dying prayer!
Drop gently on me from above
    With the soft dewdrops of Thy care;
Refresh me with Thy bounteous Grace,
And make my heart Thy dwelling-place!

The hateful weeds of sin destroy,
    The bloom of Paradise restore;
With beauty bless it, and with joy
    Fill its waste places evermore;
Refresh it with Thy bounteous Grace,
And make it Thine own dwelling-place!

It is the garden of the Lord,
    But all unfit for Him to see,
Until its tangled paths, restored
    To their primeval grace by Thee,
Become the ways where He will walk,
And by me sit, and with me talk.

O blessed Spirit! on me rest,
    And in me evermore abide;
What I should be Thou knowest best,
    What I most need Thou canst provide;
Refresh my drooping soul with Grace,
And make it God's own dwelling-place.

THOMAS DAVIS.

Incumbent of Roundhay, Yorkshire. From his Hymns Old and New, 1864.

COME, Holy Spirit, come,
   Mercies revealing;
Make every heart Thy home;
   Quicken its feeling.
Then shall our songs ascend,
Breathing glad love, and blend
With notes that never end,
   Through Heaven pealing.

Come like the morning light
   Tranquilly beaming,
Chasing the shades of night,
   Waking the dreaming.
So the sweet peace from Thee
Shall for the spirit free
Like a calm river be
   Ceaselessly streaming.

Come, Holy Spirit, come,
   Thou that delightest
Gladness to give for gloom,
   And all invitest.
Let every mourner go
Where healing waters flow,
And love and pleasure know
   Purest and brightest.

ETERNAL SPIRIT, THEE WE PRAISE.

MISS B. E. BISHOP.

In *Lyra Eucharistica*, 1863. Verses 5 and 6 of a hymn of eight, to the Trinity.

EUCHARISTIC THANKSGIVING.

WE give Thee thanks, Good Spirit,
    For Thy life-giving power,
Shining with mystic splendor's light
    In eucharistic hour.
O teach us how to worship God
    As angels do on high,
And join our loved communion with
    Their altars in the sky.

We thank Thee, Holy Spirit;
    Rise Thou within our hearts;
Illuminate the mystery
    This Sacrament imparts.
O sanctify the offerings
    We bring our God to-day;
Reveal Thy glorious presence,
    And teach us how to pray.

ANONYMOUS.

J. S. *Juvenile Hymn-Book*, 1862. I find it in *The Primitive Methodist Sabbath School Hymn-Book*, 1864.

ETERNAL Spirit, Thee we praise!
    Order from chaos Thou didst raise.
Upon my darkness brightly shine,
Vouchsafe the Light of Life divine.

'Tis Thine the Father to reveal,
'Tis Thine the child of God to seal,
'Tis Thine the Son to glorify,
'Tis Thine the soul to sanctify.

Thou canst my stubborn will subdue,
Thou canst my evil heart renew,
Thou canst my every foe o'ercome:
Descend and make my heart Thy home.

The seers of old Thou didst inspire,
The Apostles crown with holy fire;
O Fount of Life! O Source of Good!
Come, fit my soul to dwell with God.

FOR THE YOUNG.

From the same.

O LORD, Thy Holy Spirit send,
    To be our Counsellor and Friend:
This promised blessing we would claim
In our exalted Saviour's name.

Spirit Divine! Thy Grace impart
To guide and sanctify each heart:
To us the things of Christ display,
And lead us in the narrow way.

Enable us to learn Thy Truth,
And by Thy Grace direct our youth.
O may Thy power Thy Word attend,
And on our souls like dew descend.

'Tis not by our own might or skill
That we can know or do Thy Will:
But Thou the appointed means wilt bless
With Thine own power and great success.

O may Thy blessing like a shower
From Heaven upon our bosoms pour,
And may Thy copious floods of Grace
Descend on all our youthful race.

THOU BLESSED SPIRIT.

From R. H. BAYNES' *Canterbury Hymnal*, 1863. Altered by him from another piece, to me unknown.

THOU blessed Spirit, by Whose aid
    Life's path is safely. trod,
Its varied scenes and duties made
    True progress home to God:

Come to our hearts, Lord, and abide
    A welcome Guest therein:
Help to withstand assaults of pride,
    To fight and conquer sin.

The Grace and Peace of Christ reveal,
    His everlasting Love;
Disperse the doubts that would conceal
    Our hope of Rest above.

Come with the joy Thy Love imparts,
    Sweet sense of sin forgiven:
With patience fill our restless hearts,
    And guide us home to Heaven.

O SPIRIT, LORD AND GOD.

From E. Monro's *Supplementary Hymns*, Leeds, 1864. The refrain is to be used after each verse.

O SPIRIT, Lord and God,
   Come dwell and rest with me,
And kindle here the fire
   Of living love to Thee.
For I Thy child have been
   Through all my youthful days,
Since at the fount of Love
   I first received Thy Grace.
   For I am weak, alone,
      And need Thy present power
   Through life's uncertain daily strife,
      And through my dying hour.

O Fount of Life and Peace,
   Flow through my thirsting soul;
Sustain a holy life
   Until I reach the goal.
When I grow faint, refresh:
   When I have erred, renew:
When I am dull, shed forth
   The showers of Thy dew.

O Beam of living Light,
   Sun of my shadowed way,
Pour forth upon my soul
   The brightness of Thy ray.
And when the Tempter's power
   Shall too successful be,
O pierce those mists of sin,
   And bid those shadows flee.

O Breath which Jesus breathed
  Upon His Church of yore,
Fill me with heavenly Life,
  As Thou hast done before.
May every day I live
  Be sacrificed by me,
That when those days are past,
  I still may be with Thee.

O Dove Who singeth peace,
  Lull every passion here;
Raise me when I am faint,
  Encourage when I fear.
The music of Thy voice
  Shall give my spirit rest,
If Thou wilt deign to make
  This heart of mine Thy nest.

O Thou Who once didst move
  Upon the watery waste,
And gave Creation's work
  Of life and joy to taste;
Each rite divine move o'er,
  Move through my every prayer;
Grant in Communion's hour
  I still may find Thee there.
    For I am weak, alone,
      And need Thy present power
    Through life's uncertain daily strife,
      And through my dying hour.

DAVID THOMAS, D.D.

Pastor of "Stockwell Congregational Church," and author of various books. From his very interesting Collection, *The Augustine Hymn-Book*, 1866.

JOHN i. 32.

O SPIRIT, descend as the beams of the morn,
  In the brightness of God our natures adorn.
Come down as Thou didst on chaos of old;
Bring forth those creations Thy prophets foretold.

O Spirit, descend as the rain and the dew,
That the beauties of Eden may spring up anew.
Come down as the wind on the dry bones of old,
Breathe Life into souls that are withered and cold.

O Spirit, descend as on Pentecost hour,
When thousands that met were changed by Thy
    power:
Come down as a fire from Thy altar above,
And kindle within us the flames of Thy Love.

W. R. PERCIVAL.

A clergyman in East London. He contributed three hymns to *The Augustine Hymn-Book*, 1866.

THE SPIRIT OF LIBERTY.
2 COR. iii. 17.

UNSEEN Spirit, Lord of Life,
    Teach us Thee in all to see:
Strengthen for the glorious strife
All who seek Thy liberty.

Thou hast formed the earth and skies:
  All things fair and bright are Thine.
Make us in Thine image rise,
  Let us in Thy glory shine.

From Thee come the gifts of men;
  All the might of mind Thou hast:
New dost Thou make all again,
  Filling future, present, past.
Time and space are forms of Thee,
  Dwelling in Eternity:
The meek heart Thou makest free
  In Thy Love's immensity.

Thou art Health and Peace and Power
  In Thy life of mighty Love:
From Thee is our spirit's dower:
  Thou dost raise to things above.
Beauteous is Thy Holiness;
  On us let Thy Beauty be:
From Thy fulness Thou dost bless,
  Giving us our all in Thee.

All Thy works and ways are good:
  Order is Thy living Law.
By Thee Christ poured out His Blood;
  Thou to Him our hearts dost draw.
In Thy Life atoned we are,
  Children of our Father's Love:
Thou dost call Thy sons from far
  To our native Home above.

All our glory is of Thee,
    Source of sanctity and Grace:
Like to Christ we all shall be
    When we see Him face to face.
Let us see Thy glory now
    In the face of Him who died,
That we all to Thee may bow,
    Pardoned, healed, and purified.

"THE LAW OF THE SPIRIT OF LIFE."

Romans viii. 2.

SPIRIT of Life and Light,
    Whose Mind is Law,
Make us in Thee delight;
    All to Thee draw.

We are Thine own offspring:
    O make us pure!
Into Thy Kingdom bring;
    Make our call sure.

The heavens are Thine abode,
    The earth and sea;
All being from Thee flowed;
    We dwell in Thee.

Let us be born again
    By Thy great might:
May we with Thee remain
    In glorious Light!

A. JACKSON.

A deacon of Dr. Thomas' parish, now dead. From *The Augustine Hymn-Book*, 1866.

"HEAR MY PRAYER, O LORD."

LET Thy wondrous way be known,
And let every nation own
Thou art God, and Thou alone.
    Spirit, hear our prayer.

Let each one Thy glorious Name
Magnify, and spread Thy fame,
And Thy Love let all proclaim.
    Spirit, hear our prayer.

Let the nations join to sing,
And let hallelujahs ring
To the righteous Judge and King.
    Spirit, hear our prayer.

Then shall blessings from Thy hand
Fall in showers upon our land,
And the world in rapture stand.
    Spirit, hear our prayer.

Shine upon us, God of Grace!
From Thy holy dwelling-place
Deign to bless our fallen race.
    Spirit, hear our prayer.

JOSEPH TRITTON.

The date of this is 1861. I take it from the Psalms and Hymns of the English Presbyterians, 1867.

OPENING A PLACE OF WORSHIP.

SPIRIT of Glory and of Grace,
    Thy favor we entreat;
Thou true Shekinah of the place
    Where true disciples meet.

O let the labor of our hands
    Be precious in Thy sight;
And long as this our temple stands
    Thy Presence be its Light.

Here float the gospel-banner wide
    O'er faithful hearts and brave;
And here, O Jesus crucified!
    Come forth in power to save.

Make bare Thine arm, Thou King of saints,
    To bring dead souls to life;
And when Thy children's courage faints
    Renew them for the strife.

No Bochim this — no place of woe,
    But Pisgah's holy steep,
Where dying ones their heaven shall know,
    Ere yet they fall asleep:

While we who live shall urge the race,
    If Jesus be but here:
Spirit of Glory and of Grace,
    Revealing Christ, appear!

SAMUEL JOHN STONE.

Curate of Windsor, and author of Lyra Fidelium: Twelve Hymns on the Twelve Articles of the Apostles' Creed, *1866; a little volume of merit and importance.*

"I BELIEVE IN THE HOLY GHOST."

"The Lord is that Spirit."

GOD the Spirit, we adore Thee,
    In the trinal GODHEAD One,
One in love and power and glory
    With the Father and the Son;
Prayer and praise to Thee we bring,
Our devotion's offering.

Once the desolate world-ocean,
    Quickened from its long death-sleep,
Woke to light and life's emotion
    At Thy brooding o'er its deep:
Spirit, ever may Thy breath
Quicken us from sleep and death!

Holy Fount of Inspiration,
    By Whose gift the great of old
Spake the Word of Revelation
    Marvellous and manifold,
Grant to us who see and hear
Reverence of eye and ear.

Priceless Gift of Christ for ever,
    Righteousness and Peace and Joy,
Which the evil world, that never
    Can receive, cannot destroy:

Shall the Church or faint or fear
While the Comforter is near?

Author of our new creation,
  Giver of the second birth,
May Thy ceaseless renovation
  Cleanse our souls from stains of earth,
And our bodies ever be
Holy temples meet for Thee.

When we wander, Lord, direct us,
  Keep us in the Master's way,
Let Thy strong, swift sword protect us.
  Warring in the evil day;
Paraclete for every need,
Come to strengthen and to lead!

Come, Thy glorious gifts providing,
  Foretaste of the future now;
Bring that sweet sense of abiding
  Thou canst give, and only Thou.
One in Thee, we shall be one
In the Father and the Son.
                Amen.

JAMES GRANTHAM FAITHFULL.

Vicar of Cheshunt, Herts. From his *Confirmation Hymns*, 1867.

DAY OF CONFIRMATION.

O THOU Whose special work it is
  The things of Christ to men to show,
And make the souls, by purchase His,
  Their blessings of salvation know:

Shed from Thy calm celestial light
    One sweetly-penetrating ray,
That every eye may see how bright
    Our solemn consecration day.

Were not the souls of these our youth
    Once holy temples fit for Thee?
O make them now to feel in truth
    The glory of their infancy.

The spirit meek, submissive, mild, —
    Such blessing may it still be theirs!
The simple trusting of the child,
    O is it lost in after years?

Not if Thy power subduing be shed!
    Then make such light on these to shine:
By Thee belief is perfected,
    Subjection of our reason Thine.

Spirit of Truth and Knowledge true,
    Spirit of life and light and power,
Thou only canst the soul renew:
    Be this Thine own renewing hour.

Spirit of Christ, Thy Grace bestow;
    Be Thou our Guide, our Strength, our Stay;
And make us by Thy presence know
    How blest our consecration day.

GERARD MOULTRIE.

Vicar of South Leigh, near Oxford, and one of the editors of *The People's Hymnal*, 1867.

VENI, JAM VENI CONSOLATOR.

COME Thou, O come;
　Sweetest, and kindliest,
　Giver of tranquil rest
Unto the weary soul;
　In all anxiety
　With power from heaven on high,
　　　　Console.

Come Thou, O come;
　Help in the hour of need,
　Strength of the broken reed,
Guide of each lonely one;
　Orphans' and widows' stay,
　Who tread in life's hard way
　　　　Alone.

Come Thou, O come;
　Glorious and shadow-free,
　Star of the stormy sea,
Light of the tempest-tost;
　Harbor our souls to save
　When hope upon the wave
　　　　Is lost.

Come Thou, O come;
　Joy in life's narrow path,
　Hope in the hour of death,

Come, blessed SPIRIT, come;
Lead Thou us tenderly,
Till we shall find with Thee
    Our home.

RICHARD FREDERICK LITTLEDALE, D.C.L.

From *The People's Hymnal*, 1867.

LITANY OF THE HOLY GHOST.

GOD the Father, God the Word,
    God the Holy Ghost adored,
Blessed Trinity, One Lord:
    Spare us, Holy Trinity.

Holy Spirit, wondrous Dove,
Dew descending from above,
Breath of Life, and God of Love;
    Hear us, Holy Spirit.

Lord of strength and knowledge clear,
Wisdom, godliness sincere,
Understanding, counsel, fear;
    Hear us, Holy Spirit.

Giver of Love, meekness, peace,
Patience, pureness, faith's increase,
Mercy, joy that cannot cease;
    Hear us, Holy Spirit.

Teacher of all innocence,
Goodness, virtue, temperance,
In temptation strong defence;
    Hear us, Holy Spirit.

Strength of age, and Guide of youth,
Lord of tenderness and ruth,
Leader into perfect Truth;
    Hear us, Holy Spirit.

Thou Who, overshadowing
Blessed Mary with Thy wing,
Madest her to bear the King;
    Hear us, Holy Spirit.

Thou Who brooding o'er the wave
Poured the stains of sin to lave,
Comest in the font to save;
    Hear us, Holy Spirit.

Thou, Whose might from Heaven shed
On the Wine and on the Bread,
Bringeth to us Christ our Head;
    Hear us, Holy Spirit.

Lightener of eyes that seek,
Thou Who pleadest for the weak
With those groans no tongue may speak;
    Hear us, Holy Spirit.

From sin's dark and woeful night,
From the world and vain delight,
From the devil and his might;
    Save us, Holy Spirit.

From all pride and heresy,
From all lack of purity,
From the tempter's enmity;
   Save us, Holy Spirit.

Thou, with Thine own cleansing dew,
Our polluted hearts renew,
Hearken ever as we sue,
   We pray Thee, Holy Spirit.

Thou with Thine own union bind
Soul and body, heart and mind,
In peace with God and all mankind,
   We pray Thee, Holy Spirit.

That we never quench Thy grace,
But at last may reach the place
Where shines Jesu's glorious Face,
   We pray Thee, Holy Spirit.

THOMAS BENSON POLLOCK.

From his *Metrical Litanies*, 1870. The refrain, "Hear us, Holy Spirit," is meant to be added to each stanza.

PART I.

SPIRIT blest, Who art adored
   With the Father and the Word,
One eternal God and Lord,
   Hear us, Holy Spirit!

Spirit of the Only Wise,
Thou in Whom all knowledge lies,
Reading all with searching eyes:

Spirit guiding to the right,
Spirit making darkness light,
Spirit of resistless might:

Spirit Who dost fear impart,
Giving love to every heart,
Making mortals what Thou art:

Thou by Whom in days of old
Men did write as they were told,
And the truths of Heaven unfold:

Thou by Whom the Virgin bore
Him Whom Heaven and earth adore,
Sent our nature to restore:

Spirit falling like a dove
From the opened skies above,
With the Father's power and love:

Spirit, by Whose gifts of Grace
Jesus blessed our fallen race,
Raising them from lowly place:

Comforter, when Jesus rose,
Promised to be sent to those
He was leaving with their foes:

Thou Whom Jesus from His throne
Gave to cheer and help His own,
That they might not be alone:

Thou Whose power inspiring came,
Falling down like tongues of flame,
Where they met in Jesus' name,
　Hear us, Holy Spirit!

Part II.

Comforter, to Whom we owe
All that we rejoice to know
Of our Saviour's work below:

Thou Whose sound Apostles heard,
Thou Whose power their spirit stirred,
Giving them the living Word:

Thou Whose Grace the Church does fill,
Making Jesus present still,
Showing her God's perfect will:

Coming with Thy power to save,
Moving on baptismal wave,
Raising sinners from their grave:

Thou by Whom our souls are fed
With the true and living Bread,
Even Him Who for us bled:

Spirit, showing us the way,
Warning when we go astray,
Pleading in us when we pray:

· Spirit, Whom our failings grieve,
Whom the world will not receive,
Who dost help us to believe:

Spirit, guarding us from ill,
Bending right our stubborn will;
Though we grieve Thee, patient still:

Holy Ghost, when sinners fall,
And when snares their souls enthrall,
Leading back with gentle call:

Spirit, bidding terror cease,
When from sin we pray release,
Bidding us to go in peace:

Calming Spirit, always nigh,
Helping our infirmity
When in lonely doubt we lie:

Spirit, Strength of all the weak,
Giving courage to the meek,
Teaching faltering tongues to speak:

Spirit aiding all who yearn
More of Truth divine to learn,
And with deeper love to burn:

Spirit, Fount of faith and joy,
Giving peace without alloy,
Hope that nothing can destroy:

Source of love and light divine,
With that hallowing Grace of Thine,
More and more upon us shine.

Holy, loving as Thou art,
Come and live within our heart,
Never from us to depart.

May we soon, from sin set free,
Where Thy work may perfect be,
Jesu's face with rapture see.
Hear us, Holy Spirit!

TWELVE FRUITS OF THE SPIRIT.

GALATIANS V. 22, 23.

From *Resting-Places*: a Manual of *Christian Doctrine, Duty, and Devotion,* 1870: edited by this author's brother, the Rev. JAMES S. POLLOCK.

SPIRIT of *Love*, be in our heart,
And make us loving as Thou art;
And grant us holy *Joy* to find
In loving God and all mankind.
So in our hearts Thy *Peace* be known,
And in our lives its power be shown.
In days of trial make us strong
To bear our cross and *Suffer long:*
Give *Gentleness* in heart and mind,
A voice and manner always kind:
And may our inward feeling lead
To *Goodness* shown in word and deed:
May we in *Faith* on God rely,
And judge our neighbor hopefully.

In *Meekness* may our hearts be still,
And yield to all our Father's will.
And may we, strong in *Patience*, bear
What God may send of grief or care.
May *Modesty* of thought ensure
That all our lives be *Chaste* and pure:
May *Temperance* with careful rein
And *Continence* our flesh restrain.

EDWARD WILTON EDDIS.

<small>A member of the Irvingite body, and compiler of their *Hymns for the Use of the Churches*, 1864: Second edition, enlarged, 1871. These noticeable volumes contain many lyrics of his own: of which this one bears date 1868.</small>

SPIRIT of Christ, Thou speakest
  On earth His living word:
Again Thy voice of warning,
  Thy song of praise, is heard.

Thou in Thy Love restorest
  The riches of Thy Grace,
And pourest Thine anointing
  On all who seek His face.

Help us with Him in meekness
  To tread the path of shame;
To keep His word of patience,
  And not deny His name.

Few upon earth, and strangers,
  We follow, day by day,
Where He has trod before us,
  The strait and narrow way.

But soon the word of witness
  Shall sound from land to land;
And in the hour of darkness
  The wise shall understand:

When through the fires of judgment
  And through the waves of strife,
The saints of God returning
  Shall pass from death to Life;

And as the stars of Heaven,
  As sand upon the shore,
His holy ones, unnumbered,
  Shall rise to fall no more.

JAMES GABB.

Rector of Bulmer. From his *Hymns and Songs of Pilgrim Life*, 1871.

WHIT-SUNDAY.

HOLY Ghost, this day descending
  On Thine infant Church to bless,
Tongues to the Apostles lending,
  God's great mercy to express:

To their inward sight unfolding
  All the mystery of Love,
Which, His majesty withholding,
  Brought the Saviour from above:

Every heart with ardor filling
  Jesus' Name to glorify:
Dews of heavenly Grace distilling,
  Holy influence from on high:

Consecrate us now with fitness
  For the work we would fulfil:
Be in us a living Witness
  Of the Father's perfect will.

With a word of truth in season,
  Thou our waiting souls inspire;
Purge our sense, inform our reason,
  Raise our minds with pure desire.

Fill us with a holy passion
  Souls of dying men to save:
Let our walk and conversation
  Christ for its example have.

On the world, which shadows darken,
  Shed the glory of Thy light;
May repentant souls that hearken
  To Thy voice, receive aright

All the promises, whose beauty
  Makes the trusting spirit glad;
May they seek the path of duty,
  Choose the good and flee the bad:

While the earth and sky and ocean,
   Gladdened with Thy saving rays,
Murmur songs of deep devotion,
   And all creatures hymn Thy praise.

O descend, in might and blessing,
   Holy Spirit, from above!
Till the world, Thy Grace confessing,
   Praise Thee, Lord of light and love.

ANONYMOUS.

"ERIPHAS," in the *Evangelical Magazine*, 1821. This was overlooked in its proper place, being found only in NETTLETON's *Village Hymns*, New York, 1824.

WHO but Thou, almighty Spirit,
   Can the heathen world reclaim?
Men may preach, but till Thou favor,
   Heathens will be still the same:
     Mighty Spirit!
Witness to the Saviour's Name.

Thou hast promised by the prophets
   Glorious light in latter days:
Come, and bless bewildered nations,
   Change our prayers and tears to praise;
     Promised Spirit!
Round the world diffuse Thy rays.

All our hopes, and prayers, and labors
  Must be vain without Thine aid:
But Thou wilt not disappoint us,
  All is true that Thou hast said:
    Faithful Spirit!
O'er the world Thine influence shed.

AMERICAN HYMNS.

ANONYMOUS.

From *Gospel Melodies: By the Author of Several Fugitive Pieces.* Petersburg, Va., 1821. This is a paraphrase of ANNE STEELE's hymn on p. 119.

ETERNAL Spirit, wilt Thou dwell
  Within my bosom's sinful cell?
And can a Saviour send to me
A holy Comforter like Thee?

When in my doubts and dangers blind
Despair has darkened all my mind,
Eternal Spirit! didst Thou deign
'Mid all my darkness to remain?

To guide me through the mental night
Till Grace restored the living light:
To save me by Thine equal power
In every darksome, doleful hour?

When some kind promise cheers my heart
And bids each lingering fear depart,
Sweet Spirit! it must be Thy voice
That makes that faltering heart rejoice.

Jesus, what bids me call Thee mine?
Sure 'tis the Comforter divine!
He animates my heart's desires,
My faith sustains, my love He fires.

O sacred Spirit, with me stay!
Sustain me till that glorious day
When faith no more shall time employ,
Lost in the certainty of joy!

LYDIA HUNTLEY SIGOURNEY, 1792–1865.

This familiar hymn appeared in Dr. NETTLETON's *Village Hymns*, New York, 1824; and afterwards, somewhat altered, in JOSHUA LEAVITT's *Christian Lyre*, 1830, where it is untruly stated to have been "Written for the Lyre." In both it is marked "H." I credit it to Mrs. SIGOURNEY on the authority of Mr. DANIEL SEDGWICK.

BLEST Comforter Divine!
   Whose rays of heavenly Love
Amid our gloom and darkness shine,
   And point our souls above:

Thou, Who with "still small voice"
   Dost stop the sinner's way,
And bid the mourning saint rejoice,
   Though earthly joys decay;

Thou, Whose inspiring Breath
   Can make the cloud of care,
And even the gloomy vale of death
   A smile of glory wear;

SPIRIT OF HOLINESS, DESCEND.

Thou, Who dost fill the heart
  With love to all our race,
Blest Comforter! to us impart
  The blessings of Thy Grace.

SAMUEL F. SMITH, D.D.

Editor, with BARON STOW, of the *Baptist Psalmist*, 1843: it contains 26 hymns by him.

SPIRIT of Holiness, descend!
  Thy people wait for Thee:
Thine ear in kind compassion lend;
  Let us Thy mercy see.

Behold, Thy weary Churches wait
  With wishful, longing eyes:
Let us no more lie desolate:
  O bid Thy light arise.

Thy light that on our souls hath shone
  Leads us in hope to Thee:
Let us not feel its rays alone,
  Alone Thy people be.

O bring our dearest friends to God,
  Remember those we love;
Fit them on earth for Thine abode,
  Fit them for joys above.

Spirit of Holiness, 'tis Thine
  To hear our feeble prayer;
Come, for we wait Thy power divine;
  Let us Thy mercy share.

THOMAS HASTINGS. Born 1784.

From his Devotional Hymns, 1850.

O SPIRIT of Holiness, breathe
  On every lone dwelling afar,
Surrounded by shadows of death
  And regions of guilt and despair.
O breathe on each desolate place
  Where darkness and sorrow are found,
Till millions our Saviour embrace,
  And songs of deliverance abound.

O breathe on those heralds of Thine
  Who speak in the name of the Lord;
And cause Thy salvation to shine
  Wherever they publish Thy Word.
Thou, Thou art our Hope and our Trust,
  We look to Thy influence alone
To crumble the idols in dust
  And set up Thy heavenly throne.

O let the rich dews of Thy Love
  Abroad on the nations distil,
Till thousands the influence prove,
  Till all shall submit to Thy Will.
Now hasten that hallowèd hour
  When error and darkness shall flee;
And the honor and glory and power
  Shall ever be given to Thee.

WILLIAM CROSWELL, D.D., 1804-1851.

Rector of Christ Church and the Advent, Boston. His *Poems* appeared 1861.

CREATOR Spirit! come and bless us;
Let Thy love and fear possess us;
With Thy graces meek and lowly
Purify our spirits wholly.
Paraclete, the name Thou bearest,
Gift of God the choicest, dearest,
Love, and Fire, and Fountain Living,
Spiritual unction giving,
Shower Thy benedictions seven
From Thy majesty in heaven.

Be the Saviour's Word unbroken,
Let Thy many tongues be spoken;
In our sense Thy Light be glowing,
Through our souls Thy Love be flowing;
Cause the carnal heart to perish,
But the strength of virtue cherish,
Till, each enemy repelling,
And Thy peace around us dwelling,
We, beneath Thy guidance glorious,
Stand o'er every ill victorious.

RAY PALMER, D.D. Born 1808.

Secretary of the Congregational Union at New York. His Hymns and Sacred Pieces appeared 1865.

O HOLY Comforter,
    I hear
Thy blessed name with throbbing heart,
Pressed oft with sorrow, sin, and fear,
And pierced with many a venomed dart:
    Come, Messenger divine,
    Come, cheer this heart of mine.

O Holy Comforter,
    I know
Thou art not to dull sense revealed;
Thou com'st unseen as the sweet flow
Of the soft wind that woos the field:
    Breathe, Messenger divine,
    Breathe on this soul of mine.

O Holy Comforter,
    Thy Light
Is light eternal and serene;
Shine Thou, and on my ravished sight
Visions shall break of things unseen:
    Come, Messenger divine,
    Make these bright glimpses mine.

O Holy Comforter,
    Thy Love
O'erfloweth as the flooding sea;
Give me its tenderness to prove,
Visions shall break of things unseen:
    Come, Messenger divine,
    Make these bright glimpses mine.

O Holy Comforter,
    Thy Grace
Is life and help and hope and power:
By this I can each cross embrace,
Can triumph in the darkest hour:
    Come, Messenger divine,
    The strength of Grace be mine.

O Holy Comforter,
    Thy peace,
The peace of God, impart and keep
Unruffled till life's tumults cease,
And all its angry tempests sleep:
    Come, Messenger divine,
    Thy perfect peace be mine.

ANONYMOUS.

From the New York *Churchman's Monthly Magazine*, July, 1856. It is there said to be "Selected."

O THOU, Whose influence wakes
    The soul to praise and prayer,
Whose voice of consolation breaks
    Through sin and death's despair!

Come, with Thy gifts of heavenly Love,
Holy, uncreated Dove!
Speak to the trembling tempest-tost —
Light of ancient Pentecost.

As once Thou didst of old
   Descend in cloven flame
With sacred influence manifold,
   So spread the Saviour's name.
Come to our holy Mother's heart,
The gift of speech to her impart,
To win the weary, wandering, lost —
Spirit-tongue of Pentecost.

With sin and fear opprest,
   Could we life's journey make
Without Thy presence, heavenly Guest,
   Our confidence to wake?
Come when our days are young and fair,
Teach us the way to Heaven by prayer,
Ere beauteous youth in age be lost —
Blessed Dove of Pentecost.

HOLY GHOST, THOU SOURCE OF LIGHT.

From the Andover Sabbath Hymn-Book, 1858.

HOLY Ghost, Thou Source of Light!
   We invoke Thy kindling ray:
Dawn upon our spirits' night,
   Turn our darkness into day.

To the anxious soul impart
  Hope, all other hopes above;
Stir the dull and hardened heart
  With a longing and a love.

Give the struggling peace for strife,
  Give the doubting light for gloom;
Speed the living into life,
  Warn the dying of their doom.

Work in all; in all renew
  Day by day the life divine;
All our wills to Thee subdue,
  All our hearts to Thee incline.

SPIRIT, POURED ON PENTECOST.

From *Hymns for Church and Home*, Philadelphia, 1860: preliminary edition, 1859.

SPIRIT, poured on Pentecost,
  Paraclete and Holy Ghost,
Resting on the Eternal Son,
Holy, uncreated One!
Breath of Life, Thine aid impart;
Waken every slumbering heart,
Every grovelling soul refine
With Thy Power and Grace divine.

Sanctifier, seal our hearts
With the Truth Thy Word imparts:
Sacred truths and themes instil,
And Thy pleasure all fulfil.

There let Christ replace His throne,
And possess us for His own,
Till our bodies all shall be
Temples to Thy Deity.

Everlasting Spirit, come,
Teach us life's imperfect sum.
All on earth is dark and drear,
Changeful as the changing year:
Raise our thoughts from things of earth,
Subjects of a better birth;
And our song shall be of Thee
Through a blest eternity.

FOR INWARD PEACE.

From Hymns of the Spirit, Boston, 1864.

O FOR a heart of calm repose
   Amid the world's loud roar,
A life that like a river flows
   Along a peaceful shore!

Come, Holy Spirit, still my heart
   With gentleness divine:
Indwelling peace Thou canst impart,
   O make that blessing mine!

Above these scenes of storm and strife
   There spreads a region fair:
Give me to live that higher life,
   And breathe that heavenly air!

Come, Holy Spirit, breathe that peace!
   That victory make me win:
Then shall my soul her conflict cease,
   And find a heaven within.

BISHOP WILLIAM PINKNEY, D.D.

Now Assistant Bishop of Maryland. From his *Songs for the Seasons, from Advent to Trinity*: New York, 1865.

MONDAY IN WHITSUN WEEK.

O SPIRIT of the Lord of Hosts!
   We feel Thy presence near;
Not more in gifts miraculous,
   Than in the first warm tear

That gathers on the eye of faith,
   When by the font we stand;
Or when, in Confirmation robes,
   We grasp the sword in hand.

Thy first great gifts were wonderful,
   Breathed on a faithful few;
But now Thy sevenfold gifts descend
   Like sparkling drops of dew,

Within the vineyard, where the vines
   Creep o'er the trellis fair,
And with rich clusters recompense
   The dresser's watchful care.

There are diversities of gifts
　　Now, as in days of yore;
But still the Lord works all in all,
　　As once He wrought before.

One Gift there is surpassing all
　　Earth's glories, O how far;
It floats along life's firmament
　　Like evening's ruling star.

It sheds its light on all alike,
　　Who look by faith, to see
The wonders streaming silently
　　Through that deep azure sea.

It is a Gift which all may share,
　　From prince to peasant rude;
It glows not more in palace halls
　　Than in dark solitude.

It is the Gift of Love divine,
　　Which all may covet here,
From those who bask in sunny smiles
　　To those who drop a tear.

Wisdom may die, and knowledge cease,
　　And miracles may fail;
The gift of tongues, and healing too,
　　And prophecy's sad wail;

But Love remains the heart to cheer,
　　Its marvels to renew;
And o'er the darksome vale it sheds
　　A bright celestial hue.

O Spirit of the living God!
  Breathe on us from above
This rarest, noblest Gift of Thine,
  This cherub flame of Love.

We seek not wisdom, knowledge, power;
  We ask not fame or wealth;
We seek not pleasure's brimming cup;
  We ask not flush of health;

For these, though treasures rich indeed,
  When loaned to us awhile,
Can never give the bliss we crave,
  The soul's bright inner smile.

We ask for love, the bird of peace
  That sings the livelong hour,
And fills with music's sweetest note
  Earth's ruined, faded bower.

We ask, when faith and hope shall fail,
  To hear that music still,
And, with this bird within the soul,
  To rest on Zion's hill.

O give us then the grace to wait
  Thine own appointed time,
Till these dull hearts of ours shall be
  Of love the golden shrine.

JOHN HENRY HOPKINS.

Of Burlington, Vermont. From his Carols, Hymns, and Songs, 1863. This fine poem "was written in 1860 or earlier."

BLOW on, Thou mighty Wind!
   The cloven tongues descending,
Fanned by Thy dewy Breath, shall blaze and burn,
   A sacred Flame unending.
   Soon shall that Fire behold
Vile earth transformed to fine wrought gold;
   And gloom of shadowy night
That Flame shall kindle into light:
Therefore, Thou mighty Wind, blow on.

Blow on, Thou mighty Wind,
   And waft to realms unbounded
The notes of Faith and Hope and tender Love
   The Gospel trump hath sounded.
   Those sweetly piercing tones,
That charm all wars and tears and groans,
   Through earth and sea and sky
Upon Thy rushing wings shall fly;
Therefore, Thou mighty Wind, blow on!

Blow on, Thou mighty Wind;
   For tempest-tost and lonely
The Church upon the rolling billows rides,
   And trusts in Thy Breath only.

She spreads her swelling sails
For Thee to fill with favoring gales,
  Till through the stormy sea
Thou bring her Home where she would be;
Therefore, Thou mighty Wind, blow on.

Blow on, Thou mighty Wind,
  On hearts contrite and broken,
And bring in quickening power the gracious
    words
  That Jesu's lips have spoken.
  Lo then, from death and sleep,
The listening souls to life shall leap;
  Then Love shall reign below,
And Joy the whole wide world o'erflow:
Therefore, Thou mighty Wind, blow on.

To God, the Father, Son,
  By all in earth and heaven,
And to the Holy Spirit, Three in One,
  Eternal praise be given:
  As once triumphant rang
When morning stars together sang,
  Is now, as aye before,
And shall be so for evermore,
World without end. Amen. Amen.

FOR REUNION.

A verse from his Processional for the Reunion of Christendom.

COME, O God the Holy Ghost!
  O strong Wind, with thunder,
Blow, till all our scattered host
  Part no more in sunder.
  Light, O Flame all glorious,
Light once more Thy tongues of fire:
Breathe on us, till Thou inspire
  Thine own Love victorious.

INDEX OF SUBJECTS.

(THIS is of necessity very meagre and partial, aiming to indicate, not the chief attributes and ordinary operations of the SPIRIT, which are celebrated everywhere throughout this volume, but merely some of His more especial relations, occasionally noticed.)

CREATION: 9, 205, 340, 354, 416, 421, 445, 497, 528, 543, 595.
ANALOGIES OF NATURE: 135, 142, 308, 479, 590.
THE BIBLE: 115, 334, 359, 361, 392, 595.
THE CHURCH: 112, 278, 293, 362, 480, 490, 540, 626.
EXTENSION OF CHRIST'S KINGDOM: 16, 375, 444, 472, 519, 520, 537, 609, 613, 614, 624.
THE MINISTRY: 448, 462, 477.
PUBLIC WORSHIP: 373, 404, 441, 464, 470, 485, 499, 564.
BAPTISM: 372, 399.
CONFIRMATION: 447, 531, 571, 596.
HOLY COMMUNION: 335, 336, 529, 535.
PENTECOST: 13, 45–102, 299.
WHIT-SUNDAY: 264, 311, 383, 402, 446, 458, 491, 512, 565, 607.
ASCENSION: 568.
FOR THE STATE: 251, 293, 353.
    ,,   YOUNG: 476, 586.
    ,,   SICK: 467.
FRIENDSHIP: 350.
FAITH, HOPE, AND LOVE: 469.
LOVE: 570.
PEACE: 620.
THE THIRD HOUR: 8.
THE NINTH COMMANDMENT: 144.
THE BEATIFIC VISION: 396.
MEEKNESS: 548.
SIMPLICITY: 452.
CONSISTENCY: 143, 291, 358.
PENITENCE: 294, 297, 338.
PREPARATION FOR DEATH: 237–239, 305, 541.
INVITATION: 130, 131.
VANITY OF EARTH: 194, 195, 523.
PILGRIMAGE: 150, 151.
PROGRESS: 158, 554.
LITANIES: 305, 599, 601.
THE SPIRIT AND THE LETTER: 132, 487.
    ,,   UNLIMITED: 136, 417, 418, 497, 556, 557, 590.
    ,,   OMNIPRESENT: 126.
    ,,   OF THE FATHERS: 10, 275.
    ,,   OF LAW: 592.
    ,,   GRIEVED: 121, 157, 302, 303, 312, 351–353, 558.
THE GLADDENER: 116, 155, 156, 242, 527.

INDEX OF AUTHORS.

LATIN.

	PAGE
ADAM of St. Victor	54, 211–222
Ambrose?	45, 47, 198, 199
Charlemagne?	167–180
Hilary?	50, 52
Hildebert	222
Hildegarde	207, 208
Notker	58? 201, 203
Robert II. of France	181–190
Unknown	49, 53, 57, 191–197, 200, 201, 205, 210, 563, 598

GREEK.

St. Cosmas	61
St. John Damascene	60
St. Joseph of the Studium	62
Unknown	59

ITALIAN.

BIANCO da Siena	225

GERMAN.

BOGATZKY, Charles Henry	112
Bruhn, David	272
Crasselius, Bartholomew	109
Frank, John	258
Gerhardt, Paul	111, 243–255
Gregor, Christian	267
Lavater, John Caspar	274
Luther, Martin	230–241
Neander, Joachim	260, 263
Schirmer, Michael	256
Schmolk, Benjamin	264
Spitta, Charles J. P.	275, 278
Tersteegen, Gerhard	269, 270

DANISH.

	PAGE
CHRISTENSEN	280
Unknown	281–284

FRENCH.

GUION, Jeanne	285, 286
Malan, César	286, 287

ENGLISH.

tr. following an author's name indicates that he appears in this volume as a translator only: following the number of a given page, that the hymn thereon is translated from another language.

ADDISON, Lancelot	312
Alexander, Cecil Frances	91, 572
Alexander, John Henry	138–140
Alexander, William Lindsay	574
Alford, Henry	484
Allen, Oswald	573
Allen, William?	472
Arnold, Jane E., *tr.*	286, 287
Auber, Harriet	141
Austin, John	183 *tr.*, 307–310
BARCLAY, John	127, 129
Bathurst, William Hiley	9–12, 453–456
Beaumont, Joseph	71, 304, 305
Beddome, Benjamin	122, 134, 413–415
Benedict, Erastus C., *tr.*	203
Bishop, B. E.	585
Blenkinsopp, Edwin L., *tr.*	197
Blew, Wm. J.	5, 50 *tr.*, 192 *tr.*, 213 *tr.*

INDEX OF AUTHORS. 629

	PAGE
Bonar, Horatius	195 *tr.*, 537-543
Bridges, Matthew	507
Brontë, Anne	498
Browne, J. E.	495
Browne, Simon	78, 318, 421
Bunting, William Maclardie	487
Burbidge, Thomas	576
Burnham, Richard	419
Burton, John	6
Butterworth, Joseph H.	531
Cambridge, Ada	144
Campbell, Robert	65. 179 *tr.*, 187 *tr.*
Caswall, E.	45 *tr.*, 184 *tr.*, 220 *tr*, 508
Cennick, John	370-372
Chambers, John David, *tr.*	57, 58
Chandler, John, *tr.*	199, 200
Charles, Elizabeth, *tr.*	212
Cobbin, Ingram	135
Conder, Josiah	23, 465
Coney, Thomas	321
Cosin, John, *tr.*	171
Cotterill, Thomas	90, 423, 430
Coverdale, Myles	231 *tr.*, 237 *tr.*, 291
Cowper, Maria Frances	409, 411
Cowper, William, *tr.*	285, 286
Cox, Frances E., *tr.*	274
Cox, George V.	63
Craig, James	324
Crewdson, Jane	142, 199 *tr.*
Crippen. T. G., *tr.*	208
Croly, George	522
Croswell, William	615
Davies. Samuel	390
Davis, Thomas	584.
Dayman, Edward A., *tr.*	47
Dix, William C, *tr.*	59-61
Doddridge. Philip	378-380
Drummond, William, *tr.*	169
Dryden, John, *tr.*	175
Duffield, Samuel W., *tr.*	218
Dunderdale, R.	452
Dunn, Samuel	561, 562
Edhis, Edward Wilton	606
Edmeston, James	470, 471
Elliott, Charlotte	466-468
Evans, Jonathan	404
Evans, Robert Wilson	543-549
Faber, Frederic W.	186 *tr.*, 503, 505
Faithfull, James Grantham	596

	PAGE
Fallow, Eliza Jones	461
Fawcett, John	121
Fellows, John	399, 401
Flesher, John	519
Ford, Charles Laurence	66
Forsyth, Christina	532, 534
Gabb, James	607
Gadsby, William	432
Gibbons, Thomas	130
Gill, Thomas H.	100, 101, 147-157, 550-559
Gough, Benjamin	13-16
Grimani, Julia C	494
Gurney, Archer Thompson	93
Hall, C. Newman	535
Hammond, William	80, 376
Harding, John	493
Harrison, Thomas	323
Hart, Joseph	82, 382-386
Harvie, Christopher	69
Haslam, S. B.	132, 133, 446
Hastings, Thomas	614
Haweis, Thomas	20, 407-409
Hawker, Robert	437
Heber, Reginald	446
Herbert, Daniel	426
Herbert, George	299-303
Herrick, Robert	305
Hollis, Benjamin S.	499-502?
Hopkins, John Henry	624, 626
Hull, William W.	461
Humphreys, Eliza	94. 529
Irons, Joseph	433-435
Jacobi, John Christian, *tr.*	233, 242
Jackson, A.	593
Jones, Joseph	481, 483
Judkin, Thomas J.	453, 456
Keble, John	96, 98, 447-450
Kelly, Thomas	19
Kempenfelt, Richard	395. 396
Kempthorne. John	428
Kennedy, Benjamin Hall? *tr.*	270
Kinwelmersh, Francis	294
Kynaston, Herbert	205 *tr.*, 580
Leifchild, John	485
Littledale, Richard F.	95, 207 *tr.*, 210 *tr.*, 225 *tr.*, 599

INDEX OF AUTHORS.

	PAGE
Lowe, Henry	445
Lynch, Thomas Toke	524–529
Mackay, Margaret	521
Mant, Richard	469
Mason, John	116
Massie, Richard, *tr.*	111, 239, 240, 253, 275, 278
Medley, Samuel	406
Meeres, Nathaniel	484
Monsell, John S. B.	581, 583
Montgomery, James	442–444
Montgomery, Robert	497, 498
More, Henry	21, 73, 307
Morgan, Arthur Middlemore	160
Moultrie, Gerard, *tr.*	598
Neale, James	394
Neale, John Mason	8, 62 *tr.*, 188 *tr.*, 201 *tr.*, 491
Neville, S. C. E.	463, 464
Newman, John Henry, *tr.*	198
Noel, Baptist W.?	457
Noel, Charlotte Margaret	107, 560
Onderdonk, Henry Ustic	131
O'Neile, Henry	477
Palmer, Ray	189 *tr.*, 616
Pattison, Samuel	416, 417
Pearson, Charles B., *tr.*	53, 54
Percival, W. R.	590, 592
Pinkney, William	621
Pollock, Thomas Benson	601, 605
Pott, Francis, *tr.*	563
Rawlet, John	311
Rawson, George	516, 518
Rawson, Thomas	380
Reed, Andrew	439, 440
Row, Thomas	436
Russell, Arthur Tozer	234 *tr.*, 238 *tr.*, 510–516
Ryland, John	118, 405
Schæffer, Charles W., *tr.*	263
Scott, Elizabeth	392
Seagrove, Robert	373, 375
Sigourney, Lydia Huntley	612
Smith, Samuel F.	613
Sparks, William Prescott	479
Spenser, Edmund	298
Steele, Anne	119
Stewart, John	427
Stocker, John	423
Stone, Samuel John	595
Tait, Gilbert, *tr.*	280
Tate, Nahum, *tr.*	174
Tayler, Charles B.	535
Taylor, Jeremy	72
Teate, Faithfull	114
Thomas, David	590
Thrupp, Diana A.	476
Thrupp, Joseph F.? *tr.*	194
Tomkins, Henry George	523
Tonna, Charlotte E.	462
Toplady, Augustus M.	17, 245 *tr.*, 388, 390
Tritton, Joseph	594
Vaughan, Henry	75
Vennard, Richard	295
Washburn, Edward A., *tr.*	52, 216, 222
Watts, Isaac	315–317
Wesley, Charles	23–39, 83–90, 123–127, 319–369
Wesley, John	21, 303
Wesley, Samuel, Jr.	327
Williams, Isaac	49 *tr.*, 177 *tr.*, 191 *tr.*, 193 *tr.*, 201 *tr.*, 488–490
Williams, John, *tr.*	178
Williams, William	387
Willison, John	393
Winkworth, Catharine, *tr.*	109, 112, 235, 247–257, 261, 264, 269
Wither, George	67, 168 *tr.*
Woodd, Basil	425
Wordsworth, Christopher	136, 565–571
Wright, John	325
Unknown, *tr.*	172, 241, 267, 272, 281–284
Unknown	143, 292, 297, 319, 402, 419, 431, 450, 451, 457, 458, 472–475, 478, 492, 520, 564, 578–580, 585–589, 609, 611, 617–620

INDEX OF FIRST LINES.

LATIN HYMNS.

	PAGE
ADESTE, summa Caritas	563
Adsis, superne Spiritus	193-197
Almum Flamen, Vita mundi	205
Amor Patris et Filii	210
Anni peractis mensibus	57
Audimur; alma Spiritus	49
Beata nobis gaudia	50, 52
Eya musa dic quæso	53
Jam Christus astra ascenderat	45, 47, 80
Laudes Deo devotas	58
Lux jucunda, lux insignis	54
Nunc sancte nobis Spiritus	198, 199
O Fons amoris Spiritus	200, 201
O ignis Spiritus Paracliti	207, 208
Sancti Spiritus adsit	201, 203
Simplex in essentia	216, 218
Spiritus sancte, pie Paraclite	222
Veni, Creator Spiritus	167-180
Veni, Creator Spiritus, Spiritus Recreator	211
Veni, jam veni, Consolator	598
Veni, Sancte Spiritus	181-190
Veni, summe Consolator	213
Veni, superne Spiritus	191, 192

GERMAN HYMNS.

BRUNQUELL aller Güter	258
Dir, dir, Jehovah, will ich singen	109
Geist des Glaubens, Geist der Stärke	275
Hochgelobter Geist und Herr	267
Komm, Gott, Schöpfer	240, 241
Komm, heiliger Geist	230-235
Komm, O komm, du Geist	260, 263
Nun bitten wir	236-239
O du allersüssste Freude	242-248
O Geist des Herrn	274

	PAGE
O Gott, O Geist	269, 270
O heil'ger Geist, kehr'bei uns ein	256
O komm, du Geist der Wahrheit	278
Schmückt das Fest mit Maien	264
Wach auf, du Geist	112
Zeuch ein zu deinen Thoren	249, 253

ENGLISH HYMNS.

ABOVE the starry spheres	45
Alas these pilgrims faint and worn	151
All laud and worship o'er the earth	58
Almighty Comforter and Friend	540
Almighty Spirit, we	436
And art Thou grieved	302, 303
And where shall Mother's bosom	443
And will the mighty God	518
As blows the wind	135
At Pentecost, illustrious day	78
Author of every work divine	340
Awake and blow, Thou purest Wind	370
Awake, awake, Thou Spirit sweet	325
Awake, Thou Spirit, Who of old	112
Away with our fears	123
A year's swift months have passed	37
BE joyful in the Lord, ye lands	140
Be our support, O Ho'y Ghost	283
Blessed Spirit, that preparest	548
Blessed Spirit! Thou Who deignest	466
Blest be the God Who men inspired	132
Blest Comforter, Balm of the	492
B'est Comforter, come, Lord	234
B est Comforter Divine	612
Blest Comforter, Who didst inspire	513
Blest God, that once in fiery tongues	383
Blest Harbinger of future joys	401
Blest Spirit, from the Eternal Sire	487

632 INDEX OF FIRST LINES.

	PAGE
Blest Spirit of Truth, eternal God	384
Blest Spirit, One with God above	109
Bow on, Thou mighty Wind	624
Breathe, descending Holy Spirit	394
Breathe, Holy Spirit, from above	475
Brethren, let us join to raise	143
Bright Presence! may my soul	147
But who shall comfort	107
CHRIST had regained the sky	47
Christ our Sun on us arose	95
Come, blessed Spirit, descend	312
Come, blessed Spirit, Source of light	414
Come, Creator Spirit high	212
Come, deck our feast to-day	264
Come, descend, O heavenly Spirit	380
Come down, O Love divine	225
Come from the four winds, O Breath	14
Come, heavenly Spirit, come	192
Come, heavenly Spirit, come, Kind	195
Come, holy, celestial Dove	338
Come, Holy Ghost	331, 332
Come, Holy Ghost, and warm	419
Come, Holy Ghost, celestial Dove	323
Come, Holy Ghost! come, Lord	233
Come, Holy Ghost, Creator, come	174
Come, Holy Ghost, eternall God	294
Come, Holy Ghost, eternal God	172
Come, Holy Ghost, in love	189
Come, Holy Ghost, my soul inspire	469
Come, Holy Ghost, on us	515, 516
Come, Holy Ghost, our hearts	334
Come, Holy Ghost, our souls inspire	171
Come, Holy Ghost; the Lamb	580
Come, Holy Ghost, the Maker	168
Come, Holy Ghost, Thine influence	336
Come, Holy Ghost, Thou heavenly	393
Come, Holy Ghost, Thou Lord	362
Come, Holy Ghost, Who ever One	198
Come, Holy Spirit! calm my mind	427
Come, Holy Spirit, come and	307, 309
Come, Holy Spirit, come, Let Thy	382
Come, Holy Spirit, come, Mercies	584
Come, Holy Spirit, come; O hear	476
Come, Holy Spirit, come, With energy	413
Come, Holy Spirit! from the height	186
Come, Holy Spirit, God and Lord	215
Come, Holy Spirit, God of might	292
Come, Holy Spirit, heavenly Dove	317
Come, Holy Spirit, heavenly Dove	318

	PAGE
Come, Holy Spirit, heavenly Guest	371
Come, Holy Spirit, heavenly Power	375
Come, Holy Spirit, Love divine	411
Come, Holy Spirite, most blessed	231
Come, Holy Spirit, mystic Dove	493
Come, Holy Spirit, now descend	387
Come, Holy Spirit, send down	183
Come, Holy Spirit, with Thy Grace	203
Come, mighty Spirit, penetrate	538
Come, mild and holy Dove	309
Come, O come, Thou quickening	263
Come, O God the Holy Ghost	626
Come, O promised Comforter	514
Come, O Spirit. graciously	197
Come, O Spirit, Lord of Grace	187
Come, Spirit from above	191
Come then, and dwell with me	356
Come, Thou all-inspiring Spirit	365
Come, Thou almighty Comforter	426
Come, Thou beatific Spirit	357
Come, Thou Creating Spirit blest	177
Come, Thou everlasting Spirit	335
Come, Thou heavenly Spirit pure	194
Come, Thou Holy Paraclete	188
Come, Thou, O come	598
Come, Thou soul-transforming	404
Come, Thou Spirit of contrition	336
Come to our poor nature's night	516
Come to Thy temple here on earth	249
Come, ye who desire	16
Comforter, to Whom we owe	603
Creator, Holy Ghost, descend	169
Creator Spirit, by Whose aid	175
Creator Spirit I come and bless us	615
Creator Spirit, come	178
Creator Spirit, Holy Dove	240
Creator Spirit, Lord of Grace	179
DAY divine! when sudden streaming	100
Dear Comforter of pious souls	324
Dear Dove, Thy prisoner may I be	114
Dear Lord, and shall Thy Spirit rest	119
Deep Spirit of divinest calm	498
Descend, celestial Dove, And make	399
Descend, celestial Dove, In every	372
Descend, immortal Dove	378
Descend from Heaven	385
Do we only give Thee heed	155
Draw, Holy Spirit, nearer	278
Drink deep of the Spirit	127

INDEX OF FIRST LINES.

	PAGE
EARNEST of future bliss	388
Enthroned on high, Almighty Lord	20
Ere Nature, lovely child, arose	416
Ere the world, with light invested	9
Eternal Former of the holy mind	497
Eternal, Holy Spirit, bend	485
Eternal Spirit, by Whose power	453
Eternal Spirit, come	349
Eternal Spirit, let me know	435
Eternal Spirit, Lord of Light	461
Eternal Spirit, mighty Lord	406
Eternal Spirit, Source of good	414
Eternal Spirit, Source of light	390
Eternal Spirit! Source of Truth	429
Eternal Spirit, Thee we praise	585
Eternal Spirit! 'twas Thy Breath	392
Eternal Spirit, we confess	316
Eternal Spirit, wilt Thou dwell	611
Exceeding faithful in Thy word	67
Expand Thy wings, celestial Dove	354
FAIN would I mount	390
Father, admit our lawful claim	33
Father, glorify Thy Son	26
Father, if justly still we claim	21
Father, if Thou my Father art	23
Father of everlasting grace	85
Father of our dying Lord	25
Fountain of Life, most pure	479
Fountain of Love, Thyself true God	503
Fountain of sweets! Eternal Dove	304
Full of weakness and of sin	12
GENIAL Spirit, earth's Emotion	205
Gentle Spirit, waft me over	395
Gift of the Father's living Love	583
Gladsome feast!	52
Glory, Holy Ghost, to Thee	490
God Holy Ghost, teach us in faith	284
God of all consolation	363
God of peace and consolation	467
God the Father, God the Word	599
God the Spirit, we adore Thee	595
God the Spirit, we aspire	529
Grace Increate	508
Gracious, free, and sovereign Spirit	478
Gracious Spirit, Dove divine	403
Gracious Spirit, dwell with me	524
Gracious Spirit, from on high	521
Gracious Spirit, Holy Ghost	570
Gracious Spirit, Source of bliss	463

	PAGE
Granted is the Saviour's prayer	83
Great Spirit, by Whose mighty	407
Great Spirit of Immortal Love	379
Great Spirit, like a rushing wind	499
HAIL, blessed Source of holy Light	452
Hail, Father of the poor	193
Hail, Holy Ghost, Jehovah, Third	327
Hail, Holy Spirit, bright immortal	421
Hail the joyful day's return	65
Hasten, hasten, sweetest Dove	396
Health of the helpless	213
Hear all the Saviour's cry	34
Hear, gracious Sovereign	379
Hear, Holy Spirit, Fount of Sweetness	563
Hear, Holy Spirit, hear	328
Heavenly Spirit, may each heart	470
He's come! let every knee be bent	319
He Who with His mighty hand	61
His Holy Spirit dwelleth	111
Holiest Source of consolation	457
Holy Comforter, Who guidest	468
Holy Ghost, anointing Dove	371
Holy Ghost, apply Thy word	363
Holy Ghost, by Him bestowed	355
Holy Ghost, come down	505
Holy Ghost, dispel our sadness	245
Holy Ghost, divine Creator (v. 4)	566
Holy Ghost, Illuminator	568
Holy Ghost, inspire our praises	425
Holy Ghost, regard our prayers	362
Holy Ghost, remove the grief	357
Holy Ghost, the Comforter	417
Holy Ghost, the Infinite [see Come to our poor nature's night].	
Holy Ghost, the power inspire	356
Holy Ghost, this day descending	607
Holy Ghost, Thou God and Lord	267
Holy Ghost, Thou satest brooding	543
Holy Ghost, Thou Source of Light	618
Holy Ghost, Thy power impart	464
Holy Ghost, we know Thou art	356
Holy Ghost, we look to Thee	432
Holy Ghost, Whose fire celestial	431
Holy Ghost, Whose potent word	501
Holy Ghost, Who us instructest	513
Holy Ghost, with grace inspire	358
Holy Ghost, with light divine	439
Holy Gift, surpassing	62
Holy, sanctifying Dove	350
Holy Spirit, come renew me	471

INDEX OF FIRST LINES.

	PAGE
Holy Spirit, dwell in me	358
Holy Spirit! dwell with me	551
Holy Spirit, Fount of blessing	459
Holy Spirit, from on high	456
Holy Spirit, gent'y come	376
Holy Spirit, given	510
Holy Spirit, heavenly Dove	433
Holy Spirit, heavenly Witness	434
Holy Spirit! long expected	581
Holy Spirit, Lord of Light	184
Holy Spirit, mystic Dove	481
Holy Spirit, now descend	419
Holy Spirit, once again	261
Holy Spirit, Source of Light	535
How dare we pray Thee	450
I WILL not leave you comfortless	63
I would not grieve my dearest Lord	133
In the houre of my distress	305
Inspired by Thee	446
Inspirer of the ancient seers	359
JEHOVAH, let me now adore Thee	109
Jesus is gone up on high	19
Jesus, Lord, in pity hear us	36
Jesus, our exalted Head	29
Jesus, plant Thy Spirit in me	358
Jesus, we hang upon the word	27
Jesus, we on the word depend	31
KINDLER of seraphic fire	364
LEAVE us not comfortless	23
Let songs of praises fill the sky	90
Let Thy wondrous way be known	593
Listen, sweet Dove, unto my song	399
Lord, am I precious in Thy sight	157
Lord God, by Whom all change	554
Lord God, the Holy Ghost	442
Lord, show Thy glory, as of old	11
Lord, 'twas a time of wondrous love	134
Lord, when we come at Thy dear call	557
Love of Father and of Son	210
MAY Thy Spirit, bright and holy	144
Midnight clouds are rolled away	66
Mighty Comforter, to Thee	539
My faith is weak	415
My soul doth magnify the Lord	116
NAY, startle not	69
Not bound by chains	136

	PAGE
Now Christ ascends above the skies	80
Now crave we of the Holy Ghost	239
Now is the Church's joyous feast	512
Now may the Spirit's holy Fire	373
Now our prayers are heard on high	49
Now pray we all God	338
Now prompt, O Muse, the fitting	53
O BREATHE upon this languid	465
O come, Consoler, vivifying Dove	578
O Comforter, Thou uncreated Fire	208
O enter, Lord. Thy temple	253
O Fire of God the Comforter	207
O for a heart of calm repose	620
O for that flame of living fire	10
O for those solitary hours	507
O God of love and power	8
O God, O Spirit, Light of all	269
O God, our Strength, our Refuge	580
O God, when wilt Thou come	139
O heavenly Spirit of especiall power	295
O holy Comforter	616
O Holy Ghost, by Whom we live	571
O Holy Ghost, the Comforter	495
O Holy Ghost, Thou God of peace	490
O Holy Ghost, Thy heavenly dew	274
O Holy Ghost, we praise Thy Name	500
O Holy Ghost, Who didst descend	488
O Holy Ghost, Who down	550
O Holy Ghost, Whose pitying	579
O Holy Spirit, assist me	297
O Holy Spirit, blessed Comforter	286
O Holy Spirit, come, And Jesu's	573
O Holy Spirit, come With energy	472
O Holy Spirit! Comforter Divine	534
O Holy Spirit, enter in	236
O Holy Spirit, Lord of Grace	200
O Holy Spirit, now	241
O Holy Spirit, now descend on me	532
O Holy Spirite, our Comfortoure	291
O Holy Spirit, send	519
O Holy Spirit, Who art One	199
O Holy Spirit, Who didst shed	460
O Holy Spirit, with Thy Grace	203
O inexhaustive Fount of Light	220
O invincible Compeller	545
O Lord, Thy Holy Spirit send	586
O Lord, Thy wing outspread	5
O love ye the Spirit indwelling	129
O Messenger of dear delight	286
O pious Paraclete! O Holy Spirit	222

INDEX OF FIRST LINES.

	PAGE
O sacred Spirit, within my soul repeat	311
O smitten soul	153
O Son of God	160
O Spirit, descend	590
O Spirit, Fount of Love	201
O Spirit, Lord and God	588
O Spirit of Holiness, breathe	614
O Spirit of Love	493
O Spirit of our spirit	560
O Spirit of Remembrance, tell	579
O Spirit of the living God, In all	444
O Spirit of the living God, Whose	520
O Spirit of the Lord of Hosts	621
O Spirit sweet and pure	558
O Thou eternal Spright	307
O Thou meek and injured Dove	352
O Thou propitious Paraclete	321
O Thou sweetest Source of gladness	242
O Thou that hearest prayer	6
O Thou Who by the Lord wast given	511
O Thou Who by Thy Blood	37
O Thou, Whose influence wakes	617
O Thou Whose special work it is	596
O turn, most Holy Spirit, turn	451
Once more the Christian Pentecost	458
Once the soft dews of night	94
One the descending Flame	96
Our blest Redeemer	141
Our God, our God! Thou shinest	158
PRAISE be Thine, most Holy Spirit	576
QUICKEN, Lord, Thy Church and me	13
REJOICE, rejoice, ye fallen race	87
Returned is sacred Pentecost	281
Round roll the weeks	50
SAVIOUR and Prince of Peace	28
Saviour, I Thy word believe	17
Saviour, Lord, Who at Thy Death!	32
Saviour, Thy Father's Promise send	484
Single in essential place	218
Sinners, lift up your hearts	124
Sinners, your hearts lift up	89
Son of God, for Thee we languish	38
Source of good, Whose power	258
Spirit blest, Who art adored	601
Spirit, by Whose operation	275
Spirit Divine! attend our prayers	440
Spirit divine, from Whom	477

	PAGE
Spirit, Jehovah, glorious Lord	437
Spirit of Beauty	528
Spirit of Bondage unto fear	561
Spirit of Charity, dispense	285
Spirit of Christ, descend	562
Spirit of Christ, Thou speakest	606
Spirit of everlasting Grace	537
Spirit of Faith, come down	337
Spirit of Glory and of Grace	594
Spirit of God and glory, send	408
Spirit of God! descend	522
Spirit of God, I cannot rest	502
Spirit of God, mysterious Power	450
Spirit of God, on Thee we call	428
Spirit of God, that moved of old	572
Spirit of God, Whose sacred fire	457
Spirit of Grace, of Truth and Power	462
Spirit of Grace, Thou Light of Life	270
Spirit of Grace, we bless Thy name	341
Spirit of Holiness and Root	344
Spirit of Holiness, descend	613
Spirit of Holiness, look down	455
Spirit of interceding Grace	355
Spirit of Life and Light	592
Spirit of Life and Light, descend	484
Spirit of Life, go forth	472
Spirit of Life, Thy influence shed	454
Spirit of Love, be in our heart	605
Spirit of Love, return	368
Spirit of Mercy, dwell	461
Spirit of mercy, truth, and love	402
Spirit of might and sweetness too	447
Spirit of power and might, behold	443
Spirit of Power and Truth and Love	574
Spirit of Power, descend	409
Spirit of Power, 'tis Thine alone	342
Spirit of Power, to Thee I cry	474
Spirit of revelation	369
Spirit of sacred happiness	527
Spirit of supplication	366
Spirit of Truth and Holiness	473
Spirit of Truth, be Thou my Guide	498
Spirit of Truth, descend	346
Spirit of Truth, essential God	361
Spirit of Truth! my mind illume	483
Spirit of Truth, O Holy Ghost	431
Spirit of Truth, on this Thy day	446
Spirit of Truth, the Comforter	355
Spirit of truth, Thy grace impart	430
Spirit of Truth, Thy gracious beams	287
Spirit of Wisdom, guide Thine own	531

INDEX OF FIRST LINES.

	PAGE
Spirit of Wisdom, pure and perfect	498
Spirit, poured on Pentecost	619
Spirit, that dwellest where the stream	494
Spirit! Whose various energies	526
Stay, Thou departing Spirit, stay	353
Stay, Thou insulted Spirit, stay	351
Sweetest Fount of holy gladness	247
Sweet Spirit, would Thy Breath	555
That we might walk with God	122
The day of Pentecost	93
The glory of the Spring how sweet	552
The God of grace will never leave	121
The Grace of the Holy Ghost	201
The illustrious day	54
The Lord is gone	564
The Love of the Spirit I sing	118
The Spirit in our hearts	131
The Spirit in the Word	130
The tuneful sound of music	60
Thee will we praise	443
There was a little lowly upper room	91
Thou blessed Spirit, by Whose aid	587
Thou Holy Spirit, Comforter sublime	280
Thou Holy Spirite, we pray to Thee	237
Thou Source of all vigor divine	405
Thou Spirit of eternal Truth	409
Thou Who camest from above	491
Thou Who framedst this goodly	138
Thou Who lovest us as a Father	272

	PAGE
Thou Who One in Essence livest	216
Thy happy ones a strain begin	196
Thy heavenly kingdom here below	71
Till the day dawn	537
Tongues of fire from Heaven descend	72
Tune we our heart-strings high	305
Unseen Spirit, Lord of Life	590
Vouchsafe then, O Thou most	298
We cannot see the wondrous Hand	142
We give Thee thanks, Good Spirit	585
We keep the Feast of Pentecost	59
Welcome, white day!	75
When across the inward thought	523
When Christ His body up had borne	73
When God of old came down	98
When the blest day of Pentecost	82
When the leaves of life are falling	541
When the Lord of Hosts ascended	565
Wherefore, most sacred Spirit	300
Whither shall a creature run	126
Who but Thou, almighty Spirit	609
Why hasteth on this pilgrim throng	150
Why should the children of a King	315
Wind of the North, awake	535
Would the Spirit more completely	101
Yet, O most blessed Spirit	298

Cambridge: Press of John Wilson & Son.

www.ingramcontent.com/pod-product-compliance
Lightning Source LLC
Chambersburg PA
CBHW021220300426
44111CB00007B/377